CONTEMPORARY
NEWS
REPORTING

Random House • New York

CONTEMPORARY NEWS REPORTING

DOUGLAS A. ANDERSON
Arizona State University

BRUCE D. ITULE
Chicago Tribune

First Edition
987654321
Copyright © 1984 by Random House, Inc.

Library of Congress Cataloging in Publication Data

Anderson, Douglas A.
   Contemporary news reporting.
   Includes index.
   1. Reporters and reporting.   I. Itule, Bruce D.,
1947-   . II. Title.
PN4781.A594   1983   070.4'3   83–9648
ISBN 0–394–32891–4

Cover Design: Barbara A. Grodsky
Text Design: Nancy Bumpus

Manufactured in the United States of America

Acknowledgments

For permission to use personal quotations and printed material, we are grateful to the following:

pp. 8–9 From "A Child of the Century," copyright © 1954 by Ben Hecht. Reprinted by permission of Julian Messner, a Simon & Schuster division of Gulf and Western Corporation. *pp. 10–11*, Bob Greene. *p. 26* (top), Chicago Tribune. *p. 26* (bottom), Montrose (Calif.) Ledger. *p. 27*, Adam Yeomans. *p. 29*, Chicago Tribune. *p. 30*, The Associated Press. *p. 36*, Detroit Free Press. *pp. 39–40*, Chicago Tribune. *p. 49*, © Chicago Sun-Times, 1982. Article by James Warren, reprinted with permission. *p. 50*, Chicago Tribune. *p. 51*, Rick Alm. *pp. 55–56*, Neil H. Mehler. *p. 57*, Reprinted by permission of the Kansas City Star Co., © 1982. All rights reserved. *pp. 59–63*, Katherine Rodeghier. *p. 62*, Reprinted from Discovery, the Allstate Motor Club Magazine. *pp. 72–73*, Kenneth Reich. *p. 86*, Chicago Tribune. *pp. 91–93*, Rick Alm. *p. 93*, Reprinted by permission of the Kansas City Star Co., © 1981. All rights reserved. *p. 94*, Reprinted by permission of the Kansas City Star Co., © 1981. All rights reserved. *pp. 97–98*, Rick Seifert and Andre Stepankowsky. *pp. 99–100*, Allen F. Schmahl. *p. 109*, Mistie Witt. *pp. 109–10*, Seaton Publishing Company, Inc. *pp. 110–12*, Tempe (Ariz.) Daily News. *pp. 115–16*, Frank Partsch. *p. 116*, Mead Summer and State Press. *pp. 117–22*, Frank Partsch. *p. 118*, Omaha World-Herald. *pp. 126–27, 129*, Robert Rawitch. *pp. 133–34*, Tom Spratt. *pp. 134–35*, Reprinted with permission of the Arizona Republic. *pp. 135–36*, Reprinted with permission of the Phoenix Gazette. *p. 136*, Reprinted with permission of the Arizona Republic. *p. 137*, Reprinted with permission of the Phoenix Gazette. *pp. 146–47*, Robert Rawitch. *pp. 154–55*, Chicago Tribune. *pp. 156–58*, Andre Stepankowsky. *pp. 159–60*, Ted Hartzell. *p. 160*, La Porte Herald-Argus. *pp. 161–62*, Ted Hartzell. *p. 171*, FOI Service Center, a joint project of the Reporters Committee for Freedom of the Press and the Society of Professional Journalists, Sigma Delta Chi. *pp. 173–75*, Max Jennings. *p. 177*, Mesa Tribune. *p. 178*, Max Jennings. *pp. 181–83*, Jack Anderson. *pp. 195–97*, Andrew Leckey. *pp. 198–99*, Janet Key. *pp. 204–05*, Mary A.M. Perry. *pp. 206–07*, Education Writers Association. *p. 207*, Daily and Sunday Herald, Arlington Heights, Ill. *p. 208*, Reprinted from the Observer-Dispatch, Utica, N.Y. *p. 210*, Bruce Buursma. *pp. 211–12*, Eric Mink. *pp. 219–22*, Reprinted and excerpted with permission from the Minneapolis Star and Tribune. *pp. 223–24*, Reprinted with permission of the Arizona Republic. *p. 224*, Chicago Tribune. *pp. 224–26*, William Recktenwald. *p. 226*, (middle), St. Louis Post-Dispatch. *pp. 226–30*, Thomas A. Knott. *pp. 229–30*, Chicago Tribune. *pp. 241–43*, Mary Bishop and Thomas Ferrick, Jr. *pp. 244, 245–46*, Reprinted by permission of The Philadelphia Inquirer. *p. 247*, Telegraph Herald, Dubuque, Iowa. *pp. 248, 249*, University News Bureau, University of North Carolina. *pp. 254–55*, Wally Provost, Omaha World-Herald. *p. 256* (top), Reprinted with permission of the Arizona Republic. *p. 256* (middle), Reprinted with permission of the Phoenix Gazette. *p. 257*, Terry L. Henion. *p. 259* (top), Omaha World-Herald. *p. 259* (middle), Fort Lauderdale News and Sun-Sentinel. *pp. 259–60*, Reprinted with permission of the Miami Herald. *p. 260*, Copyright 1980, The Oklahoma Publishing Company. *pp. 261–62*, Douglas Looney, © 1983 Time Inc.

pp. 262–63, Wally Provost, Omaha World-Herald. *p. 264,* Omaha World-Herald. *p. 265,* Omaha World-Herald. *p. 267,* (top and middle), Reprinted with permission of the Arizona Republic. *p. 272,* From Joe Alex Morris, "Deadline Every Minute." Reprinted with permission of Doubleday & Company, Inc. *pp. 272–75,* Gavin Scott, The Associated Press. *pp. 274, 275,* The Associated Press. *p. 278,* Edward C. Nicholls. *p. 279* (middle), The Salt Lake Tribune. *p. 279* (bottom), The Associated Press. *p. 280* (middle), Chicago Tribune. *p. 282,* The Associated Press. *p. 283,* The Associated Press. *p. 284,* Leon Daniel. *pp. 289–94,* Donald E. Brown. *pp. 294, 295, 296, 297* (top), The Associated Press. *pp. 297–98,* Reprinted with permission of the Phoenix Gazette. *pp. 297–98,* Dan Fellner. *p. 299,* KPNX-TV. *pp. 300–01,* Dan Fellner. *pp. 302–03,* Paul Louderman, John Powell and KHAS-Radio News. *pp. 303–04,* Dan Fellner. *p. 305,* KOLD-TV. *pp. 306–07,* Benjamin Silver. *p. 310,* Gavin Scott, The Associated Press. *pp. 321–22,* From "Synopsis of the Law of Libel and the Right of Privacy," by Bruce W. Sanford. Used with permission of Scripps-Howard Newspapers. *pp. 327–28,* New York State Newspapers Foundation, "A Survival Kit for Reporters, Editors and Broadcasters" (1980), p. 35. *p. 335,* Gannett Co., Inc. *p. 349,* Robert J. McCloskey. pp. 349–50, William L. Green. *pp. 351–52,* Society of Professional Journalists. *p. 369,* From "Facts About Newspapers 1981," American Newspaper Publishers Association.

PREFACE

We wrote *Contemporary News Reporting* to give you the flavor of what it is like to be a reporter. We wanted to make the drama of news reporting come alive—to kindle an excitement while painting a realistic picture. Thus we used numerous anecdotes, case studies and tips from working reporters so that you would like reading the book while acquiring essential journalistic skills.

The book takes you on the beat, into the newsroom, into the press box, into the courtroom, into the wire service bureau, and introduces you to reporters, editors and current issues. You will be with Kansas City Star reporter Rick Alm as he covers the tragic collapse of the aerial walkways at the Hyatt Regency hotel, with Sports Illustrated senior writer Douglas Looney as he prepares for a Nebraska-Oklahoma football game, with Walter Berry of The Associated Press during his coverage of a sensational trial in Phoenix, Ariz., with Andre Stepankowsky of the Daily News, Longview, Wash., as he reports on the eruption of Mount Saint Helens and with scores of other newspeople as they report the day's news.

These "inside looks" focus on real reporters in real situations, but the story telling does not cloud the lessons of the text. The book provides a fast-paced overview of newswriting and interviewing principles before moving to concepts of primary importance to students who are ready for in-the-field reporting of press conferences, speeches, standard beats, breaking news and developing stories. The book also examines specialty, in-depth, investigative, sports, wire service and broadcast reporting.

Contemporary News Reporting also discusses news-gathering techniques when seeking access to public records or meetings, examines standard library sources and shows how reporters use social science methods to gather information. It provides an extensive overview of the reporting process by examining the ethical and constitutional frameworks within which reporters operate and uses relevant examples from metropolitan dailies, small dailies and student newspapers.

Opportunities beckon for journalists. It is not surprising, then, that some of the reporters and editors featured in this book have moved to other jobs. References to these journalists and their work, however, remain within the context of their jobs at the time they were interviewed.

One further note: Most newspapers follow Associated Press style; this book will also.

Many people contributed to the research and preparation of this text. Individuals who were particularly helpful through their insights and counsel were Tom Allan, Omaha (Neb.) World-Herald; Roger Boye, Society of Professional Journalists, Sigma Delta Chi; Casey Bukro, Chicago

Tribune; Leon Daniel, United Press International; Dan Fellner, KOLD-TV, Tucson, Ariz.; Robert B. Gaston, Daily News, Longview, Wash.; James Geladas, Dubuque (Iowa) Telegraph Herald; Terry Henion, Gazette-Telegraph, Colorado Springs, Colo.; Max Jennings, Mesa (Ariz.) Tribune; the late William H. Jones, Chicago Tribune; Brad Kalbfeld, The Associated Press; Neil H. Mehler, Chicago Tribune; Edward C. Nicholls, The Associated Press; Ann Nykanen, WWBM-TV, Chicago; Mark Nykanen, NBC News; Frank Partsch, Omaha (Neb.) World-Herald; Mario Petitti, Chicago Tribune; John Powell, KHAS-Radio, Hastings, Neb.; Wally Provost, Omaha (Neb.) World-Herald; Robert Rawitch, Los Angeles Times; William Recktenwald, Chicago Tribune; Al Schmahl, Grand Island (Neb.) Independent; Edward Seaton, Manhattan (Kan.) Mercury; Tom Spratt, Phoenix (Ariz.) Gazette, and G. Fred Wickman, Kansas City Star. Thanks also go to reporting instructors at Arizona State University: Donald Brown, George Flynn, Robert Lance, Benjamin Silver and Edward Sylvester.

We would like also to acknowledge those professors who reviewed all or parts of the manuscript: James Bow, University of Iowa; Jane Briggs-Bunting, Oakland University; William Folger, University of Northern Colorado; Ted Glasser, University of Minnesota; Mike Kautsch, University of Kansas; Thomas B. Littlewood, University of Illinois; David Nord, Indiana University; Jay L. Perkins, Louisiana State University; Daniel W. Pfaff, Pennsylvania State University; Henry H. Schulte, Ohio State University; Charles Self, University of Alabama; Paul S. Underwood, Ohio State University, and Roy Vanderburg, Western Illinois University.

Those professors who read the manuscript at several stages were particularly helpful: Randall L. Murray, California Polytechnic State University; Stan Soffin, Michigan State University, and Robert Taylor, University of Wisconsin. Professor Taylor helped us shape the manuscript from proposal to completion. We owe him a special debt of gratitude.

Formal thanks should be given to the editors in the College Department at Random House, particularly Roth Wilkofsky, senior editor, humanities, who worked with us throughout; Kirsten Olson, assistant editor, who field-tested the manuscript and enthusiastically steered us through revisions, and Laurel Miller, project editor, who carefully applied final copy editing and organizational touches.

Credit for typing the manuscript goes to Norma Kennedy, a thoughtful and efficient secretary in the Department of Journalism and Telecommunication at Arizona State University.

Special appreciation is extended to our families for their patience, understanding and willingness to handle extra responsibilities while we wrote this manuscript: Claudia, Laura and Mary Anderson, and Priscilla, Dena and Justin Itule. To them this book is dedicated.

Douglas A. Anderson • Bruce D. Itule

CONTENTS

ix

3 THE INTERVIEW   43

4 ON ASSIGNMENT: PRESS CONFERENCES AND SPEECHES   69

Rapid technological advances have changed the way news is processed and delivered, but in America's newsrooms many traditions endure. This chapter discusses traditional methods of reporting news and shows how some have changed. It also shows how reporters operate in large and in small markets.

You will be introduced to:

• The similarities between metropolitan and community newspapers, and points of contrast. Differences between morning and evening newspapers also are discussed.

• Changes in newsrooms in the last decade and the way reporters meet the challenge of functioning in a new environment.

• The newsroom hierarchy, from the editor down to the beginning reporter. The chapter gives an example of a "first story" and points out how all reporters experience similar emotions.

• The emergence of reporters as stars. Bob Greene, a syndicated columnist for the Chicago Tribune and a contributing editor for Esquire magazine, is interviewed. He calls himself a storyteller and reporter and offers tips to young journalists.

A lull between editions makes the Chicago Tribune newsroom look peaceful. During peak times, many of the 600-plus editorial staff members work here.

Courtesy, Bruce D. Itule

1 THE REPORTER IN A CONTEMPORARY ENVIRONMENT

It is 5 p.m. in Chicago, rush hour on the fourth floor of the 36-story Tribune Tower. Many of the 600-plus editors, reporters, copy clerks, artists, photographers and others who make up the editorial staff of the Chicago Tribune are in the massive city room.

An editor on the news desk yells, "Copy." Instantly, one of the Tribune's copy clerks (John Chancellor of NBC News was a copy clerk in this newsroom in 1944) answers the call and rushes to the editor's desk. "Take this proof to composing right away, and on the way back get me a large cup of coffee with cream," the editor tells the clerk, who in the morning is a journalism student at one of the area universities.

As the clerk passes the city desk, an assistant city editor, whose local story on train service in Chicago had been accepted by the news desk, is telling a reporter, "Trim two graphs out of this. We need only 13 inches. It can trim from the bottom, right?"

Another assistant city editor is talking on the telephone with a woman who says she is Elizabeth Taylor's daughter. "Ma'am, I've talked to you before," the assistant city editor says before he hangs up the phone. The woman had called twice the day before, saying that she had been kidnapped by the Mafia years ago and drugged, and only now did she realize her true identity.

So far today, four editions of this 800,000-circulation, 24-hour newspaper have been produced. Five more will appear tonight. Copy clerks now are delivering the Midwest Edition—which begins the cycle of the next day's editions—to the city desk, the news desk, the financial desk, the national and foreign copy desk, the picture desk, the local copy desk, the graphics desk, the sports desk and the features copy desk. There is no busier time in the newsroom. Most of the reporters and editors who work "dayside" are about to go home, and the "nightside" crew is beginning to arrive. Some people are in the middle of their day. It is a time when people who seldom work together cross paths, as students do in between classes at a high school.

"Cityside" reporters, who cover Chicago day and night in an effort to beat the rival Chicago Sun-Times, report to the city editor. Reporters stationed in bureaus throughout the United States, ready to cover a major hotel fire in Las Vegas, a volcanic eruption in Washington state, the murder of a child in Atlanta or the attempted assassination of the president in Washington, D.C., report to the national editor. The foreign editor is in charge of reporters whose assignment is the world—from foreign posts, they recount a war in the Middle East, an uprising in South America, a harvest in China. In addition there are about 100 feature, financial and sports reporters. All these journalists are competing for a spot in today's editions. Some will make it; others will not.

Meanwhile, 65 miles away in the newsroom of the evening La Porte (Ind.) Herald-Argus, Managing Editor Ted Hartzell is editing a story for the editorial page of tomorrow's edition. He has been at work since 6:30 this morning, but he has to take care of some administrative problems and finish the editorial page before he goes home. Most of his staff has left for the day because today's paper has been out since shortly after 1 p.m. Reporters who have to cover stories tonight will be back later.

The 13,500-circulation Herald-Argus produces a single edition a day, six days a week. Unlike the Chicago Tribune, which publishes every day of the year, there is no Sunday Herald-Argus, nor are there editions on New Year's Day, Memorial Day, Thanksgiving or Christmas. Hartzell heads a staff of 13 full-timers, and nearly everything they produced today went into the paper. Their newsroom shares the same floor with the paper's business office, composing room and pressroom. Though officially the managing editor, Hartzell also serves as copy editor, assignment editor, layout person and answer man. He and his reporters often write editorials.

MEETING THE CHALLENGE

These examples point out some of the differences between giant metropolitan newspapers and community newspapers, but there also are two important similarities:

- A goal of all editors and reporters is to give their readers the best product they can in a limited amount of time and space.
- The techniques used in gathering information are the same at any size newspaper. Wherever they work, reporters must be aggressive yet diplomatic enough to handle any type of interview, willing to give up their homelife when a newsworthy event occurs, consistently ethical and as objective as possible. They must write so that their audience understands them, never hesitate to ask a question more than once and understand the legal framework within which they work. And of course they must meet their deadlines.

Often when young journalists think of the newspapers for which they would like to work, they think of the huge metros, the papers that pay the best wages and have scores of "specialists" traveling around the world— papers that can make national stars of their reporters. The truth is, most reporters never will work for a huge metro. The majority will work for the hundreds of community newspapers throughout the United States. Some reporters will use community newspapers as springboards to a medium-size metro, and then they will move up to a big paper in a major U.S. city. Others will spend their careers at a community newspaper, learning every aspect of journalism. They will cover social club meetings; they will interview presidential candidates in town for a whirlwind tour; they may even sell ads and do paste-up.

THE CHANGING NEWSROOM

The way reporters and editors produce a newspaper has changed drastically in the last 10 years. Indeed, methods of production have changed as much in the last decade as they have in the entire history of printing before it. In the early 1970s, printers in newspaper composing rooms set stories and headlines on Linotype machines, which cast the lines one at a time from molten lead. A story that had been typed and then edited was sent to the composing room to be set into type. After the story was set, the type was put into a metal *galley,* or tray, and from it a proof was made and sent to the proofroom, where a proofreader read it for typographical errors. Next, the story was taken to another printer who placed the type in a page *chase,* a frame for holding pages of type, according to an editor's *dummy,* or layout sheet. Each page of the paper was made up the same way.

That all has changed. In today's computerized newsrooms, editors—and at some newspapers, reporters—also do the job of printers and proofreaders because stories can be set directly from a video display terminal (VDT). With computerized page *layout* (pagination), the composition of the entire newspaper can be done from the newsroom. In some communities, the newspaper can be sent via telephone lines or cables from the editor's computer to readers who have home video display terminals and subscribe to an "electronic newspaper." Newsrooms were computerized in the 1970s. Homes will be by the 1990s, and to survive, newspapers must meet the challenge of this changing environment that allows viewers to scan and digest their newspaper as quickly as they can push a button.

These changes in production methods are good news for journalism students because they ultimately will mean an increasing supply of jobs. They are bad news for printers, who are facing extinction at most newspapers. It seems only a matter of time before retraining, reduced work loads, retirement, normal attrition and increasingly stronger cash incentives eliminate what once was the strongest craft at American newspapers.

THE WIZARDRY OF ELECTRONICS

Because journalism is changing so rapidly, today's reporters face an important question: Will the new era of electronic information delivery do to us in the 1990s what it did to printers in the 1970s and 1980s?

Probably not. To begin with, it still is much more expensive to reach people with an electronic newspaper than it is to deliver to them the printed product. More importantly, people always will be needed to report stories, edit them and push the buttons necessary to set them into type. In the coming years, the wizardry of electronics will bring more news into readers' homes more quickly and as the audience grows, so will the need for people to provide electronic newspapers. Therefore, reporters should view computers as an asset.

It is important that today's reporters also have a working knowledge of computer technology. Many of the nation's journalism schools have installed electronic copy-processing equipment to help prepare students for the current technology. Several schools have adopted a philosophy similar to that articulated by John B. Adams of the University of North Carolina. He said his school has "enough equipment now to provide the essential ingredient—a hands-on experience to overcome the initial trauma at the thought of using new technology."

THE NEWSROOM HIERARCHY

Despite the new environment provided by electronic reporting and delivery systems, the traditional hierarchy remains in most newsrooms. At the top is the editor, whose role changes depending on the size of the newspaper. At a community newspaper, the editor also may be a publisher, a business manager, a reporter, a photographer and an advertising salesman. At a metro, the editor may have nothing to do with the day-to-day operation of the editorial process. In these cases, the managing editor is in charge. At the other end of the scale are the beginning reporters, who are trying to make their mark on the profession and hoping to get a bylined story on Page 1. The number of newsroom personnel between the beginning reporter and the top editor is determined by the circulation of the newspaper and its budget.

The managing editor runs the newsroom at most newspapers. It is his or her job to make sure that the newspaper is out on time each day and that costs are kept within a budget. The managing editor usually is responsible for hiring and firing newsroom personnel and serves as a spokesperson for the paper. At smaller newspapers, the managing editor also is involved in story selection, assignments, editing and laying out pages.

In a typical newsroom the managing editor's main subeditors are:

- *The news editor*. This editor is in charge of the copy desk, where makeup editors and copy editors work. Their job is to dummy pages and edit and write headlines for the wire and local copy that goes on the news pages each day. (Some papers have universal copy desks that handle stories from every section, but most rely on individual departments to handle their own copy and pages.) Most daily newspapers are members of The Associated Press (AP) and/or subscribers to United Press International (UPI) and several supplemental news services, so they have a steady flow of stories from cities and battlefields throughout the United States and the world. A story is sent to the copy desk for processing after a decision is made to run it in the paper. This desk is the last to see a story before it appears in print.

- *The city editor.* This editor runs the city desk and is in charge of a newspaper's general assignment and beat reporters. Assistant city editors may help hand out assignments and review stories. Reporters come to the city desk for ideas, with ideas, for counseling and with stories ready for editing. It is the city editor's job to make sure that the news in the city is covered and that as many local stories as possible get in each edition.

  General assignment reporters cover breaking news or features as they come up. Stories can range from a 72-year-old man's claiming to have a rooster that lays eggs to a state official's suffering a heart attack while playing golf. The remaining reporters have specific beats, including the police, fire, city hall, court, state capital and county government beats. The larger the paper the greater the number of beats, many of which require reporters who are specialists in specific areas. These areas include transportation, energy, education, aviation and religion. Beat reporters find and write stories that originate in their areas. Most write at least one news story a day, and they also are responsible for features.

- *The photo editor.* This editor assigns to a newspaper's photographers the news stories and features they are to cover. At many papers the photo editor sits at or near the city desk, so that photographers often can accompany reporters on assignments. Some papers have one photographer who handles everything, including pictures for advertisements. Others have several who share assignments; a few have dozens who are specialized in the types of events they cover. Sometimes the photo editor is also a graphics editor, although many newspapers today have a separate editor in charge of the maps, charts and other illustrations that go with stories. An artist or a staff of artists works for the graphics editor.

- *The sports editor.* This editor is in charge of sportswriters and the desk people who process their copy. The writers cover sports events and features in a community's high schools and colleges. They also cover professional sports in their area. The desk people on the sports staff edit stories and lay out the daily sports pages. The sports editor also often writes a column.

- *The lifestyle editor.* This editor heads what usually is a paper's main features section. It may include articles by lifestyle writers, a food editor, an entertainment writer, a drama critic, a television writer and other reviewers and critics. The lifestyle editor, like the sports editor, is responsible for editing and laying out pages each day.

- *The financial editor.* This editor is in charge of handling the business news that goes into the newspaper. Most papers have a business page or section each day, and many have a staff of financial reporters who cover area businesses. Financial news has grown in popularity in recent years, and many papers are expanding their staffs to cover it. Newspapers always have printed closing stock averages and press releases on business openings, expansions and closings, but now they are assigning their own reporters to cover financial news as aggressively as other news is covered.

THE HUDDLE

At least once each day, the city, news and photo editors join the managing editor in a *news huddle,* an editorial conference in which they discuss the top foreign, national and local stories. They will decide in the huddle which stories will make it into the paper and which of those will be on Page 1. A breaking news story could change their plans, but after about 20 minutes of give and take, these editors have determined what their readers will get that day. The sports, lifestyle or financial editor will be called into the huddle if he or she has a story that is being considered for the news section.

At an evening newspaper, the news huddle is held early in the morning, often before many of the reporters come to work, because the deadlines are early in the day. Evening newspapers (they are called *PM*s) try to get the latest news to their readers, but they realize that by the time the paper is printed and distributed, most of their readers will have had a chance to hear the news on the radio or watch it on television. Therefore, they try to offer their readers a bigger and more comprehensive news report and more local feature stories than radio or television can. In theory, if radio and television are the appetizers, the newspaper is the meal. Larger evening papers also have more than one edition each day, which helps in their never-ending battle to print the latest news possible.

Work on an evening paper is done primarily during the day, and by late afternoon, when the last edition is out, many of the staffers are off work. Beat reporters at a morning newspaper (called an *AM*) generally work during the day, but many staff members work during the late afternoon and evening, for deadlines are in the evening and the papers are printed during the night. Thus, the news huddle at a morning paper is held during the afternoon. The later deadlines at AMs mean that their reporters have several hours longer each day to work on stories than reporters for PMs. Morning newspapers also face fewer challenges from radio and television and require fewer editions because they are printed and delivered while most of their readers are sleeping.

YOUR FIRST STORY

Now, back to the beginning reporter trying to make a mark on the profession: You.

The biggest challenge you will face is your first story written as a professional journalist. That is when everything you have learned is condensed into lines on a VDT. There will be plenty of mistakes, and the copy editors probably will tear it apart, but if you have done your job, you will be proud when the paper is out and readers have a chance to see your name. There is magic in that first byline. You see it and you are convinced that people will stop you on the street to tell you how much they enjoyed your story. No one does, and only your mother will ask you for your autograph, but you still are convinced that everyone in the world will memorize your words and think of you as the next Hemingway.

Here is how Ben Hecht, a Chicago newspaper reporter in the early 1900s and coauthor of "The Front Page," "Twentieth Century" and other stage hits, described the first news story he wrote. It was about 1911, and he was working for the Chicago Daily Journal. This description of his first story appeared in his 1954 autobiography, "A Child of the Century." The story was about a woman being sued for divorce on the charge that she had slept with 20 different men:

> I sat at a typewriter in the local room for two hours writing the story of Mrs. Chandler. I still remember the lead: "We think that one of the greatest injustices ever done against a pure and noble woman has been done to Mrs. Bertha Chandler by a madman who calls himself her husband and protector."
>
> I sent the story to the city desk, page at a time. The bulging Romanoff, head copy boy, stood beaming at my side as I wrote. I wrote seventeen pages. And as I wrote I saw an unprecedented thing happening. Mr. Finnegan (the assistant city editor) read each page carefully and then handed it to Mr. Dunne (city editor). Mr. Dunne, in turn, poured over each sheet, obviously not skipping a word, and then carried the "take" in person to Mr. Hutchens (managing editor) at his desk. Mr. Hutchens' eye remained glued with similar fascination to my writing. As if this were not enough triumph for my first flight as a journalist, Mr. Hutchens handed the accumulated pages to Mr. Boyer (head compositor) who chanced to be passing. I watched Mr. Boyer, eyes wide with wonder, read my copy. At this point Mr. Duffy (sports editor, reporter) came out from behind his glass panel and joined my group of literary disciples. I was on page eighteen, with the story of Mrs. Chandler's sweetness, purity and woes still only half told, when Mr. Duffy came to me. He stood looking at me, his pipe held to his mouth, his lips puffing, his eyes twinkling, sneering and glaring all at the same time.
>
> "That's enough of that," he finally said.
>
> "I'm not through yet."
>
> "Don't be a horse's ass," said Mr. Duffy. "Come on, we'll go have a drink."

I heard a guffaw from the far end of the room. Mr. Murphy, our police reporter in for a chat with Mr. Dunne, was reading my story. Mr. Murphy laughed loud and long and cried out in delight, "What God-damn Gussie Mollie wrote this crap?"

This query and another look at Mr. Duffy puffing his pipe told me the truth. I was a clown belaboring a typewriter. I had poured out my heart and talents and earned the title of idiot again.

Later, Duffy gives Hecht some advice:

"I suggest you learn how newspaper stories are written. This is done by reading newspapers, particularly the Chicago Daily Journal, which I notice you have not deigned to peruse yet."

THE REPORTER'S ROLE

In some ways the reporter's role has not changed since the days of Hecht. The emotion and the editing Hecht went through still are there. It still is important to read newspapers, but much more goes into the training of today's reporters. They no longer simply are thrown in with the sharks to sink or to come up with an understandable news story. Most are trained professionals who have been through university journalism programs that emphasize liberal arts education. Many have had internships at newspapers or radio or television stations. By the time they get to their first jobs, they can handle basic news situations.

Today's reporters are called to handle a wider variety of stories, a skill that demands more than just journalism training. For instance, newspapers are conducting more polls than ever today, which requires not only someone trained to make the survey, but someone trained to interpret it for the paper's readers. Today's papers also have scores of special sections—home, entertainment, fashion, science, technology and more—that require writers who are more than skilled reporters.

In the early 1970s, newspapers and wire services recruited regularly at journalism schools and departments because they had plenty of jobs to offer. That all has changed now, a situation that has helped to improve journalism. Since competition is fierce for the jobs of print and broadcast reporters, there is usually a better group of people from which to pick. Newspapers and broadcast outlets are looking for reporters who are technicians in a variety of fields and languages. Today's reporters are interviewers and writers, historians and lawyers, mathematicians and economists. Still, the first step to being a good reporter is to be a good speller who knows how to write a simple sentence. The next step is enthusiasm.

Robert Wiedrich, a reporter and columnist for the Chicago Tribune, has been an eyewitness to humanity for more than 30 years. Here is how he describes his three decades as a reporter:

No reporter, however skilled, can succeed without news sources that believe in his integrity and that of the newspaper he represents. And no reporter can properly do his job unless he is enthusiastically willing to learn something new every day.

That is what brings life to your writing, the conveying to readers things you just have learned yourself, facts that piqued your fancy or broadened your knowledge and you want to share.

Without that enthusiasm, you're dead as a reporter and so is your writing. That enthusiasm pervades your professional life.

You cannot escape it because it surrounds your every moment in a newsroom filled with inquisitive minds and quick wit that makes the shifts pass too quickly.

REPORTERS AS STARS

Aside from everything else, it takes stamina to be a good reporter. Besides the frustration that comes from trying to report a story without error and still meet a deadline, the reporter must contend with irascible sources, cranky editors, lousy hours and often low wages. Any one of these factors will cause some reporters to leave the profession, but most of those who remain are assured of a professional career filled with excitement, fun and a great deal of satisfaction.

A few of those who remain also become star reporters who are highly paid and easily recognized. Some are syndicated writers who have been around the world. For a few, salaries of $150,000 to $300,000 a year—and even higher in the case of network television anchors—are not uncommon; private offices are a must; secretaries are a need, and unlimited travel is part of the job.

Besides the higher salary and other advantages that come with reporter stardom, there also is the disadvantage of being too easily recognized, which can hinder a reporter's work. Some reporters, especially those from network television, have had to learn how to deal with eager fans seeking autographs or with hostile sources who do not want to be involved in a national story. In some cases these reporters draw bigger crowds than the news sources that they are assigned to cover. For these reasons they must learn to do their jobs under different circumstances than those faced by local reporters.

Television even has had an effect on print media reporters. Some have become local or national celebrities after appearing on television panel discussions or talk shows. Indeed, journalism has become more glamorous for reporters everywhere, and with the glamour have come better salaries for everyone and stardom for a few.

One reporter who has gained a national reputation, but who refuses to call himself a star, is Bob Greene, a columnist for the Chicago Tribune. In 1969 Greene was a senior at Northwestern University, where he was associate editor of the school's daily newspaper. Today, besides writing a column four days a week for the Tribune, Greene is syndicated in more than 150 newspapers in the United States and Canada, is a contributing editor for Esquire magazine, appears on television and travels all over the world. He also answers his own telephone, although he does have a secretary, and he works on Sundays.

Greene calls himself a storyteller and a reporter. His answer to his alleged stardom is:

> I'm a reporter who has a very lucky forum. I'm uncomfortable with the idea of journalists as stars. Sure, people like to talk quite a bit about what I do, but I hope they are responding to my writing rather than to me as a personality.
>
> I consider myself a reporter. The column I do is reporting; the news-gathering aspect of my job is the same as any reporter's. What's different is my picture is with the column and it goes around the country. As a columnist you become part of the readers' lives. They get up in the morning and there you are. I have a continuing dialogue with my readers.
>
> There is a lot of justified resentment from my colleagues because I make more money, but I am the same thing I was when I was 16. I'm a fellow who likes to tell stories. I just found someone who wants to pay me for it.

Greene is a success story in the highly competitive field of big-city newspaper journalism because he has been indefatigable in his quest. When he was in high school, he worked during vacations as a sportswriter and general assignment reporter for the Columbus (Ohio) Citizen-Journal in his hometown. When he was graduated from Northwestern in 1969, he was hired as a summer tryout by the Chicago Sun-Times. He was 22 years old. By the end of that tryout, Greene was spending afternoons and nights with the defendants in the Chicago Seven trial. Reporters from throughout the world were in Chicago covering the trial of the seven men who were charged with inciting riots during the 1968 Democratic National Convention, but Greene's approach was original: He "hung out" with the defendants and then wrote sidebars on their lives.

The Sun-Times kept Greene on as a general assignment reporter after his successful coverage of the Chicago Seven. Next, he spent six months on the paper's Sunday magazine before becoming one of its columnists in 1971. By the time he moved to the Tribune in 1978, he had written five books.

His advice to young reporters is not to let anyone set timetables for them:

> If I had waited around for people to tell me it's time to write a column, I probably wouldn't be writing one now. Move when you think it is time. If you think you are good, take it for what it is worth. The walls of one city room are not the confines of the world. Extend yourself to your limits. If your city editor says, "No, we are going to keep you on the police beat here," go someplace else.

SUGGESTED   EXERCISES

1. Compare a community newspaper and a metropolitan newspaper in your area. How do their stories on Page 1 differ? Which paper uses more wire service stories? Try to find three to five stories that appear in both papers. How do the two papers differ in their treatment of the same stories? Count the stories that have local bylines. How many stories carry local bylines in the community newspaper? How does it compare with the metro paper?

2. Invite an editor from an area newspaper to your class. Find out how his or her newsroom has changed in the last five years. What is in store for the next five years?

3. Plan a field trip to the newsroom of a metropolitan newspaper in your area. Do the same at a smaller daily or weekly. What are the major similarities and differences in how they produce their products?

Reporters must know the basics of newswriting before they can effectively report the news. This chapter reviews newswriting guidelines that reporters must follow.

You will be introduced to:

• The term *news* and its many interpretations.

• The inverted pyramid form of newswriting. Guidelines for writing an inverted pyramid are discussed and a story is dissected so that you can see how this traditional newswriting form works.

• The differences between "hard news" and "soft news." Alternatives to the inverted pyramid writing form are presented.

• Different types of leads. The chapter explains the types of lead paragraphs that reporters can use on news and feature stories.

• The use of attribution.

• The importance of following style rules. The chapter stresses that reporters must use stylebooks and dictionaries.

• Tips for effective newswriting.

Most reporters in the 1980s write news stories on video display terminals.

NYT Pictures

2 WRITING THE NEWS

"Those crazy kids are jumping off the Central Avenue bridge into the creek," the woman screams into the telephone. She tells the newspaper city editor the same thing she had told the police: "Someone is gonna get killed."

Within seconds after hanging up the phone, the city editor goes into action. She is well aware that there is at least a 20-foot drop from the bridge railing to the 3-foot-deep creek below. The caller was right. Someone could get hurt. The city editor sends a reporter and photographer to the bridge. She tells the photographer to take a few shots and come back, but she instructs the reporter to stick around at the bridge, just in case something does happen.

Is it news that people are jumping off a bridge into a creek on a summer day? Will it become news only when the police arrive? Will it become news only if someone is killed or injured? Will it become news simply because the newspaper decides to send a reporter and photographer to "check it out"?

Two persons are injured in an automobile accident in a small town. The local newspaper and radio station jump all over the story because it is news. Three persons are injured in a traffic accident in Denver, and none of the media touch it. Why? Isn't a traffic accident just as newsworthy in a big city as in a small town?

What makes news? Is there a rating system for events, with a clear line between those that are news and those that are not? Or does an event become news only when one of the media decides to cover it? Moreover, does an event that already is news become even bigger news when the media are involved?

For instance, the county assessor decides to hold a press conference to announce new tax assessments for residential owners. He schedules the conference for noon, and he makes sure that print and broadcast reporters in the area know about it. His office is crowded by 11:55 a.m. with broadcast crews and newspaper, television and radio reporters.

The assessor walks in 10 minutes late and looks around to make sure that he sees the reporters he hoped would be there. He begins to make his announcement, but a television reporter stops him. "Hold on, Jim, we're having some problems with the camera," the reporter says. Several more minutes pass, and the reporter tells the assessor, "Now." The official makes his five-minute announcement, several questions follow and the "news" event is over within 20 minutes.

There is no doubt that what the assessor had to say was important because the increased assessments would hit the public in the pocketbook. They would mean higher taxes during a period of high inflation. So why did he have to call in the reporters and the lights? Why not send a press release to the newspapers and broadcasters? He made his announcement and squeezed all the news out of it that he could. His motive could have been to reach as many people as possible through today's instantaneous communication system. Or it could have been to give himself additional exposure and defend his action to the voters. Whatever his reasons, because the media decided to cover the event, it became bigger news.

DEFINING NEWS

People always have been hungry for news, but they have not always had such a wide variety of news forums from which to pick. Less than 300 years ago, before the first newspaper was launched in the American colonies, people had to be satisfied with letters of news written to merchants, packets of newspapers from England delivered to America by sailing ships, pamphlets and even songs.

Then on Sept. 25, 1690, Benjamin Harris of Boston issued Publick Occurrences, Both Forreign and Domestick, the first attempt at an American newspaper. His unauthorized paper was shut down by Massachusetts Bay officials after the first issue—and the next newspaper in the colonies was not printed until 1704—but Publick Occurrences began a wave of American newspapers that over the last three centuries has brought readers news of anything and everything.

In his issue of Publick Occurrences, Harris said that he would furnish his readers "with an account of such considerable things as have arrived unto our notice." That might be as good a definition of news as there is.

In today's media-conscious world, news comes from many print and broadcast fronts. There is no single definition for the term. It is a four-letter word. Sometimes it is bad; sometimes it is good. It can be "hard"; it can be "soft." And today, it often is defined by the media. Any event can be news, but the public will find out about it only when one of the media thinks it is newsworthy. What the media consider newsworthy in Detroit may not be newsworthy in Miami. What the Los Angeles Times decides to cover may not be touched at all by the suburban newspapers in Los Angeles County. The lead story on one newscast may not even be included in a competing newscast.

Media use many factors to determine what events they will report. These include timeliness, proximity, consequence, the perceived interest of the audience, competition, editorial goals and even pressure from advertisers. *Hard news events,* such as disasters, speeches by leading government officials and police and fire news, are reported almost automatically. These are events that affect many people, and the primary job of the news media is to report them as they happen. There also are *soft news events,* which are not considered immediately important and timely to an audience. They still contain elements of news, however, and some media think they are important enough to report. Examples of soft news include an unemployed widow's journey to the state capital to solicit funding for a statewide job bank, a car wash by fourth-graders to raise money for a fifth-grader with cancer or reactions by residents to a new ordinance that bans smoking in public buildings.

THE INVERTED PYRAMID

SEOUL, South Korea—A North Korean pilot flying a Russian MiG fighter landed in South Korea Friday and asked for asylum, officials said.

Brig. Gen. Park Jong Sik of the South Korean Defense Ministry did not give the name, rank or unit of the pilot or disclose at which base the pilot landed.

Park said the defection is being investigated. Four other military pilots from communist North Korea have defected to the south since the end of the Korean War in 1953.

The Form

Most news stories are written in a traditional form that puts the most important details first, like the one above. The form is called an *inverted pyramid*. It begins with a terse opening paragraph, called a *lead,* that summarizes the principal items of a news event. The second paragraph and each succeeding paragraph contain secondary or supporting details in order of decreasing importance. All the paragraphs of the story contain newsworthy information, but each paragraph is less vital than the one before it. This writing form puts the punch of a story at the beginning, so it is different from the writing form used for novels, short stories, drama and some news features where an author begins with background and works to a climax.

Examples of the inverted pyramid form can be found in writing done before the mid-nineteenth century, but most journalism historians say that the concept was developed during the Civil War. Newspaper correspondents in the field sent their dispatches by telegraph. Because they were afraid the enemy would cut the wires or the system would malfunction, the correspondents squeezed the most important information into the first few sentences. Wire services, which used telegraphers to transmit stories until computers were introduced in the early 1970s, have continued to use the inverted pyramid form extensively. Stories written in this form are a staple of wire service reporting.

Newspapers also adopted the inverted pyramid form of news reporting because it allowed readers to comprehend the news quickly. Few people budget hours a day for reading news. It is convenient for the reader to grasp quickly the most important news of the day by simply skimming lead paragraphs. The form allows readers to decide if they want to continue. Readers can leave the story at any one of the easy "breaks" the form provides.

Finally, the inverted pyramid form is useful in the preparation of the copy. It enables copy editors to slice a story quickly from the bottom, and it helps them write headlines because they do not have to search through a story to find the key point for the headline.

Guidelines for Using the Inverted Pyramid

The following guidelines are useful for writing in an inverted pyramid form:

- *Avoid a "buried lead."* The essential ingredients of an inverted pyramid are the who, what, when, where, why and how of a news event. The most important of these are put in the lead paragraph and the rest are saved for subsequent paragraphs.

  For example, a beginning reporter handed this story to his editor:

  > Police Chief John Jones discussed Riverdale's crime problem with interested townspeople at a meeting Monday night.
  > Jones agreed to meet with residents who have grown increasingly concerned about the safety of their neighborhoods.
  > The chief said there were more serious crimes reported in the last 12 months in Riverdale than during any year in the city's history.

  The editor scolded the reporter for "burying" the lead—the item of primary importance that occurred at the meeting. The news peg obviously was not that the police chief discussed the city's crime problem—citizens knew the topic of the meeting *before* it was held—but what the chief said about it.

  The lead paragraph should have read:

  > Police Chief John Jones said Monday night that there were more serious crimes reported in Riverdale last year than during any 12 months in the city's history.

- *Keep the lead as brief as possible.* If you can do it in 25 words or fewer, fine, but never write a lead with more than 35 words.

  For instance, look at the following lead. It tells the key point of a lengthy story in only 17 words:

  > Philadelphia's 7,500 police officers will not get a raise until July 1983, an arbitration panel ruled yesterday. (Philadelphia Inquirer)

  Now look at the lead of an Associated Press story that the Inquirer ran on the other side of the page. Its 54 words make it a chore to read and understand. The writer should not have attempted to put two ideas into one sentence:

Efforts at the United Nations to avert an all-out war in the Falkland Islands entered the "final stage" yesterday as British Prime Minister Margaret Thatcher reportedly warned Argentina that it has 48 hours to make peace, and the military junta in Buenos Aires accused Britain of negotiating in bad faith while bombing Argentine targets.

In this case, the lead would have been more effective if it had said:

British Prime Minister Margaret Thatcher warned Argentina yesterday that it has 48 hours to make peace in the Falkland Islands.

Now the readers are given the news in 20 words. The United Nations peace effort and Argentina's accusations can be used in the second paragraph:

As efforts continued in the United Nations to avert an all-out war in the South Atlantic, Argentine military leaders accused Britain of negotiating in bad faith while bombing Argentine targets.

- *Keep all sentences as simple as possible.* Trim superfluous or hard-to-understand words. Do not clutter sentences with unnecessary adjectives, adverbs or subordinate clauses. Readers will leave a story that contains cumbersome writing. And they do not have time to look up words in a dictionary.

- *Whenever possible, write in active voice (subject acting upon object) rather than passive voice (subject is acted upon).* Active voice is considered more direct and vigorous. Here is an example:

An Arabian sheik gave a Pennsylvania mill town $35,000 Saturday to help pay the depressed community's debt.

Passive voice should be used only when the person or thing receiving the action is more important than the person or thing doing the acting, as in:

Sen. Alan Smith was killed Monday when a car crashed into his roadside office.

- *Write in past tense because you are describing past events.*

An Example

Here is an example of a news story that illustrates the inverted pyramid form.

Lead:

> Chicago firefighters battled dense smoke for nearly six hours Saturday to bring a multialarm blaze in a downtown frozen foods storage building under control.

The 24-word lead answers the five Ws:

- Who: firefighters
- What: battled dense smoke in a multialarm blaze
- When: Saturday
- Where: downtown Chicago
- Why: to control a fire

Second paragraph:

> The approximately 150 firefighters on 30 pieces of equipment called to the four-alarm blaze at the Booth Cold Storage Co., 121 W. Kinsie St., were hampered by the building's insulated construction, which is designed to keep food frozen.

This paragraph explains the lead. It answers the "how" of the story (on 30 pieces of equipment), tells how many firefighters battled the blaze and mentions their major problem. Most importantly, it gives the address of the building. All of this information is vital to the story, but it cannot be crammed into the lead. The reporter writes in general terms (downtown, frozen foods warehouse, multialarm) in the lead and then is specific in the second paragraph.

Third paragraph:

> The blaze broke out at about 12:15 a.m. Fire officials said the building was operating automatically overnight, so no employees were inside.

If there had been injuries, that would have been in the lead, but because there were none, the reporter saves this information for the third paragraph. The time the fire broke out also is important to the story, but it is not as vital as the information in the first two paragraphs.

Fourth paragraph:

> The fire was confined to the top floor and roof in the eastern third of the 8-story red-brick building.

None of the information in this paragraph is vital to the story. The reporter is giving readers additional information and also is providing them with a good break. They can leave the story at this point and still be satisfied that they have been given the news.

Fifth paragraph:

> Police and arson detectives were called in to make a routine investigation.

This paragraph clearly is the least important. It can be dropped from the story because it merely tells readers that response to the news event is routine.

In a longer story, the writer could have added more supplemental or background information, such as quotes from police and fire officials or details on other recent multialarm fires downtown. In this case, however, it was decided that the story was worth only five paragraphs. That decision could have been made by the reporter when writing the story, by an editor when editing it or by a makeup editor when placing it on a page.

HARD NEWS VS. SOFT NEWS

Today's reporters must be able to use alternatives to the traditional inverted pyramid form when they write. Hard news written in inverted pyramid form still is the cornerstone of American journalism, but more and more media are using a softer approach in covering everyday stories. In these stories, the key point is not necessarily put into the lead paragraph.

For example, a student reporter is assigned to write a story about the increasing burglary rate in the apartment buildings near her university. She calls the police department and sets up an interview with the officer in charge of the burglary detail. She finds out that the increase is alarming. The officer tells her that unless his department is given additional funding, his staff can do little to check the skyrocketing rate.

The reporter can handle the story as hard news and write it in inverted pyramid form, or she can handle it as soft news. Here is an example of each approach.

Inverted pyramid:

> Burglaries have increased in apartment buildings here by more than 200 percent in the last year, and police say there is little they can do about it.
>
> "Without a bigger budget and more manpower, we are powerless to reduce the wave of crime," Lt. Felix Ramirez of the burglary detail said. "The best we can do is hope witnesses will come forth and help us capture the criminals."

Ramirez blamed much of the increase on a climbing unemployment rate. He said another major reason is that most apartments in the area are occupied by students, who are at school all day long.

A softer approach:

It was about 5 p.m. Tuesday when Herbert V. Williamson walked in on three men who were burglarizing his apartment.

Panicking, the three thieves ran out and took off in their car. Williamson called the police immediately and then started to cry as he stared at his worldly goods dumped on the floor.

Fifteen minutes later, three men were arrested by police near the Saxton Street Mall after their car stalled. On the back seat were three paintings and hundreds of dollars worth of silver coins and clothing taken from Williamson's apartment.

Williamson and the three suspects are only a small part in the city's skyrocketing burglary rate, which has increased more than 200 percent near the university in the last year. Police blame much of the increase on a rising unemployment rate, and they say there is little they can do about it.

Of course, not all events can be covered either way. There are hard news events—a murder, a traffic accident, a speech—that need to be written in an inverted pyramid because they have immediate news value. Soft news stories, however, are meant to entertain or educate, so the reporter has more flexibility in choosing writing form and more room for creativity. Writers of soft news do not have to follow the rigid inverted pyramid form, but they still must tell all of the story as objectively as possible in easy-to-understand language.

A Little of Each

Most newspapers give their readers a mix of hard and soft news, even on Page 1. Usually the hard news story is on top, but many newspapers are beginning to put more soft stories on Page 1.

One newspaper that offers its readers both hard and soft news is the Wall Street Journal. Every day, the Journal prints sober business and finance reports. It also runs a "What's News" column that summarizes the top news stories. Mixed in with these are how-to human interest stories that center on the business world. The variety offered to readers by this blending of hard and soft news has helped make the Wall Street Journal the most-read daily newspaper in the United States.

Here are two examples of stories published in the Journal on the same day. They illustrate how the paper approaches news.

Story one:

WASHINGTON—Producer prices rose a moderate, seasonally adjusted 0.5 percent in November, the Labor Department said, and many analysts contend the inflation outlook will brighten further as the recession continues in coming months.

The increase, equal to 6 percent at an annual rate before compounding, followed a rise in October of 0.6 percent, or 7.2 percent at an annual pace, and a slim rise in September of 0.2 percent, or 2.4 percent at an annual rate.

This story is a traditional, hard news account written in inverted pyramid form. Although the story has many more inches, the first two paragraphs provide the reader with the most important information. Readers could quit reading after these two paragraphs and feel confident that they know what is happening to prices in the United States.

Story two:

NEW YORK—It was a real-life episode with elements worthy of a television drama:

A young woman is rushed to an emergency room with internal bleeding. An astute piece of medical detective work reveals that she has a rare blood disorder. While medical teams labor heroically to help her, the nation is scoured for supplies of a rare drug that she must have.

After reading two paragraphs of this story, most readers would think that it is about a young woman who has a rare blood disorder. But it is not. The story deals with dazzling hospital bills that must be paid by the hospitals themselves. Its main point is that a single patient's inability to pay a huge bill will mean that other patients will have higher bills or that, ultimately, hospitals will be forced to eliminate some services.

One story is hard news that will affect readers directly. The other is soft news that is meant to arouse their interest and educate them. Soft news also can entertain readers, make them angry, make them laugh, surprise them or teach them a lesson.

"Jello Journalism"

The success of the Wall Street Journal is not a signal for reporters to abandon the inverted pyramid and write only soft news leads. Some editors refer to the present overemphasis on soft news as "Jello journalism," and they want nothing to do with it. But there is a place for it. Very simply, soft news leads are useful on soft news stories. Generally, however, they should not be used on hard news stories.

For example, after a motorcycle gang roared into a national forest in southeastern Illinois and allegedly raped and beat two women, 10 motorcyclists were indicted on charges of rape, deviate sexual assault, aggravated battery, armed violence and unlawful restraint. In a follow-up story, the St. Louis Post-Dispatch reported that the cost of prosecuting the motorcyclists could plunge a rural county in Illinois into a financial emergency. There is nothing soft about that, but the readers were not given this information until the 11th paragraph of the story. The opening paragraph said:

> The two-lane road winds through the hills of Hardin County deep into the Shawnee National Forest in southeastern Illinois, carrying visitors far from the interstate highways and backward in time.

The next nine paragraphs build up to the paragraph that gives the news. Even the headline was written on the 11th paragraph. It said, "Cycle Gang Violence Jars Rural County's Budget."

In this story, a hard news lead should have been used. There was no reason to take the reader through 10 paragraphs before giving the thrust of the story. A soft lead approach would have been more appropriate had the focus of the story been the psychological effects of the attack on the two women.

THE LEAD—A FORMIDABLE CHALLENGE

The media might be placing more stress on soft writing approaches that emphasize people, but the basics of solid, accurate, concise and responsible newswriting remain important. The lead is the key to any successful story. It is the invitation. It also must be appropriate for the story and clear to the reader.

Even reporters with several years of experience contend that writing the lead often is the most challenging part of putting together a good news or feature story. In most cases, the type of lead is determined by the type of story. A hard news story usually is topped with a terse, hard news lead. *Features*—soft news stories that include human interest stories, personality profiles, in-depths, analysis pieces and backgrounders—can begin with any of several leads, all of which create a mood for readers. Types of leads include summary, anecdotal, contrast, staccato, direct address, question, quote and delayed.

Summary Lead

The *summary lead* is used on most hard news stories. In fewer than 35 words, it gives readers the gist of the story and lets them decide right away if they are interested enough in the story to continue. Reporters usually use summary leads on traditional news stories because readers who spend little time with the news demand the most important points high in the story. That way, if they do not read the entire article, at least they have been told the major points. Here are some examples:

WASHINGTON—President Reagan was shot and wounded in the chest Monday when a gunman lurking in the crowd fired a rapid volley of close-range shots as the chief executive emerged from the hotel. (Chicago Tribune)

BROOKFIELD—High winds at the center of a thunderstorm did major damage to four homes in the Imperial Estates subdivision here Saturday afternoon, but police said no injuries were reported. (Milwaukee Journal)

When James Freedman arrives April 1 to take his new position as UI president, he will be accompanied by a questionable record on affirmative action issues. (The Daily Iowan, University of Iowa)

Anecdotal Lead

Whereas the summary lead is the most common lead used on hard news stories, the *anecdotal,* or *narrative, lead* is the most popular on features because it paints a picture for the readers, placing them in the action of the story and then drawing them through it. Summary leads usually do not contain names of people unless they are well-known, but in an anecdotal lead it is acceptable to use the name of one of the people discussed in the story. Indeed, this type of lead allows readers to identify with an individual. It usually is written in a block of paragraphs and thus builds up to the major point of the story, so readers are deeply involved with the individual and with the train of events before they are told the real reason for the story. When anecdotes are used throughout, readers should become so emotionally attached to a character that they want to read the entire story, no matter how long.

Here is an anecdotal lead from a feature story in the Montrose (Calif.) Ledger. The first paragraph identifies one of the main characters but readers do not know until the third paragraph what the story is about:

Anderson L. Brooks was about to leave home for another day at work. He adjusted his black, narrow necktie the way he had for 40 years. He slipped on his favorite brown hat, the one with a sweat ring showing through the band. He lit a cigarette and left for downtown Los Angeles.

Brooks has seen downtown L.A. grow into an asphalt giant. His office is a three-sided box with three chairs, bottles, cans, brushes, peeling paint and girlie magazines. It's an office where he and his clients have aged. Brooks has been in the city's heart since 1937. He's 63 now, but he refuses to talk about retirement. He's too old to talk about another profession.

Brooks is a bootblack, a shoeshine man, one of a vanishing breed. He has been polishing boots and shoes in the middle of one of the world's largest cities for four decades. Brooks and his 60-year-old brother, Joseph H., operate a stand at Broadway and Second Street in the middle of smog and concrete. Before that, when Franklin D. Roosevelt was president, they had a stand several blocks away on Main Street.

Here is another example of an anecdotal lead. It was taken from the Daily Forty-Niner at California State University in Long Beach. The story, written by Ron Prichard, won first place in the annual general newswriting competition in the William Randolph Hearst Foundation Journalism Awards Program. The story dealt with the family of Ron Settles, a Cal State–Long Beach football player who police said hanged himself in jail after he was arrested on drug charges and for pulling a knife on two officers. A jury at a coroner's inquest after the death ruled that Settles did not commit suicide but died "at the hands of another." The story began on the day Settles' mother and father learned he had died. The lead effectively drew readers into the Settles' home, where the action of the story took place:

> At about 8 p.m., Helen Settles pulled her car into the driveway of her Carson home. She was greeted by neighbors who told her that police had stopped by several times that afternoon. A few minutes later, a Carson police car pulled up, and the officer asked if she was the mother of Ron Settles, Cal State–Long Beach running back.
>
> "They asked me about Ronnie," she recalls. "He asked me if he could come inside. . . . He asked 'May I fix you a cup of coffee,' and I said 'In my own house?' It was like he was nervous too."
>
> She said the first thing she thought of was an accident.

Contrast Lead

A *contrast lead* contrasts or compares one thing with another or several things with each other. These "old and new" or "short and tall" leads usually tell readers what the story will be about. They can be used in any type of news or feature story, but they are particularly useful in historical pieces because they show the differences between the way something used to be and the way it is now. Here is an example of a contrast lead:

> Scott Lovelace went to camp this summer.
>
> He swam, played basketball and ate three solid camp meals a day. He woke each morning to 7 a.m. wake up calls from a bullhorn. He went to sleep each night after a singalong around a blazing campfire.
>
> Yes, Scott Lovelace went to camp this summer. But at the John Birch Society summer youth camp high in the South Georgia mountains, Scott and 125 other teenagers learned more than just first aid and how to tie double half-hitches.
>
> Scott learned that marijuana is ruining America's youth. He learned that abortion is murder. He learned that newspapers and television lie. He learned that federal welfare is equivalent to stealing. (The Independent Florida Alligator)

Adam Yeomans, a University of Florida student, won second place in the annual Hearst Foundation general newswriting competition for the article from which this lead was taken. His "contrast" lead effectively introduced what Scott Lovelace learned at the John Birch Society camp.

Here is another fine example of a contrast lead:

> CAPE CANAVERAL, Fla. (AP)—Alan Shepard took a brief ride into space and became a millionaire businessman. John Glenn orbited Earth and today serves in the Senate. Neil Armstrong took a giant step for mankind and now promotes an El Dorado, Kan., oil firm.
>
> John Young was, is and will remain an astronaut. (Associated Press)

Staccato Lead

The words in a *staccato lead* help set the mood for the piece. This type of lead emphasizes a short burst of phrases that carry readers into the story by dangling some of the story's key elements in front of them. It is meant to tease readers and can be used on news or feature stories. Two examples:

> Friday. 6 p.m. In a tavern. Everyone's talking—until she walks in.

> The first day of his prison term. 3,649 to go.

Direct Address Lead

In the *direct address lead,* the writer communicates directly with the reader by using the word *you* in the lead. Such leads usually are not acceptable in hard news stories, where the writers should not communicate directly with readers, but they sometimes do work in features. Be careful with them, though, because some editors do not like them at any time. Here are two examples:

> Hard starting, black smoke and poor fuel economy are some symptoms that indicate it is time to check your car's spark plugs. (St. Louis Post-Dispatch)

> TGIF! You've had a hard week, and you deserve to be able to plop down and let the entertainment flow. (Judy Flander's syndicated television column)

Question Lead

Question leads are easy to write. They ask readers a question in the first paragraph and then give the answer in the second or a later paragraph. But be careful with them because some editors ban question leads. Their reason: Readers want answers in the lead. Also, editors contend that writers rely on question leads as crutches, using them when they cannot decide what the key point is. Still, these leads are used, sometimes effectively, on news and feature stories. For instance, a question lead worked on this story on Mehmet Ali Agca, the 23-year-old Turkish terrorist who shot Pope John Paul II in 1981, because it contained elements of news:

> ROME—Was it the lonely odyssey of a single-minded, criminally insane fanatic or the carefully planned movements of a paid killer, picking up money and support from international organizations? (Chicago Tribune)

In the next example, the question lead did not work as well because the readers were not given any news:

> LANSING—Is the bloom off the conservative movement in Michigan? (Detroit News)

Quote Lead

A *quote lead* is used on news or feature stories to entice readers. The quote may be the most powerful one in the story, or it may set the tone for what is to follow. Be careful when using quote leads, though. Some editors would say that using good, strong quotes in leads is effective writing; others would not allow it because they want a summary in the opening paragraph. When writing a quote lead, try to put the attribution in the first paragraph. That way, the reader is not forced into the second paragraph to find out who is speaking. An example:

> OWINGS MILLS, Md., Nov. 10—"What's the big deal?" Bert Jones wanted to know. Over and over during perhaps a half-hour session with reporters outside the Baltimore Colts' offices today, he kept saying that, until his voice sounded like a squeal. "It's not me. I'm not doing a thing. It's hilarious to me that a major obstacle can come out of something like this. You'd think we were having a second coming of (the Battle of) Gettysburg." (Washington Post)

Attribution is used in this combination quote-question lead, so readers know immediately who the main character is. But giving Jones' second quote in the lead makes it too long. It would have been better to have started the second paragraph with the second quote.

Here is another example of a quote lead:

> MICHIGAN CITY—"The closing of the Washington Park Zoo has never entered my mind, not the minds of anyone I know and it never will." (South Bend Tribune)

This strong quote lead would have been better if it had contained the speaker's name. Here, it was the mayor of Michigan City, Ind., so his name would have given the lead authority. By putting the name in the second paragraph, the writer risked the chance that some readers never would know who was speaking.

Delayed Lead

Delayed leads introduce suspended-interest stories that string along readers until the end, when the news peg or the main point of the story is given. Readers still are given news in the lead paragraph, but the "kick" of the story is saved for last. These leads are popular for the short, humorous "brites" that are used in newspapers. They also can be used on features or to give a news story a different twist. Here is an example:

> GRAND RAPIDS, Mich. (AP)—Big losers, 93 of them, were named the winners in a sports editor's challenge to his rounder readers: take off pounds and "Beat Becker's Bulk."
>
> Altogether, 973 readers of the Grand Rapids Press lost more than 4 1/2 tons in the six-week slimming contest, the newspaper said Sunday.
>
> About 2,400 people, who entered the contest to try to shed pounds faster than sports editor Bob Becker, weighed in at official stations around the city. After the six weeks, 973 people were game enough to weigh themselves again. The total loss was 9,148 pounds.
>
> Becker demonstrated his powers of reduction could match at least some readers. He dropped 17 pounds, from 238 to 221 pounds.
>
> The 93 contestants who equaled or surpassed Becker's performance are being offered a prize they might love to hate—the newspaper has invited them to an ice cream party next Saturday.

SECOND-DAY LEADS

Second-day leads are used to update stories, giving the audience something fresh. For instance, a morning newspaper reports that a businessman was wounded during the night by an armed bandit. The lead says:

> A jewelry store owner was shot four times late Tuesday by an armed bandit who burst into his store and took more than $5,000.

An evening newspaper and the evening news do not want to repeat exactly what the morning paper said, and so their reporters must focus on something new, such as the condition of the businessman or the arrest of a suspect. They look for a second-day angle. Their lead may be:

> A local jewelry store owner was in critical condition today after being wounded in a robbery at his store.

Or:

> A 32-year-old unemployed carpenter was arrested today in the shooting and $5,000 robbery of the owner of a local jewelry store.

In this case, new facts of significance were gathered, which warranted a second-day lead. Of course, in some cases reporters cannot find any new information, and their editors must decide whether the story is important enough to rehash old news. Usually, they decide to hold the story until there are new developments because readers and viewers are not interested in old news.

If the old news is run again—either because it is an important story that occurred after deadline or because the newspaper or broadcasting outlet missed it the first time around—the time element usually is "buried" in the second paragraph. Then the lead may read:

> A local jewelry store owner has been shot four times by an armed bandit.

The second paragraph could say:

> The gunman, who burst into the store Tuesday night and demanded money, took more than $5,000 in cash and checks.

THE TIME ELEMENT

In a news story, the time element belongs in the lead with the key points of the news because it conveys immediacy to the reader. It gives the "when" of the story. In a feature, immediacy may not be important, so the time element can be saved for a later paragraph.

Wherever it is used, the time element needs to be placed so that it does not disturb the flow of the sentence. Usually the best position for the time element is immediately after the verb. Some examples follow:

> A suspect was arrested Monday in the slaying of two nurses outside of Memorial Hospital.

> At least three persons were killed and 10 injured Tuesday when a tornado ripped through the west side of town.

> The legislature is deadlocked on the Equal Rights Amendment, State Sen. Nancy Neary said Monday.

Sometimes the time element cannot follow the verb directly and must be moved to a "comfortable" spot in the sentence to avoid awkward construction:

The City Council approved an ordinance Friday to fund the city's $200,000 tree-removal project.

Here the time element follows the object of the verb. The City Council cannot, after all, "approve Friday."

Although the time element should be moved to avoid awkward construction, do not place it between the subject and verb unless the sentence will not read any other way. For instance:

British jets on Monday bombed the airfield at Stanley, capital of the Falkland Islands.

Here the time element is put between the subject and verb so that the sentence will not read as though the jets "bombed Monday." The appositive after "Stanley" prevented the writer from placing the time element immediately after that noun, and it would have been awkward at the beginning or the end of the sentence.

ATTRIBUTION

Attribution tells an audience who gave the information to the reporter. It adds authenticity to a story and authority to the source or sources. An audience looks at what the sources say and then evaluates the worth of their statements.

Attribution is not needed when a fact is reported or when it is presumed that a reliable source was interviewed:

Two persons were killed Thursday in a two-car crash on University Drive.

The annual Fourth of July parade has been moved to Sixth Street this year.

Attribution is needed, however, when a reporter is repeating the opinion of a source, as happens most of the time.

Attribution usually identifies the source by name:

Drug-impregnated sheets of blotting paper are being sold to city schoolchildren, Police Chief Herman Mehring said Tuesday.

It also can be a vague identification if the source is being protected or a spokesperson is repeating an official position:

Mayor John P. Jones is using city funds to support a $200-a-day drug habit, an aide who wants to remain anonymous said Monday.

Prices on new cars will not be increased this year, the Ford Motor Co. said Tuesday.

Where to Put It

In these examples, the attribution is put toward the end of the sentence because the news is more important than who said it. If the attribution itself is the major point of a sentence, use it first:

> Arizona Sen. Barry Goldwater said today that he will not run for re-election next year.

Attribution also can be put at the beginning if it introduces a direct quote that is longer than one sentence:

> Mayor Kevin Jackson said: "I want to be able to work with the powers that be for the benefit of the community. I am sure we can cut crime and improve the quality of life. All we need is the necessary communication."

Notice that a colon is used after the word *said*. It is used because the attribution is introducing a multiple-sentence direct quote. If it were introducing a single-sentence direct quote, a comma would be used after the word *said*. Punctuation would not be used if the attribution were used before an *indirect quote,* a summary of a direct quote that uses no quote marks:

> Mayor Kevin Jackson said he wants to work with community leaders to cut crime and improve the city's quality of life.

Usually attribution for a multiple-sentence direct quote is put after the first sentence:

> "We must convince them that peace must win," protest leader Carl Hume said. "No country will win if a war is fought with nuclear weapons. There would be no world left."

Because attribution is put after the first sentence, there is no need to use it again after the last sentence. Even if the quote is more than one paragraph long, there is no need to repeat the attribution. In that case, each paragraph of the continuing quote would begin with quote marks, but no end quotes would appear until the quote actually ends:

> "There is no reason why we should have lost today," the coach said.
> "We have the talent to go out and win, but for some reason we are not putting it together. We have solid pitching and hitting, but our opponents always seem to do better.
> "There will be some changes in our starting lineup next week. That should help us."

It would be incorrect to write a multiple-sentence direct quote and put the attribution at the end of the last sentence because readers would keep wondering who is speaking.

If direct quotes from two people follow each other, introduce the second quote with its attribution:

> "We can't do it that way," Fire Chief Raymond Garcia said.
> Police Chief Frederick McAuley said, "It can be done if we have the necessary funding and manpower."

Writers can avoid using attribution with every sentence by using direct quotes. Attribution must be used with every indirect quote, sometimes at the beginning and other times at the end to vary the writing. If a partial quote is followed by a complete quote, use attribution between them:

> No decision has been made on whether Israel will attack "with all we have," Eitan said. "We are sitting and waiting."

Be Objective

Because *said* is a neutral verb, it should be used in the attribution for news stories. *Added* also can be used because it, too, is an objective verb. Do not use verbs that have connotations. There are many verbs to avoid, but here are some of the worst offenders:

- asserted
- claimed
- contended
- cried
- declared
- demanded
- emphasized
- hinted
- maintained
- opined
- stated
- stressed

There also are attribution words that should not be used simply because of improper usage. Here are some examples:

> "We will be there," he smiled.

> "We'll see what happens," he winked.

> "That's impossible," she moaned.

If a source did smile, wink, moan or whatever, use this construction:

"We will be there," he said with a smile.

WORDS THAT LAST FOREVER

As a reporter you should recognize that putting together a news story is not the same as writing to your sweetheart or doodling in your notebook during psychology class. As you sit in front of your video display terminal, carefully writing a concise, accurate, appropriate lead and then painstakingly weaving the remainder of the story together with logical transitions, you are aiming your writing at an audience that could number in the millions, for your words will last forever.

Your words will be printed today or tomorrow, but they will last for centuries—in a library, on microfilm, in a scrapbook, in an attic trunk. If you are covering a major event such as an earthquake, a war, an assassination, the return of hostages or a spectacular trial, thousands of people will save your words. They will compare your version with what they remember, or they will read your words to learn about the event. Readers save stories that affect them. Even the two-paragraph obituary you write late at night your first week on the job will be saved. Your stories become part of the permanent record of humankind.

Everything you write must be clear, terse and free of grammatical, spelling, punctuation and stylistic errors. All errors, even the "small" ones, point out that you did not do the best that you could. Some of your readers will catch even your smallest mistakes and, suspecting that you have erred elsewhere, will wonder whether they can believe anything you have written.

Use Vivid Verbs

The key to a good sentence is a strong, colorful verb. A vivid verb can indeed animate a sentence, as in, "The hostages snaked their way along the tarmac to freedom." Any photographer will tell you that a picture must tell a story; it should stand on its own and not need words to explain its meaning. Conversely, the words you write can paint a picture. Your sentences can so accurately describe a snowstorm, a riot, a trial or a parade that your reader can see the event.

Do It with Style

Following established style rules goes along with choosing the best words for a story. Some newspapers have their own stylebooks, but most use

The Associated Press or United Press International stylebooks. Style is more than punctuation, abbreviation and capitalization. It is a guide for a newspaper's uniformity. When reporters and editors follow the established style, their newspaper automatically becomes better reported, better written and better edited.

The current edition of the style guide used by the Detroit Free Press tells the staff:

> Most rules of newspaper work require no elaboration: Be accurate, be honest, be fair, be readable and so on. Adherence to these rules is absolutely essential for Free Press writers and editors.
>
> Rules of style, alas, are not so easy to summarize. Hence the development of this style guide. It is based on previous Free Press practices, and on the joint wire service stylebook, and on the ultimate rule, common sense.
>
> This guide is not intended to hinder the style of any writer or editor. There are no restrictions in that area except good sense and good taste.
>
> But each writer, each editor, each department is expected to spell the same way, capitalize the same words and so on. If we are sloppy with such relatively minor but eye-catching matters, the reader is justified in wondering whether we are sloppy with our facts as well. Let us not raise such doubts.

No stylebook is meant to lay down the rules of correct grammar. It is up to the reporter to know them. Nor will any stylebook be all-inclusive, but it can begin to show reporters and editors how they can make their newspaper uniform. Ask newspaper editors what the main function of a newspaper is, and they probably will say that it is to convey to its readers important, useful and interesting information in a relatively small amount of space. That means that the greatest story you ever write will go unnoticed by your readers unless it is simple, to the point and follows rules of grammar and style. Remember, as a reporter and writer, you are communicating with people who depend on you to give them an account of what is happening in their world, their state, their town, their neighborhood. They will continue to read your story if they can understand it and believe in it. They will turn to another page of the paper if they cannot.

WHAT'S THE SECRET FOR GOOD WRITING?

"The Editor's Exchange," edited and produced at the Newspaper Center in Washington, D.C., has published 20 rules for good writing. The tips were contributed by San Bernardino (Calif.) Sun editor Wayne Sargent, who noted that most of them came from columnist Jim Bishop. These are the tips:

- Be fair. Presenting all sides of a story is not copping out.
- Observe good taste.
- Make leads provocative, clear and simple.
- Sentences should be short.
- Quotes improve stories. Use them.
- An important story need not be long.
- Select adjectives carefully. Too many are dangerous.
- Don't be impressed with an important assignment.
- Go directly to the source on every story when possible.
- Leave no reasonable question unanswered. Do not assume readers know the background. And don't be afraid to write a good story you think readers already know.
- Be polite, but don't be servile.
- Get details. If your congressman wears high-top shoes, scratches his ears and uses a spittoon, you've created a word picture.
- Don't be afraid to try something that isn't in the book.
- Even if you have mastered the language, use short, easy words.
- Stories are improved by injection of time element.
- After the lead, blend the story from paragraph to paragraph.
- Don't insult a race, an ethnic group, a minority or other entity. Identify when it adds information. The distinction is thin at times.
- Don't abuse your privileges or the weapons of your industry.
- Admit errors quickly and fully.
- Name the source of your story when possible. If it is an exposé from a confidential source, protect that source.

If you are interested in being a superior reporter, make note of these tips. In addition, read everything you can get your hands on. Read novels, history, old books and new books.

Read newspapers, too. Besides teaching you current events and the distinction between hard news and soft news, newspapers let you see how other writers report. If you have the time, read at least three newspapers each day: a national paper such as the New York Times, the metropolitan daily that covers your area and a community newspaper in your area. All three will supply you with many different types of stories. They also should more than satisfy your appetite for news and newswriting.

Each newspaper has a style of its own that its reporters must follow, but basically writing is the same no matter where you are. You must:

- *Know how to spell every word you use in every story you write.* If you do not know how to spell a word, look it up in the dictionary sanctioned by your newspaper. Never guess. Never assume that a word is spelled the way it sounds.

- *Know grammar well enough to teach it.* Get a good grammar handbook. And again, use a dictionary. It will tell you not only how to spell a word but if the word is a noun, verb, adjective or adverb.

- *Follow the stylebook your newspaper has adopted.* Many metropolitan newspapers have their own stylebooks, but most of them are based on the AP or UPI stylebooks. Buy one now; it is an investment that will pay for itself many times over. It is a book that you can use throughout your entire career.

- *Remember that you are writing for some people who were not at an event but wanted to see it anyway.* You are their eyes. Use strong verbs to paint an accurate picture for your readers. It is your job to lift them out of their chairs and put them into an event. Make sure that they have a ringside seat for every event you are describing.

- *Report only what you see.* Unless you are writing an editorial or an analysis, it is not your job to interpret or editorialize. Your job is to paint a precise picture of the event. Do not retouch it. Readers really do not care what you think. Like a photographer, you are recording an event for your readers. Let them interpret it.

- *Never quit learning.* Do not think that just because you have had a college education in journalism you need no further education. College merely whets your appetite.

- *Never let the routine of the job overwhelm you.* You will dislike some of the assignments given to you, but stay enthusiastic and professional.

- *Learn from your mistakes.* When you make an error, admit it and do not make it again. And admit when a rival reporter does a better job than you. Better yet, do not let him or her do it again!

S U G G E S T E D   E X E R C I S E S

1. Use the following set of facts to write a five-paragraph hard news story. Then use the same facts to write a soft news story.

This is going to be a hot year for personal computers. Retail sales for home computers were $4.5 billion for this year and they are expected to double in two years. International Resources Development, Inc., a market research firm that specializes in electronics, estimates that from 50 million to 80 million people will buy computers during the 1980s, not because they need them but because they feel a need to become "computer literate."

Christine Munoz has a home computer. She bought hers because she is writing a book and the computer is making her job easier. She is writing a novel. "I can store everything in the computer's memory," she says. "If I need to make corrections, it's easy to call up a page, erase what I want to and make the correction. I also have a desk-top, high-speed printer so I can send parts of the book to my editor."

Right now, Christine has a Timex-Sinclair computer, for which she paid $200, but she plans to buy another computer soon with greater memory. Her computer has 48K RAM (random access memory), which stores 48,000 characters of data. It's not enough for writing books, but it was inexpensive and got her hooked on computers.

Many American and Japanese manufacturers are producing personal computers now, ranging in price from $10,000 to $60. Some have disc drives to run programs and some have palm-sized plug-in cartridges.

Personal computers are becoming big business for several reasons. First, there has been a strong buildup in recent years of software programs available to put computers to good use. The hardware has become smaller and sleeker and prices have gone down. There has also been heavy-duty advertising. And, everywhere we go today, we see computers—in store windows, at banks, in grocery stores, at the office. According to International Resource Development, Inc., one of the main reasons people are buying computers for their homes now is they fear they will be left behind in a computerized world.

2. Find a news story in a daily newspaper that is written in inverted pyramid form. Analyze it paragraph by paragraph to see how it is constructed. Are the most important points in the lead? Which major elements are saved for the second and later paragraphs?

3. Clip five hard news stories from a local daily. Rewrite the leads so they are people-oriented soft news. Then rewrite five soft news stories into hard news.

4. Listen to a radio newscast and a television report on the same story. How are they different? How do they compare with newspaper coverage of the same story?

5. Here is a news story from the Chicago Tribune. What type of lead is on it? Write as many different leads for the story as you can:

When you pay your bus fare, you should get a ride on a bus, not a camper with folding chairs in the back, the Regional Transportation Authority has decided.

You also should get a bus that runs, has heat in the winter, is equipped with working brakes and is on time.

These findings probably will be good news for commuters in Lombard, who have been complaining for nine months about service by a company the RTA hired to operate two of its routes in that west suburban village.

The RTA staff announced Monday it will ask the RTA board to cancel a contract with Sanders Charters, 10028 S. Hoxie Ave., Chicago, and replace it with a Lombard firm.

"We've had numerous complaints," said Joseph DiJohn, head of the RTA bus system.

Sanders has operated the routes since May 3, after being awarded a $43,333 contract. The next day, the RTA received 15 complaints about late buses on both routes.

On Dec. 23, the RTA sent Sanders a warning "after a camper was used in place of a bus taken out of service for apparent lack of a valid safety sticker."

The best reporters are those who know how to gather meaningful, relevant information during an interview. This chapter discusses effective techniques of interviewing.

You will be introduced to:

• The methods used in researching and setting up an interview. These two stages require as much attention and expertise as actually asking the questions.

• Closed-ended and open-ended questions, and when to use them most effectively. The chapter also explains funnel and inverted funnel interviews and when to use them.

• Ways to handle hostile sources.

• Taking notes effectively. The chapter explains when it is best to use the telephone and when it is best to conduct face-to-face interviews. The advantages and disadvantages of using tape recorders also are discussed.

• The similarities and differences in interviews for breaking news stories, features and investigative pieces.

• How to treat direct and indirect quotes and anonymous sources.

Sound interviewing techniques are necessary for reporters to write complete, meaningful stories.

© Hazel Hankin/Stock, Boston

43

3 THE INTERVIEW

An *interview*—the exchange of information between a reporter and a source—is vital to preparing a news story. When a reporter asks the right questions with finesse, a source becomes a window to the news. Conversely, a story can fail if the reporter asks the wrong questions, does not ask enough questions, does not know how to ask them or gives up too early on an irascible or close-lipped source.

Interviewing requires patience, confidence and an uncanny ability to listen, participate, observe and absorb everything that is said. Reporters must be able to ask a question and then listen to the entire response, all the time zeroing in on its key points. Reporters who are well-prepared should be able to tell when a source is telling the truth, embellishing it or lying.

An interview is divided into three stages:

1. The research
2. Setting up the interview
3. The questions and answers

Each stage requires careful attention and expertise. A shoddy job on any of the stages will show up in the final product. A thorough job on each stage will mean the best, most professional story possible.

Besides the general procedures that reporters must follow before and during the interview, there also are specific guidelines for conducting interviews for inverted pyramid news stories, features and investigations. The specifics will be discussed later, after the rules applicable to most interviews are examined.

THE RESEARCH

The key to a successful interview is establishing rapport with the source. To do so, reporters must do their homework so that they can go into an interview knowing both the background of the source and something about the subject matter of the story. Sources are most likely to relax and open up when they feel that they are talking to reporters who speak with knowledge and authority. Sources often volunteer little information when they think reporters are not asking intelligent questions or do not understand what they are talking about.

Most newspapers have their own libraries—called *morgues*—in which clipping files are kept on sources and subjects, and the paper's reporters can do much of their research there. Some newspapers close their morgues to the public, however, so aspiring reporters may not be able to use them. Check on local policies. If the local morgue is closed, the newspaper may have an index of its articles, which will make it easier to find the correct microfilm or clips at public or campus libraries. (A more complete discussion of newsroom and library sources is found in Chapter 9.) These libraries also have a wide selection of "Who's Who," encyclopedias and other reference books and indexes to material in books, magazines and major newspapers. In addition, many have copies of area newspapers as well as microfilm of newspapers from cities throughout the country. You will therefore be able to look up anything that has been written about the person you are interviewing. If nothing has been written on the source, thoroughly research the subject of the story. You should spend as much time as possible finding out about the source and/or subject of your interview.

If earlier stories have been written on your source, it is a good idea to talk to the reporters who wrote them. They can provide insight into a person's character and mannerisms and can tell you how easy the person is to interview. Profiting from the experience of other reporters will help make the job easier.

Some of the people you interview will be writers themselves. If they are, take a look at what they have written. A book does indeed reveal much about its author, and there is nothing like saying to a person, "I read your book" or "I read the article you wrote." Those few words really will relax your source.

When preparing for an interview with someone who never has been interviewed, you would be wise to talk to some of the person's friends or professional acquaintances. Any bits of information that can be gathered before the interview will make the entire process easier, and so do not hesitate to call one person to ask questions about another.

SETTING UP THE INTERVIEW

Once the preliminary research has been completed, it is time to set up the interview. Here are some guidelines:

- If you are not on deadline, telephone or write the person in advance to request the interview.
- Say that you are a reporter and name the organization for which you work.
- Establish a time and a place that are convenient for the person being interviewed.
- Tell the person the type of information that interests you.
- Tell the person approximately how long the interview will take.

In features and investigative stories, where the deadline is more flexibile, there usually is time to set up the interview in advance. In a breaking news story, however, reporters seldom have the time to call or write in advance to arrange interviews. In this situation, time is critical, and interviews are instantaneous. For example, there is a three-alarm fire in an apartment building, and six people are killed. Reporters are on the scene almost as quickly as the fire trucks. Firefighters are interviewed. Scores of questions are addressed to survivors and families of people who died. The reporters ask the questions quickly, often speaking with anyone they can get to.

In stories with less deadline pressure, setting up an interview helps curb the adversary relationship that can exist between reporters and sources. It allows sources to look their best and prepare for the interview. It also allows reporters to be well-prepared.

Phoning or writing in advance helps reporters get past the secretaries, public relations people and others who are on the source's payroll and often speak for him or her. Keep calling, writing or hanging around a person's office until the appointment is made. Explore every ethical avenue to arrange interviews with sources who are not interested in talking.

As soon as you contact the person, state that you are a reporter and identify the publication for which you work. If you are writing for class only, say so. When people know that they are being interviewed for publication, it becomes their responsibility to control what they say.

Whenever possible, make the interview convenient for the person being interviewed. Sources tend to be more talkative if they are on their own turf, and so let them decide on the time and place of the interview. Many times, they will ask, "When is it convenient for you?" If they do, then think of deadlines, dinner dates and growling editors. Otherwise, ride with them. Some of the best interviews take place late at night, in a meat locker at a butcher shop or in a helicopter dropping tons of water on a brush fire. The point is that you are stepping into someone else's world; therefore, an interview should be convenient for the source, not for you.

When setting up the interview, be sure to tell the person the type of information you are interested in. Tell the source something about the story and how his or her information will fit into it. That will help relax the source before the questioning begins.

It also is important when setting up an interview to tell the person approximately how long the interview will take. Newsmakers usually are busy people who must budget their time, so it is courteous to give them an idea of how much time you need.

Ask for plenty of time. Of course, if the person will give only a few minutes, take it. That is better than nothing. The important thing is to get the interview, because once people start talking, they often keep going past the predetermined time limit.

Once the appointment for the interview is made, keep it. If the interview is scheduled for 11 a.m., be there at 10:50. The only thing worse than coming to an interview unprepared is showing up late or out of breath. Getting to an interview early will show initiative and should impress the source. One other thing: Do not schedule one interview immediately after another. That way, the only person looking at a watch will be the source.

Also dress the part. There is no need to wear a coat and tie or high heels when covering a yacht race as a working crewmember. On land, do not wear a T-shirt, shorts and deck shoes or a sundress to interview the defense attorney in a murder trial. The best thing to do is try to dress at the same level as the person being interviewed.

ON THE INTERVIEW

Once you are on the interview, you need to pay particular attention to the ways in which questions are asked, the structure of the interview, observable details, hostile sources, the possible use of the telephone, taking notes and closing the meeting.

Asking the Questions

The timing and wording of questions during an interview can affect the source's response. Some interviews require only quick questions and specific "yes" or "no" answers. For these, it is best to ask *closed-ended questions,* which are structured to elicit precise answers. For instance, when a reporter from the Phoenix Gazette was ready to close in on the superintendent of a state institution for juvenile delinquents, he asked such closed-ended questions as, "Is it true that on Nov. 23 a 16-year-old girl was assaulted sexually by two boys in the recreation room?" and "You have been unable to stop students from harassing guards, haven't you?" By asking carefully worded questions such as these, the reporter forced the superintendent to be precise.

Open-ended questions are used when a "yes" or "no" answer is not immediately necessary. Because they allow a source flexibility to develop an answer, open-ended questions sound less intimidating. They are a good way to break the ice between a reporter and a source. Here are examples of open-ended questions: "In a coeducational institution such as this, how do you keep the boys and girls separated?" and "How do you handle students who harass guards?" Open-ended questions give sources an opportunity to elaborate in considerably more detail than would be the case with closed-ended questions.

Two factors determine which type of question—open-ended or closed-ended—the reporter should use:

- *How the subject seems to react to certain questions.* The reporter needs to gauge how the interview is going and then decide if specific, potentially threatening questions are necessary. Closed-ended questions should be reserved for a point in the interview when the source is relaxed and beginning to open up.

- *The length of the interview.* If an important source who is rushed for time is being interviewed, get to the heart of the interview right away. Chances are that sources such as these have been interviewed many times before, so that they are used to specific questions.

Funnels and Inverted Funnels

Interviews follow one of two patterns that are determined by the subject matter and the type of person being interviewed. One is structured like a funnel; the other like an inverted funnel.

The *funnel interview* is the most common and is the most relaxing for both the reporter and source because the toughest and most threatening questions are saved for near the end. These interviews begin with background talk, such as:

- "How long have you been in the city?"
- "How old are you?"
- "Tell me about your family."
- "Where did you get your experience?"

The background questions are followed by open-ended questions, which are followed by closed-ended or adversary questions. Funnel interviews are most useful when the source never has been interviewed, the length of the interview is not important or particularly touchy closed-ended questions need to be asked. By beginning with general, easy-to-answer questions, the reporter has a good chance of establishing a rapport with the source. Then, once the adversary questioning begins, the source is more likely to respond candidly.

In an *inverted funnel interview,* the key questions are asked immediately. This style of interview is used with people, such as law enforcement or government officials, who are experienced in fielding closed-ended or adversary questions. It also is used in breaking news stories when there is little time for the interview.

For instance, a U.S. representative has just voted for a controversial bill that will cost his state millions of dollars in lost federal aid. He is ready for the adversary questioning that is sure to come from reporters: "How could you do it?" "Don't you realize this vote might cost you your job?"

Memorizing Questions

Before entering an interview, memorize the list of questions you would like to have answered. Of course, the interview might take an unexpected turn and some of the questions might have to go unanswered, but still know in advance what you want to ask. During the interview, if you think of additional questions, jot them down on your notepad when you get a chance. Do not go into an interview with a long list of questions on a piece of paper that you must consistently look down at and read from. You do not want to appear as though you are merely checking off questions one by one as they are answered. That could intimidate the source. Once you have asked a question, it is important to be open for any response. Do not be so wrapped up in the eloquence of your questioning that you ignore what the other person is saying. Remember that responses to questions tend to be signals for additional questions, some that you might not have thought of while you were preparing for the interview.

Ask a terse, easy-to-understand question and then really *listen*. Let the person being interviewed feel that he or she really is conversing with you rather than responding to a list of questions.

The Need for Observation

In an interview, reporters are the ears and eyes of their audience. When they report accurately what a source has said, the audience can "hear." When they observe and then report the mannerisms and surroundings of the source, the audience can "see." Observations by the reporter are especially important in features because they add color to the stories.

During an interview, reporters should keep in mind the following:

- What is unusual—or common—about this person or place? How is the person dressed? How is the office decorated?

- Does the source articulate well? Is the source "comfortable" discussing this subject? Are there any outside sounds that can be heard during the interview? Is the source distracted?

- Are there any pleasant, unusual or unpleasant smells about this place or source?

Observations are important to stories because they paint sharp pictures for an audience. They are vital to features, but they also can be used effectively in news stories.

Here is a paragraph out of an in-depth feature on federal Judge Julius J. Hoffman, who at age 86 was about to be stripped of most of his duties. Hoffman had gained notoriety more than a decade earlier when he presided over the "Chicago Seven" trial of the 1960s (when seven men were charged with inciting riots during the 1968 Democratic National Convention in Chicago). The story appeared in the Chicago Sun-Times:

"I have no thought of retiring," said the proud Hoffman as he sat in his chambers, dressed to the nines as always, surrounded by walls of laudatory citations, awards and enlarged editorials. Some inscriptions he knows by heart.

Here is a paragraph out of a hard news story that appeared in the Chicago Tribune. It illustrates how a reporter's observations added color to a story on the sentencing to death of a man who had been convicted of killing a Chicago police officer:

> The prosecutor paced and pointed to the many Chicago police officers who filled the gallery of the 5th-floor courtroom. He then grabbed the murder weapon and waved it at the jury. "This gun is talking to you. What it says is worth more than 10,000 words. It killed a man who wears this badge," he said, picking up Doyle's police star.

Hostile Sources

Not every source is cooperative, easy to talk to and ready to admit wrong-doing. Often sources are hostile, especially if they are asked to reveal something they do not care to share with the public. In these cases, it becomes the reporter's responsibility to try to make a hostile source open up.

Of course, if someone does not want to talk, that is his or her right. No reporter can force a person to talk. Sometimes the reporter simply must give up on a source and look for another. In these cases, an audience must be told (for instance), "The senator refused to comment."

Here are some ways to convince a hostile source to open up or to keep a source from becoming hostile:

- *Do not act like a prosecuting attorney.* Avoid hostile questions. If you must be heavy-handed, try to save it for the end of the interview.

- *Be sympathetic and understanding.* That does not mean you have to be on the side of the source when you are sitting at your video display terminal.

- *Genuinely try to understand the source's position.* Try to find a reasonable explanation for any charges against a source.

- *Ask questions that show that you are knowledgeable.* Let the source know that you have done your homework.

- *If you have heard some damaging things about a source, repeat some of the charges.* Often hostile sources will open up to respond to charges against them.

- *Keep asking questions.* As long as the source does not hang up the telephone or ask you to leave his office, you can continue asking questions.

Rick Alm, one of the Kansas City Star reporters who covered the July 17, 1981, aerial walkway collapse at the Hyatt Regency hotel in Kansas

City that killed 114 persons and injured nearly 200, offers some additional advice on handling hostile sources:

> Do not be afraid to trade information. You can tell sources a little about what will be in the story. People don't like being interviewed cold. They want information, too. You can't just *take* as a reporter, especially in political stories. Sometimes, you have to be a conduit, trading information between sources.
>
> For example, we printed many stories about the Hyatt Regency. If I needed to interview a lawyer who did not want to talk, I had no trouble giving him some of the information out of the other stories if I thought it would help me get information.
>
> I sometimes have found that in dealing with hostile sources, it helps to say nothing. If you ask a question and the source says nothing, try saying nothing yourself. Wait until the source responds. There may be silence for 30 seconds, but if the source gives you a crumb, then you can keep asking questions.

Using the Telephone

The telephone is a valuable tool in an interview, and it is used more and more today in routine news stories. When reporters are covering breaking news near deadline, when they need to talk to a source who is out of town or when they are interviewing a source who knows them well, they almost always use the phone.

Of course, in many interviews, especially where the source does not know the reporter or there is no immediate deadline, face-to-face contact is important. The telephone should not be used as a crutch by a reporter who is too lazy to go out in the field. The rule of thumb is this: If you have the time, if the source is nervous or if you need to make observations for the story, interview the source in person.

Video display terminals are a big help in telephone interviews because they are quick and the source cannot hear them. The sound of a typewriter might bother the person being interviewed, so if one is being used for note taking, explain the noise in advance.

Taking Notes

During an interview, the reporter must understand and at the same time transcribe what the speaker is saying. To do that, it is necessary to write fast, perhaps devising some system for shortening words. Many reporters also use tape recorders, particularly in face-to-face interviews.

Tape Recorders
By using a tape recorder, the reporter can establish and maintain direct eye-to-eye contact with the source and conduct the interview as if it were a

conversation. Reporters who do use recorders usually take notes, too. Every experienced reporter probably has lost at least one interview because of a malfunctioning recorder, which is enough to make some reporters abandon the machines altogether. Tape recorders have two other disadvantages:

- Sometimes they intimidate and inhibit a source. Some people simply do not like talking into a machine that will record everything they say.

- They can waste time because the reporter has to go back and listen again and again to the recording until useful quotes are found. This problem can be eased if the reporter uses a footage meter with the recorder and makes notes of the location of pertinent quotes.

The great advantage of a tape recorder is that it provides a precise record of what is said. Especially in in-depth interviews, it is impossible to write down everything that is said, and so the recorder is useful to back up the quotes. The reporter takes notes to remember key points of the interview; then when it is over, the notes can be filled in by going over the tape.

A warning whenever using a tape recorder: Check the machine *before* the interview and take along extra batteries and tape.

Tips on Note Taking
Here are some tips on note taking:

- *If you are conducting an in-person interview, put your notepad and tape recorder, if you are using one, in an inconspicuous place.* The best spot for a notepad is in your lap. That way, the person is talking to you rather than to the notepad.

- *Do not worry about lines or neatness when you are taking notes.* Just write as fast as you can. You do not need to keep your eyes on the notepad; keep them on the person you are interviewing.

- *Do not be afraid to ask the source to repeat a quote.* It is not rude to say: "Excuse me, but I did not get down everything you said. Can you repeat it?" After all, both of you want to make sure a quote is accurate. Reporters usually wait until the end of the interview to do this. They make a note to themselves to come back to a certain point in the interview at an opportune time.

- *If the person you are interviewing is using terms that you do not understand, stop the interview.* You can say: "I'm sorry. I do not understand that. Can you explain it better?" Doing so will make the story better and will show the person being interviewed that you are conscientious.

- *Take as many notes as you can.* You always should have more notes than you ever would need to write the story. It is not unusual to write a two-page story from 15 pages of notes.

- *Do not forget where you are getting the information.* People being interviewed give reporters their opinions; therefore, what they say should be attributed. Make sure you attribute everything that is not fact.

- *Get in the habit of putting some type of symbol, such as a star, next to key phrases or quotes.* That is a good way of identifying possible leads or areas that need additional probing. Reporters facing a tight deadline often compose their stories mentally during an interview; then when it is over, they can head directly to a phone to call in the story.

- *Listen for key phrases and then write them down.* Do not try to write everything verbatim; it cannot be done. Let a tape recorder do that. All reporters have "systems" for quick note taking. They may leave out the vowels in words, use symbols for words, learn shorthand or have their own list of abbreviations. Any system that makes the job quicker is useful, but remember that best way to learn effective note taking is to keep practicing.

Recording Telephone Interviews

Some reporters tape-record interviews they conduct over the telephone. Doing so poses no legal or ethical problem if the person being interviewed is told that the conversation is being recorded. The problem occurs if the person is not told.

According to Los Angeles Times reporter David Shaw, 13 states—California, Florida, Massachusetts, Illinois, Pennsylvania, Delaware, Georgia, Maryland, Michigan, Montana, New Hampshire, Oregon and Washington—have laws that prohibit the taping of a telephone conversation without telling the other party. But in a comprehensive article published in the Times, Shaw said that the wording of the laws in at least four states "is so ambiguous that they may not, in fact, make all such secret recordings illegal."

Shaw cited the California law, which applies to "confidential communications," defined as "any communication carried on in such circumstances as may reasonably indicate that any party to such communication desires it to be confined to such parties." Thus, Shaw said, some newspaper attorneys interpret that statement to mean that newspaper reporters who conduct interviews via the telephone are sheltered provided that they identify themselves as reporters. Because the person being interviewed is talking with a reporter, he or she should recognize that the conversation may not be a "confidential communication." A spokesman for the California attorney general's office, however, told Shaw that some judges and juries might not agree with that "reasonable interpretation."

Aside from the issue of ambiguity, Shaw noted that most state laws exempt persons who are seeking information on felony crimes. This, then, could provide protection to investigative reporters.

Despite the practice's being illegal in 13 states (the Florida Supreme Court, in upholding the law there, said that such a practice "would pose a threat to citizens' justifiable expectations of privacy"), Shaw wrote that reporters in some of these states continue to record telephone interviews secretly. Because there is no federal law prohibiting the practice in the other 37 states (although telephone company regulations may call for the removal of a phone for secret recording), reporters in these states can secretly record telephone interviews legally.

That, of course, raises an ethical question.

In his survey, Shaw interviewed about 100 reporters from 12 newspapers across the country. About 40 said that they secretly tape-record interviews. Some said that they saw no ethical problem with the practice; others said they felt "uneasy" about doing it. Shaw found that those reporters who investigated criminal activities were more likely to justify secretly using tape recorders. Several reporters said that they recorded conversations simply to ensure accuracy and fairness to all parties.

Shaw found that editors were more likely to regard the practice as unethical. Many called it "a kind of entrapment."

Los Angeles Times Editor William F. Thomas issued a memo to his staff that said, "To clear up any misunderstanding, it is the Times' policy that telephone or other conversations be taped only after notification and with approval of the other party or parties." Shaw reported, however, that some Times reporters said they would continue to secretly tape-record conversations.

When questioned after his story was published, Shaw said that some reporters at the Times were not happy with it: "There was considerable resentment here among those people who believed that they should be able to tape."

According to Shaw, younger reporters—those who grew up in the electronic age—are more likely to use tape recorders than are older reporters. Shaw noted that some reporters are so enamored of the devices that they "take recorders to the toilet with them."

Shaw's opinion on the ethics of secretly recording interviews did not change as a result of his survey.

"I think when you tape somebody you ought to tell them," he said. "What it really comes down to is that journalism is not a game of, 'Gotcha: Gotcha to say something you shouldn't have.' We are supposed to be doing our best to get the facts before the public and to get people to level with us. I don't think the best way to do this is to lie to the person being interviewed—even by omission."

Shaw cited memos that were distributed at the Boston Globe, the Chicago Tribune and the Philadelphia Inquirer informing reporters that the practice was illegal in their respective states. He also cited oral policies at the Milwaukee Journal and the New York Times prohibiting the practice.

When It Ends

The more you and the source talk, the better the interview and resulting story, and so you should try to keep the interview going as long as possible. Keep asking questions until you have asked every one you can think of or until the person being interviewed has had enough. Keep your ears open until it is over because key points for the story often are made at the end of the interview when the source has relaxed fully.

At the end of the interview, thank the source and ask, "Where can I reach you by phone if I have additional questions while I am writing the story?" You then will have quick contact if you do need help, and you will show the source that you are trying to be accurate. Also, doing so forestalls a request from the source to see the story before it is printed.

Under no circumstances should you agree to show a source the story once it is written. People almost always want to retract or edit their statements once they see them on paper. If you are confused by something a source said, phone the person to ask for clarification or additional information.

As soon as you walk out of the interview, review your notes. Read them carefully to make certain you understand your own writing. Many reporters type their notes after interviews to help them fill in empty spots. If you used a tape recorder that malfunctioned, call back the source immediately and set up another interview.

Tips From a Pro

One reporter who has interviewed thousands of people is Neil H. Mehler of the Chicago Tribune. He has owned a weekly newspaper, been news editor of a daily and spent many years as the political editor of the Tribune. Mehler is now a copy editor at the Tribune, and it is his job to pick apart what reporters write.

"In interviewing a person in the news or a person who is anxious to be quoted—as with a senator or governor—a reporter naturally focuses on the news of the day or—as with an author or actress—the subject's area of specialization," Mehler said.

He added that the most difficult people to interview are those who are thrust into the news for the first time, such as a small-town official who is not used to vigorous and adversary questioning. "In this situation, I have found it useful at times to ask such an outrageous question that it produces an instantaneous angry or emotional answer," Mehler said. "For example, a village manager left the employ of a municipality I was covering. It was of some interest to me and others whether he had been fired or had left on his own. I put the question to a village trustee this way: 'You finally got rid of Mr. X.' He shot back, with obvious anger, 'We didn't get rid of him!' I had an answer that, I am satisfied, was truthful and put down all speculation. The same answer said with less emotion would not have satisfied me as to the truth of the matter."

Mehler also recommends using a tape recorder, especially when covering government officials who tend to change their minds. He said: "I covered the governor of Illinois for many years. One governor was a skilled media manipulator and attention-getter, but he often would deny on Tuesday what he had said on Monday. To counter this, I would tape all of his press conferences, type notes from tapes immediately and then have them available for his next media event, which was usually the next day."

Mehler added that when the governor attempted to skin back or lie about what he said previously, "I read to him from his press releases or my notes of his taped utterances. It was effective. His reputation, through this sort of behavior, suffered greatly and he was defeated in a bid for re-election. That gave me satisfaction, not in a partisan sense, but in the sense that a reporter had been able to accurately convey to the readers-voters what this elected official was like and let them decide whether they wanted to retain him in office."

Research before an interview is essential if the reporter wants to guard against liars, charmers and obfuscators, Mehler said. "But there is nothing wrong," he added, "with letting a person use your newspaper or broadcast outlet for personal gain—as with a person running for office—if there is news value in what he says and it is clear at all times that you are merely quoting him or making a reasonable reference from what he said. If the senior senator from your state tells you in a press conference or interview that the Earth is flat, he is to be quoted precisely. Then, in the story or in a sidebar, it is mandatory that the reporter note that this is not the accepted belief."

SPECIFIC KINDS OF INTERVIEWS

Although the general guidelines already discussed hold true for all interviews, different kinds of interviews pose different challenges for the reporter. The following sections discuss procedures for interviews for news, feature and investigative stories.

News Stories

To prepare for an interview for a news story, a reporter should concentrate on researching the subject of the story. In these stories, sources generally are interviewed to support or criticize the news peg of the story. Of course, news stories can be made from an interview with a single source, but generally the sources of a story are supplementary to the news event itself. For example, before a city council meeting, a city hall reporter would review the agenda of the meeting. Interviews are conducted after the agenda is reviewed or after the council meets. The lead of the story would be on the major accomplishment of the meeting.

Here is a portion of an inverted pyramid news story from the Kansas City Times. It illustrates how interviews are used to supplement the key point of a story.

Lead paragraph:

> Legislation designed to reduce auto thefts in Kansas City by placing tight restrictions on salvage yards—where missing cars sometimes end up—was derailed Thursday by the City Council.

This 29-word summary lead gives the "what" (legislation derailed), "who" (City Council), "where" (Kansas City) and "when" (Thursday) of the story. Now the readers know the major news of the story.

Second paragraph:

> "You have to create an environment that is not conducive to handling stolen vehicles," said Councilman Joe Serviss, who pushed the proposal. "If there's no market for stolen cars, ultimately there will be fewer stolen cars."

Now the readers know that at least one person was interviewed for the story. The quote is not important enough for the lead, but the reporter felt it was the top quote of the story. By using a quote, the reporter lets the source tell readers that legislation was needed. The paragraph shows opposition to the council's action.

Third paragraph:

> But, as 35 salvage yard operators looked on, the City Council rebuffed Mr. Serviss. Deeming the legislation too tough, the council sent it back to a committee for more consideration.

Here readers are given more of the Ws of the story: "why" (legislation too tough) and "what" (sent back to committee).

Fourth paragraph:

> "Finally, somebody is listening to what we have to say," said Eileen Hager, the president of the Greater Kansas City Auto Dismantlers and Recyclers Association.

A quote supporting the council's action is used. It shows readers that people from both sides of the issue were interviewed. Again, one of the sources talks directly to the readers, giving them an opportunity to draw conclusions. The paragraph shows that the reporter tried to be as objective as possible.

Now the tone is set for the story. There are 10 more paragraphs, but they follow the same pattern: Quotes and indirect quotes from Serviss and Hager are woven in with the news elements of the story, leading down to the least important. In the final paragraphs quotes are used from other council members who supported or did not support the legislation.

To prepare this story the reporter listened to the meeting and then conducted interviews afterward. The final product was 12 inches long. It contained two direct quotes and one indirect quote from Serviss, two direct quotes from Hager and one direct quote each from two council members. Although considerable time was spent interviewing the sources, the reporter had to choose only the very best quotes for the story.

Features

In an interview for a *feature,* an umbrella term for a variety of soft news stories, a reporter must find out as much as possible about the person being interviewed. In this type of story, the interviewee often is the key point; therefore, the interview can make or break the final product.

A feature can be:

- *A human interest story,* which offers an audience a greater understanding of a particular subject. These stories are reported because of their oddity or their emotional or entertainment value. Examples include stories on how the community is coping with city hall's order banning the watering of lawns and outside plants, how to repair your bicycle and the effect a recession is having on the town with the highest unemployment in the nation.

- *A personality profile,* which brings an audience closer to a person in or out of the news. Examples include an interview with the judge in a sensational murder trial and the story of a man in a wheelchair who just completed a trek across the country to raise funds for handicapped children.

- *An in-depth,* which through extensive research and interviews provides a detailed account well beyond a basic news story. Examples include stories on the effect cancer has had on a family that has lost three sons to the disease, how illegal aliens get into the United States and what is being done to keep them out and how one rock group made it to the top and another one failed.

- *An analysis piece, or backgrounder,* which adds meaning to current news by explaining the how and why of an event.

Features are not meant to deliver the news firsthand. They do contain elements of news, but their main function is to humanize, to add color, to entertain or to educate. They often recap major news that was reported in a previous news cycle or elsewhere in the same edition.

Because the deadlines for features are more flexible, reporters have plenty of time to thoroughly research and set up the interview. They also have more time to polish their writing, which is not constricted by the traditional inverted pyramid form.

An example of an actual feature interview follows. It illustrates the types of questions a reporter writes down (or memorizes) before the interview, after having completed the research; questions asked during the interview, which often expand upon or differ from the list of anticipated questions, and the way the interview guides the story, in this case a personality profile.

The story was written by Chicago free-lance travel writer Katherine Rodeghier for Discovery, the travel magazine of the Allstate Motor Club. Rodeghier began her professional writing career shortly after she finished her bachelor's degree in journalism at Northern Illinois University. She spent four years as education reporter and then four years as travel editor at the Daily Herald in Arlington Heights, Ill. She began her free-lancing full time in 1980, and since then has sold travel articles to scores of magazines and newspapers.

Rodeghier first queried the magazine to see if it would be interested in buying the article, a profile of 30-year-old Odessa Piper, who got her start baking bread in a commune and now owns L'Etoile, one of the finest French restaurants in Wisconsin. In its acceptance letter, the magazine told Rodeghier that it would pay $300 plus expenses to and from Madison, Wis., for a 1,000-word story. It also would assign a photographer.

After making the appointment for the interview, Rodeghier conducted her research. She prepared the following list of questions that she hoped would be answered during the interview:

- How did you get your start in the restaurant business?
- When did L'Etoile open?
- What is your background? You learned to bake in a commune— when and where? What led you there?
- Where are you from?
- How old are you?
- What do you think of Madison? What attracted you here?

- Do you have a published menu? May I have one?
- What are your most unusual dishes? What are some of the favorites with your customers?
- Where do you get your ingredients?
- What is your clientele? Do you get many tourists?
- What should a visitor see in Madison?
- What are your prices?
- What is the best time to dine here? Are reservations needed?
- How many do you seat?

In any interview, a reporter may not stick to the prepared questions simply because there is no way to tell in advance what direction the interview will take. The anticipated questions are a guide; they help the reporter prepare for the interview.

In this interview, which was conducted over lunch, Rodeghier used a tape recorder and took brief notes. It is a challenge to eat, talk and write at the same time, but it is something reporters must learn to do.

By the time the one-and-a-half hour interview was completed, Rodeghier had several pages of notes and two tapes of what was said. Here is a partial transcript of the actual interview:

Q—How did you get started in the restaurant business? (Rodeghier knew the answer to this question after her research, but by asking a background question first, she helped relax the interviewee and got the woman to talk about herself.)

A—After high school, I went to a commune and lived there for a year and we used very basic technology. We grew almost all of our foods except our grains. Our farming efforts were not always successful that first year, and we had to rely heavily on the grains. I really did a lot of bread baking and just fell in love with it. All of us were somewhat sheltered and certainly very indulged children who grew up in nice homes and had many opportunities, and here we were out in the commune practicing things that were really rough. It was quite an adventure.

Q—Why did you go to the commune?

A—Many of the commune members were Dartmouth College students I knew. We were exploring a different kind of lifestyle than going off and taking over Dad's company.

Q—How did the commune prepare you for the restaurant business?

A—I learned a great deal of respect for food because we worked so close to the land and did live right on the edge. What we grew is what we subsisted on. I think that's the part that prepared me. At the time I had absolutely no intention of running a restaurant. That seemed so, well, among other things, capitalistic. It seemed too indulgent for me.

Q—What did you do when you left the commune?

A—I moved to Wisconsin to a farm outside of Madison, near my sister. I continued to grow vegetables and bake. I experimented with other things using white flour and some sugar. That prepared me for a job I took at the Ovens of Brittany, which is another fine restaurant in the city.

Q—Did you have any problems in your early days of professional cooking?

A—My croissants would turn out to be these horrible tough things and the French bread would be flat. I refused to follow a recipe. I had the idea that if I was going to do this, I was going to learn about the process myself to create my own recipes, and it was very important to me for some reason. Madison didn't quite care if the French bread was kind of droopy and the croissants were hard. Madison gave me this ample opportunity to keep at it.

Rodeghier continued to ask background questions, which are important to any interview. The reporter must find out spellings, ages, addresses and other background information to make the story accurate.

Next, Rodeghier concentrated on questions about the menu, clientele and unusual things about the restaurant. The writer also made notes about the atmosphere in the restaurant, what Piper was wearing and how she spoke. In an earlier answer, Piper had mentioned a partner, something Rodeghier did not know about, so Rodeghier wanted to pursue that point:

Q—When you first opened, you had a partner? What happened?

A—In the beginning, we were equal partners. What made the partnership end is that it quickly became unequal. All the lawyers and the bankers and suppliers would talk to him. This shows how times have changed because I don't think this would necessarily happen now. Women's liberation wasn't as developed then as it is now. I know a lot of women in business now. I think it's delightful. It's wonderful. My partner was interested in the limelight. Then things went wrong. Everything that could go wrong did. We lost a lot of money. I became ill. My partner was disillusioned and decided to leave. We were deep in debt. I knew I had to pick it up and rebuild it and carry it on. I felt an extraordinary love for the place.

These are only six of the dozens of questions that were asked during the interview. Many answers led to questions that Rodeghier had not anticipated. Near the end of the interview, Rodeghier quickly referred to her notes to ascertain that she had asked all the questions she wanted to.

"I told her I was going to check my notes," the writer said. "I think it is important for a reporter to make sure all the questions are asked because an editor might want some very specific things covered."

When she sat at her typewriter to write the story, Rodeghier had to condense all of the information into 1,000 words, about four typewritten pages.

A key point of this personality profile is that a former commune member has become the owner of a successful French restaurant. Rodeghier's two-paragraph contrast lead showcases that point for readers:

When Odessa Piper was baking bread in a New Hampshire commune 10 years ago, few guessed she would one day own one of the finest gourmet restaurants in Madison, Wis.

Today, at the tender age of 30, Piper has already put in more than five years as proprietor of L'Etoile, a tiny shrine to fine cuisine on Madison's star-shaped capitol concourse.

Next, the writer brings the readers into the restaurant. More background information will come later:

Gourmet doesn't necessarily mean stuffy. Piper personally greets diners—among them state Supreme Court justices, legislators and members of Madison's artistic and academic communities—and recites selections from the blackboard menu.

"It's an opportunity for me to talk with my clientele," says Piper. "I tell them about nouvelle cuisine without a lot of falderal. I don't want my customers to feel anxious or afraid. Unfortunately, so many people make that connection with a gourmet restaurant. Delivering the menu to them is a chance to ease their mind."

By using a direct quote in the fourth paragraph Rodeghier allows one-on-one communication between the source and the reader. Establishing that source–reader relationship early in the story is important.

Rodeghier comes back to the background questions in the middle of the story. Before that, she uses words to paint a picture of the restaurant. She sprinkles in plenty of quotes and gives readers necessary information, such as the prices. Because she has only a limited number of words in which to tell the story, she must pare any information that is not absolutely vital to it. For instance, Piper told her quite a bit about the doomed partnership that started L'Etoile, but in the story Piper's statements were boiled down to this sentence:

Through serious financial reverses, and the loss of her partner, she struggled to make L'Etoile a commercial as well as culinary success.

By the end of the story, readers should feel that they know Piper, what she serves, how she prepares it, how much it costs, who eats it and what the atmosphere of L'Etoile is like. Rodeghier finishes the story with a quote, an effective way to end features. Piper is put in direct communication with the readers:

For Piper, Madison's appeal lies in its intellectual and artistic atmosphere—its theater, dance and art openings—and its proximity to the lakes and forests and rural areas of central Wisconsin. When she takes time off from L'Etoile, she enjoys day trips in the country to bike, canoe or simply explore a small town and "find a good restaurant at the end of the day."

Rodeghier said her eight years as a newspaper reporter prepared her for her career as a free-lancer. "I established many contacts in my four years as travel editor," she said. "I think it is important to have experience on a publication. It exposes people to editors and how they think and the deadline pressures and other pressures of writing."

Investigative Stories

In preparing for an investigative piece, a reporter must research both the topic and the source. Because this type of story often entails probes that reveal wrongdoing by an agency or official, the interviews tend not to be as easy as those for news stories or features. Instead, an adversary relationship often exists between the reporter and the source, making the interviewing process more difficult. To succeed, investigative reporters try to know the answers to many of their questions before they ask them, and thus thorough research before the interview is imperative. Investigative stories also require more interviews than news stories or features, especially if the reporter is trying to expose corruption. Investigative stories may deal with international topics, such as how and where terrorists receive funding to travel throughout the world; national topics, such as congressional sex scandals, or local topics, such as graft in the police department or city hall. Clearly, when reporters work with stories like these, sources are not going to be helpful or friendly. They even may be frightened.

Often the ideas for investigative stories come from news tips. For instance, a terrified guard at Arizona's medium security institution for juvenile delinquents called the Phoenix Gazette. She did not want to give her name, but she did want to talk about what she termed the "total breakdown" in control at the "school." The reporter immediately asked her name, but she was afraid to give it. She said she would lose her job if the institution's superintendent found out that she called the newspaper.

Her story was a shocking account of harassment, drugs and sex. She called back the next day and told more, but she still refused to go on the record. She did give her phone number to the reporter, who told her repeatedly that unless she went on the record, her story might never be told. The reporter told her that the story was so important that the public's right to know superseded even her own fears.

By the second day, the reporter began calling other guards named by the woman. He also arranged an in-person interview with a state legislator who was leading an investigation of the institution. On the third day, when he talked to the woman again, the reporter had enough information to substantiate many of her charges that drug use and sex were rife at the institution. Because several other guards agreed to go on the record, the woman did, too.

After gathering all the evidence necessary to make a story, the reporter called the institution's superintendent—the story's central character—and requested an interview. It was set up in the superintendent's office—his own turf—at a time most convenient for him. The reporter told the superintendent that he was planning a series on the institution.

The reporter began the interview by shaking hands with the superintendent and other officials at the school. Next came background questions on the superintendent's experience. (Actually, the reporter already knew most of this information, but he wanted the superintendent to feel relaxed. He wanted to establish a rapport before he began asking adversary questions.)

Next the superintendent conducted a tour of the institution, something he enjoyed doing. He pointed out the openness with which students were allowed to move, the cleanliness of the buildings and the well-equipped classrooms. He did most of the talking.

By the time he returned to his office, the superintendent felt comfortable with the reporter. He had talked for more than an hour, and none of the questions had challenged him. Then the reporter began asking adversary questions:

- "Is there a sex problem here?"
- "Do the inmates have access to drugs?"

Because these questions were not specific, the superintendent was able to answer them simply by saying, "I'm positive we have less dope and less sex here than at a public school." Then the reporter unfolded a series of questions that included specific names, dates and experiences. The superintendent could have denied that the specific incidents had occurred, but it was too evident that the reporter had done all of the necessary homework. By the end of the interview, the official admitted that he wished things were better and that he faced some monumental problems he probably could not solve. Within six months, as a result of the four-part Gazette series and an investigation by the state legislature, the superintendent was fired.

WRITING THE STORY

Once the interview is completed, the reporter is ready to write the story. In doing so, reporters must determine whether or not to quote and how to treat anonymous sources.

Quotes

To quote or not to quote is a major consideration reporters face after conducting an interview. Some use direct quotes sparingly because they do not want their stories to read like speeches. Others use quotes as often as possible because only then can the speaker talk directly to the readers.

There are no definite rules on when to use a direct quote. Still, direct quotes should not be wasted on commonplace statements. Reserve direct quotes for the most specific, vivid statements the source makes. For example, do not waste a direct quote on a statement such as, "We will consider several important items at our next regularly scheduled council meeting." That statement could have been paraphrased and attributed. Direct quotes should be saved for this kind of statement: "Our next council meeting will be a blockbuster. The zoning issue must—and will—be hammered out at that session."

Misquoting is a cardinal sin. That does not mean that quotes cannot be altered slightly to clean up grammar or to take out profanities; it means that quote marks around a sentence are somewhat sacred. They mean the words are exactly—or nearly exactly—what the person said.

Generally, it is a good idea to sprinkle direct quotes throughout an interview story. Let the speaker talk to the readers, but make sure that the direct quotes are accurate. When in doubt, use an indirect quote. Remember, an indirect quote also is attributed; it simply is not in the exact words the speaker used. Never make up direct quotes. They often can make a story read better, but made-up quotes do not say much for the scruples of the reporter.

At times, reporters must use the "words-in-your-mouth" technique for interviewing people, especially when the source never has been interviewed or dislikes reporters. Be careful here, though, because it is too easy to make up quotes when using this technique. For example, a reporter is interviewing an inarticulate person who seems to answer every question with a "yep." The reporter appreciates the terse responses and the easy note taking, but a story cannot be filled with "yeps." The reporter says to the person, "Did the pain feel like a sharp, blinding jab in your head?" The response is, "Yep, that is how it was." The reporter then uses an indirect quote in the story, which reads, "Smith said the pain felt like a sharp, blinding jab in the head."

Use the technique when it is needed but use it sparingly, and never fake it and pass it off as a direct quote.

Anonymous Sources

Each time reporters conduct interviews, they face the risk that their sources will request anonymity. Therefore, reporters on any size newspaper—from a college weekly to the largest metros in the world—must learn how to deal with people who are willing to provide information as long as their names are not used in the story. There are no hard and fast rules on dealing with requests for anonymity because every story is different, but there are general guidelines that all reporters can follow.

Unless the story is a secret investigation that requires anonymity on the part of the reporter, sources always should be told immediately, "I am a reporter and what you say may be published." Then it is the source's responsibility to practice self-control. Of course, some sources know that they are talking to a reporter and still ask for anonymity after they have talked far too long and too much. When that happens—and it does quite often—reporters must make a decision either to use the name anyway or respect the other person's wishes. In making this decision, the reporters must consider the importance of the story, the value of the source, the laws of their state and the editorial policies of their newspapers.

Sometimes anonymous sources are government or corporate officials who do not want their names used because they believe that their bosses or the institutions for which they work want credit for the statement. For instance, a "high ranking official" may be the secretary of state making an important policy statement about diplomatic relations with a foreign nation. The reporters know who said it, but they use the nameless attribution because that was the condition of the interview. They also may use phrases such as "the Department of State said today" or "the White House said today" when quoting officials who wish to remain anonymous.

In most cases reporters will use anonymous sources only when they cannot find other sources who will go on the record. In nearly all cases, newspapers will not run a story based on a single anonymous source because the chances of error are too great.

Anonymous sources sometimes are valuable because they can lead you to other sources, and so do not turn them off simply because they do not want to have their names used. Explain to them newspaper policies regarding the use of anonymous sources and the importance of their being identified in the story. Often people can be convinced to go on the record if they realize how vital the story is and that without identified sources it may never be printed. If nothing works, look for other sources, using the unnamed source for guidance.

"Reporters must name the source of information in every story whenever possible," the Denver Post's policy regarding sources states. "Exceptions must be thoroughly discussed with editors and house counsel." The paper also tells its reporters to avoid using unnamed sources if possible and when confronted with them to seek alternative sources and documentation.

The Bangor (Maine) Daily News instructs its reporters: "If reporter and editor see clear need for confidentiality, the reason for anonymity should be explained in the story as fully as possible short of identification. If the reason isn't good, scrap the source and the quote." Also, "Information from an anonymous source should be used only if at least one other source substantiates the information."

At the Detroit Free Press, reporters are not allowed to promise news sources absolute confidentiality on their own. At least one editor must know the identity of the source, and it is up to a supervising editor, in consultation with the reporter, to make the decision on whether or not to use the unnamed source. "What's involved here is not a question of trust but rather a question of protecting the staff and the newspaper from possible problems," Managing Editor Neal Shine said. "Sources for stories will be named in the story unless the reason not to do so is an overriding consideration."

The best guideline to follow is this: Avoid using unnamed sources. Even if you are in a crowd at a breaking news story, ask people their names, addresses and phone numbers. Don't be lazy. If one person will not give his or her name, find someone who will.

S U G G E S T E D   E X E R C I S E S

1.   Practice interviewing a fellow student while taking notes on a video display terminal or typewriter. Do it again and take notes by hand. Which way was the quickest for you? Where do you need practice?

2.   Start a list of words that you have shortened for note-taking purposes. Look at the following examples and then try to think of more: u r—you are, w/—with, cty—city, ctrm—courtroom, sch—school.

3.   Interview a government official who has been interviewed many times. Do the same with someone who never has been interviewed. Which was easier to set up? Who was easier to interview?

4.   Pick a government official or celebrity in your area and thoroughly research his or her background for a personality profile interview. Then set up an appointment with the person, conduct the interview and write the story.

5.   Interview a fellow student, using both a notepad and a tape recorder. Compare your notes with the tape to see how accurate you are.

People hold press conferences and give speeches because they want to get a message across to an audience. Sometimes they also want to be on Page 1 of the newspaper or on the evening newscasts. This chapter discusses how reporters take the newsworthy points of press conferences and speeches and put them into understandable news stories.

You will be introduced to:

• The differences and similarities between covering Washington, D.C., and local politics. Lesley Stahl, CBS News White House correspondent, calls the White House "the ultimate stakeout."

• Preparations for a press conference. The chapter offers tips from Kenneth Reich, political writer for the Los Angeles Times.

• The steps a student reporter takes from receiving an assignment to cover a press conference to actually writing the story. The chapter explains how the reporter strings together her story.

• How to prepare for and cover a speech. Examples of a speech and the resulting news story are given.

President Reagan calls on reporters at a news conference.

UPI

69

4 ON ASSIGNMENT: PRESS CONFERENCES AND SPEECHES

Imagine that you are a reporter in Washington, D.C., and you are about to cover your first presidential press conference at the White House. You work for a major metropolitan newspaper that has a Washington bureau, and you are one of five reporters in the bureau who cover the nation's capital. Washington was not your initial assignment; first you had to prove yourself on a local level.

It is early in November and trees are losing their summertime dress of green. Crews around government buildings clear away the brown, fallen leaves as squirrels gather nuts. The air is crisp, the sky overcast and for the first time in your life you honestly feel alone and small. The beauty and vastness of the buildings and the history they represent overpower you. The people inside of them try to.

You are young, but youth does not exclude a reporter from such a choice assignment. It takes talent and perseverance. The competition is fierce, and only the best reporters make it. You can smile simply because you are one of them.

Even when you were in college dreading your next assignment in public affairs reporting, your main goal in journalism was to be a Washington correspondent. So here you are, sitting in a crowded room with some of the best-known reporters in the world. Within seconds, in will walk the most powerful person in the world. Then it will be you and the other reporters against the president. There will be about 300 reporters in the room. The press conference will last 30 minutes. You don't even know whether you will have a chance to ask a question.

MEDIA EVENTS

Presidential press conferences are major media events, usually staged in prime time, when the nation's top reporters challenge the president. They are big shows for both sides because millions of people will be watching every move, every statement.

It wasn't always that way. The presidential press conference began during Theodore Roosevelt's administration when reporters gathered around the president's desk for a chat. When Herbert Hoover walked into his first meeting with the 30-member Washington press corps in his office on March 5, 1929, he said, "It seems that the whole press of the United States has given me the honor of a call this morning." By the time Harry Truman was president, the press conference drew big crowds. At his last conference, on Dec. 31, 1952, there were 322 reporters in the Executive Office Building.

Television and radio coverage of presidential press conferences began during Dwight D. Eisenhower's term. In the early days of his presidency, portions of film and sound track were released for broadcast hours after the conference, which gave Eisenhower's staff time to delete questions and answers they felt needed to be cut, but after several months, the entire transcript was released for broadcast and newsreels. Eisenhower also started the practice of having reporters identify themselves and their connections before asking their questions.

Instead of holding regular press conferences, which his aides considered too much of a political risk, President Ronald Reagan has turned to the safety of radio and TV addresses to the nation and informal, less challenging interviews in the Oval Office with friendly reporters.

In his early press conferences, Reagan also eliminated other traditions. At Reagan's first press conference, instead of allowing reporters to jump from their seats and yell "Mr. President" to be recognized, the administration required them to remain seated and raise their hands until Reagan called on them. At his second conference, Reagan and his aides picked the questions by a lottery. Names were selected from a jelly bean jar.

"THE ULTIMATE STAKEOUT"

At a speech before the Society of Professional Journalists in 1981, Lesley Stahl, CBS White House correspondent, called the White House "the ultimate stakeout." She said, "We all sit around waiting for someone to call us or a chance to shout a question. There is a natural instinct, a feeling of them [administration officials] against us [Washington reporters]."

Like it or not, most of the reporters who cover the White House only have access to certain people and news, which is one of the ways the administration manages the news each day. Although reporters would like to get all the news, administration officials would like to give out only the news that is favorable to them. They must protect the president and national security.

With hundreds of reporters covering the president, an individual has little chance of easy access. Exclusive stories are few and far between, which can make the job tedious and give a reporter a real sense of helplessness. The best reporters are the ones who go beyond the press conferences, speeches and White House handouts to dig up news.

Despite its problems, the White House and/or Washington assignment probably is the most prestigious in journalism. America's heart beats in Washington, and journalists and their organizations attach great importance to the coverage of politics there. Indeed, many of the nation's most famous and best-paid reporters are covering or have covered stories in the nation's capital, one of the world's great news centers.

There are plenty of stories in Washington. Although the president and other top officials in the administration are hard to get to, every member of Congress is ready to fill any news vacuum. Senators and representatives want their views known, and reporters have no problems getting stories on Capitol Hill. There are scores of stories every day in federal departments, too, but few news organizations have the staffs to cover each department daily.

Finally, the Supreme Court is covered daily by a handful of highly specialized reporters. They follow major cases and then write understandable accounts of the justices' decisions.

For many reporters, covering politics in Washington is the pinnacle of their careers. Early in their professional lives they made becoming a Washington correspondent their goal. For many other reporters, however, the best place to cover politics is on the state or local level, where there is more ready access to the people in power. On these levels, reporters often can talk to top government officials simply by telephoning them. Exclusive stories are much easier to obtain.

THE PRESS CONFERENCE

Candidates, officials and other people hold press conferences for one or all of the following reasons:

- They feel an obligation to make information public.
- They want to get a message to as many people as possible.
- They would like to be seen on Page 1 of the newspaper and on the evening newscasts.

A press conference is a gang interview, which means that every reporter present is going to get the same information. There is another drawback, too. People who hold press conferences usually know in advance what they want to say. They will get their message across and will not say much more, especially if they are experienced at fielding adversary questions from reporters. Therefore, even before the press conference begins, reporters should research the subject and speaker thoroughly. That way, they make sure that their questions are on target. Being prepared helps them to dig out the key information from all the rhetoric.

"Most press conferences are simply canned information," according to Kenneth Reich, political writer for the Los Angeles Times. Reich should know. In his 17 years at the Times, he has covered politicians at every level of government. "An experienced person holding a press conference is able to control it more than the reporters can," Reich added. "They pretty much know what they are going to say and they do not go beyond that. Inexperienced people, or people who lose their temper, such as Richard Nixon, are the people who hold interesting press conferences."

Reich said that even on the local level, the press conference has become a highly stylistic show. "People use press conferences to get 30 seconds on television," he said. "In the case of a candidate, what print journalists say months before an election is important because that's when people are interested in an in-depth look at a candidate. But when you get closer to the election, everyone who is voting is looking at TV. When a candidate calls a press conference at this time, it is going to be for TV. Every remark is going to be 30 seconds long."

Telephone interviews and careful attention to what candidates and officials say on television and in mail to constituents usually provide more useful information than a press conference, Reich added. Still, press conferences should be covered, especially on the local level where they are often more spontaneous. Reich offers the following tips to reporters who are covering a press conference:

- *Read as many clippings as possible about the person who is holding the press conference.* This point should be especially followed if you have not covered the person before. Never go into a reporting situation uninformed. "If you are assigned to cover a press conference in a tiny town where there has just been a sensational murder, you had better know something about that town before you go in."

- *Talk to other reporters.* They can help you get the lay of the land.

- *Be flexible.* Thus, if an issue comes up that you had not expected, you are ready to jump in and ask the appropriate questions. Again, doing your homework before the press conference will help prepare you for unexpected events. Do not be too rigid in your questioning. Too many reporters enter a press conference with the story's headline in mind. Do not be afraid to change your approach if you have a gut reaction or hear something unusual.

- *Listen carefully.* Often you will need to read between the lines.

Preparing for a Press Conference

Broadcast reporters have an advantage over print reporters during a press conference because the speaker wants to be seen as well as heard. Hence broadcast reporters are more likely to control the questioning, which usually is limited in time. All reporters at the conference, however, have the same function: They are there to ask questions and to make the person answering them say something newsworthy. Because of time or space limitations, the reporters may be there to obtain answers to only a couple of specific questions. They all know they cannot report everything that is said, and so they try to get their specific questions answered. They also listen to the other questions and their answers just in case something new or unexpected pops up. It is up to the reporters to challenge the speaker to provide something more than rhetoric.

Let's examine a specific case to see how reporters handle press conferences. A candidate for governor plans to visit a university campus to try to win student and faculty votes. He also agrees to hold a press conference for student journalists and reporters from local papers and television stations who are covering his visit to the campus. A reporter for the campus newspaper is assigned to cover the press conference.

First, the student reporter must do her homework. She goes to the library and looks up past clippings on the candidate. She needs to find out everything she can about this person who wants to run the state for the next four years. So far, all she knows is that the candidate is a lawyer who works for a major law firm. What is his background? Has he been in public office before? How does he stand on issues affecting journalists, such as open meetings and freedom of information laws? Are there any skeletons in the candidate's closet that perhaps other reporters have not found?

Second, the reporter checks with her city editor to find out if there are any specific questions her editors would like asked. Editors and fellow reporters also might provide useful information that was overlooked during research.

After completing her research and talking with her editors, the student reporter decides that she wants to ask about the candidate's dealings with the state as a lawyer. Two years ago, the candidate's law firm was awarded a state contract to conduct an ongoing study to determine how the state can introduce new mass transportation bills in the legislature that have a chance of passing. The reporter wants to find out:

- Is the law firm still on a retainer from the state?
- If the candidate is elected governor, will he continue to let his law firm conduct state business?

She goes to the location of the press conference early so that she can get a good seat. The closer she is to the candidate, the more likely her chance to ask a question. The candidate will be looking into some powerful lights, and it may be difficult for him to see anyone in the back of the room. He also will be more likely to answer questions from the broadcast reporters, and so it is important for the reporter to be as close to the candidate as possible.

Asking the Questions

The first question at the press conference is from the political editor of the local daily, who asks the candidate what he will do to improve minority hiring in the state. Currently, there is a 25 percent minority hiring goal in the state, but some legislators are suggesting that the state increase the quota to 40 percent. The reporter wants to know the candidate's views on the proposed changes. His answer:

It depends on what the proportion of minorities is in both state government and in the population of the state. If we find that 25 percent is too low, I think we would have no trouble supporting an increase in the goal. But if the proportion of minorities is closer to 25 percent, I would have trouble supporting an increase in the hiring goal.

By now, most of the reporters in the room are raising their hands and calling out the candidate's name. He calls on a television reporter, who says:

BBX Freight Lines filed a class-action suit yesterday on behalf of the state's taxpayers challenging the collection of motor fuel taxes from users of the state's toll roads. The current governor says both the fuel taxes and the collection of tolls are needed to keep our highways in operating condition. What is your opinion?

The candidate's answer:

I think we should eliminate the toll roads. No one should have to drive through our state and face having to stop every few miles to pay for the use of a road. The roads are paid for, and we do not need tolls anymore. It also is getting too expensive to collect the tolls. I checked the figures the other day, and by the time the state funds the support system to collect the tolls, there is not much of a profit. I will scrap those toll roads.

Several more questions are asked, and the candidate seems to field them quite well without getting himself into any trouble. On his answer on the toll roads, the candidate sounded very much like someone stumping for office. Even as a student, the young reporter knows that people seeking political office often make promises they may not be able to keep if they are elected.

Then the candidate calls on the student. She stands up and gives her name and the name of her newspaper. Then she asks:

Sir, two years ago your law firm was hired by the state to offer advice on transportation bills. Is your firm still doing business with the state, and if it is, would you let it continue to do business with the state if you are governor?

The candidate shifts in his chair and glares at the student journalist. It is obvious that he was not prepared to answer this adversary question. All of the other reporters in the room are listening carefully, too, as the candidate says:

Why, yes, we still are conducting the study for the state. Our firm is one of the only firms in this part of the country that specializes in transportation, and we are providing the state with valuable information that it could not obtain anyplace else. As governor, I will no longer be working for the law firm, and I see no problem in it continuing its relationship with the state.

The student reporter asks an immediate follow-up question:

But don't you think you are committing an impropriety? You are employed by a firm that is working for the state and you are campaigning for governor. Don't you see a conflict of interest there?

His answer:

Of course I do not see a conflict. We are charging the state less than our usual fee and are giving it first-class advice. So far the state has supported six important transportation bills in the legislature that have benefited everyone. There will be more bills. If you want to go hunting witches, go hunt them elsewhere. There is nothing improper here.

Score one for the student reporter. She now has her probable lead. The candidate has revealed that his law firm will continue to be awarded state funds if he is elected governor.

The reporter does not jump out of her chair yet. She puts a big star next to her two questions and answers. There will be more questions and answers, and something even more exciting may come up. The star means that this information is her lead so far. But reporters do not quit once they think they have their leads. They know a new and more powerful lead can come any time in a press conference, so they listen to each question and answer carefully. The time to rush to the door is when the press conference has ended.

Picking Out the News

Once the press conference is over, some of the reporters head right to the pay telephones near the room in which it was held. They are reporters who work for evening newspapers with morning deadlines or radio reporters who must phone in information for an hourly newscast. Here reporters must be at their best. They do not have a video display terminal or a typewriter in front of them on which to compose a story, erasing mistakes and rewriting if necessary. Reporters who phone in their news stories must rely on their notes and experience to dictate a story that makes sense the first time. It also helps to have a good rewrite person on the other end of the phone to polish the rough edges, shuffle paragraphs if necessary and look up additional information. The student reporter's campus paper comes out in the morning, and so she can take most of the afternoon to write her story and meet her 5:30 p.m. deadline. She heads back to the office, thinking about the press conference. Which questions were the best? Who were the best reporters? Did the candidate skirt any issues? Was he honest? What is the best lead?

How the student reporter organizes her story is determined by several factors:

- Are the responses to her questions good enough for the lead paragraph?

- What are the other key points of the press conference? Would any of them make better leads? What are her editors looking for? Do they want a specific lead or a specific angle to the story?

- Is a second-day lead required? It may be if other reporters use her lead first.

She decides to lead with what the candidate said about the law firm. Other reporters might choose something else, but that does not mean that she is wrong and they are right. Five reporters might cover the same press conference and produce five different leads because they all were interested only in their questions and the following responses. Or they all might choose the same lead.

The student reporter's main competition comes from the stories that will be in the evening papers and newscasts. They may use her lead before she has a chance to. She does have an advantage, however, because she still has several hours to do more research on the candidate's law firm.

Writing the Story

It is now late afternoon and the reporter is sitting at a VDT. She has made several phone calls to find out about the law firm's dealings with the state. She has read one other story on the press conference, seen one television newscast and listened to two radio newscasts. Two reporters based their leads on the responses to her questions. Two went with the candidate's view on the minority hiring goal.

The student reporter decides to string together (organize) her inverted pyramid news story this way:

1. Begin with a summary lead highlighting what the candidate said about his law firm. Get in additional information that the earlier stories missed.

2. Provide quotes and indirect quotes to back up the lead. Also tell where the press conference was held.

3. Move into the minority hiring goals.

4. Follow up with quotes and indirect quotes.

5. Come back to candidate's law firm.

She decides not to use anything on what the candidate said about toll roads because he did not clarify his answers sufficiently. Her story begins:

Gubernatorial candidate John M. Jenkins said Monday his law firm will continue to do its $65,000-a-year business with the state even if he is elected governor.

The lead paragraph gives several key points of the story: who (candidate John Jenkins); when (Monday), what (will continue to do business with the state). It also tells readers how much the business is worth, something Jenkins did not say in the press conference but which the reporter dug up afterward.

Second paragraph:

"If you want to go hunting witches, go hunt them elsewhere," Jenkins said in a press conference at State University. "As governor, I will no longer be working for the law firm, and I see no problem in it continuing its relationship with the state."

This paragraph lets Jenkins tell readers directly that there is nothing improper in his dealings with the state. By using a strong direct quote in the second paragraph and attributing it to Jenkins, the reporter moves from a summary of the story to direct communication between a central character and the audience. That removes the reporter from the story and allows readers to begin to draw conclusions.

Third paragraph:

Jenkins' firm was hired by the state to advise it on mass transportation bills. He said that, so far, his firm has provided information on six bills dealing with a statewide mass transit system.

The reporter continues to explain the lead further. Readers are told why the state hired Jenkins' firm and how many bills the firm has worked on so far.

Fourth paragraph:

"There will be more bills," Jenkins said. "Our firm is one of the only firms in this part of the country that specializes in transportation, and we are providing the state with valuable information that it could not obtain anyplace else."

Again, the reporter lets Jenkins talk directly to readers. The candidate actually uttered these sentences before the ones used in the second paragraph, but the reporter uses them in what she considered their order of importance.

Fifth paragraph:

Jenkins also said he would not support an increase in the state's minority hiring goals unless he found that the current 25 percent was less than the proportion of minorities in the general population.

Now the reporter moves to what she considers the second most important point made at the press conference. She summarizes the point with an indirect quote and then explains it further, as she did in the first four paragraphs with her lead.

Sixth paragraph:

"It depends on what the proportion of minorities is in both state government and in the population of the state," the candidate said. "If we find that 25 percent is too low, I think we would have no trouble supporting an increase in the goal."

This paragraph explains further the summary paragraph before it. Like the other paragraphs, it also is attributed to the source. In this case, however, the reporter uses "the candidate said" to avoid using "Jenkins said" in every paragraph.

Seventh and eighth paragraphs:

The six bills for which Jenkins' firm has provided information deal with funding a statewide agency to oversee mass transportation.

The state has attempted for years to create the agency, which it says will cut the costs of mass transportation by millions of dollars. Jenkins' firm was hired to help draft legislation acceptable to a legislature stalemated on the issue.

The reporter ends the story by moving back to the central point. By stringing together summaries followed by quotes and indirect quotes, she gives her readers news on two newsworthy points high in the story. Background information and additional quotes on the top point are saved for late in the story, when there is the greatest chance of losing readers.

SPEECHES

Like press conferences, speeches are used by people to get a message across to an audience. Reporters cover a speech a little differently, though, because they do not come armed with a set of specific questions. It is more difficult to challenge the speaker, and so many of the story leads are more likely to be on the same point. In this case, reporters are the eyes and ears of people who cannot attend the speech.

Speeches build up to a major point. Hence they are organized differently from news stories, which put the major point at the top. Reporters need to recognize this difference. They must be able to understand the organization of the speech, anticipate its main points and cut out all the unnecessary information.

Reporters know that a 30-minute speech would take up considerable space in the daily news hole if it were printed in its entirety, and so they must pick it apart and give their audience the new, the important and the unusual. (In some instances, such as a presidential speech, entire texts are printed.) Clever speakers realize the reporter's function, too, and so they will make every attempt to put in something new, important or unusual.

Preparing for a Speech

As in preparing for a press conference, it is important for reporters to do their homework before covering a speech. Only under the most unusual circumstances, such as an extremely tight deadline, would they cover a speech without first researching the subject and the speaker. Even if the assignment is given only a short time before the speech, it is easy to go to the library or a newspaper clipping file to find out what has been written previously on the speaker or the topic of the speech. Here are some hints on how to prepare for covering a speech:

- *Rely on library research, news clippings, friends of the speaker and fellow reporters for background information on the speaker.* Try not to go into a reporting situation cold. Remember, people who give speeches usually have said the same thing before and you do not want to report something old. Make sure you have the correct spelling of the speaker's name. Go into research asking, "Who is this person?" Come out satisfied that you know the answer.

- *Prepare a list of questions that you hope the speech will answer.* If the questions are not answered during the speech, use reporting skills to get them answered after the speech.

- *Try to obtain an advance copy of the speech.* Advance copies are useful because they provide most of the information that the speaker plans to get across. Do not use the advance copy in place of the actual speech, though, because speakers often wander from their prepared texts. They will add some things and omit others, and so avoid the embarrassment of relying solely on the advance text. Instead, use it as a guide for covering the speech and making sure the direct quotes are exact.

- *If you plan to use a tape recorder during the speech, make sure it is working properly.* You don't want it to malfunction during an important part of the speech. Keep extra batteries and tapes on hand. Also, make certain that your pens are not out of ink, your pencils are sharpened and you have plenty of paper for taking notes.

- *Try to interview the speaker before the speech.* Every reporter covering a speech will be told the same thing, so if possible, break away from the pack beforehand to obtain exclusive information. Here is where homework is important. Make sure you know plenty about the speaker before the interview begins. Find out where the speaker will enter the room and wait there. Then it is possible to get off a couple of quick questions before the speaker gets to the podium. When speakers come to university campuses, they often will visit classrooms or officials first or will stop for a cup of coffee someplace on campus, and so try to catch them early.

Covering a Speech

When the speech begins, listen carefully and take copious notes, even if you are using a tape recorder. That way, if the recorder does malfunction, you still will have a record of what was said. Listen for the new, important or unusual parts of the speech—something that could be a lead—and put a star next to it in your notebook so that you find it easily after the speech. If you have an advance text of the speech, follow along as the speaker talks, adding new phrases and crossing out sentences or phrases omitted during the speech. Listen for topic sentences, numbered points, transitional words and summaries at the beginning and end of the speech.

Since it is impossible to transcribe the entire speech, listen for information and quotes that you think can be used in a story. If you hear something and start to write it down and then get mixed up, put some type of symbol next to it so that you can have it clarified after the speech. If you are writing a direct quote, put quote marks around it in your notebook so that you will be able to pick it out quickly when you are writing the story.

Often you will be writing down a sentence when you hear the speaker say another important sentence. Keep calm. Forget the first sentence and begin writing the second if you think that it is more important to the story. People are always going to speak faster than reporters can write, so just try to write down the key points and quotes. Since tape recorders and advance texts are excellent aids for getting precise quotes, use them if you can, especially until you have perfected your own system of fast note taking.

The end of the speech does not signal the end of your job. If there is time for questioning, ask for the clarification of points you did not understand. Do not be afraid to ask the speaker to repeat a quote, explain an unclear statement or expand any of the topics of the speech. Experienced speakers know that reporters can get mixed up and they do not want to be misquoted, and so they usually are willing to clarify points of the speech.

After the speech is also the time to ask questions on subjects that you had wanted covered but that were not. Try to get the speaker alone after the other reporters have left. Remember, your story could read just like all the others unless the speaker gives you exclusive information. If there is time, follow-up phone calls to the speaker may be helpful, too. No story can be definitive, but reporters do want to make sure that everything they write is accurate and as complete as possible.

The Result

Here is an example of a speech and the final, five-paragraph story. Notice how the reporter drew on the key points and used them in a traditional, inverted-pyramid news story.

The speaker is a U.S. representative from a neighboring state who is visiting the university from which she was graduated. She is in her second term in Congress, and she is on a subcommittee that is studying gun-control legislation. Her speech:

Thank you for inviting me to your campus today. I have not been on campus since I graduated from here many years ago, so it really is neat to come back and see all of the changes. There certainly are many of them. I wasn't here in horse-and-buggy days, but I have to admit I sort of felt that way walking through campus. It's hard to believe I ever was that young. You people are indeed fortunate. You have so much in front of you. The future of our nation does, indeed, belong to you. You are more educated and better equipped than any college graduates in our history.

Today, I would like to talk to you about gun control, and what I consider unbridled crime in this great country of ours. Like it or not, when you leave the relative safety and the idealism of university campuses, you are taking your lives into your own hands. The ease with which anyone in this country can obtain any type of gun has resulted in an ever-increasing crime rate. Americans are captives in their own homes, afraid to go outside, sometimes even in daylight. They seem to be unable to exercise their political franchise to turn things around. This nation simply cannot tolerate this constant slaughter anymore.

The Reagan administration has offered Congress the key to national survival by recommending mandatory prison sentences for people who use firearms in the commission of a felony. Even if the U.S. Congress acts favorably on this recommendation, the 50 states should adopt similar legislation of their own. Mandatory sentences should be the law in every state and in every city and town.

If such a law were passed and enforced, our nation's prisons would overflow within six months, but the costs of housing the felons would be worth it. It would give all of us law-abiding citizens a chance to enjoy our parks, to walk along inner-city streets without fear of being killed or injured. Guns in this country have destroyed the safety of our streets, and we need a strong law to make potential criminals think twice before they pick up a gun.

If President Reagan can convince Congress and the states to enact tough anti-gun legislation that provides for mandatory sentencing and insist that it is enforced, the American lifestyle surely will show dramatic improvement within a few years.

The mandatory gun-sentencing law will eliminate misplaced leniency by judges. It will make it clear to all offenders that if they carry a pistol, even in the commission of a burglary, they will go to the penitentiary when they get caught. The time is right for such a law; so is the legislative climate. Citizens are demanding relief, and it is time for the American criminal justice system to be reformed nationally and locally to reflect equitably the rights of victims, too.

There are strong lobbies in this nation that will continue to try to block any type of gun-control legislation. They must be stopped, and only we can do it. With mandatory sentencing, we all will be able to enjoy this beautiful country anytime, anyplace for the rest of our lives. Without it, our lives are in danger every second. Your killer could be just around the corner.

The mandatory-sentencing law should be dovetailed with another recommendation when Congress begins weighing the federal criminal code package proposed last month by Attorney General William French Smith. In that package, the administration suggested that courts be allowed to deny bail to persons who would present a danger to society if they are released before trial. An armed felon certainly would fit into that category. That class of criminal should be kept in jail so that some policeman's or citizen's life is not placed in double jeopardy because the person with the gun is freed on bail and allowed to prey again on society for his lawyer's fees.

I really wish I could spend more time with you today to convince you how important these proposals are to the safety of all of us, but I have to catch a plane back to Washington in an hour. I would have liked to answer questions from all of you, but there simply is not time. Thank you for inviting me to your campus and taking the time to listen to me. I hope all of you will continue to pressure your elected officials at all levels to help make our country safe again. Thank you.

Before writing this story, the reporter must ask—and answer—several questions:

- *What is the key point? What will be in the lead?* The key point here is obvious: The congresswoman is urging people to support anti-gun legislation. First, she supports the passage of a bill that would require mandatory sentencing for anyone caught using a gun in a crime. Second, she thinks bail should be denied to any gun-toting criminal who could be a threat to society. There should be big stars next to these items in the reporter's notebook.

- *Which quotes are the best ones to illustrate the speaker's views and make the story readable?* Here is where reporters pore over their notes, looking for the best quotes. There are several sensational quotes in this speech.

- *What has been said before? Has this official given the same speech before? Is any of this new? Is it newsworthy?* Only the reporters who have done their homework can answer these questions. If in doubt, check the clips again.

- *When is the deadline? Is there time to obtain an opinion from the other side?* Here is where reporters check with their editors, who may ask for another opinion. In most speech stories, however, editors simply ask for a few paragraphs on what the speaker said. If they ask for the other side, the reporter must start the research again to find the best possible rebuttal.

Now, the story:

Laws requiring mandatory prison sentences for anyone using a gun in the commission of a felony should be passed by the Congress and by each state, a visiting U.S. representative said on campus Tuesday.

Notice that the congresswoman's name was not used in the lead. Here the reporter made a judgment call and decided the "what" of the story— mandatory prison sentences—was more important than the "who." In this case, the speaker's title adds more strength to the story than the actual name does. The name will be used in the next paragraph.

"Guns in this country have destroyed the safety of our streets," Rep. Joanna Sanders, R-Iowa, said in a talk sponsored by the campus chapter of the Young Republicans. "With mandatory sentencing, we all will be able to enjoy this beautiful country anytime, anyplace for the rest of our lives. Without it, our lives are in danger every second."

Sanders, who is on a congressional subcommittee studying gun-control legislation, also urged Congress to approve a Reagan administration proposal that the nation's courts be allowed to deny bail to suspects who would be dangerous if they were released before trial.

The 1962 graduate of NSU said, "An armed felon certainly would fit into that category. That class of criminal should be kept in jail so that some policeman's or citizen's life is not placed in double jeopardy because the person with the gun is freed on bail and allowed to prey again on society for his lawyer's fees."

Notice that the reporter was able to find the year Sanders was graduated from the university. That's where homework comes in. Sanders did not mention the year in her speech.

Sanders admitted that strong pro-gun lobbies in the United States would continue to work against gun-control legislation, but she added, "They must be stopped, and only we can do it."

Most speech and press conference stories follow the same pattern: a terse (35 words or less) lead paragraph followed by a strong quote in the second paragraph. If the "what" is more important than the "who," the lead will present the key point first and the attribution will follow. If the "who" is well-known, the name is used in the lead. If the "who" is not well-known, a title is put in the lead to give it authority and the speaker's name is used in the second paragraph. For instance, look at the difference between these two leads:

> The Soviet Union is waging biological warfare campaigns in Southeast Asia, a biochemist from State University said Monday.

In this case , the scientist's title—not a name—gives more authority to the lead.

> The Soviet Union is waging biological warfare campaigns in Southeast Asia, President Reagan said Monday.

In this lead, the "who" is as important as the "what." The lead just as easily could have started, "President Reagan said Monday . . . "

The second paragraph contains the story's strongest quote and names the speaker or, if the name was used in the lead, gives the speaker additional authority. The rest of the paragraphs in the story can follow the pattern of summaries, quotes and indirect quotes.

A FINAL NOTE

Reporters often do not agree with what a speaker is saying. That's fine, and if possible, there should be plenty of adversary questions before and after the speech or during the press conference. But once it is time to write the story, the reporter's opinions should be left out. Let the speaker's quotes speak for themselves; the readers can decide whether or not the speaker is full of hot air. Like reporters, readers are not so gullible that they will believe everything that is said.

Whenever you cover a press conference, speech or any other type of story, just remember the advice the old Chicago editor gave one of his cub reporters many years ago: "If your mother says she loves you, check it out."

SUGGESTED EXERCISES

1. Here is a part of a column by Stephen Chapman, an editorial writer for the Chicago Tribune. Treat the column as though it were a speech given on your campus and write a news story:

Transportation Secretary Elizabeth Dole suggests that the [Reagan] administration may finally implement one of its nobler campaign pledges—raising the 55-mile-per-hour speed limit.

Posterity will note that the decline of the U.S. auto industry came only after Washington pitilessly revoked the right of every natural-born American to drive 70 miles per hour. A Toyota is fine at 55; but at the speed God intended us to cruise, you'd really rather have a Buick.

President Nixon imposed the 55-mile-per-hour limit—the double nickel, as it is known by us critics—as a fuel-saving measure in the wake of the 1973–74 Arab oil embargo. It was a nice public relations gimmick, giving the impression we were doing something to strike back at OPEC, but not a serious conservation measure. Even by the most sanguine estimates, it has reduced our total oil demand by only 3 percent, and our total energy consumption by less than 1 percent.

When bankruptcy of that rationale was exposed, the advocates of 55 came up with another: safety. Higher speed limits, they warn, would mean unrestrained carnage. The picture they paint of life after 55 resembles Gettysburg after Pickett's charge. Here too, the claims of the defense are conveniently inflated to serve the requirements of the melodrama.

It is true that traffic fatalities declined after the speed limit was lowered, but it is often overlooked that much of the decline was due to people driving less. Traffic volume is the biggest single factor in determining the accident rate, and it fell by about 5 percent in the wake of the 1973–74 gasoline shortage. In fact, the fatality rate reached its lowest level before the states began seriously enforcing the new speed limit.

The neat correlation between safety and lower speeds is also largely imaginary. In the half-century before 1974, the traffic fatality rate fell by 80 percent. This occurred even as legal speeds were going the opposite direction. The drop in fatalities in the last nine years only continued a long-established trend.

The double nickel offends almost everything the president stands for, besides offending a lot of people who voted for him. Repealing it is the least he can do to lighten the burden of Leviathan. Reagan may not be able to lead us to prosperity, but if he'll just let us, we can find our own way back to 70.

2.   Cover a speech on campus. Practice using symbols in your notes for what you consider the key points of the speech. Compare your lead and story with those of other students to see how many agree and disagree with your news judgment.

3.   Rewrite the story of the press conference covered by the student reporter in this chapter. Use a different lead than she did. Can you make the story stronger?

4.   Reread the speech by the congresswoman who advocated strong anti-gun laws. Rewrite the story with the same lead and different quotes. Rewrite it with a different lead and different quotes. Can you make the story stronger?

A large portion of daily news coverage is devoted to disasters and police and fire news. This chapter examines how these stories are covered by reporters in different size markets.

You will be introduced to:

• Coverage by reporters at the Kansas City Times and Kansas City Star of the worst hotel disaster in the United States since 1946.

• Steps reporters should follow when covering disasters to ensure that they obtain the best possible story without interfering with rescue efforts.

• Tips from two Pulitzer Prize–winning reporters of the Daily News in Longview, Wash., who covered the eruption of Mount Saint Helens.

• How a medium-circulation daily, the Grand Island (Neb.) Independent, responded when seven tornadoes devastated much of the town. Managing Editor Al Schmahl explains what his staff went through to produce the newspaper.

• Working with police and fire officials. The chapter examines the daily routine of a reporter assigned to cover police and fire news.

Wayne Lischka, left, structural engineer whom the Kansas City Star hired to aid coverage of the collapse of a four-story-high walkway at the Hyatt Regency hotel, confers with reporter Rick Alm.

© 1981, The Kansas City Star Company

89

5 ON ASSIGNMENT: DISASTERS AND POLICE AND FIRE NEWS

Friday, July 17, 1981. Kansas City, Mo. It was the night the music stopped.

It was 7:05 p.m. in Kansas City. Newspersons who did not work nights were enjoying their summertime Friday evening. It was a time for dancing, laughter, drinking and playing. Mike Waller, managing editor of the Kansas City Star, was with his paper's photo editor, several photographers, reporters and copy editors drinking in a bar after they had won, by forfeit, the last game of the season for the Star's softball team. Rick Lyman, assignment editor at the Star, was driving home from a movie. David Zeeck, Star city editor; Darryl Levings, one of his assistants; Rick Alm, Star city hall reporter, and their wives were having dinner in a restaurant three blocks from the Hyatt Regency hotel. At the same time, 1,500 to 2,000 people were in the glittering lobby of the year-old Hyatt Regency for a tea dance. The casual party featuring free admission, inexpensive drinks and Big Band-era music was a popular weekly event, and attendance had grown dramatically. The Steve Miller Band was playing Duke Ellington's "Satin Doll."

Suddenly, a four-story-high walkway in the lobby collapsed, hurling concrete, steel and people onto more people below. Within seconds, 111 people would be dead and 188 injured. The toll would climb to 114 dead and nearly 200 injured. "It was the worst thing I have ever seen," one of the survivors said. "You could watch the people on the walkway grab a hold of the walkway. Then they disappeared."

WHEN DISASTER STRIKES

The collapse of the "skybridges" at the Hyatt Regency was the worst hotel disaster in the United States since a fire killed 119 people in Atlanta in 1946. It was the worst loss of life since 274 persons died in the crash of a DC-10 airliner shortly after takeoff from Chicago's O'Hare International Airport in 1979. For the reporters and editors at the Kansas City newspapers and the radio and television stations, it was a night when they were forced to hide their tears so that they could report a disaster. Their job was to marshal all of their experience to produce a news story about chaos, terror and death. In disasters such as this, no one has to tell professional reporters and editors what to do. They know.

Besides two staffers who were attending the tea dance with their families and were caught in the disaster, the first person on the Star to hear of the collapse was Bill Norton, the paper's Johnson County, Kan., bureau chief. He was working late at his suburban bureau, about a half hour southwest of the city, when he heard an urgent call come across his police scanner: All available ambulances in the county were asked to go to the Hyatt Regency as quickly as possible. Norton tried to call an editor, but Waller was celebrating after the softball game, Zeeck was out to dinner and Lyman was at a movie. Finally, he reached Mike Zakoura, an assistant city editor, and they decided to go to the Star office to start organizing coverage for the Sunday paper.

The Star publishes Monday through Friday evenings and Sunday mornings; its sister paper, the Kansas City Times, publishes Monday through Saturday mornings. The collapse occurred on the Times' news cycle, so its staff would be responsible for initially reporting the disaster in the Saturday morning paper. The Star would carry the story into the Sunday edition.

Meanwhile, Lyman was caught in a traffic jam in the city's midtown Crown Center urban renewal district, an area of shops, offices, apartments, condominiums and hotels. Police were at every intersection directing traffic out of the area. For Lyman, it was like stumbling into a war zone. The buildings were lit by flashing blue and red lights of emergency vehicles. Ambulances were headed in both directions.

At the restaurant near the Hyatt where Zeeck, Levings and Alm were dining, two middle-aged women rushed into the foyer to use the telephone. Blood covered their clothes. The three newsmen went right to work. "We thought there had been a car accident," Alm said. "I took one woman aside and started getting the story from her. I couldn't figure it out because I'd never been in the hotel. She kept saying the balconies fell. It was only minutes after it happened. We decided to go to the hotel."

While Alm was interviewing the woman, Zeeck called the office to get a photographer. From all over the city, Star editors and reporters were doing just what any professional newsperson does when a spectacular news event occurs. They were heading for the scene or the office or calling their supervisors to find out what to do. The members of the softball team went to the office, and many of them spent the night working in their blue uniforms.

At the Scene

Alm and the two editors got to the hotel before the ambulances. There were only a couple of police officers there. "When we first got there, we thought it was a fire," Alm said. "We thought all the dust was smoke. We couldn't see much because of the dust. We saw some people sticking out of the rubble and we knew it was terrible."

At first, Alm was confused. He knew he had to get a story, but for a moment, he stood there in shock like the people in the lobby. Here is what he saw:

> It was almost like a dream with a huge cloud of dust rising. It was like slow motion. Everyone was just looking around trying to figure out what happened. There was no panic. It was about 10 minutes after the collapse. There was no frantic rescue effort yet. There were bleeding people. I saw

dead people. People were just sticking out of the rubble. There was a slab above them, a slab below them, like a sandwich. The first thing I heard was gushing water. A water line that had been attached to the fourth-floor skywalk burst. I could see water coming out of the wall.

Within minutes, Alm saw the extent of the disaster, and he knew he had to find out who was in charge. By now, the police had arrived, and the rescue attempt had started. One of the first things officers did was rope off the area outside the hotel. Alm went to the chief of police, who had arrived at the scene.

"I was with the chief of police when I got thrown out," the reporter said. "He told me he was trying to figure it out. I never argue with police who have to clear a scene. They have a tough job, too. Reporters have to comply, but they should keep asking questions as long as they can."

Alm was inside the hotel from 10 to 15 minutes. Once the police arrived, reporters were not allowed inside the lobby, but they could look in through the doors. They had access to survivors on the grass and sidewalks outside the hotel.

A hotel office away from the lobby was set up as a command information post. Alm just kept asking questions, trying to reconstruct what happened. He recalled:

> The most difficult thing was talking to survivors. Everyone told a different story. One of the hardest things I've ever done is trying to talk to someone bleeding on a stretcher. Some people just had to be let alone. They could not talk. There were 250 to 300 people outside who were hurt. There were thousands of spectators. The place was a mob scene. I just tried to stay calm. I asked people their names, addresses, if they were with friends or relatives, what they were doing when the skywalks fell. When someone was too hysterical, I went to someone else. I know it's callous, but we had to get the story.

Covering the Story

Back at the office, editors had set up the staffing plan. Initially, six reporters were sent to the hotel to talk to people and write down names, quotes and impressions. (There would be 30 to 40 Star reporters at the Hyatt by the end of the night.) A reporter was sent to every hospital in the city where a victim might be sent. Three reporters were assigned to cover the city's emergency services system to find out how well it held up under the strain of such an enormous tragedy.

Reporters at the scene had responsibilities for both reporting and writing. They had to gather information for the story they were assigned to write and also had to make sure that any information they received that might fit into another story was passed along to the person in charge of that story. Many reporters fed information to rewrite people in the office who were writing stories for a special section planned for the Sunday paper. To make sure that reporters were not repeating what already had been done, editors kept a running, descriptive list of all stories and who was writing them.

Alm spent about three and a half hours at the hotel before he went to the office, where he would work all night. "Instinct kept me going," he said. "We had tremendous pressure on us to get the story. Within 20 minutes, we knew the magnitude of the thing. At the office, we sorted out what we had. We broke up into teams to handle different types of stories, such as victims, background and hospitals. That night, I was assigned the 'why' story— why these things fell."

By the middle of the first night, the Times released its final edition with the headline "46 killed in Hyatt collapse as tea dance turns to terror." The lead story carried a byline reading "By the Times Staff." It began:

> A quiet evening of tea dancing in the lobby of the Hyatt Regency hotel erupted into chaos and terror Friday night when a four-story-high walkway in the lobby collapsed, killing at least 46 persons and injuring at least 82 others.
>
> Dozens of early evening revelers were catapulted into the air at 7:05 p.m. as the walkway collapsed onto a second-floor walkway directly beneath it. That too collapsed, trapping spectators beneath tons of tangled metal and crumbled concrete.
>
> The number of dead seemed certain to increase as firefighters and other rescue workers worked feverishly with pickaxes, shovels and their hands to rescue people still trapped beneath the mass of broken glass and steel of the fallen walkways.
>
> Police spokesman Sgt. Jim Treece said early this morning that there were still bodies inside the building in addition to the 46 already confirmed dead.

Besides the main story on Page 1, there were two large photographs and a sidebar story that focused on the people involved in the disaster. The sidebar, which was written by Laura Knickerbocker and James C. Fitzpatrick, began:

> "An old lady was on top of my ankle, screaming. I said to her, 'Be calm. Breathe deep,' but she just kept struggling. I felt her last movement. She's dead."
>
> Betty Nelson, 46, remembered the gruesome scene. She was trapped for 40 minutes, along with dozens of others, when the suspended fourth-floor walkway collapsed at the Hyatt Regency hotel Friday night. Luckily, she was not badly hurt.

Besides the front page, the Times devoted four inside pages of its first section to the collapse.

Writing the Follow-Ups

As the night wore on, it was up to the Star staff to pick up where the Times left off. The death toll had risen considerably and still was climbing. Security officials at the hotel also began cracking down on who was admitted to the lobby and adjacent makeshift morgue and emergency treatment room, making the work of reporters more difficult. One Star reporter, Brian Burnes, got into the hotel by carrying buckets of water with Red Cross volunteers. Photographers were kept in the background, so that they were forced to snap and retreat.

By midmorning Saturday, every reporter at the Star, including three who were on vacation, either had called the paper or had shown up. The entire staff, including suburban bureau reporters, were in and out of the newsroom. Plans for the Sunday paper called for a chronology story with a minute-by-minute account of the tragedy, 8-inch stories on survivors, a list of the dead and plenty of people stories. A large color picture would be used on Page 1 of a 10-page special section, which would be the first section of the paper. There would be no ads in the section. Another full page of color photographs would be used on the back page of the section.

John M. Wylie II, the Star's editorial training director, was given the task of putting together a comprehensive list of the dead and injured. He was given a staff of three to help him. Extra help was hired to aid in the writing of obituaries for the Sunday paper. It was a massive job, but thanks to quick-acting reporters and editors, by late Saturday, when the Sunday paper was ready to go to press, the Star was able to give its readers a package of news stories and features on the collapse. The main story on Page 1, written by Steve Woodward and Robert J. Pessek, carried the headline "The Hyatt horror: 111 dead, 188 hurt and a city in shock." It was topped by a second-day lead because by now the disaster was more than 24 hours old. The story began:

> A gray sky rained tears Saturday on a city overcome with grief.
> As bulldozers raked away tons of rubble that choked the once-glittering lobby of the Hyatt Regency hotel, funeral preparations began for the 111 persons killed when two massive aerial walkways plunged onto the crowded floor.

Other stories told of critics of the skywalk designs who said that the avalanche of steel and concrete was inevitable, the hard work of volunteers, the outpouring of aid from city residents and the grief of the survivors and families of the dead.

In the first week after the collapse, the Star and Times published more than 50 full pages of related news. By the end of the year, they had printed more than 340 stories, hundreds of pictures and scores of editorials. The papers still were running stories on the disaster months later when they found out that their concerted coverage of the Hyatt collapse earned them the 1982 Pulitzer Prize for general local reporting.

Organizing the Coverage

The major reason that the Star and Times were able to provide such complete coverage of the Hyatt disaster so quickly was the high degree of organization in the newsroom, the key to successful coverage of any disaster. Just as rescue work must start immediately whenever a disaster strikes, so must the reporting of the event. Police and firefighters are directed by a commander; reporters are directed by an editor. Usually the editor is someone who has covered disasters before and can make sure that the right stories are covered, reporting is not duplicated, the most current information is gathered and deadlines are met.

Imagine how it must have been inside the Hyatt Regency minutes after the collapse of the skyways. It was dark, and the dust was blinding. Survivors were moaning for help or their families. People around them were dead or dying. Many were injured seriously. Some could not move. Meanwhile, emergency crews and reporters and photographers were crowding into the hotel.

Police officials do not want reporters hampering the rescue attempt; reporters do not want the police hindering their effort to gather information and meet their deadines. What is needed in these situations, besides organization, is cooperation. Emergency services officials realize that the media can help them get vital information to the public, and reporters know that the officials can help them in gathering the information. It is possible for all of them to do their jobs professionally without stepping on toes. It must be remembered that both the reporters and the emergency workers are in an unpleasant situation. They are facing possible personal danger, and they are dealing with human emotion and suffering. It is not an easy task, and it is filled with stress.

Guidelines for Covering Disasters

Reporters at any level—from college newspapers to huge metros—tend to head for disasters as soon as they hear about them. Indeed, a driving force inside all reporters carries them to the scene of an emergency, where they immediately start taking notes, talking to police and interviewing survivors. It is an inner drive that clicks during emergencies, causing reporters to drop everything they are doing and head right to the scene of a news event. Should you be involved in covering a disaster, there are guidelines you should follow to make sure that your news organization gets the best possible stories and that the rescue effort can proceed as smoothly as possible:

- *If you hear of a disaster, call your editor.* Find out if coverage is being planned and/or how the disaster is to be covered. Remember, organization is the key to successful coverage of a major story, so let the editor call the shots.

- *If you cannot reach an editor and you feel that you should be at the disaster site rather than at your office, go with care.* Make sure you pay attention to warnings from emergency officials to avoid being injured yourself.

- *If you can, identify yourself as a reporter to everyone you talk to.* Although not always possible, it is best to let survivors, rescue workers and law enforcement officials know why you are there. You do not want to be accused later of being underhanded.

- *Do not do anything that might lead to your arrest or ejection from the site.* You cannot write a story if you are not there to cover it. Cooperate with police and fire officials. If you feel that they are being unreasonable, check with their supervisors or your editors. Do not argue with front-line officers because they are only doing what they perceive to be their duty. Their supervisors can handle the problems.

- *Listen to everything that is going on and take copious notes.* Talk to whomever you can, and make sure you get names, addresses and phone numbers. Even in these situations, editors and readers are suspicious of anonymous sources. You are there to cover three types of stories: spot news, public service and people features. Don't forget basic reporting. Find out who, what, where, when, why and how.

- *If you can find a telephone at the scene, call your editor and try to keep the line open.* If you need to, hire someone to stay at the phone and keep the line open while you gather your information.

- *If you are one of the first people on the scene and there are survivors who require immediate aid, help them.* That will make a great story, too.

- *Never feel that you should not cover a disaster because you are a student journalist.* Even if you do not work for the campus newspaper, you could be the first reporter at the scene of a disaster. Wire services or metropolitan newspapers might buy the story that you write.

Two reporters who are experienced at covering a disaster are Andre Stepankowsky and Rick Seifert of the Daily News in Longview, Wash., one of the closest towns to Mount Saint Helens, the volcano that erupted violently in 1980. The staff of the 27,000-circulation Daily News won the 1981 Pulitzer Prize in general reporting for its coverage of the eruption.

Stepankowsky and Seifert offer these additional tips for reporters covering disasters:

- *Remember that the first responsibility of the press in the minutes immediately following a disaster is rumor control.* Since you cannot ignore rumors, you have to spend considerable time checking them out. You have to tell your readers or listeners what is rumor and what is not.

- *Double check sources of information.* Do not settle for one version of the truth. Always try to get two eyewitnesses. Consider all versions, and remember that the experts may not actually know what is happening. Because official sources often are worried that the press is going to distort the story, they may sanitize information before releasing it to the press. At the same time, reporters must realize that public officials are trying to avoid unnecessary panic.

- *Realize when the disaster requires a team effort.* Usually a disaster becomes too big for one reporter or editor to handle. Staff meetings and plenty of planning are important.

- *Also cover the tragedies that follow the initial shock.* Disasters spawn disasters; for instance, disasters often knock out water and sanitary systems, which can cause disease and other problems. Looting becomes a problem when mass evacuations are ordered. Essential services and transportation are disrupted.

- *Be aware that few bureaucracies are prepared for disasters.* Disasters also spawn bureaucratic disasters. Often cleanup and aid efforts are duplicated, and there is little cooperation with the press. Seek out blind spots from other sources. Moreover, remember that disasters often bring in a whole new bureaucracy to dole out aid. This new layer of government interacts with the old, and the public and the press have to learn to deal with both bureaucracies. It is important to analyze how well the new officials are doing their jobs in helping the needy.

- *Find out how well prepared your own newspaper or broadcast outlet is for disasters.* How would you do your job if roads were destroyed, phone service were interrupted and power were out? How would the newspaper be printed and distributed? (The Daily News had to buy a four-wheel-drive vehicle to negotiate rugged roads and invest in a two-way radio system.)

- *Find out where any government money provided for recovery efforts is going and whether it is being distributed fairly.* Make sure that public officials are not using the money to make their friends and themselves richer.

- *Expect the national media to pour into town and learn to put up with them.* Remember, their responsibility is not to the local audience, so that they tend to simplify and sensationalize. That can breed rumors, and because local residents are watching national television coverage they notice the discrepancies between the network stories and the local coverage. Local reporters must therefore deal with the national stories, either by correcting them, refuting them or putting them in perspective.

- *Do not scare readers or viewers unnecessarily, but tell them what is happening.* If there is a threat of widespread flooding, you must tell your readers, even if the story causes public alarm.

- *Remember that scientists who are involved in disasters, or threats of disasters, seldom give a straightforward prediction of what is going to happen.* They speak in probabilities and scenarios. Do not expect science to have all of the answers.

- *Seek out academics who are experts in fields pertinent to the disaster.* (For example, psychologists were right when they said that people in Longview would suffer from delayed stress as a result of the volcano's eruption.)

- *Be prepared to do the unusual.* Helicopters cost hundreds of dollars an hour to rent, but they are worth it if that is the only way to get photographers or reporters to the scene of a disaster. Be ready to walk into crumbling buildings or on the roofs of flooded homes.

Planning for Emergencies

Covering a disaster is different from everyday reporting because much of it is based on gut reactions and instant decisions. Despite advance planning and organization on the part of editors, reporters must be ready for the unusual when they are assigned to cover a disaster. At no other time will they have to hide their emotions and personal suffering so completely as when they are in the middle of human agony and must calmly ask questions, take notes and report what they have seen.

While reporters and photographers are trying to work their way into restricted areas, editors and circulation officials face the problem of getting the newspaper to readers. If there is flooding, newsprint may be damaged and roads may be closed. In major emergencies, law enforcement officials often close entrances and exits to towns, which can prevent delivery trucks from moving and employees from getting to work. Indeed, covering a disaster is a battle, and reporters have no way of knowing when it will strike. All they can do is plan for it and hope they will be ready.

Besides instantaneous organization, reporters and editors should have emergency plans that can be implemented when disaster strikes. Editors know that disaster can hit in the middle of the day or night or right on deadline. They also know that it can affect the printing of the newspaper, and so they do not want to be caught unprepared. In most cases they have two emergency plans, one for covering the disaster and the other for maintaining the production of the paper.

For example, the Grand Island (Neb.) Independent put its newsroom emergency plan into operation when seven tornadoes devastated much of Grand Island, a community of 38,000. Five persons were killed and more than 135 injured. The twisters caused $300 million in damage and destroyed or damaged 80 businesses and 2,000 homes.

The Independent's emergency plan had been developed several years earlier after an airplane hijacking in Grand Island. The paper, which has a 21-member newsroom staff, found out then that it needed plans for:

- Coping with the deluge of news requests from the national media.
- Handling local officials.
- Using reporters and writers in the best way.

"We kept our fastest writer in the office for the rewrites, and our toughest reporters out gathering the information," Managing Editor Al Schmahl said. "We also designated a couple of staffers to answer outside requests, providing other media with copies of what we had written and making arrangements for them to use our typewriters, VDTs and darkroom.

The Independent's newsroom emergency plan was put into effect long before the staff knew the seriousness of the tornado disaster. Two base stations were set up, one at the newspaper and the other at an assistant managing editor's house in case of communications problems. "Approximately half the staff worked through the night," Schmahl said. "Our plant was undamaged, but we had no power and no water. We broke out typewriters and began pounding hard copy. We used water from the toilets to process film." Because of the power loss, the editors decided to print the paper in York, a community about 40 miles east of Grand Island.

Every member of the staff was used to cover some aspect of the story. Schmahl became a reporter and wrote a sidebar story on the storm system and the weather bureau's role. Sportswriters helped gather information, and the family editor checked with funeral homes. "As much as we could, we kept our beat reporters in contact with their regular sources," Schmahl said. "Our police reporter stayed with the public safety folks, the city hall reporter was with city utility representatives and the education reporter checked on damage to schools."

Besides spot news coverage, public service stories had to be developed to tell residents how to make certain that water was safe to drink, how long food could be kept without spoiling, how to avoid price gouging, how to cope with government bureaucracy and where to go for assistance. People stories also were important. "We did articles on each of the people killed, we tramped around devastated neighborhoods to talk to victims and we looked for human interest in the hundreds of helpers who came to town for the cleanup," Schmahl said. "We just tried to tell what these tornadoes had done to peoples' lives." The Independent also let people tell their own stories in a month-long series of "Tornado Tales," which were submitted by readers affected by the twisters.

"At the end of the first day's coverage, we held a planning meeting for the next day," Schmahl said. "For approximately the next 10 days, we moved our morning editors' meeting up to 7 a.m. and included key reporters in it. We met again every afternoon at 2 to plan the next day's product. We also had special planning sessions for our Saturday and Sunday editions." Because of damage to businesses and a weeklong loss of power, little advertising appeared in the Independent for the first week after the tornadoes, but the paper continued to published.

The first day's edition printed in York contained eight pages, which were filled with tornado stories and photographs. After an initial press run of 25,000 copies, the paper twice reprinted 3,500 issues and placed a five-paper purchase limit per customer, but the edition still sold out in hours. Issues for the next three days also were overprinted, and they also sold out. The Independent sold the papers for 25 cents each and donated all of the money to the Grand Island Charitable Foundation's tornado disaster fund.

COVERING THE POLICE AND FIRE BEATS

In many ways reporters are doing the same job as police officers and fire officials: They all are protecting the public. Like the police, reporters are investigators who search for wrongdoing and try to correct it. It is a reporter's job to expose injustice at all levels. Because their jobs are similar, there usually is a spirit of cooperation between reporters and law enforcement officials.

That is the good news. The bad news is that the two sides often are in bitter conflict. Why?

- Whereas the ends of honest reporters and honest police may be the same, the means may require stepping on each other's toes.
- The timing of news stories may conflict with police investigations.
- The press is charged with criticizing law enforcement officials for abuse of power or other questionable actions.
- Law enforcement officials may believe that they need notes and other evidence gathered by a reporter, and they may go to court to get them. That often conflicts with commitments made by the reporter to protect confidential sources.

Reporters should not let these potential problems interfere with the daily gathering and writing of the news. It is wise to be aware of the problems but not let them hinder professional reporting.

Developing Sources

Reporters who will be working with police and fire officials should first introduce themselves at the police and fire stations before there is an emergency. Then when there is a story to be covered, the police and fire officials will be more likely to cooperate because they have seen the reporters before. Student journalists also should visit their local fire and police officials, introduce themselves, become familiar with how and where records are filed and explain that they will or may be involved in reporting police and fire news. As in any interviewing situation, a reporter never should barge in and say, "I'm here to get the story." Police and fire officials may need some stroking before they appreciate and respect a reporter, and it is the reporter's responsibility to take the time to gain that respect.

Once the preliminary work is done, it is time to cover the news—either at the scene or from reports and interviews in the station. The size of the newspaper usually determines how its reporters cover police and fire news. At small papers one reporter may be responsible for covering both police and fire news. In this case the reporter would call or stop in at the police station, fire headquarters and perhaps even the county sheriff's office at least once a day to check reports on crime and fire news. Larger papers usually have a pressroom at police headquarters where their reporters are available to cover crime news 24 hours a day. The larger papers also usually have more than one reporter covering police and fire news.

A Case Study

Let's look at an example of a reporter who covers police and fire news for a small evening newspaper in a suburban market. Each day he has to cover two local police stations, a substation of the county sheriff's department and fire stations in two communities.

Because he is the paper's only police and fire reporter, he is supplied with a police scanner so that he will find out about stories as they break. If there is an emergency, he calls his editor immediately to find out how the paper wants to cover the story. If the editor is not available, the reporter will make the decision either to go to the scene or to the police or fire station.

As soon as he arrives at work each morning at 8 o'clock, the reporter calls the two fire stations and speaks to the commanders in charge of the morning shift. He has been covering this beat for some time, so that the fire officials recognize his voice and know that he will be calling at about the same time every day. The commander will run through the reports quickly for the reporter, who will decide which ones are important enough for stories. The only stories his paper will run are ones involving serious fire damage to a building, injury, death or other unusual circumstances. The commander also is aware of the paper's policy, so that he and the reporter quickly pass over the routine fire calls.

On this day, the reporter is interested in the report on a house fire in which a 5-year-old boy was injured seriously. The boy had been playing with matches in his bedroom and accidentally started his bed on fire. By the time his parents reached him, he had second- and third-degree burns on his legs.

The reporter listens as the commander reads the report, which contains the boy's name, address, age and the circumstances surrounding the incident. The report also provides the names of the fire officials who investigated the blaze and the name of the chief in charge of handling the call. The reporter's next step is to talk to the people involved for quotes and to check some of the information in the report. He also calls the hospital where the boy was taken to find out his condition.

The next step is to call the police department because police were called in to investigate the fire. The reporter will be going to the police station soon, but he wants to get the information on the fire over the phone so that he can write his story before covering the police stories of the day. He is told that the police do not suspect foul play; the boy simply was playing with matches and started his bed on fire. Now the reporter is ready to write his story on his video display terminal. The lead reads:

A 5-year-old boy playing with matches suffered second- and third-degree burns on his legs Tuesday after he started his bed on fire.

The next paragraph names the boy and gives his parents' names and address. It also gives more details on the fire. The seven-paragraph story also includes direct and indirect quotes from fire and police investigators.

It is now about 9:30 a.m., and the reporter must visit the two police stations and the sheriff's office before his noon deadline. Because he has been covering the same beat for some time, he is able to walk right into any of the stations and begin his work. He knows where the reports are filed, and many of the officers know him by name.

Police stories are based largely on what the investigating officers wrote in their reports, which then are filed in a loose-leaf notebook or on a clipboard in the police station. The reports, which are public property, give the basic details. The reporter then can interview individual police officers for more information and quotes. Because police officers are not trained in journalism, there are often points in the reports that must be checked before they can be used in a news story. The reports should be used as a guide; it is not a good idea to write a story based solely upon one officer's perception of an event. Reporters should verify addresses and spellings. Because police also are not trained in libel, reporters need to be careful not to use potentially libelous parts of a police report.

The reports include a description of the scene of a crime, names of victims and witnesses, the circumstances surrounding the incident, names of people arrested if there were any, a list of any property that was damaged, names of the investigating officers and a narrative from the officers.

On a typical day the reporter spends about 15 minutes looking through the notebook at the first police station, picking out the reports he thinks can be the basis for a story. He will do the same thing at his two other stops.

By 11 a.m., the reporter has collected information on two burglaries, one robbery and one shooting. He has interviewed two police officers and a sheriff's deputy, and when he gets back to the newsroom, he will need to make a couple of phone calls before he writes his stories. By his noon deadline, he will give his city editor stories on the burglaries, robbery and shooting. After lunch, he will call the fire station, police stations and sheriff's office to see if anything new has broken. He also will spend part of the afternoon completing a feature story on a new training program the fire department is using.

Most reporters who cover police and fire news handle their assignment in much the same way as the reporter in the preceding example. They set up some type of routine to fit their tight deadlines and then follow it. A major breaking story that requires them to be on the scene can change the routine at any time. In emergency situations, reporters must be at their best because then more than at any other time they must follow their instincts, compete with other reporters covering the same story, deal with officials trying to cope with an emergency and even watch out for their personal safety.

Reporters are not on the scene of a major police or fire story to aid or interfere with officers. They are there to chronicle the event and the agony that accompanies it. The key to successful coverage is listening to the people involved—the law enforcement officials, the witnesses and the victims. In these situations reporters do not need to ask many questions because there is constant chattering. There will be plenty of excellent quotes.

Handling the Tough Ones

Reporters and photographers on the scene run the risk of being perceived by officers as interfering with the investigation or with rescue attempts. Police do have the power to arrest people. Charges such as criminal trespass or interfering with police officers are hard to prove, but they successfully remove reporters from the scene of a major story. It is a fact that some front-line police officers and firefighters dislike talking to reporters, and here the reporters face the greatest risk of being arrested. Officers do not have to cooperate with reporters. In these cases begging or shouting usually do not do much good. It is best to go to fire or police supervisors, who should provide information or instruct those under them to provide it.

For example, when the Kingsport (Tenn.) Times-News began its own investigation of a local double-murder case, it had to do it without the cooperation of Tennessee Bureau of Investigation officers. On the day the agency arrested a suspect, an agent, upset by the newspaper's probe, called the paper to say that his agency had nothing to report so that there was no need for reporters to call. The newspaper found out about the arrest from other media in the area and called "foul," forcing the director of the bureau to remind his agents that although they can deny the press their comments, they cannot mislead reporters or lie to them.

Public information officers who are trained to present their agencies in the best possible light also create a hurdle reporters must clear. Reporters covering police and fire news learn quickly from experience how to handle tough law enforcement officials and their spokespersons. It might take several shouting matches, but they will learn. The problem is one that all reporters, especially young ones, must learn to handle in an individual and professional way.

S U G G E S T E D   E X E R C I S E S

1. Use the following information from a police report to write a news story:

Dwight C. Valentino, 22 years old, of Apt. 104, 1721 Poplar Place, Schaumberg, and Kenneth P. Wangerin, a visitor to Valentino's apartment from Lyndon, Kan., have been found shot to death in Valentino's apartment.

The shooting occurred Tuesday afternoon.

It is a ground-floor apartment.

The bodies were discovered by Valentino's mother, who wondered why she could not contact her son. She called police at 2:35 p.m.

Wangerin is 24 years old.

So far there are no motives or suspects.

The apartment shows no signs of a struggle or a forced entry.

Valentino was shot in the face.

Wangerin was shot in the upper body.

Both bodies were found fully clothed in the living room.

Five .22-caliber cartridge casings were found in the apartment.

Police also found two live .22-caliber cartridges.

Employees of the complex said Valentino had lived at the apartment for six months.

2. Have reporters in your area been arrested for allegedly interfering with police or fire officials at the scene of a disaster? If so, how did the individual reporters and their news organizations handle the situation? Do your local police and fire officials have guidelines for handling the media during emergencies?

3. Devise a newsroom emergency plan for your campus paper. If there already is one, how does it work?

4. If you have not done so yet, visit your local fire and police headquarters. Familiarize yourself with the operations so that you are prepared to cover breaking stories.

Reporters regularly cover local and state government. This chapter discusses this facet of reporting.

You will be introduced to:

• Local government coverage by a small-city afternoon daily, the Manhattan (Kan.) Mercury. The chapter discusses local government systems and the types of stories local government reporters write. It traces a day on the job with Mistie Witt. It also provides specific suggestions for the effective coverage of local government.

• State government coverage by a metropolitan newspaper, the Omaha (Neb.) World-Herald. The chapter describes state government systems, the types of legislative stories the World-Herald publishes and the primary sources of information necessary to report effectively on state government. It also traces a day on the job with legislative reporter Frank Partsch.

Coverage of city councils is a staple of newspaper reporting.

© Chicago Tribune, 1983

107

6 COVERING LOCAL AND STATE GOVERNMENT

Most newspapers take pride in their coverage of local and state government. Whether their circulations run to the hundreds of thousands or are less than 15,000, newspapers devote considerable space to issues of close-to-home relevance.

The editor-in-chief of the Manhattan (Kan.) Mercury would agree that many of the nation's major metropolitan dailies are excellent newspapers. Still, none of the metropolitan newspapers covers Manhattan city government or Riley County government as extensively as the Mercury does.

Many reporters launch their careers by covering government at the grassroots levels.

COVERAGE OF LOCAL GOVERNMENT

Coverage of city and county government often is one of the first assignments young reporters receive—particularly if they go to work for small- or medium-circulation dailies or weeklies.

Extensive coverage of local government is a primary goal of many of these newspapers, including the Mercury, a 13,500-circulation afternoon daily. The Mercury, which has won scores of state and national awards for excellence, is published in a community of 35,000 that is the home of Kansas State University.

"I see our role as the newspaper of record for Manhattan and Riley County and, to a lesser extent, for the surrounding communities where we have home delivery," said Edward Seaton, publisher and editor-in-chief. "This means in Manhattan and Riley County government matters, we cover virtually everything. Every item on the agendas of the governing bodies receives some sort of coverage. While our focus is on substantive matters, we mention even such items as mayoral declarations of special weeks. We also cover in considerable detail all court news with the exception of minor traffic violations."

Manhattan is governed by a city manager who implements policy legislated by a five-member city commission. One of the commissioners serves as a chairman with the title of "mayor." A new mayor is selected each year. Riley County is governed by a three-member commission. The commissioners function both as legislators and executives. City and county commissioners run at large.

The Mercury covers all city commission meetings and work sessions. It also covers all Urban Area Planning Board sessions, some meetings of the Planning Appeals Board, all sessions of the Downtown Development Committee (a city board) and some meetings of other city boards, such as the human relations, environment, park, recreation and airport boards. Most of these boards function only in an advisory capacity to the city commission; the issues they face ultimately come before the commission.

The Mercury also regularly covers the city manager's office, as well as other appropriate offices of the city staff, such as the planning director and the works director. The newspaper reviews all police reports and publishes those that are significant. Fire coverage is handled through police reports except in cases of major fires.

A Day on the Job with Mistie Witt

Mistie Witt is the Mercury's full-time local government reporter. The newspaper also has one reporter covering Riley County government half time; one reporter on the police beat half time; one full-time reporter on area news, which generally focuses on the county and city; one full-time reporter on local schools, and two reporter-editors who write on any of these subjects.

Witt begins her days at about 8 a.m. with a check of the mail for agendas, memorandums and other information. Her mornings are spent "writing anywhere from one to three stories for that day's paper," she said. Her stories come from a variety of sources; no day during the week is the same.

On Monday mornings, the city manager and other city staff members hold a press conference. These conferences give Witt an opportunity to ask questions about relevant issues. The conferences almost always produce a story and quite often provide ideas for follow-ups.

"My afternoons are more flexible than my mornings," said Witt. "A lot of that time is spent working on a feature or other type of story for our Sunday edition. I conduct interviews, do my research and write during the afternoons. Also, if I have spare time during the day, I try to read other newspapers for ideas and to see what they are covering."

One thing Witt learned early in her coverage of city government is that the "complete story" about significant issues seldom is revealed during a meeting. Often she will develop stories from information mentioned during regular meetings but examined more fully later on.

For example, she wrote a story that tied together various complex elements of the Manhattan redevelopment plan. Most Manhattan residents undoubtedly had heard of the plan but knew few specifics. Witt's story led with a broad, local angle on redevelopment before moving to the specifics that mattered:

> Downtown redevelopment began as a simple effort to save Manhattan's central business district from the decay experienced by similar areas of many other cities.
>
> But that simple effort is growing into a much more complex project encompassing revitalization of the whole economy.
>
> Downtown redevelopment has mushroomed into a variety of projects, each dependent upon downtown revitalization for success. City officials

say each project may also contribute to the realization of the proposed mall project.

Potential increases in business opportunities which would be generated through a regional mall in the downtown area and the need to relocate businesses now situated in the proposed mall acreage have led to several secondary projects in addition to the main mall proposal.

And, evidently U. S. Department of Housing and Urban Development officials in charge of allocating a grant the city wants for the project support such secondary projects.

Witt then discussed in detail five secondary projects under consideration. She provided background on a meeting between city officials and HUD officials concerning requirements for an Urban Development Action Grant (UDAG). Witt went on to discuss the requirements for a UDAG:

> UDAG requires a certain amount of private investment for federal funds received. Grants for small cities require approximately $6 private investment for every $1 of federal funds allocated to the cities.

The reporter put this in perspective for her readers by explaining that if the mall developer spent an estimated $40 million on construction, the city then could apply for $6 million in UDAG funds. She then explained how the federal funds would be used to aid the redevelopment project and closed her story with some specific figures on the number of grants allocated to small cities during the last quarter of the year.

Clearly, local government reporters are expected to be enterprising and diligent. They must be capable of separating the significant from the insignificant at board meetings, pegging story angles to issues of interest to readers and piecing together stories that explain complex local issues in a way average readers can understand.

Covering the City Council

The Tempe (Ariz.) Daily News, a 12,000-circulation daily, also covers city government extensively. It is not unusual for the Daily News to publish three or more stories the morning after a council meeting. Katherine Corcoran led one story with:

> The Tempe City Council rejected eight companies' bids for city towing business and voted Thursday to advertise for new bids.
>
> On a 5-2 vote, with Mayor Harry Mitchell and Councilman William Ream dissenting, the council rejected the towing bids it received in December.
>
> The city now rotates towing among seven companies, but the council decided in October to divide the city into two zones at Rural Road and use one company each.

The story went on to provide details on proposed fees, estimated response times and quotations from council members and towing company owners. Obviously, the reporter had done her homework. She wrote a straightforward lead explaining action taken at the meeting, followed it with the precise vote and details on how the city is divided and then provided background to the reader on previous action by the council concerning the towing issue.

City government reporters should remember that it is not enough merely to report what happened *at* the council meeting. They also must provide sufficient background and conduct interviews to fully explain the significance of the action.

A second story flowed from the same Tempe City Council meeeting. Though the council did not reach a final decision, Susan Carson recognized the news value. She began her story:

> The Tempe City Council decided Thursday to continue negotiations with the Fiesta Bowl over payment of costs incurred by the city during the New Year's Day football game.
> The council also delayed a decision on imposing a 1 percent city sales tax on Fiesta Bowl tickets until the expense question is resolved.
> The city provides police protection and traffic control for the annual game at Arizona State University's Sun Devil Stadium. Councilman William Ream, who asked for the delay, said the Fiesta Bowl's executive committee has agreed to pay the sales tax.
> But the committee has not yet agreed to reimburse the city for all of its expenses, Ream said.
> "We're negotiating how much they should pay and what the expenses really are," Ream said.

Carson's story also provided attributed estimates on when the issue might be resolved; it gave details on how the city and Fiesta Bowl had handled finances during previous years, and it provided specifics on how much money the city would have collected in sales taxes from the most recent bowl game.

Again: It is not enough to report action taken at a meeting. Background information and direct quotations are necessary to make the story understandable to readers.

City and county government reporters do more than report what happens at meetings and provide sufficient background. Pre-meeting stories are written to keep readers informed on issues that will be considered by councils or boards. Corcoran, for example, recognized the news value of one item as soon as she examined the agenda for an upcoming meeting. She wrote:

> The Tempe City Council plans to increase residential water rates by 20 percent and raise garbage-disposal fees by 9 percent.
> The proposals will be introduced at Thursday's council meeting.

Any time a city proposes to raise rates for services, readers need to know *how* it will affect them individually and *why* the increase is being sought. Corcoran wrote:

> The water increase is needed to repay millions of dollars the city has borrowed for construction projects, said James Alexander, the city's management services director.
>
> The council plans to increase the monthly basic water service charge for a single-family home from $4 to $5 and raise the usage rate from 42 to 50 cents per 1,000 gallons for houses, town houses and apartment complexes.
>
> Monthly garbage-collection rates for single-family homes and town houses would increase from $5.50 to $6; from $8.25 to $9 for duplexes, and from $3.50 to $3.80 for apartment complexes.

Some readers no doubt would wonder what could be done to make their opinions known. Corcoran provided the answer:

> The council will hold a public hearing on the proposals before voting.

Clearly, Corcoran took an agenda item and developed it into an informative pre-meeting story. Local government reporters sometimes fall into the trap of thinking that readers understand completely the background and significance of an issue. That certainly is not the case. Reporters must work hard to provide complete details on each important item being considered by a governing body.

Suggestions for Local Government Reporters

More than anything else, coverage of local government requires hard work. Whether the local government reporter is starting the job immediately after college or with decades of journalism experience, settling into a new position is challenging. Often the most frustrating part of covering local government is getting to know the system and determining the true power structure.

Local government reporters should do the following:

- *Learn the system.* Check the newspaper morgue to see if stories about the hierarchy of the local government (city and/or county) have been done. If they have, they should provide good background. If they have not, consider writing such a series as one of your first major undertakings.

    Most American cities have either a mayor-council form of government or a city manager-city council form. Under the *mayor-council system,* the mayor is a primary source of news; for he or she is attuned to all city government activity. As more cities moved to a city manager form of government in the 1970s and 1980s, however, the mayor became more of a figurehead. The main source of city government expertise became the *city manager,* a trained professional adept at administering a community's affairs.

There is, of course, more to city government than the ranking official. Popularly elected city council members and commissioners fill important positions, as do city clerks, city treasurers and city attorneys. Other officials such as the fire chief, the police chief, the health department head, the director of the public works department, the city engineer, members of the planning and zoning commission, members of the parks and recreation commission and members of the civil service commission occupy just a few of the rungs on a city government ladder. County government is a system unto itself that includes officials such as commissioners, clerks, treasurers, recorders of deeds and attorneys.

A textbook can do no more than generalize about a local government system. Each is unique. Reporters must immerse themselves totally to become familiar with the local government structure of the city in which they work. This requires diligence, patience and concentration. This familiarization also must be accomplished quickly; reporters cannot adequately report on local government unless they thoroughly understand its structure.

- *Get to know the personalities.* It is one thing to master a local government organizational chart; it is another to pick out who among those occupying positions listed on the chart is truly significant. Once this determination has been made, reporters should get to know these persons as well as possible. If the city attorney is a Boston Celtics fan, the reporter should learn about the Boston Celtics and mention the team to the official. It might help the reporter get a local government story sometime.

- *Develop reliable sources.* Many local government stories are obtained directly from persons who occupy elected or appointed positions. Reporters obviously should build a network of sources from within these ranks. It is just as important, however, for reporters to develop a subnetwork of sources. Administrative assistants, secretaries and other staff members can be important sources. Reporters should choose them wisely, cultivate them and build a bond. But they should never take advantage of them.

- *Never let friendship interfere with the job.* Reporters who cover specific beats sometimes spend as much time with officials— their sources—as they do with their personal circle of friends. It is not surprising, then, that reporters and news sources sometimes become friends. Reporters must handle this situation with care—striving always to be fair in their handling of news stories.

- *Always be prepared.* To succeed, city government reporters must know more about city government than any other journalists in town. They must have more sources, do more homework on the issues and work longer hours. Good reporters never skim an agenda casually and write a meeting off as unimportant. Instead, they work harder to find *something* of value in an otherwise routine meeting.

- *Make note of story possibilities.* Many good local government stories do not evolve from coverage of meetings. Rather, they evolve from in-depth follow-ups of news tidbits tossed out at meetings or in informal conversations with local government sources. Even if reporters are working on another story at the time and do not have time to develop the new angle, the idea should be noted and carefully filed away for future reference.

- *Read other newspapers and listen to radio and television news.* Reporters should not operate in a vacuum, smugly assured that their sources will keep them informed of all possible stories. Other media should be surveyed constantly. Some of the best story ideas arise from less-than-satisfactory handling of stories by other reporters.

- *Write to inform, not impress, readers.* Develop local government stories from the standpoint of what the issue means to the readers. For example, if a city intends to raise an additional $14 million in property taxes during the next fiscal year, reporters should explain to readers what this increase means to them as homeowners. What will the increase do to taxes on a $50,000 house, a $75,000 house or a $100,000 house? That is what is important to the readers.

These suggestions are not limited to local government coverage. They also apply to coverage of state government—another formidable challenge.

COVERAGE OF STATE GOVERNMENT

Coverage of state government is a demanding assignment. Statehouse reporters must be resilient. They work long days when the legislature is in session, always having to be alert to hastily called meetings and position changes by key legislators.

Legislative coverage entails far more than merely writing stories about official votes taken on a particular day; it involves extensive behind-the-scenes work and reporting. An examination of the hectic pace kept by a statehouse reporter makes clear the demands placed on him.

The Responsibilities of a Legislative Reporter

Omaha (Neb.) World-Herald statehouse reporter Frank Partsch, who lives in Lincoln (the state capital) and works out of the bureau there, begins this pre-dawn winter day scratching around in the snow on his front porch to find the morning newspaper. The newspaper contains about 20 legislative stories, six of which he wrote the previous day. His eyes search for what he considers to be his best story: a report of a lobbyist's change in position on a tax bill.

A senator who had helped change the lobbyist's mind alerted Partsch to the story. Of course, publicizing the story would bolster the senator's position on the measure, which was scheduled for debate that day. Partsch knew the lawmaker's motive, but the reporter also realized that the story was an important one, especially when he was able to report that the legislator offered the lobbyist help with a special-interest bill that would be considered later.

Partsch reads the rest of his stories to spot errors and see if they were changed at the copy desk.

Compared with that of many states, Nebraska's government structure is compact. The state has a budget of about $1.5 billion and a relatively small government apparatus of about 25,000 employees. It also is known for its one-house Legislature—often referred to as the Unicameral. Forty-nine members serve in the officially non-partisan Senate.

The World-Herald, Nebraska's only statewide-circulation newspaper, maintains two non-sports reporters in its bureau in Lincoln. One concentrates on water and natural resources matters and is the No. 2 legislative reporter; Partsch is the other. His assignments include the Legislature, politics, spot news, features and routine state government coverage. He also writes a weekly column.

The newspaper depends on Partsch and one other reporter to cover the Legislature extensively. The World-Herald, however, also makes good use of Associated Press and United Press International stories on state government. In addition the newspaper's city desk is attuned to Lincoln stories and frequently sends specialists from Omaha to cover stories ranging from the judiciary to agriculture, commerce and medicine.

Partsch strives to be first with exclusives: analysis, enterprise and well-documented spot news coverage. He assumes that the wire services will provide broad coverage on major stories and floor votes. "I am in Lincoln to provide cutting edge stuff for my newspaper," he said.

Partsch has many story topics to choose from most days, but generally finds himself able to select only a handful. In choosing his topics he considers whether:

- They are important and exclusive to the World-Herald.
- They are subjects on which he has more background and expertise than do the wire service reporters who also would cover them.
- They are important enough to warrant his byline.
- They are particularly interesting to a segment of readers (e.g., farmers, Omaha city residents and so on), and thus deserving of World-Herald coverage even though the wire services probably would not cover them because they do not have widespread interest.
- They are issues judged particularly newsworthy by World-Herald editors or, more important, by World-Herald readers.

Reporters for small-circulation dailies and campus newspapers need to consider similar questions in deciding whether they should provide staff coverage of selected legislative issues. Generally, small dailies and campus papers will rely on the wire services for the brunt of their statehouse coverage. Sometimes, however, if an issue is of primary interest to their readers, editors at these papers will assign staffers to follow its progress. Students at state universities, for example, logically are interested in tuition costs. Editors at the State Press, Arizona State University's campus daily, assigned a reporter to concentrate on this issue. At the beginning of the legislative session, Mead Summer wrote:

> An increase in tuition and eventual elimination of student health services at the three state universities will be proposed to the Senate Appropriations Committee, the chairman of an appropriation subcommittee said Wednesday.
> Sen. Jack Taylor, R-Mesa, said the subcommittee will recommend resident registration fees be increased from $710 to $770 for the 1983-84 school year, and to $805 for the 1984-85 school year.
> The subcommittee's recommendation would increase tuition for out-of-state students, who currently pay the resident registration fee in addition to $2,540 tuition, to $2,750 for 1983-84.

The story went on to quote Taylor and other state representatives on the tuition proposal and to provide statistics on students who use health centers.

Reporters for the State Press, whose readership is made up almost entirely of students, faculty and university employees, certainly would follow progress of the tuition proposals in the legislature more closely than would wire service reporters or statehouse reporters for metropolitan newspapers.

Obviously, it is important for reporters to understand the informational needs of their readers. Partsch is a firm believer that a legislative reporter also should understand the state and its people.

"You can be magnificent interviewer and a brilliant wordsmith, but you cannot fool the natives," he said. "You need to understand them—not only their present, but their past."

A native of the state, Partsch earned an undergraduate degree at the University of Nebraska and a master's degree at Ohio State University. He was a reporter for the Wall Street Journal and editor of a tri-weekly Nebraska newspaper, the Sidney Telegraph, before being named the World-Herald's legislative reporter.

"I am much more capable of being a Nebraska legislative reporter than I would be of manning a legislative desk in another state," he said. "Were I to move, I could master the issues quickly, but it would take years to understand the history, the people and, ultimately, the perspective of what happens."

Legislative coverage can seem overwhelming to the beginning reporter, but after grasping the basic issues, the reporter is ready to develop an informational pipeline—a dependable network of sources. Partsch does not make formal "rounds," as a reporter on the city beat might. Rather, he talks to some sources frequently and to others as the occasion demands. His primary information network includes the following:

- A dozen members of the Legislature who individually tip him on the comings and goings of their opponents or on the executive branch.
- A dozen lobbyists who are keen—and frequently underutilized—observers of senators, issues and the executive branch.
- A handful of key departmental assistants, who help him flesh out stories before he goes to their supervisors or the governor for quotes.
- Specialists in departments who occasionally provide good ideas for stories if they are not involved.
- Former officials who keep in touch through former employees.
- Fellow reporters who sometimes trade information.
- Academics in various disciplines, who are especially valuable if they also are politically astute.

In each case, sources must be watched closely. Their information is valuable only if their motives for parting with it are understood.

Partsch tries to develop a lot of tax-trend stories, political-trend stories, development-of-policy stories and how-government-works-behind-the-scenes stories. "Many of these require the trust of sources who will share complex situations and examine my perspectives," he said. "My idea of the most complex story is a spiral in which I hear a rumor or generate a question; check it with experts in the lower levels of government to establish its validity; go to departmental assistants for background; check with lobbyists for points of view; touch base with key senators to ascertain movement, and, finally, zero in for on-the-record stuff at the bottom of the spiral."

One enterprise story that earned Partsch good play culminated three months of behind-the-scenes work. "I liked this story because I had been the only reporter with sufficient entree to both sides to do the running story," Partsch said.

The story focused on the maneuvering for leadership in the Legislature. It began:

> The Legislature organized itself Wednesday along lines that appeared to give previously influential senators—described as the "old guard"—an upper hand.
>
> In a day beginning with a prayer, punctuated with talk of partisanship and flavored with traditions—one broken—senators set up the formal machinery for handling legislation in the remainder of the 90-day session.
>
> It included several dramatic moments in addition to the tradition-breaking re-election of Hastings Sen. Richard Marvel as speaker—the first time that has happened since the one-house Legislature was established in 1937. Only once before, in the old State Senate, was the state's top legislative officer re-elected.
>
> "Old guard" and "new guard" are shorthand terms for the two coalitions maneuvering for leadership in recent months.

Partsch elaborated on the organizational fights that "had been raging behind the scenes for months, with State Republican Party officials proclaiming neutrality in that battle while pushing for Republican leadership." The reporter effectively wove direct quotations into his analysis. He quoted the "old guard" senator who urged other lawmakers to avoid partisanship "or you will watch this place be destroyed." Partsch said that the senator had challenged his colleagues to put a constitutional amendment before the voters to repeal the non-partisan election if they wanted a partisan body.

The story on the legislative reorganization is an example of the type of stories statehouse reporters must be capable of compiling. Without extensive sources and a strong "feel" for the political movements within a governing body, this type of story would be impossible to write.

Partsch exemplifies the aggressive, thoughtful journalists who make good legislative reporters. The work is sometimes tedious, but it always is challenging.

"I cannot emphasize enough the time and effort I put into attempting to avoid whim and tangent, including second-guessing my own judgments and motives," Partsch said. "I constantly am doubting and testing whenever possible, and building scenarios to explain people's behavior and uncover irrational actions that demand further reporting."

Mixed with these intellectual exercises are long, hard work sessions. In the next section Partsch constructs a typical composite day when the Nebraska Legislature is in session.

A Day on the Job with Frank Partsch

7:30—Arrive at the office and read the morning Lincoln newspaper. This gives me a look at other reporters' perspectives on the stories I covered as well as a chance to compare their exclusives with mine.

8—Have the first of the day's 20 telephone conversations with the regional editor in Omaha. We review the previous day and decide on necessary follow-ups. He requests a new lead on the lobbyist's change of position story, which will permit him to keep the story on Page 1 for the afternoon. (The World-Herald is a 24-hour newspaper with multiple editions.) I begin work on that. The lobbyist calls, upset, wanting to know where I got the information on the rest of the deal. I don't argue with angry people. Sometimes I tell them how this is a stage and we all have our assigned roles. Sometimes I say I just couldn't resist the urge. I don't mind apologizing when I'm wrong, and it's very easy to say, "I understand how you feel." A senator telephones to ask for coverage of a bill-signing ceremony in the governor's office. I'm quick to say, "Sorry, another commitment." In the case of bill-signing ceremonies in the governor's office, another commitment could be sharpening pencils. The morning mail arrives with a letter that makes for a short story on a pending issue.

8:50—A fellow World-Herald reporter and I cross the street to the Capitol, where we pick up the agenda. The senators will consider a dozen bills, some on final votes and others at amendment stages. We run through the list, each of us selecting bills by our specialty and interest. Some of the issues are left to the wires or ignored as insignificant or non-newsworthy. We telephone the regional desk to inform the editor of our selections and possible changes.

9—Opening gavel. My associate will cover the first bill. I don't know whether it will take two minutes or two hours, but I suspect it will be the latter. I remain in the chamber, using the time to read bills and other paperwork available at the press table, chat with senators, gossip with other reporters. This is watching and listening time. Who is huddling with whom? Who is lighthearted? Who is wary? What is moving, where and why?

Two senators confer at the rear of the chamber. They have been feuding over a hospital issue. I ask a senator who is friendly to one whether they are burying the hatchet. "No," he says. "I think they're planning a bottle-bill amendment [a mandatory five-cent deposit on pop and beer containers] to the tax bill." I ask the other senator's aide about the bottle bill. He confirms it, but asks me not to involve him. The conference ends, and I approach the senators separately. Another story. I confer with my fellow World-Herald reporter. She predicts that her bill will be settled momentarily, and she is right. She goes to the press room to transmit the story, and I begin listening to floor debate on a banking bill.

10—If this were Friday, we would have had to free one reporter to cover the governor's weekly press conference. Debate continues, with several amendments offered by both sides. The lobby is crowded with bankers. I read the bill, and, not understanding the reasoning behind some of its language, go to the bill's sponsor. He explains it. Then I go to the lobbyist who wrote the bill. I go to more than one source on everything about which there is the slightest doubt when time permits. Sources on different sides of issues are best. In this case I proceed to the lobbyist for the opposition. He has a different idea of why the bill is worded as it is. A lobbyist motions me over and invites me to lunch with a client who has a point to make. Although the lobbyist is a helpful source, I decline. It is too time-consuming, and it is not good to be seen in such company on the day of the debate.

10:45—Debate continues. My notes include a sketch of the proceedings with a few direct quotes. I mentally frame my lead and turn phrases over and over. Deadline for the afternoon paper is 11:15.

11:05—Telephone the regional editor and dictate the bottle-bill story. He agrees to hold 10 inches until noon for the banking story. Suddenly, the senators stall the bill procedurally without resolving any of the questions and go on to a road-construction issue. No story, I inform the editor, but the road-bond issue is highly significant to Omaha-area readers of the afternoon paper. He agrees to hold the 10 inches for the road-bond story.

11:14—The road-bond bill is amended and advanced without debate. My notes contain three quotes, but I have enough background to do the 10-inch story. My associate returns to the floor, and I begin to write on the portable electronic terminal at our desk in the Capitol pressroom.

11:24—Story completed. I let my mind wander for a few minutes. It was too easy. Indeed, the senators who were involved had explained the agreements that had enabled them to break the logjam, but something was missing. As the debate proceeds I begin making telephone calls in the pressroom (I can follow the debate on a speaker either in the pressroom or in our own office across the street). I call an assistant attorney general, an accountant in the Highway Department, a budget specialist in the Legislature's research office. A picture begins to emerge that will explain why the opposition to the road-bond bill had vanished in exchange for what seemed to be an insignificant amendment. It involved powerful politicians and businessmen—apparently nothing illegal, but certainly a financial and political power play that would benefit some regions and businesses over others. I decide to develop the story for the morning paper instead of using these fragmentary findings in the afternoon paper.

Noon—Senators recess for lunch. I interview three in a hallway to obtain pieces of the road-bond story. So far, I am cautious not to reveal the main direction of the story. I buy a cheese sandwich at the Capitol cafeteria and eat it while I walk back to the pressroom. Another two calls, and the story appears ready to write.

12:20—Return to our office across the street and write the road-bond story, look at late-morning mail and catch messages that may have been left there.

1:05—The road-bond story is finished and transmitted. I rewrite the bottle-bill story, using fresh quotes I picked up at noon, plus a historical sketch of previous bottle-bill fights.

1:15—We plan the afternoon's activities from the agenda. I call the regional desk to inform the editor of our afternoon plans. He suggests a third bottle-bill story, this one concentrating on the political motives of the sponsor.

1:30—The Legislature convenes, several members short because of the committee meetings. The first bill is insignificant and drones along until a generally colorless lawmaker makes a particularly articulate and interesting speech. My first reaction is to write a story saying that. But the speech had the ring of a lobbyist who favors this issue. I saunter out. "Quite a speech you wrote for the senator," I say and wink. The lobbyist grins and winks. This isn't worth a story, but it might work into print some day as part of a column, a profile of the senator, a profile of the lobbyist or an analysis of either the issue or of relations between the floor and the lobby.

2:20—A couple of bills have gone by, each worth a 5-inch story. I am following a rumor that a senator is under heavy pressure from the elderly back home to change his vote and support a bill to build a state home for the elderly. He downplays the pressure but his once harsh opposition to the bill is moderating. No story yet. On impulse I call a senior citizens' center in his district and ask for anyone interested in the issue. The voice on the other end of the phone explains that a petition campaign is being planned that will prove a major embarrassment to the senator. Among other things his grandmother is planning to pass petitions. Next step (always) is to call the grandmother (before you go to the senator). She confirms it, though she speaks lovingly of her grandson. Warmth amid conflict. Time for the senator now. He is angry when he hears what I have.

2:55—Floor activity drones along, so I go to the pressroom to start the story about the senator and his grandmother.

3:10—The sponsor of the tax bill featured in my morning story attempts a surprise procedural motion on that bill, which was not on the agenda. I rush upstairs to the chamber. The two committee work sessions have disbanded; several senators also are heading for the chamber. The idea of the procedural motion is to move the bill quickly ahead to avoid a crippling amendment that opponents were planning to file on the following day. Drama runs high. Debate includes criticism of the tactic of agenda-busting. The vote is short.

3:46—Adjournment. I return to the office and write the tax story and the story about the senator and his grandmother.

4:45—The governor calls. He is irritated by the momentum he perceives on the tax bill and wants to comment (in hopes of slowing the bill).

5:15—My next major deadline (Lincoln edition) is 11 p.m. I rewrite the tax bill story, pulling together the governor's comments and signs of momentum, as well as comments on the earlier change of position by the lobbyist. This story probably will be rewritten again for the next day's afternoon editions.

6—Read the afternoon Lincoln paper. Should have read it earlier. Begin thinking about my Sunday story, based on interviews and thoughts I have had at various times during the week. Our Sunday stories are supposed to be important news stories, not soft stuff, and there is pressure to produce well-researched and well-written copy. So this is not a sluff-off period.

S U G G E S T E D   E X E R C I S E S

1. Invite the city clerk, a council member, city administrator or mayor to your class. Ask the official to explain and discuss the city government structure in your community. Ask the official to discuss his or her perceptions of media coverage of local government.

2. Obtain a copy of an agenda for an upcoming city council meeting. Carefully review the agenda and get background on issues you do not understand. Attend the meeting. Write a story.

3. For a one-week period clip stories written by statehouse reporters for competing newspapers when the state legislature is in session. Notice how their stories on similar topics might differ. How many "exclusives" did each statehouse reporter have published during the week?

Reporters who cover the courts are responsible for gathering and writing some of the most complex, sensitive information that newspapers publish. This chapter discusses this coverage.

You will be introduced to:

• Coverage of the courts by one of the country's leading newspapers, the Los Angeles Times. Robert Rawitch provides tips for effective court reporting.

• The judicial system on both the federal and state levels. Differences and similarities are discussed.

• Coverage of civil cases. The chapter describes types of civil cases that often merit media attention. Examples of stories illustrate potentially newsworthy junctures in the often long and complex lives of many civil actions.

• Coverage of criminal cases. The chapter traces, with examples, the step-by-step evolution of a criminal case.

• Suggestions for the effective coverage of trials.

A reporter monitors trial proceedings while watching the courtroom drama on television.

© Michelle Bogre 1979/Sygma

7 COVERING THE COURTS

Coverage of the courts is one of the most demanding assignments a reporter can receive. During one day of testimony in a criminal trial, enough words can be spoken to fill 200 manuscript pages. From the testimony the reporter must extract the significant points and construct a readable, concise newspaper account of perhaps fewer than 500 words. Broadcast reporters face even more stifling word restrictions.

"The biggest challenge in court reporting is getting a grasp of the system," said Robert Rawitch, suburban editor of the Los Angeles Times, who covered the federal courts in that city for more than four years. "It is difficult to develop an understanding of legal procedures and jargon. You must strive diligently not to exaggerate or underplay the importance of any happening."

The Times assigns one reporter to the federal courts, one reporter to the state criminal courts and one reporter to the state civil courts in Los Angeles. In addition, a legal affairs reporter who is not responsible for daily developments in the various court systems writes on broader issues, such as the workings of grand jury systems, civil rights prosecutions of police officers, sentencing patterns of judges, unaccredited law schools and the trend toward national law firms. The Times also has a reporter who covers the U.S. Supreme Court full time in Washington, D.C., and a reporter based in San Francisco who spends about 50 percent of his time covering the California Supreme Court and the 9th U.S. Circuit Court of Appeals.

Rawitch had no particular training in legal reporting when he began work on the federal court beat. "I was assigned initially to the federal courts to see if the beat was worth covering on a full-time basis," he said. "After three weeks, I concluded it not only should be a full-time beat, but that the Times probably had not been covering it extensively enough. I was offered the job, but I turned it down. The assistant metro editor asked me to stay on that beat for a couple of weeks until someone could be assigned."

Before Rawitch's temporary shift was over, the Times instituted a hiring freeze. Rawitch had to remain until it was lifted. Meanwhile, he grew accustomed to the job, liked the challenge and decided to stay. It took him six months, however, to develop a sound understanding of the system and the people who were involved in it.

"Some judges would talk to me, some would not," Rawitch said. "Those who would not thought it was inappropriate. Others would see me only when their law clerks were present as witnesses to the conversations. Still others would have lunch with me, joke with me and join me for a cup of coffee."

Judges, however, are not the only sources of information for most court reporters. Reporters depend most heavily on the clerk of the court and other office personnel for calendar information and tips on upcoming proceedings.

"Clerks are good sources because they do not have a vested interest in most cases," Rawitch said. "Prosecuting attorneys and defense lawyers, though they can be helpful, do have such a vested interest. As a reporter you must be wary of that."

THE JUDICIAL SYSTEM

Reporters need to have a basic understanding of the judicial system, on both the federal and the state level. Aspiring court reporters should take appropriate college courses to help develop that understanding. The following overview serves as a starting point.

The Federal Judicial System

The United States Supreme Court is the nation's highest court. The wire services, the largest newpapers and the networks assign reporters to regularly cover the high court. The term of the court begins the first Monday in October and usually lasts until late June or early July. It is divided between sittings and recesses. During *sittings,* cases are heard and opinions announced. During *recesses,* the nine justices consider the business before the court and write opinions. Sittings and recesses alternate at approximately two-week intervals.

Public sessions of the court begin at 10 a.m. There is a one-hour recess starting at noon. Sessions end at about 3 p.m. The justices conduct private conferences to discuss cases on Fridays preceding argument weeks.

Reporters, of course, can cover the public sessions. When decisions are handed down, the justice who wrote the majority opinion normally highlights the facts and *holding* (outcome) of the case orally. Complete written opinions also are available to the press.

Reporters who cover the Supreme Court must have a solid understanding of the law and legal procedures in addition to being capable journalists. Complex legal language filling scores of pages must be deciphered when the written opinions are distributed. The facts of the case and the significance of the holding must be grasped. Reporters often select pertinent direct quotations from the majority, concurring or dissenting opinions. For background, law school professors or practicing attorneys sometimes are consulted for an interpretation of the significance of the case, for additional background or direct quotations.

The various circuits of the U.S. Court of Appeals occupy the intermediate level in the federal judicial system. With the exception of the circuit court that sits in the District of Columbia, each of these intermediate-level panels hears cases on appeal from several jurisdictions. The numbered circuits start in New England. For example, the 1st U.S. Circuit Court of Appeals sits in Boston. It serves Maine, Massachusetts, New Hampshire, Rhode Island and Puerto Rico. The 9th U.S. Circuit Court of Appeals sits in San Francisco. It serves Alaska, Arizona, California,

Hawaii, Idaho, Montana, Nevada, Oregon, Washington and Guam. Courts of appeals sit to review results of trials or decisions made in lower courts. Appeals usually are limited to the facts and record of the case at the trial level.

Trials in the federal system generally are confined to the U.S. District Courts. There are 94 such courts. Each state has at least one; some of the more heavily populated states have more than one. Written transcripts of the proceedings usually are available. Sometimes written opinions from the U.S. District Courts are published, bound by volume and shelved in libraries.

The federal system also includes several specialized courts such as the Court of Customs and Patent Appeals, the Customs Court and the Court of Claims.

State Judicial Systems

There are about as many types of state court systems as there are states. Usually, a state's judicial system has three layers:

- *Trial courts,* where proceedings are initiated.
- *Intermediate courts,* where appeals are first heard.
- *Supreme courts,* which are panels of final resort.

The names assigned to the courts at each of these levels vary, but generally the highest is called the *state supreme court.* The intermediate level (used by about half the states) is called an *appellate court.* Trial-level bodies, often called *superior courts,* are the highest trial courts with general jurisdiction in most states. Sometimes they are given other names; for instance, in New York the trial-level body is called the Supreme Court.

Several other courts complete the various state systems. These, according to a West Publishing Co. chart, include *probate courts* (which handle wills, adminstration of estates and guardianship of minors and incompetents); *county courts* (which have limited jurisdiction in civil and criminal cases); *municipal courts* (where cases involving less serious crimes, generally called *misdemeanors,* are heard by municipal justices or municipal magistrates), and, in some jurisdictions, *justice of the peace* and *police magistrate courts* (which have very limited jurisdiction and are the lowest courts in the judicial hierarchy). Justice courts in Arizona, for example, hear matters that involve less than $500.

COURT CASES

Court cases can be lumped in two divisions: civil and criminal. *Civil cases* involve arriving at specific solutions to legal strife between individuals, businesses, state or local governments or agencies of government. Civil cases commonly include suits for damages arising from automobile accidents, suits for breach of contract or even suits for libel.

Criminal cases involve the enforcement of criminal statutes. Suits are brought by the state or federal government against an individual charged with committing a crime such as robbery, burglary or murder.

Civil Cases

Generally, countless briefs are filed in civil suits, and reporters must periodically check court dockets for progress in specific cases. In Superior Court for Los Angeles, the average civil suit is in the system—from time of filing until trial or settlement—approximately four years. It is not unusual for cases to extend six or seven years. Metropolitan court systems often are short on personnel for civil cases, and legal requirements force them to give priority to criminal cases. The average criminal cases in Superior Court for Los Angeles generally will conclude from two to four months after the arrest.

Understanding record-keeping systems is a critical element in good court coverage. Reporters in small cities do not face the crunch of cases that metropolitan reporters do, but regardless of the case load, reporters must watch dockets and calendars closely. In Superior Court for Los Angeles the civil courts reporter for the Times usually is following the progress of more than 500 pending suits. "It is a bookkeeping nightmare," Rawitch said.

The filing system in Los Angeles' civil division of Superior Court is efficient and detailed, but the Times reporter must spend more than an hour each day checking case numbers listed on the court calendar.

Steps taken in a suit can vary. According to "Law and the Courts," published by the American Bar Association, here is the basic process:

- The *plaintiff* (the party bringing the suit) selects the proper jurisdiction (federal or state system, and the appropriate court thereof).
- The plaintiff files a *complaint* (sometimes called a *petition*) against a party (called the *defendant*).
- A hearing is held in which the plaintiff prepares a detailed set of charges.
- *Depositions* (out-of-court statements made by witnesses under oath) are taken.
- After all the pleadings have been filed, attorneys for both parties appear before a judge at a pretrial conference to agree on the undisputed facts of the case. (Often a settlement is reached at this point without trial.)
- If no settlement is reached the case is scheduled for trial.

- Testimony as to the dispute is presented and arguments are heard at the trial.
- After the arguments, the judge instructs the jury (unless the defendant has waived his right to a jury proceeding) on legal considerations.
- The jury goes to its room for deliberations.
- The jury returns with a verdict.
- The verdict is announced, and the judge enters a judgment upon the verdict.
- If either party is unhappy, an appeal can be made.

Reporting Civil Cases

The majority of civil suits never reach trial.

Scores of civil suits are filed each day in metropolitan jurisdictions. Certainly not all of them are newsworthy. Reporters must decide which suits are important and then constantly check court dockets for developments. The following suit, because it involved one of America's best-known syndicated columnists and a former ambassador, logically would be considered newsworthy.

On April 18, 1977, Turner B. Shelton, former ambassador to Nicaragua, brought a libel suit in the U.S. District Court for the District of Columbia against "Washington Merry-Go-Round" syndicated columnist Jack Anderson and his associate Les Whitten. The action sought $15 million in damages. Because the action involved a controversy between citizens of different states (Shelton lived in Beverly Hills, Calif.), the U.S. District Court had jurisdiction. Because Washington, D.C., was the focal point for gathering the information at issue, suit was brought in the District of Columbia.

The first portion of the complaint, which was assigned Civil Action No. 77–0666, looked like this:

UNITED STATES DISTRICT COURT
FOR THE DISTRICT OF COLUMBIA

Civil Division

TURNER B. SHELTON   :
  1121 Tower Road :
  Beverly Hills, Cal. 90213 :
   Plaintiff,   :

 v.

JACK ANDERSON
    1401 Sixteenth St., N.W.   :
    Washington, D.C. 20036   : Civil Action No. 77–0666
      Defendant

    and

LES WHITTEN
    1401 Sixteenth St., N.W.   :
    Washington, D.C. 20036   :
      Defendant   :

COMPLAINT

(Libel & Interference with Contract)

1. Jurisdiction is founded upon diversity of citizenship and the amount in controversy. Plaintiff is a citizen of the State of California and resides therein. The defendants are citizens of the State of Maryland and maintain their principal place of business in the District of Columbia. The amount of controversy exceeds the sum of Ten Thousand Dollars, exclusive of interest and costs.

2. The plaintiff, Turner B. Shelton, was a career foreign service officer and the former Ambassador of the United States of America to Nicaragua, and the former Ambassador in Residence at the Naval War College in Newport, Rhode Island.

3. The defendant, Jack Anderson, is a syndicated newspaper columnist and writes and publishes a column daily in *The Washington Post* which is distributed in the District of Columbia. The said column is also published daily in more than 1,000 newspapers throughout the United States and the world.

4. The defendant, Les Whitten, is a writer and jointly with the defendant Anderson writes and publishes a daily column in *The Washington Post* which is distributed in the District of Columbia. The said column is also published daily in more than 1,000 newspapers throughout the United States and the world.

The complaint then listed four *counts* (parts of a civil complaint claiming specific wrong done) of allegedly libelous information published about Shelton by Anderson and Whitten. The complaint concluded with the following:

WHEREUPON, plaintiff prays:

1. For judgment against the defendant Jack Anderson in the amount of Two Million Five Hundred Thousand Dollars ($2,500,000.00) as compensatory damages.

2. For judgment against the defendant Les Whitten in the amount of Two Million Five Hundred Thousand Dollars ($2,500,000.00) as compensatory damages.

3. For judgment against the defendant Jack Anderson in the amount of Five Million Dollars ($5,000,000.00) as punitive damages.

4. For judgment against the defendant Les Whitten in the amount of Five Million Dollars ($5,000,000.00) as punitive damages.

5. For costs and interest against each of the defendants.

Attached to the complaint were copies of three "Merry-Go-Round" columns that allegedly contained libelous statements about Shelton.

A story about the Shelton suit—like all court-related articles—should contain certain essential ingredients:

- It should clearly spell out who is bringing the suit (the plaintiff), who is being sued (the defendant) and when the suit was filed.

- It should identify the parties as fully as possible (the occupations of the plaintiff and defendants in the Shelton action are particularly significant).

- It should provide background on the circumstances that brought about the suit.

- It should give specifics on the damages sought.

- It should give the defendants' response to the complaint.

- It should fully attribute all information. It should make absolutely clear to the readers that the information came from court records. Reporters and their newspapers can defend themselves against libel charges by accurately quoting from official court documents. (A discussion of libel defenses is presented in Chapter 17).

A story such as this could be written about the Shelton suit:

A former U.S. ambassador to Nicaragua filed a $15 million libel suit in U.S. District Court for the District of Columbia today against syndicated newspaper columnists Jack Anderson and Les Whitten.

In his complaint, Turner B. Shelton, now of Beverly Hills, Calif., charged that allegations about him published in the "Washington Merry-Go-Round" syndicated newspaper column were false. The complaint said the columnists had published the statements knowing them "to be false or having reason to believe" them to be false.

According to the complaint, Anderson and Whitten wrote a column that labeled Shelton "probably the worst ambassador of the Nixon era."

Shelton's complaint also quoted from a Nov. 10, 1976, column that mentioned "the tolerance (Secretary of State Henry) Kissinger has shown for the Foreign Service's foul balls."

Anderson and his associates were aware, or had access to information, that Shelton had received the Distinguished Service Award of Valor, the latter for superior performance during the earthquake in Nicaragua, according to the complaint.

After the suit was filed, Anderson said, "We have never been sued successfully and this is no exception. We rather welcome the opportunity to lay the record out in court."

Forty notations were made on the docket that recorded progress in the case during the 16 months after the Shelton complaint was filed. Reporters following the case should have noticed docket entries that documented the filing of an answer to the complaint, several notices for the taking of depositions, a motion of the plaintiff to amend the complaint, a motion by the plaintiff to compel answers to questions in oral depositions, an order by the court denying the plaintiff's motion to force the defendant to reveal the identities of confidential sources and finally, on Aug. 1, 1978, a notation that the case had been settled and dismissed.

Of these docket entries reporters logically would have followed up on the refusal of the judge to compel Anderson and Whitten to reveal their confidential sources. Doing so would likely have made a good news story. And certainly reporters should have written a story about the dismissal of the case. There was no monetary settlement, but Anderson agreed to publish a clarifying column—not a formal retraction—concerning Shelton. Reference could have been made in the news story about the dismissal of the suit to the column Anderson wrote. In that clarifying column Anderson wrote that although he had earlier reported that Shelton was more concerned with personal problems than with the plight of Nicaraguans during the earthquake, "we are now persuaded that the ambassador and his wife were deeply concerned about the devastation. The ambassador worked tirelessly for six days and nights with little more than a few hours sleep and refused to let a broken arm slow him down." In addition to making reference to the Anderson column in the story of the dismissal of the suit, reporters could have contacted attorneys for the parties and the parties themselves for additional comments and information.

Selecting Civil Suits to Cover

The majority of civil suits do not involve high-ranking public officials or well-known columnists. According to Tom Spratt, courthouse reporter for the Phoenix Gazette, many civil suits merely "fade away" after an initial filing. More than 90 percent never make it to trial.

Still, if a story has been written about the filing, a reporter must be diligent in following the case to its conclusion. It is important to report dismissals, settlements or verdicts. Many civil suits make headlines when they are filed, but as they become tangled in the shuffle of paperwork and forgotten in the passage of time, they are not followed up on by reporters. This, of course, is unfair to the parties involved. If a newspaper reports that

a malpractice suit seeking $15 million in damages was filed against Dr. John Jones, the newspaper owes it to its readers and to the parties in the suit to report how the case ultimately is decided.

No magic formula determines if a civil suit is newsworthy. Spratt, however, tries to systematically examine all civil complaints. He glances at the general headings listed at the tops of the complaints: *contract, tort motor vehicles, tort non-motor vehicles* (this category includes personal wrongs and often is newsworthy) and *non-classified* (which includes an assortment of cases that do not fit under common headings).

Spratt also looks at damages sought. Because a party seeks more than $1 million does not necessarily make the complaint newsworthy. "After the reporter is on the courthouse beat for a while, he or she will begin to recognize which lawyers consistently file suits seeking huge damages, but which never get very far in the judicial process," Spratt said.

After Spratt isolates cases of potential interest by reading the headings and determining the damages sought, he reads the complaints in their entirety to see if they seem to be particularly important, interesting or significant.

Once a civil suit has been filed and Spratt decides it deserves coverage, he often calls the attorney who filed it for a further explanation. "I make an effort to talk to attorneys for both parties, whenever possible," Spratt said. "This is particularly important in civil cases where filings and rulings are very complicated." Sometimes, to get additional background, he also calls attorneys who are not involved in the suit but who are experts in the area being litigated.

Newspapers do not cover most civil suits at every step in the judicial process. Often, a short story is written when a suit is filed and another story is written when the suit is dismissed or settled or when there is a verdict. Some civil cases, however, because of the huge damages sought or because of the parties or issues involved, merit expanded coverage. An example is a case filed by a Phoenix family after a natural-gas explosion in their apartment. This suit had a number of newsworthy elements: Astronomical damages were sought, the defendants included public utilities and it was a spectacular explosion.

The Filing

The story of the filing, which was published in the Arizona Republic, contained the essential items of importance. The lead paragraph focused on the damages sought:

> Members of a Phoenix family critically injured April 20 by a natural-gas explosion in their apartment have filed a $92.1 million suit in Maricopa County Superior Court.

The next two paragraphs provided background on the plaintiffs:

The complaint was filed by lawyer Charles Brewer on behalf of
Daniel and Gloria Crawley and their sons, Tracy, 9, and Jeremy, 6. They
were burned when a blast ripped through their apartment at 6565 N. 17th
Ave.

Crawley, his wife and Tracy were reported in critical condition
Wednesday at Maricopa County Hospital. Jeremy was reported in
guarded condition.

The story went on to list the defendants:

Named as defendants in the suit, filed Tuesday, are Arizona Public
Service Co., the Salt River Project, Bianco Construction Co. and the
owners of the 16-unit apartment complex, Gerald L. Emery, Richard C.
Herrerias and Stewart Kim Patberg.

The story concluded with details outlined in the complaint and with
direct quotations from affected parties:

According to the suit, the explosion was caused by a leaking gas line.
The suit accuses the defendants of negligence in the design, construction,
maintenance and installation of the line.

"We're most concerned about the Crawley family, and we're actively
investigating the circumstances of the accident," Martha McKinley, an
APS spokeswoman, said Wednesday.

"The facts will surface during legal discovery proceedings. To say any
more would be inappropriate because the matter is in litigation."

Sally Keck, an SRP spokeswoman, said that utility cannot comment
on the suit because it hasn't seen it.

Emery, one the apartment owners, declined comment.

The Developments

Procedural maneuverings are extensive in complicated civil suits; generally, they are not newsworthy. As noted earlier, civil suits can drag on for
years. Occasionally, however, between the filing and conclusion of litigation, developments arise that are newsworthy and deserving of coverage.
This was the case in the natural-gas suit filed by the Crawleys. Jeff South's
story in the Phoenix Gazette revealed a new development:

Because of their desperate plight, burn victims Gloria Crawley and
her children will get their day in court sooner than expected.

Judge James Moeller of Maricopa County Superior Court has
approved a motion giving priority to the Crawleys' lawsuit in connection
with an April 20 explosion that ripped through their apartment at 6565 N.
17th Ave.

At the request of the Crawleys' attorney, Moeller set the case for trial
next April.

The story went on to list the defendants, provide background on the $90-million-plus suit, explain the reasoning advanced by the Crawleys' lawyer for the need for the accelerated process and explain that Mrs. Crawley's husband had died from burns 30 days after the explosion. The story also quoted from documents filed by the Crawleys' attorney, Charles Brewer:

> The Crawleys' "desperate physical, financial and mental situation may become irreversible and irrecoverable" unless the case goes to trial soon, Brewer said in court documents.

The Settlement

As often is the case in civil actions, the suit was settled out of court. Naturally, this case merited a major story. Brent Whiting of the Arizona Republic used a straightforward lead:

> An out-of-court settlement of $8.1 million was reached Thursday in a suit filed by members of a Phoenix family critically injured last year when a natural-gas explosion ripped through their apartment.

Background on the suit was given in the next two paragraphs:

> The $92.1 million Superior Court lawsuit was filed by Gloria Jean Crawley, 30, and her sons, Tracy, 10, and Jeremy, 8.
> Mrs. Crawley's husband, Daniel, 32, died May 14, just one month after the explosion at the Palo Verde Apartments, 6565 N. 17th Ave.

Obviously, in a settlement story, attribution must be provided. That came in the fourth paragraph:

> Charles M. Brewer, Mrs. Crawley's attorney, said the settlement will be paid by Arizona Public Service Co. and by Palo Verde Apartments Inc., owner of the 16-unit complex.
> Brewer said that under the terms of the settlement, APS and its liability-insurance carrier will pay $7.1 million, and the remaining $1 million will be paid by the carrier for the apartment owner.

A logical question naturally surfaced: Had there been other civil suits in the state that involved such a large settlement? If the answer could be documented, it likely would belong in the lead. Here, it was merely an *opinion* that was placed lower in the story and was fully attributed:

> "This is probably the biggest settlement in Arizona history," Brewer said. "I would have liked to have tried the case, but when you have this kind of a settlement offer, you have to accept it."

The story went on to provide other pertinent particulars: an update on Mrs. Crawley and her children and background on the filing.

Stories That Require Enterprise

Diligent courthouse reporters will seek out stories that go beyond filings, developments and outcomes of individual civil suits.

Gazette reporter Spratt, for example, noticed a flurry of suits in Maricopa County Superior Court in which large damages were sought. He compiled a list of some of the suits, talked with attorneys and put together an interesting piece that was published under the headline "King-sized damage demands becoming routine in lawsuits."

Spratt started his story with a lead that emphasized the proportions of the damages sought in some contemporary suits:

> After discovering cracks in their Fountain Hills home, John and Margaret Kriegel filed a lawsuit asking for almost as much money as the United States paid for Alaska in 1867.
>
> But their $5 million complaint (compared with $7 million for Alaska) failed to raise many eyebrows in Maricopa County Superior Court. Multi-million-dollar lawsuits have become commonplace there.
>
> And the chances of convincing a jury to award $1 million or more have been rising steadily since the first such verdict in the early 1970s.
>
> Society's financial expectations have grown during the last 10 years—and with them the amount of money sought in lawsuits, Ralph Mahowald, president of the Maricopa County Bar Association, said:

As he moved into the body of his story, Spratt noted that the damages sought by the Kriegels actually were small compared to a libel suit mentioned later in the story that sought $200 million. Again, Spratt put those figures in perspective. He wrote that $200 million was slightly more than the predicted cost of producing the 1982 World's Fair in Knoxville, Tenn.

Spratt then traced the steady increase in damages awarded in Maricopa County. In 1960, the largest amount won for a client in a civil suit was $435,000; two decades later it stood at $3.9 million. The largest out-of-court settlement to date was the $8.1 million to the Crawley family.

The story by Spratt is an example of a reporter taking complicated information that involves dollar amounts almost unimaginable to ordinary readers and transforming those numbers into a readable, understandable court-related story.

Criminal Cases

As noted, criminal cases involve the enforcement of criminal statutes. In his book, "The Reporter and the Law," Lyle Denniston, veteran U.S. Supreme Court reporter, wrote: "Crime is the main staple of legal reporting. Of course, crime alone does not make all the news on the court beat. But it does dominate the beat."

As Denniston noted, "Criminal law is simply more 'newsworthy' than civil law. More often, a criminal case will have in it the ingredients of human interest, public policy and clear-cut controversy that makes news. At a more fundamental level, criminal law provides the most vivid test of a community's sense of justice and morality."

Criminal charges are brought against an individual through an indictment that is voted by a grand jury or through the filing of an information. As with civil action, the intricacies of a criminal action will vary. According to "Law and the Courts," the steps that occur are basically as follows:

- The clerk of the court issues a warrant for the arrest of the person charged (if the person has not been arrested already).

- A preliminary hearing is held at which the state must present sufficient evidence to convince the presiding judge that there is reason to believe the defendant committed the crime that he or she is being charged with. If the judge agrees that there is sufficient reason, he or she will order the defendant bound over for trial.

- After the defendant has been bound over for trial, a date for an arraignment is set.

- The defendant appears at the arraignment, where the judge reads the charge and explains the defendant's rights.

- The defendant then pleads guilty or innocent. If the defendant pleads innocent, a trial date is set.

- A jury is selected.

- Once the trial is under way, opening statements by the prosecuting attorney and the defense attorney are made (presentation of evidence by the state always is given first).

- The defense attorney then presents his evidence.

- Final motions and closing arguments are heard.

- The judge then reads instructions to the jury.

- The jury deliberates and returns with a verdict.

- The judge enters a judgment upon the verdict.

- The judge sets a date for sentencing.

- The defendant, if unhappy with the verdict, may appeal to a higher court.

All these steps are potentially newsworthy. Reporters must of course be extremely careful to attribute statements to legal documents or to individuals who make them in or out of court. Coverage of a criminal proceeding ordinarily is not as complex and laborious as sifting through five years of motions and filings in a civil case, but careful, accurate reporting is just as important.

Reporting Criminal Cases

As stated earlier, steps in criminal proceedings can vary. To illustrate general reporting procedures, however, the following fictional scenario is presented:

The case unfolds when Nancy Johnson, 33, is found fatally stabbed at home, 1002 Central Ave., Riverdale, where she lived with a friend, Linda Evans. Evans found the body at 12:30 a.m., on Monday, July 25.

According to the police report, Johnson had been strangled and had been dead less than four hours when Evans found her. Evans had been away from the house on a skiing trip since Friday afternoon.

Johnson was a fourth-grade teacher in the Riverdale schools. She was named "Teacher of the Year" by the Riverdale Parent-Teacher Association last spring. She was dating Sam E. Smith, 39, owner of a television appliance store. Friends had seen Smith and Johnson at a movie Sunday night, July 24. Smith told police he had taken Johnson home at 10:30 p.m. and she had been alive when he last saw her.

Johnson was lying nude on her bed when Evans found her.

Gathering the Information

The police reporter for the Riverdale Daily News, an afternoon newspaper with a circulation of 12,000, is alerted to the apparent slaying when, at 2 a.m., the night desk sergeant at the police station calls. He says he thought she "would like to know." She is thankful she had cultivated the sergeant as a source. On this night, it pays off. Other reporters still are sleeping.

The call gives her a running start on the story. Thirty minutes later, she is at the police station to get comments from investigating officers. She gathers pertinent information and, at 7 a.m., calls her city editor to tell of the death and the possibility of a late-morning arrest of a suspect.

The editor tells her to find background on Nancy Johnson to blend into the story. The reporter uses information gathered from the police records, interviews with investigating officers and police spokespersons, interviews with school district officials and biographical details supplied by the school district. Linda Evans refuses to comment.

The Arrest

The arrest is made at 11:30 a.m., just one hour before the newspaper's deadline. The reporter, after learning that Johnson was named "Teacher of the Year" last spring, decides to put that fact in her lead. She writes:

> A 39-year-old television appliance store owner was arrested shortly before noon Monday in connection with the Sunday night slaying of Nancy Johnson, 33, who was named Riverdale's "Teacher of the Year" last spring.

Riverdale Police Chief Don James identified the suspect as Sam E. Smith, owner of Smith's TV Land, 1216 N. Third Ave. Smith was arrested at his store, according to James.

James said police were called to Miss Johnson's house at 1002 Central Ave. at 12:30 a.m. Monday by Linda Evans, a roommate.

Police found the nude body of Miss Johnson on her bed.

James said the bedroom showed signs of a struggle.

Miss Johnson, who was a fourth-grade teacher in the Riverdale schools, was named "Teacher of the Year" last spring by the Parent-Teacher Association.

According to James, Smith and Miss Johnson had gone to a movie Sunday night.

Miss Evans, who returned home from a weekend of skiing, told police she called them the minute she walked into the bedroom and saw the body.

Police released no other details.

Kenneth Bowling, superintendent of the Riverdale schools, said he was "shocked" when he heard the news of Miss Johnson's death.

"She was one of the finest teachers in our system," he said.

The basic story of the arrest is carefully worded; it says Smith was arrested *in connection with the Sunday night slaying* (some newspapers prefer to use *in suspicion of* or *in the investigation of*). The reporter is careful not to write Smith was arrested *for* the slaying; doing so would imply guilt and could lead to a libel suit. Also note that the word *slaying*—not *murder*—is used. The AP Stylebook says: Do not say a victim was murdered until someone is convicted of murder. Instead, use *killed* or *slain.* "Do not describe someone as a *murderer* until convicted of the charge in court."

The reporter also is extremely careful to attribute all facts to the police. The quotation from the superintendent of schools also adds substance to the story.

Pre-Arraignment Developments

In most states, an arraignment in a lower court (designations of these courts vary, but they include police courts, municipal courts, magistrate courts or justice courts) generally takes place soon after the arrest. Because slayings are not common in Riverdale, the Daily News court reporter makes a particular effort to keep pace with developments in the case. She writes this lead for a pre-arraignment story:

A 39-year-old television appliance store owner will be arraigned at 10 a.m. Wednesday in Police Court on a charge of first-degree murder in connection with the Sunday night stabbing death of Riverdale teacher Nancy Johnson, prosecuting attorney Joe Morris said.

The reporter is careful to put attribution in the lead paragraph. *Arraignments*—where the charge is read to the accused—sometimes do not take place on schedule or are not held at all if last-minute information surfaces that clears the suspect. Thus, attribution to an authoritative source is imperative. The short pre-arraignment story closes with new information on the apparent cause of death and with background on the slaying:

> According to the county coroner's office, Miss Johnson died of stab wounds inflicted by a kitchen knife in her house at 1002 Central Ave.
>
> Sam E. Smith was arrested Monday morning by Riverdale police. According to police, Smith had taken Miss Johnson to a movie Sunday evening.

The Lower-Court Arraignment

Naturally, the reporter will follow with a short story about the lower-court arraignment. Most Riverdale readers now are aware of the slaying; Sam Smith and Nancy Johnson have become household words. For the first time, the name of the accused is used in the lead paragraph:

> Sam E. Smith pleaded innocent Wednesday to a charge of first-degree murder in connection with the Sunday night slaying of Riverdale teacher Nancy Johnson.
>
> Smith, owner of Smith's TV Land, 1216 N. Third Ave., was dressed in a blue pin-striped suit as he stood silently beside his lawyer, Kevin Cosgrove, during a 12-minute arraignment before Police Court Judge Andrew Gaston.
>
> The case was assigned to Police Court Judge Henry Collins for an Oct. 17 preliminary hearing. Bail was set at $100,000.
>
> When Smith was arrested Monday, police said he and Miss Johnson had gone to a movie the night before. She was found stabbed to death at 12:30 a.m. Monday in her bedroom at 1002 Central Ave.

Notice that the reporter continues to provide background on the slaying. Even when reports of judicial proceedings are in the news for an extended time, reporters always must assume that most readers do not know the background of the case.

The Preliminary Hearing

At a preliminary hearing the judge must decide if the state's case is adequate to bring the accused to trial. The state, often without revealing all the information it has, nevertheless must present sufficient evidence to convince the judge it has a good case. The reporter covers the hearing and begins her story with the following:

> Sam E. Smith was ordered bound over to Nuckolls County Superior Court Tuesday in connection with the July 24 slaying of Riverdale teacher Nancy Johnson.
>
> Police Court Judge Henry Collins found sufficient reason for Smith to stand trial.
>
> Smith was freed on $100,000 bond.

Police Chief Don James told Collins that Smith had taken Miss Johnson to a movie the evening of July 24. James said Smith was the last person to have seen Miss Johnson alive.

County Coroner Wayne Brown said Johnson died from stab wounds.

Smith, owner of Smith's TV Land, 1216 N. Third Ave., pleaded innocent in Police Court during his arraignment on a charge of first-degree murder.

The preliminary hearing story should include specifics on the testimony of law-enforcement officers. Their testimony likely will be pivotal in deciding whether there is sufficient reason for the accused to stand trial.

In lieu of a preliminary hearing, the procedure in some states is to refer the case to a grand jury to see if evidence is sufficient to bring the accused to trial. If the grand jury determines there is sufficient evidence, it will return an indictment known as a *true bill*. If the grand jury decides that a sufficient probability does not exist that the accused committed the crime, it will return a *no bill*.

The Superior Court Arraignment

If the judge at the preliminary hearing decides the evidence is sufficient (or if a grand jury returns a *true bill*), the accused is arraigned in a court that has jurisdiction in felony (serious) cases. The Daily News reporter writes this story:

Nuckolls County Superior Court Judge George Flynn Wednesday set a Jan. 4 trial for Sam E. Smith, 39, who is charged in connection with the July 24 slaying of Riverdale teacher Nancy Johnson.

Smith, owner of Smith's TV Land, 1216 N. Third Ave., was arraigned and pleaded innocent to a charge of first-degree murder.

Smith also had pleaded innocent to the charge when arraigned last month in Police Court.

Police Chief Don James said at a preliminary hearing that Smith had taken Miss Johnson to a movie the evening of July 24. James said Smith was the last person to have seen Miss Johnson alive.

Pretrial Coverage

Before a trial, newspapers generally will publish stories that summarize past developments and inform readers of new information, such as the selection of a jury. Occasionally facts will surface to make a pretrial story particularly important. The Daily News reporter recognized an item of significance before the Smith trial:

Television cameras will be allowed to film the trial of Sam E. Smith, 39, who is charged with first-degree murder in connection with the July 24 slaying of Riverdale teacher Nancy Johnson.

Smith's trial begins Wednesday.

The state legislature voted last session to allow a one-year experiment of camera coverage of trial-court proceedings beginning this year.

On Monday, Superior Court Judge George Flynn asked prospective jurors if they would be influenced by the television coverage. None replied yes.

Flynn also denied a defense request to close the trial to television coverage.

Miss Johnson, who was named "Teacher of the Year" last spring by the Parent-Teacher Association, was found stabbed to death in her house at 1002 Central Ave. According to police, Miss Johnson and Smith had gone to a movie the evening of July 24.

The possibility of camera coverage of portions of the trial, of course, makes this case even more newsworthy. With background information close at hand (the reporter has all the clips), she is ready to cover the trial. This trial has considerable news value: proximity, emotion and the uniqueness of camera coverage.

The Trial

Reporters provide gavel-to-gavel coverage of only the most important trials. Editors at the Daily News decide that their courthouse reporter should cover each day of the Smith trial. Her leads generally will focus on the key testimony of the day. As the Smith trial winds down, the woman who found Johnson's body is called to the stand. The story:

Linda Evans told a packed courtroom Thursday that her roommate, Nancy Johnson, had turned down a marriage proposal from Sam E. Smith one week before she was stabbed to death last July 24.

Taking the witness stand in Nuckolls County Superior Court, Evans testified that Miss Johnson told Smith that she was "not ready for such a big step."

Smith, 39, owner of Smith's TV Land, 1216 N. Third Ave., is on trial in connection with the slaying of Miss Johnson.

Miss Evans found the nude body of Miss Johnson during the early morning hours of July 25 in the bedroom of a house they shared at 1002 Central Ave.

Miss Evans said Miss Johnson was "very upset" because of the way Smith had reacted when she told him she was not ready to get married.

"Nancy told me she had never seen him so upset," said Miss Evans. "But Nancy thought that since they had been dating for only four months, talk of marriage was premature."

According to testimony by Miss Evans, Miss Johnson accepted Smith's invitation to go to the movie the evening of July 24 "because she wanted them to remain friends."

The Verdict

The climax to a criminal trial is the verdict. The Daily News reporter writes:

Sam E. Smith, 39, owner of Smith's TV Land, 1216 N. Third Ave., was convicted Friday in Nuckolls County Superior Court for murdering Riverdale teacher Nancy Johnson.

Note that the word *murdering* is used after the conviction. The lead often practically writes itself in a verdict story, but the reporter must work hard to assemble the remainder of the account. There is no sacrosanct formula for writing a verdict story, but the reaction of the defendant and the length of time the jury deliberates generally are placed high in the story. The Daily News story continues:

Smith, a short, well-built man with blond hair, broke into tears when the verdict was read.
The jury had deliberated 55 minutes.

Stories about verdicts also often contain quotations from attorneys, insight on the possibility of an appeal, background on the case and reactions from witnesses, jurors, friends and other interested parties. The story continues:

Deputy Nuckolls County Attorney Joe Morris, who prosecuted the case, said the state will ask for the death penalty.
Superior Court Judge George Flynn said a presentence hearing will be conducted Feb. 4 and Smith will be sentenced Feb. 8.
Smith's attorney, Kevin Cosgrove, said his client would seek a new trial.
"I didn't do it, I didn't do it," Smith blurted as he was escorted from the courtroom by the bailiff. "I loved her. I really did."
Smith fell to his knees after the emotional outburst and was helped to his feet by the bailiff and Cosgrove.
Outside the courtroom, Miss Johnson's roommate, Linda Evans, embraced friends. Her testimony was regarded as crucial to the prosecution's case.
Miss Evans told the jury Thursday that Smith was upset with Miss Johnson when she turned down his marriage proposal one week before her death.
"I know he is guilty," Miss Evans said of Smith. "I hope the sentence is harsh. He took away a beautiful life."
Miss Johnson's parents, Dr. and Mrs. Fred Johnson of Little Valley, who had attended every day of the 11-day trial, showed no emotion. They left the courtroom immediately after the verdict was read and would not comment.
Miss Evans found the nude body of Miss Johnson during the early morning hours of July 25 in the bedroom of a house they shared at 1002 Central Ave.
Miss Johnson was named "Teacher of the Year" last spring by the Riverdale Parent-Teacher Association. Superintendent of Schools Kenneth Bowling attended the trial each day.

Coverage of criminal proceedings generally does not end with the verdict. Often there will be requests for new trials, appeals and, of course, the sentencing.

Request for New Trial

Smith's attorney, Cosgrove, sought a new trial. The story:

> Convicted killer Sam E. Smith's request for a new trial was denied Monday by a Superior Court judge.
>
> Nuckolls County Superior Court Judge George Flynn said Smith must face sentencing Feb. 8 for the July 24 stabbing death of 33-year-old Riverdale teacher Nancy Johnson.
>
> Smith, 39, was found guilty last week of first-degree murder.
>
> Smith's attorney, Kevin Cosgrove, argued that the televising of portions of Smith's trial deprived him of "the judicial serenity to which he was entitled." Cosgrove had argued the jury should have been sequestered.

The Sentencing

Naturally, follow-up stories could be written on such topics as experimentation with cameras in courtrooms in other states; comments from judges, lawyers, jurors and witnesses concerning the effects of the cameras in the Smith trial, and the possibility of an appeal.

Indeed, coverage of the Smith trial and its ramifications could continue for some time. Certainly, the sentencing would merit a story:

> A tearful Sam E. Smith, described by friends as an honest, decent, gentle man, was sentenced to die in the electric chair for the stabbing death of 33-year-old Riverdale teacher Nancy Johnson.
>
> Superior Court Judge George Flynn issued the sentence Tuesday.
>
> Smith's attorney, Kevin Cosgrove, said his client would appeal.

Coverage of the Smith case illustrates that there are several newsworthy points as a case makes its way through the judicial system.

SUGGESTIONS FOR COURT REPORTERS

Reporters who cover criminal trials should:

- *Provide sufficient background for the reader.* For example, when charges are filed in an armed robbery case, refer to the crime to put the judicial proceedings in perspective.
- *Double-check facts.* Names, ages, addresses and the specific charges always should be verified. The stakes are high. Reporters never want to make errors, but there is a monumental difference between saying that John Jones was the leading scorer for his basketball team (when he really was only the second-leading scorer) and saying that John Jones was charged with driving while intoxicated (when he really was charged with running a stop sign).

- *Use complete names and addresses or occupations.* To avoid confusion—and head off potential lawsuits—list full names and middle initials, ages and addresses or occupations of persons charged with crimes.

- *Attribute all statements.* Never use hearsay in a court story. Carefully explain to the reader the source of the information.

- *Report all relevant facts.* Search for all relevant news angles. For example, when a man is on trial for armed robbery, write background information on the minimum and maximum penalties as established by law, the number of armed robbery trials in the same court during the past year and the circumstances of the arrest.

- *Write simply.* Strive to translate "legalese" into lay terms whenever possible. Reporters need to have an understanding of the law, but they should not forget to communicate as informed laymen—not as lawyers.

- *Take careful notes.* Be extremely careful to take accurate notes during proceedings. When tape recorders are allowed, they provide a good backup. If notes are not clear, or if the tape recorder malfunctions, check with the official court reporter who records verbatim the transcript of the proceedings.

- *Be alert for testimony that contradicts previous testimony or evidence.* Develop your own system for emphasizing such occurrences in your notes. As you listen to a full day of testimony, place asterisks beside such occurrences to jar your memory when you begin to write.

- *Watch for reactions (including facial expressions) of trial participants.* You should not play the role of amateur psychiatrist, but it sometimes is worth reporting when witnesses break down on the stand, attorneys raise their voices and spectators orally react to testimony.

Obviously, reporters do not become adept at covering trials by examining a list of suggestions. Suggestions can be helpful, but reporters become proficient at covering trials only by doing it.

THE CHALLENGE OF COVERING THE COURTS

Rawitch of the Los Angeles Times estimated that it takes a reporter six months to a year to become attuned to covering courts in a metropolitan setting.

"The role of the court reporter is to break through the legal jargon—to translate the special role of the court to the every day role of the reader,"

Rawitch said. "But just like the specialist on any beat, the court reporter must be careful—once he or she begins to feel comfortable with the system—not to lose sight of what is important to the reader."

Covering the courts involves more than reporting on procedural filings in civil suits and on spectacular criminal trials. Many good court-related stories are the result of a reporter's persistently searching for information that can lead to in-depth stories on the workings of the judicial system or on the interaction among those involved in the system.

Reporters who cover the courts must spend considerable time making small talk in various clerks' offices to pick up gossip and insight into upcoming matters. On days when there are no significant proceedings to cover, Rawitch suggests that reporters spend time "cultivating sources, developing feature stories, reading legal briefs, catching up on filing or tracking cases and just plain 'snooping around' in the hope of finding something no one else thought to tell you about."

S U G G E S T E D   E X E R C I S E S

1. Invite a local attorney to your class to explain the court system in your state.

2. Become familiar with the record-keeping system at your local courthouse. Ask a clerk to help you locate the verdict in a recently completed civil suit. Trace progress in the suit by examining the docket and relevant filings. Write a story on the outcome of the suit and incorporate appropriate background information.

3. Assume you are a reporter for a newspaper in your town. Using the following information and information later presented in exercises 4, 5, 6, and 7, write news stories at various junctures in a criminal case. First, use these facts to write an arrest story:

> An 11-year-old girl, who had been missing for two days, was found dead in a field four miles south of town. Her body was found by two teen-agers who were jogging on a country road. The name of the girl was Sally Jones. She was the daughter of Mr. and Mrs. Bill Jones.
> Four days after the body was found, the county coroner released a report saying the girl had been sexually assaulted and strangled.
> Exactly one week after the body was found, a 23-year-old man was arrested by police.
> According to police, the man was on probation in your state for a crime he had committed in New Mexico. The man was identified as William J. Henderson, 2000 Elm St. Henderson was arrested on a Saturday night in the county jail, where he had been held for three days for an alleged probation violation.
> At a press conference Saturday evening, Police Chief Donald South said the break in the case came when Henderson's New Mexico probation

officer notified authorities that the suspect was living in a rural area south of town.

South refused to say whether Henderson had a criminal history of sex offenses. Henderson was employed by a contractor.

He was being held for investigation of first-degree murder and sexual assault.

4. Write a story based on the following description of the Police Court arraignment:

Henderson was arraigned in Police Court on Monday. He pleaded innocent to charges of first-degree murder and sexual assault. The arraignment lasted 15 minutes. The presiding judge was Fred Walters. The case was assigned to Police Court Judge Dean Gardner for an Aug. 5 preliminary hearing. Henderson was ordered held without bond in county jail.

5. Write a story on the preliminary hearing:

A preliminary hearing was held in Police Court on Thursday. The presiding judge was Dean Gardner. Gardner found there was sufficient evidence for Henderson to be bound over for trial in Superior Court. Police Chief South said Henderson had been seen a quarter-mile from where the body of Miss Jones was found on the evening she disappeared.

6. Write a story about the Superior Court arraignment:

Henderson was arraigned in Superior Court on Wednesday before Superior Court Judge David Glenn. Henderson pleaded innocent to first-degree murder and sexual assault. He wore county jail garb. Trial was set for Nov. 10.

7. Write a story about the verdict:

Henderson was found guilty in Superior Court Thursday after a seven-day trial on charges of first-degree murder and sexual assault. The jury deliberated 35 minutes. Henderson showed no emotion as the verdict was read by Judge David Glenn. Jurors left the courtroom without comment. A court official said the six women jurors and two of the six men were crying as they left. Testimony by the county coroner, Jason Russell, revealed that Miss Jones died two to eight minutes after elastic pigtail holders had been wrapped around her neck and she had been gagged with her socks. The jury had spent most of the day listening to closing arguments by Prosecuting Attorney Terry Johnson and Paul Cummings, a public defender who represented Henderson. Cummings said he would appeal. Sentencing was scheduled for Dec. 1.

8. Attend a trial. Write a story. Be sure to incorporate background information.

The major responsibility of reporters covering breaking news is to write stories on the latest developments. But they must meet their deadlines, which means stopping their coverage while the stories go on. This chapter examines how reporters cover developing stories. It discusses how reporters decide whether and for how long coverage of a story should continue.

You will be introduced to:

• Coverage by reporters at The Daily News in Longview, Wash., of one of the decade's biggest developing news stories, the eruption of Mount Saint Helens. Andre Stepankowsky recalls some of the hundreds of stories he and other Daily News reporters wrote, which earned them a Pulitzer Prize for general reporting.

• How a community newspaper, the Herald-Argus of La Porte, Ind., reacted the day the town's mayor was wounded and his wife slain in an early morning attack.

• First-day, second-day and later coverage of a continuing story. The chapter uses examples of news stories to illustrate how stories are developed from day to day.

The body of Reid Blackburn was found in his car buried under ash from the eruption of Mount Saint Helens. Blackburn was a photographer for The Columbian, Vancouver, Wash.

Wide World Photos

151

8 THE DEVELOPING STORY

Whenever a major news event breaks—the taking of hostages, an assassination, the eruption of a volcano—coverage begins quickly. The major responsibility of all reporters covering such events is to write the latest story possible as the news develops. Reporters will stop developing the story only when every news angle has been exhausted or when their editors feel that it is time to go on to another breaking story. The story can be developed for days, weeks or longer.

Even in a local market on a routine day, reporters and editors must decide continually whether a story should or should not be developed beyond a single item. Some local news events—a train derailment, a head-on collision, the search for a new college president—may be worth several stories. Others—the opening of a new school, the closing of a business, a vacation Bible school—are worth only one.

Stories are developed from day to day when reporters and their editors feel that the news event or its aftermath has a continuing impact upon their audience. That does not mean that a story quits developing just because reporters quit covering it. It simply means that there is room each day for only so many stories, and judgments of their newsworthiness determine which ones are used and which ones are dropped. For example, if a truck carrying a load of peanuts into town skids off the highway, overturns and spills roasted peanuts all over the countryside, it certainly is worth a story. If the truck driver is not injured, the mess is cleaned up quickly and the truck leaves town two hours later, the news event deserves only a single story reporting the crash. But if the driver is hurt critically and then dies, or a reporter finds out that the peanuts were stolen or several residents of town are arrested for stealing some of the savory cargo, the story may continue to develop for days.

Other factors besides the perceived impact on an audience enter into deciding whether or not to continue developing a story. They include prejudices of reporters and editors, size of the market and what the competition is doing.

Whenever reporters cover a developing story, their primary consideration is their deadline. It simply must be met, which means that no story they write can be definitive. All they can do is to report the latest information available at the time they write their stories. There always will be more information to gather and another story to write the next day, in a week, in a month or next year.

MOUNT SAINT HELENS: A CASE STUDY

His name was Andy. But no one knew his name when his picture was taken; he was merely an "unidentified" boy lying dead in the back of a pickup, the symbol of a volcano's violence. Millions of newspaper and magazine readers throughout the world saw the dead child, his hands on his stomach, in a wrenching peace after one of the earth's most phenomenal displays, the eruption of Mount Saint Helens in Washington. It was May 18, 1980, and one of the decade's biggest stories was breaking.

In the rush to get early news of the volcano's eruption to the world, a photograher flying over the scene in a helicopter took a photograph of the child lying in the rear of a dented pickup. The photographer did not even see the boy's face. The Associated Press distributed the photo worldwide, hours before the boy's mother knew his fate.

There was not time to identify the boy. His name and the names of scores of other victims would have to wait for later stories.

The boy was 11. He raised chickens. He and his family lived in an area southeast of Seattle. He had a sister, Robin, who stayed home with her mother that weekend. He had a 9-year-old brother, Mike, who also had gone camping and was killed with Andy and their father, asphyxiated by volcanic ash that blanketed their campsite four and a half miles from the mountain.

The world's eyes focused on Washington that day. Andy's photo was one of many. Hundreds of reporters headed for the area to cover the spectacular news story. In their haste to meet deadlines, to write that breaking story before the end of a 24-hour news cycle, reporters would leave out names, omit facts, cut interviews.

In the case of a volcanic eruption, stories will continue as long as there are reporters on the scene. It will be Page One material for days; then the stories will move inside and continue for days more; then follow-ups will be written and rewritten for months afterward. The first day is the most important because that is when the story will be broken. Next will come the second-day story and scores of sidebars and follows. Victims will be identified; families will be interviewed; officials will release new information; mothers will find out what happened to sons, the world will learn Andy's name.

Breaking Stories

The Associated Press used a typical, inverted pyramid, terse lead for the volcano's breaking story:

> VANCOUVER, Wash. (AP)—Mount Saint Helens erupted in its most violent display in 123 years Sunday, shooting smoke and ash 9 miles into the sky with a blast felt for 200 miles.
> Five persons were killed fleeing down the mountainside.

In this first story the "what" was the most important element. Readers were being told a volcano erupted in Washington. As the day wore on, the first lead would be updated, and readers would be given more information.

VANCOUVER, Wash. (AP)—Mount Saint Helens blew its top Sunday with a blast felt 200 miles away, belching ash and hot gas that blotted out the sun for more than 450 miles. The eruption killed at least eight persons.

Now the number of deaths, which was rising, was moved into the lead. Readers also were being told that ash was spreading over the United States.

Mount Saint Helens was an excellent example of a developing story. It remained on Page 1 for days as more of the story unfolded. Leads were rewritten continually, but background information on the event was included in each story. Reporters try to give readers the latest and most important news in each lead of a developing story, but because some readers may not have seen the earlier stories, some previous information must be repeated.

Each day, the oldest information is put nearer and nearer the end of the story. For instance, later stories on Mount Saint Helens always gave readers new information in the first few paragraphs. Then, high in the story, "old" news, such as the number of deaths, the exact location of the volcano, weather conditions and the amount of ash covering streets in the Northwest, was repeated. Next, transition was used to return to new elements in the story.

When President Jimmy Carter visited Washington several days after the eruption, Michael Coakley of the Chicago Tribune said in his lead:

President Carter on Thursday viewed the damage left in the wake of Mount Saint Helens' eruption, describing Sunday's volcanic explosion as "one of the most devastating, but also one of the most interesting, events in recorded history."

The second paragraph also gave readers new information:

Touring the scene by helicopter, the president flew within two miles of the volcano itself before being forced to turn back by a snowstorm.

The third paragraph gave more new information, but it also began to tie in the old news with the new:

What Carter saw was 150 square miles of southern Washington state lost in a blanket of gray mud and ash. A wider area on the periphery suffered severe damage from flash floods and mudslides, causing homes, barns and even entire logging camps to all but disappear from aerial view.

In his fourth paragraph Coakley repeated more old news, which still was vital to the story:

The eruption left at least 14 dead and about 75 missing and caused billions of dollars in damage.

In the fifth paragraph a direct quote from Carter was used to bring the readers back to the latest news:

> "There was nothing remaining except bare piles of mud and what used to be mountains," said the president, shaking his head in disbelief.

The rest of the story then dealt with the president's visit, although some additional old information was given near the end.

Follow-Up Stories

News stories break on either the a.m. or the p.m. news cycle. In other words, morning papers or broadcast news shows will report the breaking news before the evening papers and shows, or vice versa. Then it will be up to reporters in the next news cycle to write a *second-day story,* a follow-up that updates the earlier stories and gives an audience something fresh. Second-day stories allow an audience to pick up a story where it was left off by an earlier news cycle. They may supply information that was not available or known when the first stories were written or they may analyze or humanize earlier stories.

Here are several examples of follow-up leads on the eruption of Mount Saint Helens. In each case the lead gave readers information that was not known in an earlier news cycle. Some are AP leads; others are combined wire service leads.

Day two:

> Airborne ash from Mount Saint Helens crossed the Mississippi River Tuesday after causing more traffic problems in the Pacific Northwest than any blizzard ever has.

Day three:

> VANCOUVER, Wash. (AP)—President Carter declared the state of Washington a major disaster area Wednesday and then flew to the Pacific Northwest to personally inspect the awesome destruction wrought by Mount Saint Helens' volcanic eruption.

Day five:

> VANCOUVER, Wash. (AP)—With 17 bodies recovered and 71 persons missing near Mount Saint Helens, search and rescue helicopters targeted 15 areas in the devastated region in which they said more dead could be found Friday.

A week after the original story:

> TOLEDO, Wash. (AP)—Two large ash eruptions from Mount Saint Helens, the second reaching 20,000 feet above sea level, spread ash over

communities far south of the mountain Saturday, a Geological Survey scientist said.

Twelve days after the original story:

VANCOUVER, Wash. (AP)—Chances of finding alive any of the 58 persons still missing after the explosion of Mount Saint Helens are "nil," an official said Thursday as an air search was suspended.

Follow-up stories may be written weeks or months after the initial story breaks if there is additional news to report or the story needs to be completed. Years later, a follow-up may tell readers what happened to the forest that was erased by the eruption of Mount Saint Helens or how two people returned, for the first time, to the site where their son was killed. Of course, in the case of a major story such as a volcano eruption, there are scores of follow-ups that can be written by an enterprising reporter in the future. These may include:

- People died in the eruption. People still are missing. Who are they? Where are their families?

- What is the effect of the blanket of volcanic ash in the Northwest? (The ash can be swept or washed away, but it does not simply disappear.) Has the ash changed the weather? Did it affect peoples' health? What has it done to livestock? How about tourism, forestry and the waterways? Are there any beneficial uses for the ash? (Yes, it can be used in the manufacture of concrete.)

- What are the chances of another eruption? How much more damage could be caused? Will other volcanoes erupt in the United States? How many active volcanoes are there? Can eruptions be predicted?

- Enough timber to build 150,000 homes was uprooted. Can the forests be rebuilt? Is there a use for all of the uprooted trees? How many homeowners were affected? Interview some of them to find out what it was like to rebuild their homes. What did the uprooted trees do to the wildlife?

- What is the history of volcanoes? How are they formed? Is the upheaval surprisingly simple? In what parts of the world do most volcanoes erupt?

Coverage by The Daily News

One of the hundreds of newspersons who witnessed much of the devastation from Mount Saint Helens was Andre Stepankowsky, a 26-year-old reporter for The Daily News in Longview, Wash., one of the towns closest to the mountain.

The volcano's big eruption in May 1980 came on a Sunday, a day off for Stepankowsky and the other 33 members of the editorial staff of The Daily News, a 27,000-circulation evening paper that publishes Monday through Saturday. On that Sunday Stepankowsky and Jay McIntosh, another reporter at the paper, had planned to go hiking.

They never made it. The story unfolding in their back yard was about to change their lives. Within a year, after months of hard work and thousands of hours of reporting and writing, the editorial staff in Longview would share a Pulitzer Prize for general reporting.

Stepankowsky started covering the mountain full time in the spring of 1980. For more than a year, he devoted all his time to the developing story. Occasionally, he would write four stories a day. He has written hundreds of stories on Mount Saint Helens.

On the way to their hiking trip, Stepankowsky and McIntosh had stopped at a restaurant in Longview for breakfast. "It was a nice day but hazy," Stepankowsky said. "We noticed the sky around the mountain was getting dark. Then the black cloud over it started to get bigger and bigger. We wolfed down our breakfast and went to the newspaper."

The newsroom was empty. McIntosh started calling the editors while Stepankowsky called the U.S. Geological Survey. He was told that there had been a major eruption. "The editors told us to toss a coin to see who would go up in a plane with a photographer, and I won the toss," Stepankowsky said. "At 9:20 a.m. I went up in a plane with photographer Roger Werth. It was amazing. We saw the first mud flow go down the south fork of the Toutle River. By noon, we were out of fuel, so we had to return. I went back to the office and started making phone calls. I worked until 2 a.m."

Daily News Managing Editor Robert B. Gaston said: "Everyone who was in town reported for work that Sunday. At midnight the newsroom parking lot was full. One editor slept at the office. A photographer worked 38 straight hours. Most reporters worked at least 80 hours that first week. In two weeks, more than 400 volcano stories were written."

For weeks after the blast, The Daily News gave its readers thorough coverage. More than 5,000 extra copies of the May 19 edition sold out within 24 hours. The paper was the first and last to interview Harry Truman, a stubborn old resort owner who lived at the base of the mountain and chose to die there. Readers were given tips on how to save their automobile engines, lungs, eyes and possessions from the volcanic ash that blanketed the town. A mental therapist gave advice to those who had lost homes, relatives and friends.

On one assignment Stepankowsky went to a subdivision 10 miles north of Longview to check residents. "I saw a whole bunch of people who were moving out," he said. "They were three houses away in this mud. I hitched a ride on a tractor, walked across two roofs, climbed down a ladder, up a ladder and into this house to interview the owners of a home."

Unlike reporters from the big newspapers, the wire services and the networks, who came to town for the breaking story and then left, Stepankowsky and the other reporters for The Daily News lived in Longview and had a sense of the community's feelings. "We have to deal with the people here from day to day," he said. "We didn't want to scare them unless we had to. We didn't want to sensationalize the story. For instance, the threat of flooding scared the hell out of me. We wrote about it and it scared people. We had to."

Thirteen months after the major eruption, the paper still was carrying a daily story on the volcanic activity of the mountain. It still was running photographs of what once was the mountain's top. Stories included accounts of area merchants sprucing up their stores for the expected onslaught of summer tourists, the battles between lumber firms that wanted to replant and environmentalists who wanted to leave much of the area untouched forever to show nature's wrath, the continued threat of flooding from new lakes formed by mud slides and an anticipated shortage in state funding for stricken areas. One story reported on the showing in Longview of the movie "St. Helens!"

"There is no shortage of stories now," Stepankowsky said. "Eventually, it will die down, but most geologists say this volcano will act up for 20 or 30 years. It always will have an impact on this community."

Indeed, Mount Saint Helens' story never will stop developing. For one thing it is an active volcano, and no one knows when it might blow its top again. Second, reporters should not let it stop. It is too good a story, and a reporter easily could go there years later and find a follow-up to write.

IT HAPPENED IN LA PORTE

La Porte is a quiet, old town of 22,500 built around several lakes in northwest Indiana. Its only newspaper is the evening Herald-Argus, which has a circulation of 13,500. The 13 full-time and four part-time members of the Herald-Argus staff focus their coverage on La Porte County, a large area that is industrial in the north and agricultural in the center and south. On a typical day the Herald-Argus is filled with the same types of stories printed in most community newspapers:

- National and international stories from a wire service. (The Herald-Argus subscribes to United Press International.)
- Syndicated columns.
- School, church, club and other local news.
- Community sports.
- Area weather.

A shooting is big news in La Porte, so imagine the impact on the town and the Herald-Argus when on Memorial Day 1982 Mayor A. J. Rumely was shot and wounded critically and his wife slain. How the Herald-Argus covered the story in the three days after the shootings illustrates how a hometown newspaper would cover a developing story.

Rumely, 71, and his wife, Frances, 69, were shot about 1:30 a.m. in their home in La Porte. "Our work began about 4 a.m. that Memorial Day when Dave Jensen, one of the four full-time cityside reporters, got a call about the shooting," Herald-Argus Managing Editor Ted Hartzell said. "Dave and I talked about whom we could contact to begin working immediately on the story. Our own people were enjoying the holiday, too."

One of the first things Jensen did was to call La Porte Police Chief Larry Miller, who Hartzell said refused to confirm or deny the report. "In the next 24 hours, Miller, who had given our reporters a tough time the last few years on even routine news, maintained his virtual silence with us and all other reporters," the managing editor said.

Hartzell went to the city police station himself but said he met with the same resistance his reporter had. "Then I walked a few blocks to the La Porte County police office and learned through a dispatcher that the county police also were tied up in investigating the wounding of the mayor and the killing of his wife," Hartzell said. "Though far from official, the offhand remark from the county police dispatcher about the investigation was confirmation enough for me that the story was true, so I began pulling people off their vacations and back to La Porte."

The Herald-Argus does not publish on Memorial Day Monday, so the staff had a full day to gather information and write stories. The main story on Page 1 would have to carry a second-day lead because the shooting itself would be reported by other media a day before the Herald-Argus would be out.

"We roughed out a plan of attack for various stories we knew had to be covered, matching reporters' beats and strengths with story angles," Hartzell said. "For instance, Associate Editor Don Benn, a longtime Herald-Argus editor, historian and writer, was a natural to write the sidebar on what other disasters La Porte mayors have faced in the past. Don's story, while not strictly necessary, was one of those touches that gave greater richness to our coverage. It was a local story that could not have been bought from a wire service or syndicate."

At a noon press conference Memorial Day, the police chief acknowledged only that the mayor was wounded and his wife slain. He refused to answer any questions from reporters, some of whom had come from Chicago, Indianapolis and the wire services.

By now, the staff members of the Herald-Argus were in high gear. Hartzell said: "Pulling in people immediately to begin the story, instead of waiting even a few more hours until a more reasonable hour of a holiday morning, proved valuable because we were able to interview several of the Rumelys' seven children within hours of the shooting. Some family members and friends of the family talked candidly with our people before the police had a chance to discourge such talk."

Day One

The Tuesday paper of 24 pages contained 14 stories on the shooting. The lead story, under the headline "Mayor wounded, wife killed," began:

> A homemade silencer for a pistol was found in the hand of slain Frances Rumely, officals close to the investigation of her Memorial Day slaying said today.
>
> They speculated the killing came during an assassination attempt on the life of her husband, Mayor A. J. Rumely Jr., who remained in critical condition today with three wounds.
>
> La Porte City Police Chief Larry Miller would not confirm what, if anything, was found in Mrs. Rumely's hand. He also refused to say if police had a suspect.
>
> Mrs. Rumely, 69, was shot twice, once in the chest and once in the hip. Mayor Rumely, 71, was shot in the abdomen, left forearm and left thigh.
>
> Mayor Rumely today was in the intensive care unit of La Porte Hospital after more than four hours of surgery Monday. He and his wife were shot early Monday morning. Funeral services for his wife will be Thursday.
>
> "There are two theories, either it was a broken burglary attempt or an attempt on the mayor's life," one ranking police officer involved in the investigation said today. "And we recovered an item that I never had seen connected to a burglary."
>
> That item, the Herald-Argus had learned, is most likely a homemade silencer found in the hand of Frances Rumely when police and Emergency Medical Service workers arrived. Officials said the silencer was believed to be on the murder weapon, which has only been described as at least a .38-caliber weapon.

This story is structured as most developing stories are after the event is a day old:

- A summary, second-day lead provides the latest news (the discovery of a silencer, an assassination attempt is suspected, Mayor Rumely's condition is critical).

- It is written in inverted pyramid form. First-day information that is still vital to the story is placed high up, but not in the lead paragraph (the Rumelys' ages, where and when they were shot, the type of weapon believed to be used).

Other stories in the Tuesday paper included a backgrounder on the Rumely family, an item on who would be running the city, an interview with the doctor who operated on the mayor and oversaw the autopsy on

Mrs. Rumely and a rundown of the other murders in La Porte since 1975. There also were editorials on Mrs. Rumely and on the news blackout imposed by the police chief.

Day Two

"On Tuesday, soon after the paper was published, the whole editorial staff sat down and brainstormed about where to take the story," Hartzell said. "We didn't know if there was a suspect. Like the rest of the town, we wanted to find out why anyone would want to shoot the mayor and his wife. We tossed about a number of mild controversies that the mayor had been involved in, seeking any clues as to whom might have been so aggrieved to try to assassinate him."

By that evening police had arrested a suspect, which provided the direction for Wednesday's Herald-Argus. The top story was headlined "Fired worker accused." It began:

> Herald Lang, 30, of La Porte, a former city employee who was fired from his job at the sewage treatment plant in April after an argument with his boss, has been charged with murdering Frances Rumely and attempting to murder Mayor A. J. Rumely early Monday.

Once again, the top story was written in a traditional inverted pyramid form, giving readers the latest news first. The next seven paragraphs of the story contained information on the suspect and his background. The mayor's condition, which remained unchanged, and notice of Mrs. Rumely's funeral now were put in the ninth paragraph. Other information still vital to the story—the homemade silencer, the caliber of the gun, how many times the Rumelys were shot—was pushed down even farther.

All of Page 1 dealt with the shootings. There was a photograph of the suspect being led to court, a story on what he said during his first court appearance and a picture of and story on the suspect's mother. She told the Herald-Argus that her son was angry with the mayor for approving Lang's termination. To get the interview, Les Lindeman, a Herald-Argus reporter, and a reporter from the nearby Michigan City (Ind.) News-Dispatch went to the suspect's house while other reporters went to city hall for official word on the arrest.

"We used our home advantage to reach Lang's mother," Hartzell said. "The story about her, written on deadline, added a rich dimension to our follow-up coverage."

Day Three

On the third of coverage, the Herald-Argus reported Mrs. Rumely's funeral. The lead story on Page 1 began:

State officials, legislators and delegates from cities throughout northern Indiana joined more than 1,000 people at the funeral today of Frances Murphy Rumely, who was fatally shot Memorial Day morning.

The LaPorte incident was an excellent example of a developing story because there were new breaks for three days:

- Day One—The shootings and speculation of a motive.
- Day Two—The arrest.
- Day Three—The funeral.

Of course, the story was not forgotten on the fourth day, but by then the Herald-Argus reporters were able to go back to their beats and report on the Rumely story as new developments occurred. Six months later they would report that Rumely died in a South Bend, Ind., hospital. The next month they would report that Lang was sentenced to 110 years in prison for murdering the Rumelys as they slept in their homes.

"The story proved to me that there is no better vantage point than the hometown paper in covering this type of story," Hartzell said. "Whatever fears we had that we would be scooped on our own turf by big-city journalists was unfounded. They relied on us. Outside reporters habitated our newsroom for a couple of days. It was the natural place to go."

HELPFUL GUIDELINES

Here is a set of guidelines to follow when working on a developing story:

- *If you are assigned a follow-up in a developing story and you did not write any of the earlier stories, check in a campus or public library or newspaper morgue for clippings.* The earlier stories are important because they provide facts and names of people you might want to interview. Also talk to the original reporter, who might have some ideas that can help you. If you did write an earlier story, review your notes.

- *Use the latest news in the lead.* You will want to use information from the original story to provide your readers with background, but that should be used later in the story. The first few paragraphs of the story should be fresh news.

- *Double check the facts in earlier stories, especially if you did not write them.* Just because something is in print does not mean that it is correct. You do not want to repeat an error. When in doubt check it out.

- *Do not continue to develop a story from day to day unless doing so is worthwhile.* Some events are worth only one story.

- *Make sure you meet your deadline.* If there is more information to dig up, save it for a later story.

- *Cooperate with other reporters who ask you to provide them with information.* Remember, you may need their help sometime. Just don't give away your lead.

S U G G E S T E D   E X E R C I S E S

1. Write a three-paragraph news story from the following set of facts:

> A police officer has been shot.
> He was found dead outside of a bank downtown.
> It happened Tuesday right near deadline, so you don't know the name yet.
> It happened at the First National Bank at 164 W. Third St.
> He was shot with a .45-caliber pistol, the same type of gun worn by local police officers.
> Police tell you they believe the man was working as a part-time security guard at the bank during his off hours.
> His body was found at 9:20 p.m.
> Police won't give you the name because the dead officer's family has not been notified.

The next day you gather additional information on the dead police officer. Now write a second-day story using everything you know so far:

> The officer's name is Dennis Albertson.
> He was 44 years old.
> He was married to Susan Albertson.
> They have two children. Joey is 3 and Mary is 5.
> Albertson was working as a part-time security guard at the bank during his off hours.
> An autopsy has been ordered.
> Police say Albertson was killed with his own service revolver.
> He'd been on the police force for seven years.
> Albertson was 6 feet tall. He weighed 190 pounds.
> Two years ago Albertson was awarded a police department medal for rescuing three infant children from a fire in an apartment building.
> You talk to Police Chief Jerome Fissel. He says, "This is such a sad thing. Dennis had so much to live for. No one considered him depressed. He was always so happy and concerned about the well-being of other people. He had such a lovely family. It's just too bad."

On the third day you gather more information on the shooting of Dennis Albertson. Use everything you have now to write another story:

Funeral arrangements for Albertson are being handled by Weiss Funeral Home, 2235 W. Appleton Road.

Visitation is from 7 to 9 p.m. Sunday. Funeral is Monday morning at 9 in Evergreen Cemetery.

Albertson's home address is 1414 N. Wolf Road.

You talk to County Coroner Robert L. Henderson, who says Albertson died of a self-inflicted gunshot wound. "I feel there is enough evidence to say on the death certificate that Mr. Albertson died by suicide," Henderson tells you.

You also find out that Albertson was scheduled to appear before a county grand jury probing a sports betting ring operated by as many as four local police officers. Albertson was suspected of being one of the officers involved, County Attorney Charles Pagel tells you. "We sure wanted to talk to him," Pagel says. "We are close to cracking this case. There will be at least 15 arrests." Pagel says officials believe that the police officers were running a betting ring while they were on duty.

2. What are the top stories developing in your city at the current time? What about at your school? Research one of the stories and write a follow-up.

3. Pick a major news story that broke today. List possible local, second-day stories that could develop from it. Research and write the story.

4. Pick a developing story and analyze how it is covered by a newspaper for a week. What is the new information each day? How much farther down is older information put in each story? Is the story covered by the same reporter each day? When do you think the story should be dropped?

Reporters can strengthen every story they write by consulting all available sources of information. Often, however, they do not know where to look for information. This chapter discusses sources of information and explains how these can be located and used.

You will be introduced to:

• The Freedom of Information Act, which can be an effective tool for gaining access to federal-level information. The chapter discusses the provisions of the act, how and when to use it and the types of material that are exempt from it.

• State-level open records and open meetings laws. Laws that can help reporters gain access to state-level information and provisions in state access laws that can prove frustrating to reporters are described. The successful quest for information by a medium-circulation daily, the Mesa (Ariz.) Tribune, is examined.

• Common newsroom sources such as directories, dictionaries, encyclopedias and thesauri. The chapter discusses library sources, such as indexes and statistical guides, and sources of information on legal topics, such as code books and court digests.

Mesa (Ariz.) Tribune Executive Editor Max Jennings, right, and Tribune reporter Mike Padgett sort out some of the information gathered in the investigation of the Arizona State University athletic department.

Peter Ensenberger

167

9 GATHERING INFORMATION

Information underlies good reporting. But information must be gathered. It can be collected through interviews or observation. It can be harvested from public documents, private diaries, memos, letters, books, library statistical guides, magazines, newspapers, waste baskets or microfilm. Information can inundate reporters. Sometimes, however, no matter how hard they try, reporters are frustrated in their quest for essential facts.

ACCESS TO FEDERAL INFORMATION

As might be expected—considering the theoretical adversary relationship between press and government—the media would like to have access to and use certain information that the government would prefer not to release. In the early 1960s members of Congress started working on legislation that would make available, for public inspection, the records of federal departments and agencies. As a result Congress passed the Freedom of Information (FOI) Act in 1966. This act unlocked doors to information that previously had been unavailable, although there were several exceptions to disclosure.

By the early 1970s members of Congress discovered the need to put teeth into the act. In 1971 a published story said that President Richard Nixon had received conflicting recommendations on the advisability of an underground nuclear test scheduled for that fall. A congresswoman sent a telegram to the president requesting immediate release of the recommendations. The request was denied.

Thirty-three members of Congress brought suit under the Freedom of Information Act. The administration said that nine of the 10 affidavits sought had been stamped "secret" by executive order. The U.S. Supreme Court upheld the right of the administration to withhold the information on that basis. Justice Byron White stated that Exemption 1 of the act blocked requests for *all* information classified "secret" by executive order. White added that the exemption was "intended to dispel uncertainty with respect to public access to material affecting national defense or foreign policy."

Justice William Brennan Jr. dissented in part. He said that White's majority interpretation of Exemption 1 as a "complete bar to judicial inspection of matters claimed by the executive to fall within it wholly frustrates the objective of the . . . act." Justice William O. Douglas also dissented. He contended that the executive branch should not have "*carte blanche* to insulate information from public scrutiny."

Congressional reaction to the majority decision was negative. Legislation was introduced to amend the act to permit, among other things, "in-camera" inspection of documents. A judge then would be able to examine materials in a private room or with all spectators excluded from the courtroom to determine whether documents stamped "secret" had in fact been classified properly. The implementation of faster and more efficient appeals procedures also was sought. Executive branch agencies lobbied against the proposals. The House, however, voted 383-8 to amend the act and later overrode President Gerald Ford's veto. The Senate then passed the bill, 65-27. The legislation took effect on Feb. 19, 1975.

The amendments were a tremendous help to the public—including journalists—who had felt unduly frustrated by the cavalier, wholesale designation of documents as "secret" by the executive branch. Essentially, the revised act gives "any person" access to the records of all federal agencies unless the information sought is a clearly defined exception.

How to Use the FOI Act

If the information sought is not an exception, journalists are advised to make informal requests to the agency. This can be done by telephone. If an informal request fails to bring results, a formal, written request for the records can be made. As emphasized in a booklet published in 1980 titled "How To Use the Federal FOI Act," "Once an FOI Act request is made, the burden is on the government to promptly release the documents or show that they are covered by one of the act's exemptions."

The agency must respond within 10 working days. If the agency refuses to supply the information or does not respond within the 10 days, the reporter can appeal to the head of the agency. If an answer is not given within 20 working days by the agency head, or if the head denies the request, the reporter can file a lawsuit in federal court. If the reporter wins the lawsuit, the agency will be ordered to release the documents and to pay attorney fees and court costs. The court also can order sanctions against the government officials responsible for improperly withholding the information. Names of responsible officials are readily available because the law specifies that any denial notification shall include "the names and titles or positions of each person responsible for the denial."

The 1974 amended FOI Act does not apply to matters that are:

(1) (A) specifically authorized under criteria established by Executive order to be kept secret in the interest of national defense or foreign policy and (B) are in fact properly classified pursuant to such executive order;

(2) related solely to the internal personnel rules and practices of an agency;

(3) specifically exempted from disclosure by statute . . . , provided that such statute (A) requires that the matters be withheld from the public in such a manner as to leave no discretion on the issue, or (B) establishes particular criteria for withholding or refers to particular types of matters to be withheld;

(4) trade secrets and commercial or financial information obtained from a person and privileged or confidential;

(5) inter-agency or intra-agency memorandums or letters that would not be available by law to a party other than an agency in litigation with the agency;

(6) personnel and medical files and similar files the disclosure of which would constitute a clearly unwarranted invasion of personal privacy;

(7) investigatory records compiled for law enforcement purposes, but only to the extent that the production of such records would (A) interfere with the enforcement proceedings, (B) deprive a person of a right to a fair trial or an impartial adjudication, (C) constitute an unwarranted invasion of personal privacy, (D) disclose the identity of a confidential source and, in the case of a record compiled by a criminal law enforcement authority in the course of a criminal investigation, or by an agency conducting a lawful national security intelligence investigation, confidential information furnished only by the confidential source, (E) disclose investigative techniques and procedures, or (F) endanger the life or physical safety of law enforcement personnel;

(8) contained in or related to examination, operating, or condition reports prepared by, on behalf of, or for the use of an agency responsible for the regulation or supervision of financial institutions; or

(9) geological and geophysical information and data, including maps, concerning wells.

"How to Use the Federal FOI Act" is advertised as a "concise and complete do-it-yourself guide for print and broadcast media, authors, scholars, students, researchers, writers and teachers." The booklet, a joint project of the Reporters Committee for Freedom of the Press and the Society of Professional Journalists, Sigma Delta Chi, includes an overview of the act, the agencies covered by the act and the records that are available; a discussion of who can use the act; suggestions on informal and formal requests; guidelines on searching and copying fees; a description of ways to have fees cut or waived; suggestions on procedures for filing formal appeals; a discussion on how to file FOI Act lawsuits, and an analysis of the nine exemptions to the act. On page 171 is a sample FOI request letter that is included in the booklet—a booklet of value to all reporters.

Tele. No. (business hours)
Return Address
Date

Name of Public Body
Address

To the FOI Officer:

This request is made under the federal Freedom of Information Act, 5 U.S.C. 552.

Please send me copies of *(Here, clearly describe what you want. Include identifying material, such as names, places, and the period of time about which you are inquiring. If you wish, attach news clips, reports, and other documents describing the subject of your research.)*

As you know, the FOI Act provides that if portions of a document are exempt from release, the remainder must be segregated and disclosed. Therefore, I will expect you to send me all nonexempt portions of the records which I have requested, and ask that you justify any deletions by reference to specific exemptions of the FOI Act. I reserve the right to appeal your decision to withhold any materials.

I promise to pay reasonable search and duplication fees in connection with this request. However, if you estimate that the total fees will exceed $____, please notify me so that I may authorize expenditure of a greater amount.

(Optional) I am prepared to pay reasonable search and duplication fees in connection with this request. However, the FOI Act provides for waiver or reduction of fees if disclosure could be considered as "primarily benefiting the general public." I am a journalist *(researcher, or scholar)* employed by *(name of news organization, book publishers, etc.)*, and intend to use the information I am requesting as the basis for a planned article *(broadcast, or book)*. *(Add arguments here in support of fee waiver)*. Therefore, I ask that you waive all search and duplication fees. If you deny this request, however, and the fees will exceed $____, please notify me of the charges before you fill my request so that I may decide whether to pay the fees or appeal your denial of my request for a waiver.

As I am making this request in the capacity of a journalist *(author, or scholar)* and this information is of timely value, I will appreciate your communicating with me by telephone, rather than by mail, if you have any questions regarding this request. Thank you for your assistance, and I will look forward to receiving your reply within 10 business days, as required by law.

Very truly yours,

(Signature)

Journalists lobbied hard for passage of the Freedom of Information Act and for the amendments that strengthened it, but Washington reporter John A. Jenkins, writing in Quill magazine, termed the act a "journalistic stepchild." Most of the requests for information under the act come from private law firms and businesses.

Impact of the FOI Act

James Kilpatrick wrote in his syndicated column that, though journalists brought the FOI Act into being, it "is being badly abused." He said that only about 10 percent of the requests made under the act come from journalists or scholars. He claimed that "the overwhelming bulk of requests have nothing whatever to do with 'the public's right to know.'"

Kilpatrick cited Department of Justice figures showing that 93 percent of the requests come from lawyers "seeking an advantage in antitrust cases, or from felons seeking access to FBI files, or from underworld figures on fishing expeditions." The columnist wrote that 60 percent of the requests at the Drug Enforcement Administration "come from the criminal element."

Sen. Strom Thurmond of South Carolina said that the act "has an admirable purpose, to give citizens more access to government and its processes." An article in Presstime, however, quoted Thurmond as saying, "Congress went too far in exposing the government to freedom of information requests and lawsuits." The senator claimed that the "capabilities of our investigative and law enforcement agencies have been unreasonably burdened by this law."

Attempts to water down the act were made during the Reagan administration. Attorney General William French Smith suspended a four-year-old Justice Department policy that required agencies to show proof of "demonstrable harm" before the department would defend an agency sued for denying a request under the act. Increasing pressure also was placed on Congress by the business community and executive branch to exempt entire agencies from the reach of the act.

The media and other groups bristled at the thought of a diluted act. Jack Landau, director of the Reporters Committee for Freedom of the Press, told a Presstime reporter that the FOI Act was threatened primarily by the federal government, which is concerned about the burdens and costs of implementing the provisions of the act (Attorney General Smith placed the annual government cost of administering the act "above $45 million"); by the FBI and CIA, which seek exemption from the act, and by the National Association of Manufacturers, which would like to cut down on the flow of information about business that is released through requests under the act.

Though the act might be abused by some, it has been an effective tool for journalists seeking to secure government information. All reporters should familiarize themselves with the provisions of the act and the procedures for using it to greatest advantage.

ACCESS TO STATE INFORMATION

Legislatures have taken measures to provide access to state-level information. Nearly all states have some type of open records laws; it is the responsibility of reporters to know the law in their states. Naturally, most state statutes have certain exceptions just as the federal Freedom of Information Act does. It is impossible to tell how "strong" or "weak" an open records law is until it is tested in court.

Max Jennings, executive editor of the Mesa Tribune, an Arizona daily with a circulation of about 44,000 owned by Cox Enterprises, Inc., found out firsthand that merely having a state access law on the books is no guarantee that public employees will necessarily—quickly, quietly and without reservation—turn over all requests for information.

Jennings spearheaded a six-person team of reporters and editors that assembled more than 25 news stories, editorials and columns focusing on the Arizona State University athletic program. At the time the university was under investigation by the National Collegiate Athletic Association for alleged athletic rule violations. Most of the material was published during a one-week period.

The effort was substantial. Still, Jennings said he was frustrated because the "whole story" had not been told. "We felt, despite the volumes we had written, that there was a great deal of information we did not have. We had to gain access to the NCAA documents and the ASU response" before the story could be regarded as complete.

Jennings and his reporters made "several informal requests" to ASU officials for the NCAA documents. The university refused to turn over any materials. Jennings told the director of university relations that a suit would be filed if the records were not made available. The editor also sent a letter by certified mail to the ASU president. Jennings did not think the president would be intimidated by the letter. "In fact, I would have been surprised had he honored the formal request," Jennings said.

The editor was convinced that ASU, a public institution, had "hired expensive lawyers at taxpayers' expense and instructed them to stonewall" the request.

Formal requests, statesmanship and persuasion had failed. Litigation was the one remaining option. At this point newspaper executives must decide whether to tenaciously pursue the information or to sit back and rationalize that the story would not be worth the effort.

Not all newspapers—particularly small- and medium-circulation dailies with limited financial bases—choose to make the economic commitment necessary to pursue the cause in the courts. Public officials often realize this and gamble that their refusal to turn over what would appear to be public records never will be challenged.

Jennings, with the support of his publisher, Charles A. Wahlheim, decided to bring suit—a suit that would entail an enormous expenditure of time, money and energy. They thought the newspaper had a "50-50" chance of winning. "It was only after a great deal of thought that we decided to file suit if necessary," the editor explained. "We were not naive about the time and expense involved. It was a last resort."

Jennings perhaps was more familiar with his state's access law than most medium-circulation daily editors because of his academic background. (He had been a university professor.) "I emphasized the importance and purpose of the law in my reporting classes," he said. "That may have had something to do with my confidence in using it. I think a lot of editors of smaller newspapers don't spend a lot of time familiarizing themselves with open meetings or open records laws—and that is unfortunate."

Jennings said that most editors probably would *want* to file suit to gain access to suppressed information. "But the sad truth is," he said, "most conversations between editors and publishers concerning access to public information stop when the question of legal fees comes up. And even large organizations sometimes are reluctant to spend money fighting cases of this nature."

Bringing access cases almost is a matter of "idealism," Jennings said. "The tangible rewards for doing something like this (filing suit) are awfully small," he said. "The information sought, if you win in court, generally is turned over to all the media. But you can go home at night and say, 'Gee, what we did was really worthwhile, and it makes me proud to be in this business.' "

Once a decision is made to file suit, editors often work closely with attorneys who, of course, dictate strategy. Attorneys for Cox Arizona Publications, Inc., the corporation that publishes the Tribune, scoured the Arizona Revised Statutes for precedent cases to seek legal justification for requesting the information.

They found that Arizona had enacted an access to public records statute in 1901—11 years before statehood. The statute states:

> Public records and other matters in the office of any officer at all times during office hours shall be open to inspection by any person.

The law also imposes a duty upon all "officers" and "public bodies" to maintain "all records reasonably necessary or appropriate to maintain an accurate knowledge of their official activities which are supported by funds from the state or any political subdivision thereof." The law permits any person to request "to examine or be furnished copies, printouts or photographs of any public record during regular office hours," and it requires that the custodian of the records furnish copies upon request.

The language, at first reading, appears clear. Jennings thought it certainly provided a right of access to the NCAA documents. But the editor found that a governmental entity that does not want to release information can be a formidable—and sometimes frustrating—foe. ASU officials contended that the Arizona statute, as interpreted, simply did not apply to the NCAA investigation documents.

Crucial Questions

What are public records? What would "other matters" include? What might constitute "all records reasonably necessary or appropriate to maintain an accurate knowledge of . . . official activities . . ."? These were crucial questions in this case—just as they often are for journalists who seek information at the state level.

The state courts, in various decisions, had considered the scope of the Arizona law, and the state attorney general's office had issued opinions to help clarify it.

The Cox lawyers found a case decided in 1952 to be the primary precedent. An Arizona state court had ruled that a public record is "one made by a public officer in pursuance of a duty." The court also had ruled that any "written record of transactions of a public officer, which is a convenient and appropriate method of discharging his duties, and is kept by him as such, whether required by express provisions of law or not" also would be considered a public record.

"Other matters" were defined as records "which are not required by law to be filed as public records, but which relate to matters essential to the general welfare of taxpayers, such as matters of taxation, revenue and the proceedings for the carrying out of governmental projects at public expense." The court held that records classified as "other matters" were subject to inspection unless they were "confidential" or if it would be against the best interests of the state to disclose them.

"Public Records": A Confusing Designation

Determining whether materials are public records or can be classified as "other matters" often is confusing and difficult. Also some public records are exempt by statute from disclosure. In Arizona, for example, the following are exempt: records of all child welfare agencies, student records from public schools (which are open only to parents or guardians), automobile drivers' accident reports (which are for administrative use only), certain state health records and state income tax returns.

Case-by-case judicial determinations must be made for those documents that are not statutorily exempt but that appear to be sensitive or confidential. The courts must balance the interest of the person seeking the information against the best interests of the state. "In-camera" inspections by the trial court to determine whether or not disclosure is appropriate often will take place.

Citing the law, Jennings requested that the Arizona Board of Regents and the ASU president permit his newspaper to examine and photocopy documents relating to the NCAA investigation. The editor was specific. He sought materials containing the charges brought by the NCAA (which had been delivered to ASU earlier in the year); written responses and correspondence from ASU to the NCAA pertaining to the charges; and all "internal correspondence and memoranda from any ASU officer, board or department . . . pertaining to the NCAA's charges."

Two months later, counsel to the Board of Regents formally denied the request. The attorney said that he did not believe the NCAA documents constituted a "public record" within the meaning of the state statute and that he considered "the NCAA charges as confidential."

Less than one month later, Cox Arizona Publications, Inc., filed suit in Superior Court. The complaint alleged that in denying the request, ASU officials had "failed to perform their nondiscretionary duty to comply with the Arizona Access to Public Records Law." The complaint also accused the university and its representatives of acting in "bad faith and in an arbitrary and capricious manner."

The complaint emphasized that the records sought were of "vital interest to the citizens" of Arizona because the charges could bring NCAA penalties and forfeiture of "certain revenues." The complaint further said that "irreparable harm to the State of Arizona, its citizens and taxpayers has resulted and will continue to result" from ASU's refusal to turn over the documents.

ASU's attorneys responded that the issue was "not as simple" as Cox Arizona Publications suggested: The issue involved "a highly complicated and sensitive matter." The university argued that disclosure of the information "would be against the best interests of the state."

Ultimately a Superior Court judge held for Cox Arizona Publications, ruling that the information sought was not a "public record" but should be categorized as "other matters" in the files of public officials or institutions. He said that this type of material must be divulged on request unless the documents are confidential or it is against the best interests of the state to disclose them.

The judge said that the documents did not fall into the "confidential" category. In fact, he said several of the allegations in the documents already had been reported in area newspapers. Because some of the material was common knowledge, the judge said he failed to "understand a plea for confidentiality." He ordered that the documents be turned over to the media.

In its editions the morning after the documents were released, the Mesa Tribune published four comprehensive articles based on the new information: a summary of the NCAA charges and the ASU responses, a summary of the ASU plan to prevent future abuses, a summary of the letter sent to the NCAA by ASU President Schwada and a reaction to the court ruling by the Tribune's counsel.

The lead story began:

> Unethical conduct by Arizona State University coaches and representatives involving gambling funds, cash for athletes and even an offer of land to a blue chip recruit were among infractions detailed in NCAA findings released Wednesday.
>
> About 80 NCAA charges and two thick volumes of responses from ASU were released at 9 a.m. Wednesday to representatives of Cox Arizona Publications, Inc., publishers of the Mesa Tribune and Tempe Daily News.

Before the story continued with the specific allegations and responses, this background paragraph was inserted:

> The release of the documents, in the office of Maricopa County Superior Court Judge Stanley Goodfarb, followed a lengthy battle by Cox to have the documents released under the Arizona Access to Public Records Law.

The excerpts from Schwada's letter to the NCAA that gave "a rare public view of the university president's perception of the athletic controversy and its effects on ASU" also provided the basis for a strong story:

> Arizona State University President John Schwada complained in writing in mid-November that the "long-term negative impact" of the mushrooming athletic scandal could affect all campus programs.
>
> He said "lurid" coverage of events at the school already had damaged the institution's reputation.
>
> In a letter to National Collegiate Athletic Association officials contained in the documents released under court order Wednesday, Schwada warned William B. Hunt, assistant NCAA executive director, and Charles Alan Wright, infractions committee chairman, that the university's ability to recruit athletes already had been hurt by ASU's own remedial actions . . . and a "continuing stream of damaging publicity, rumors, charges and litigation."

The Tribune capped its day-after coverage of the release of the documents with a reaction story. It began:

> The Mesa Tribune's success in wresting details from Arizona State University in the probe of its athletic department was a coup for all Arizonans whose tax money pays for the school, the lawyer who won the case said Wednesday.
>
> "I hope public officials are aware of this decision and will be more reluctant to take the same position as Arizona State University officials," said attorney Phil Higdon of Brown & Bain in Phoenix.

A Costly Victory

Jennings and the media had won. But the victory was costly for Cox Arizona Publications, Inc. Attorney fees were more than $14,000 (they were recovered later), and Jennings had spent scores of hours in an effort to gain the information. The Mesa Tribune did not even get an exclusive story; all media were given access to the documents.

"I hope we sensitized public officials in Arizona as to what the requirements of the law are—and that is to the benefit of all the citizenry, not just the media," Jennings said.

Jennings was convinced that the refusal to return phone calls, the refusal to cooperate in bringing the case to a hearing and the ultimate appeal to the Arizona Supreme Court were "all part of a calculated strategy on the part of the university to deny us the record. I think it is a strategy that works most of the time for public agencies. Public officials are not using their money; they are getting paid for the time such delays consume. They have nothing to lose and everything to gain if disclosure of the documents would be embarrassing, so the tactic is to jam, stall, stonewall."

Jennings offered this advice to reporters who seek state-level documents:

- Be as aggressive as you know how to be.
- Be familiar with the access statute in your state (type a summary of it and carry it in your billfold).
- Don't be afraid to cite the law to public officials who want to withhold information. If this does not get results, go back to your editor and demand support from management.

"I do not want to hire a reporter who does not feel outraged at being denied a public record," Jennings said. "I want my reporters to feel a genuine sense of outrage; and, if they don't, I think they ought to practice another profession."

ACCESS TO STATE AND LOCAL MEETINGS

State open meetings laws, like open records laws, are not uniform. Some states have stronger and more specific statutes than others. It is imperative, therefore, that reporters become thoroughly acquainted with the requirements of the laws in their states.

Iowa is among the states that recently have made their open meetings laws more specific. The Iowa law, which took effect Jan. 1, 1979, stated, "Ambiguity in the constructions or application of this chapter should be resolved in favor of openness." The law, which is very comprehensive, merits examination.

The Iowa law begins with important definitions. For example, it defines *governmental body* as:

- A board, council, commission or other governing body expressly created by the statutes of this state or by executive order.

- A board, council, commmission or other governing body of a political subdivision or tax-supported district in this state.

- A multimembered body formally and directly created by one or more boards, councils, commissions, or other governing bodies subject [to the above].

- Those multimembered bodies to which the state board of regents or a president of a university has delegated the responsibility for the management and control of the intercollegiate athletic programs at the state universities.

The law defines a *meeting* as "a gathering in person or by electronic means, formal or informal, of a majority of the members of a governmental body where there is deliberation or action upon any matter within the scope of the governmental body's policy-making duties." Meetings, however, do not include situations in which members gather socially and do not discuss policy.

Iowa's law also provides that governmental bodies, with the exception of township trustees, "shall give notice of the time, date, and place of each meeting, and its tentative agenda." The law requires notice of at least 24 hours before the meeting except when it is "impossible or impractical." Acknowledging that it might be necessary to hold a meeting on short notice, the law nevertheless requires that the reason for it be clearly stated in the minutes.

Attention is given to closed sessions. The law provides for closed sessions "only by affirmative public vote of either two-thirds of the members of the body or all of the members present." The law spells out the only acceptable reasons for a closed session:

- To review or discuss records which are required or authorized by state or federal law to be kept confidential or to be kept confidential as a condition for that governmental body's possession or continued receipt of federal funds.

- To discuss application for letters patent.

- To discuss strategy with counsel in matters that are presently in litigation or where litigation is imminent where its disclosure would be likely to prejudice or disadvantage the position of the governmental body in that litigation.

- To discuss the contents of a licensing examination or whether to initiate licensee disciplinary investigations or proceedings if the governmental body is a licensing or examining board.

- To discuss whether to conduct a hearing or to conduct hearings to suspend or expel a student, unless an open session is requested by the student or a parent or guardian of the student if the student is a minor.

- To discuss the decision to be rendered in a contested case.

- To avoid disclosure of specific law enforcement matters, such as current or proposed investigations, inspection or auditing techniques or schedules, which if disclosed would enable law violaters to avoid detection.

- To avoid disclosure of specific law enforcement matters, such as allowable tolerances or criteria for the selection, prosecution or settlement of cases, which if disclosed would facilitate disregard of requirements imposed by law.

- To evaluate the professional competency of an individual whose appointment, hiring, performance or discharge is being considered when necessary to prevent needless and irreparable injury to that individual's reputation and that individual requests a closed session.

- To discuss the purchase of particular real estate only where premature disclosure could be reasonably expected to increase the price the government body would have to pay for that property. The minutes and the tape recording of a session closed under this paragraph shall be available for public examination when the transaction discussed is completed.

The law specifies that the reason for the closed session must be provided by reference to a particular exemption, announced publicly at the open session and entered in the minutes. The body cannot discuss any business during a closed session that "does not directly relate to the specific reason announced as justification" for closure. The law also requires that "detailed minutes" be taken at the closed meeting and that the session be tape-recorded.

Of primary importance is the stipulation that a body must take final action in an open session "unless some other provision of the code expressly permits such actions to be taken in closed session."

Suits to enforce the law are to be brought in the district court for the county in which the governmental body "has its principal place of business." The burden then is placed on the body "to demonstrate compliance with the requirements" of the law. If it is found that the body violated the requirements of the law, each member who participated in its violation can be fined not more than $500 but not less than $100.

The law specifies, however, that members of a body found to have violated the law shall not be assessed damages if they prove that they voted against the closed session, that they had good reason to believe that they were in compliance with the requirements of the law or that they "reasonably relied upon a decision of a court or a formal opinion of the attorney general or the attorney for the governmental body."

Iowa's law also provides for the removal from office of any official who twice has been assessed damages for violating the act.

Obviously, open meetings laws are subject to interpretation, and not all are as carefully drawn as the Iowa statute. Still, reporters should carry copies of their states' open meetings laws when they attend governmental sessions. If a meeting is about to be closed, the reporter should take these actions:

- Ask what section of the law is being invoked.
- If the justification appears flimsy, ask that an objection be recorded in the minutes.
- Request a delay until an editor or the newspaper's attorney can be called.

Reporters who are not totally familiar with the open meetings laws in their states might be taken advantage of. Do not allow that to happen: Know your state's law from beginning to end.

THE JACK ANDERSON METHOD

"Washington Merry-Go-Round" syndicated columnist Jack Anderson, who has been labeled "the most celebrated practitioner of the muckraking tradition" and the "outstanding muckraker of the times," occasionally makes use of the Freedom of Information Act.

"We use the FOI Act," Anderson said. "But we probably don't use it as much as some other reporters. A good deal of the information we use could not be obtained through the act. It would be exempt. We do use the act, however, for historical or background information. I believe in the Freedom of Information Act, even though I do not use it extensively."

Anderson ridicules government attempts to classify documents as "secret" or "top secret." He claims that federal bureaucrats classify volumes of information as "secret" that more appropriately should be classified "censored." Many of his exclusive columns come from classified information that he intercepts.

Anderson's reporting methods often are criticized, particularly by government officials. Critics claim that he rushes to print information before he gathers all of the relevant facts.

Anderson, however, stands by his methods. He prides himself on reading "a regular diet of classified material and private memos" that often form the basis for items in his daily column.

After nearly four decades of Washington reporting, his information pipelines run deep. He has no trouble gathering a great deal of secret information. His problem is deciding how much to print.

When Anderson started work in Washington in 1947, he immediately discovered that his colleagues were getting their news from the newsmakers—a source that seemed logical. "But I quickly discovered that the newsmakers were politicians, and politicians generally are not reliable sources," he said. "They have politics to play, elections to win and policies to oppose or defend."

According to Anderson, public officials often lure journalists into news-baited traps. "I read stories all the time based on 'leaks.' Well, for the most part, these are 'authorized leaks.' For example, if the Pentagon is unhappy with an administration decision, it will 'leak' a story to a reporter. The Pentagon hopes a newspaper will publish the story, and this will influence public opinion and Congress. If the White House gets angry, the Pentagon can merely disclaim any responsibility."

Washington reporters, for the most part, do not "dig out" facts, Anderson said. "The news is pretty well controlled by the politicians at the top in each agency," he explained. "A correspondent who wants a story at the White House generally will have to go through the press office. It is nearly impossible to slip into someone's office privately. You are escorted by someone from the press office. This gives the White House almost total control over information that flows out of the White House. Obviously, little information is going to come out that is critical of the president. White House correspondents, for the most part, get only 'favorable' information about the White House—the unfavorable information comes from the 'authorized leakers' at other agencies."

Anderson, however, gets most of his information from the career civil service workers in each agency—individuals affected only remotely by partisan politics. "The career people, during the early months of the Reagan presidency, were sending the same analyses to the new administration that they had been during the Carter administration," Anderson said. "The information was updated, but the basic facts were the same. Yet Ronald Reagan gave the people a different view of the world than did Jimmy Carter. The career people give the information as *facts*—as straight as they can."

Anderson admits that bias and distortion also can exist at the career levels. "The career people generally submit their facts as they get them, though they also occasionally have their axes to grind. The information can be tilted somewhat but it still is the most objective available in Washington," he said.

The columnist said he believes that he is the only Washington reporter who regularly intercepts news at the career levels. "I go to the politicians to tell them what is happening and to ask them for comments. I know what is happening before I ask them for comments."

Anderson's methods need not be limited to coverage of the highest levels of American government. They can be used by the city-beat reporter on the smallest dailies or weeklies. The Anderson philosophy is clear: Do not rely totally on public statements made by public officials. They might be decent, honest individuals. But generally there is more than one side to an issue. Policies never are as neat and ironclad as they sound or look on paper.

When gathering information do not stop the quest with public statements or even public documents that are not exempt under federal or state access laws. To obtain every conceivable scrap of relevant information, get to know the professional staff at the city agencies, whether it be the mayor's office, the city clerk's office, the city attorney's office, the utilities department, the city engineer's office, the fire department or the police department. Find out what they are thinking; get to know them. Build up trust; gain access to their memos and policy recommendations. Then, when the mayor makes a statement that does not align with a memo from the police chief, it can be pointed out in a story.

STANDARD REFERENCES

Information gathered from volumes on library shelves or from standard references that are found in most newspaper offices can be just as valuable as information gathered from public documents, public meetings or governmental sources. Certainly, information gleaned from these sources can provide much-needed background for stories.

The following list is not exhaustive, but it contains several valuable references for the working journalist.

Newsroom Sources

Stylebooks, atlases, almanacs, dictionaries, encyclopedias and thesauri are common reference books that reporters use frequently. In addition to these sources, found in nearly every newsroom or newspaper morgue, the Guinness Book of World Records usually can be located. Reporters often consult it—not merely to provide information for stories they are working on, but to answer questions that readers bombard newsrooms with at all hours of the day.

Other newsroom sources include:

- Biographies. Standard biographical reference volumes such as Current Biography, which is published monthly except in August, are available in many newsrooms. This service provides about 30 articles on newsworthy living persons in each month's edition. The annual volumes contain about 350 biographies. The Dictionary of American Biography, another common source, contains information on distinguished Americans who are dead.

    Most small- and medium-circulation newspapers limit their biographical volumes to one or two major ones, but libraries have a number from which to choose. These range from Who's Who in Switzerland to Who's Who in Communist China. Library shelves also include such specialized volumes as Who's Who in the United Nations, Current World Leaders, The International Who's Who, Who's Who in the World, The New York Times Biographical Edition, Obituaries on File, Biography Index and Biography.

- City directories. These volumes include alphabetical lists of names, addresses and telephone numbers of adult residents. They also contain street address guides, telephone number directories, ZIP codes, elementary school districts for individual addresses and information on such things as population, average income per household, home value distribution, construction permits, utilities, news media, tax bases, airlines, buses, railroads, climate and industrial sites.

- State directories. Called "blue books" in many states, these volumes include information on the executive branch (official state rosters of elective and appointive officers, their salaries and so on), the legislative branch (rosters of officials, their districts and so forth) and the judicial branch (rosters of judges, circuits, maps and so on). These volumes also include information on things such as state schools and colleges, election returns and miscellaneous statistics.

- Facts on File. This reference, which is published weekly, summarizes, records and indexes the news. National and foreign news events are included along with information on deaths, science, sports, medicine, education, religion, crime, books, plays, films and persons in the news. The index includes subjects (grain embargo, school prayer and so forth) and names of persons, organizations and countries.

- Editorial Research Reports. Published four times a month, it deals with major contemporary news issues, presenting a balanced overview in about 6,000 words. This source is particularly valuable because of its objective approach.

Library Sources

Public or college libraries can provide scores of useful references for reporters who seek information that is not readily available in most newsrooms. These sources include the following.

General Information

- Computer reference services. Many college and university libraries and some large public libraries now have computer reference services. A computer-assisted search for information is similar to a volume-by-volume search of a printed index. The computer will respond by spitting out a reference list on the topic—an almost-instant bibliography. Sometimes, the citations include *abstracts* (brief summaries of the articles or books). Libraries are connected to computers by telephone; comprehensive systems in New York and California are "called" frequently. The librarian types questions into a terminal. The requested information then is returned electronically through telephone wires. There are advantages to computer searches that can greatly benefit reporters working on major projects: speed (scores of references can be thoroughly searched in a matter of seconds), multiple-access points (the computer is not restricted to laborious checks limited to author, title and subject; it even can scan for title words) and currency (because of lag time in printing, computer lists are more current). Most libraries charge for the service. The fee generally is based on the time the library is connected to the computer.

- Newspaper indexes. The New York Times, the Los Angeles Times, the Washington Post, the Wall Street Journal and the Christian Science Monitor, among others, are newspapers that index news events. Most contain subject and name indexes.

- Miscellaneous indexes. Reporters use these when they are researching a particular topic. They include, but are not limited to, the Business Periodicals Index, the Readers Guide to Periodical Literature, the Essay and General Literature Index and Indexed Periodicals (which is an alphabetically arranged listing of periodical and serial titles that are indexed in some 330 American, British and Canadian periodical indexes).

    Reporters who seek book-length treatments of various subjects can consult the Subject Guide to Books in Print, which lists all in-print and forthcoming titles from more than 12,000 publishers, or Books in Print, which lists books alphabetically by title. Overviews of various books can be found in Book Review Index, New York Times Book Review Index and Book Review Digest.

- American Statistics Index (ASI). This volume lists, by subject, areas in which there are federal government statistics. A counterpart, Statistical Reference Index (SRI), covers statistics gathered by organizations, university research centers and state governments.

- Monthly Catalog of U.S. Government Publications. This volume can be helpful to the reporter who is not sure where to search for specific information. Subjects are derived from the Library of Congress Subject Headings and its supplements. The catalog consists of text and five indexes: author, title, subject, series/report number and stock number. Instructions for ordering also are included.

- National Directory of Addresses and Telephone Numbers. This book includes sections on business and finance, government, education, religious denominations, hospitals, associations and unions, transportation and hotels, communications and media and culture and recreation. It also has an alphabetical list of all names included.

- Names and Numbers: A Journalist's Guide to the Most Needed Information Sources and Contacts. Part I, "Useful Logistics," provides information on airlines, airports, hotel/motel chains and the like; Part II, "Information Sources and Contacts," provides information on government agencies, institutions, businesses, sports, arts, embassies and the like; Part III, "The Media," provides information on networks, newspapers, public relations firms, press clubs and the like.

- Statistical Abstract of the United States. This book is a digest of U.S. statistical data that have been collected by the U.S. government and some private agencies.

- Gallup Opinion Index. Published monthly, this index provides analytical as well as statistical data.

- Editorials on File. Published biweekly, this source contains editorial reprints from more than 130 American newspapers. There generally are 20 to 30 editorials on each subject. Indexes for subjects are found at the end of each binder.

Information on States

- Statistical abstracts for various states. These volumes often will include information on such things as geography, climate, population, vital statistics (births and deaths), health, education, labor, employment, earnings, public lands, recreation, government, law enforcement, mining, construction, housing, manufacturing, transportation, energy, communications, utilities and real estate.

- The Book of the States. This volume provides information on the structures, working methods, financing and activities of state governments. Scores of tables list all states and comparative information about such things as income taxes, campaign finance laws and voter turnout.

- State Information Book. This source presents basic information on aspects of all 50 states, such as officers; major services; details on the legislatures; the supreme courts; Washington, D.C. representation, and the federal offices in each state.

Information on Congress and the Federal Government

- Federal Register. Administrative rules and regulations are published in this Tuesday-through-Friday service.

- U.S. Government Organizational Manual. This source describes the functions of departments and agencies in the executive branch. It includes a bibliography of publications prepared by each.

- Congressional Information Service (CIS) Index. This volume provides access to contents of congressional hearings, reports and documents. It contains testimony by expert witnesses. It is excellent for pro and con arguments.

- Congressional Digest. This source explores current controversial topics. Many of the arguments are quoted from congressional committee reports.

- Congressional Directory. This book contains short biographical sketches of all representatives (listed by state). It also lists the office and telephone numbers of members of Congress, along with the names of two principal staff members for each.

- Congressional Quarterly Weekly Report. Published weekly, this source contains voting records of congressmen, texts of presidential press conferences and major speeches.

- Congressional Record. This source contains verbatim reports on what is said on the House and Senate floors. Members of Congress also can enter materials into the Congressional Record that were not delivered on the floors of the respective Houses.

- Congressional Staff Directory. Reporters often find this source particularly valuable when gathering information on topical issues. It provides names of staff members of congressional committees and subcommittees along with nearly 3,000 staff biographies.

- Guide to Congress. The subject index of this source, published by Congressional Quarterly, includes a variety of topics on how

Congress works. For example, reporters wondering about impeachment proceedings could turn to this volume for a summary of the purpose of impeachment, its history, the procedures and a chart on votes by which federal officers have been impeached by the House.

Sources on Law

Reporters who seek information on legal topics can consult the following:

- Dictionaries. Black's Law Dictionary provides the meanings of legal terms and phrases found in statutes or judicial opinions. It also includes a guide to pronunciation.

- General legal encyclopedias. Corpus Juris Secundum and American Jurisprudence are good basic sources. Corpus Juris Secundum provides a look at American case law from the first reported case to the present. It also includes citations to such sources as treatises, form-books and law journal articles. American Jurisprudence provides overviews of various aspects of law arranged alphabetically by title. Some states, such as California, Florida, New York and Texas, have their own laws published in encyclopedias. General encyclopedias include, in addition to overviews of cases and statutory laws, definitions of words and phrases. Reporters who are exploring an area of the law for the first time will find general encyclopedias excellent starting points.

- General directories. The Martindale-Hubbell Law Directory is an annual directory of attorneys. Names are listed alphabetically by state. In addition to biographical information, confidential ratings on such matters as legal ability and promptness in paying bills are provided. There also are various regional directories, such as the Pacific Coast Legal Directory.

- Indexes. The Index to Legal Periodicals is published monthly, except in September. Bound volumes by year can be found in law libraries and in many university libraries. The topical index is particularly helpful to reporters who need to read an overview of a particular legal subject. This volume provides the current index to more than 300 American legal journals and British periodicals. Articles dealing with the law published in general circulation outlets are indexed in Legal Resource Index and Current Law Index.

- Federal laws. The United States Code and United States Code Annotated contain federal statutes. Journalists often refer to federal acts by popular names, such as the Taft-Hartley Act.

Shepard's Federal and State Acts and Cases by Popular Names lists federal acts by their popular names and provides citations to the acts. Acts also are listed by their popular names in some volumes of United States Code Annotated.

- State laws. Each state publishes its codes. These generally are compiled under a title such as Arizona Revised Statutes or Ohio Revised Code. Reporters should familiarize themselves with the system for compiling laws in their states.

- Digests. American Digest System publishes all reported state and federal cases. The cases are arranged by subject. The U.S. Supreme Court Digest arranges U.S. Supreme Court decisions by subject.

- Federal court decisions. Opinions of the U.S. Supreme Court can be found in United States Reports (official government edition), United States Supreme Court Reports (Lawyer's Cooperative Publishing Co.), Supreme Court Reporter (West Publishing Co.) and United States Law Week (Bureau of National Affairs). Opinions of the U.S. Court of Appeals, the Court of Customs and Patent Appeals and the Court of Claims can be found in the Federal Reporter series. Selected opinions of the U.S. District Courts and the U.S. Customs Court can be found in the Federal Supplement. These volumes are found in law library collections as well as in many university libraries.

- State court decisions. Some states publish volumes containing only their state court decisions; some do not. Selected state court decisions can be found in the National Reporter System's regional volumes. The North Western Reporter, for example, contains opinions from Iowa, Michigan, Minnesota, Nebraska, North Dakota, South Dakota and Wisconsin. Several regional reports are published.

S U G G E S T E D   E X E R C I S E S

1. Obtain a copy of the booklet "How to Use the FOI Act." Read and discuss the practical guidelines it outlines for prying loose information under this federal law.

2. Locate and make copies of your state's open meetings law and open records law. Invite a local journalist to class who has used the laws to gain access to state-level information. What frustrations did the reporter encounter?

3. Discuss how Jack Anderson's methods of gathering information can be applied on the local level.

4. The next time you write a story on an event or personality in the news, visit the campus library to consult applicable sources of information discussed in this chapter.

5. Write a story that will be based in part on information you are able to locate in public records. For example, if you attend a state university, locate the institution's budget in the library. Find salaries of key university administrators, department heads and faculty members.

6. Write an "obit for the file" on a prominent local person or university official. Put together this comprehensive obituary completely from library sources. No interviews are allowed.

More and more specialists are being hired by the media today to cover areas of major interest to sophisticated audiences. These areas include business, education, medicine, religion, environment, consumerism and the arts. This chapter examines two of these specialized areas—business and consumer reporting.

You will be introduced to:

- The differences and similarities between beat and specialty reporting.
- Andrew A. Leckey, an economics and banking reporter for the Sun-Times in Chicago. Leckey offers helpful tips to reporters who would like to specialize in financial writing.
- How consumer reporting has changed since the 1960s and 1970s and the types of stories consumer reporters are covering today.

When seven people were killed in 1982 by poisoned Extra-Strength Tylenol capsules, consumer reporters had to explain the complex issue—how and why the killings happened and what would be done to prevent more—in language their audiences could understand.

© Steve Leonard/Sygma

10 BUSINESS AND CONSUMER NEWS

There is a fine line between a beat reporter and a specialty reporter. In fact, it can be argued that all reporters are specialists. Most reporters, however, are generalists who can peer into any field, learning just enough at any given time to cover a story before deadlines and daily journalism pressures push them into the next field and story. Many newspapers, especially weeklies and small dailies, simply do not have enough time or reporters to cover a single subject in depth day after day.

DIFFERENCES BETWEEN BEAT AND SPECIALTY REPORTING

Reporters who become sufficiently informed in one field to report and write on it exclusively and intelligently are considered specialists. As world, national and local issues reached new levels of sophistication and complexity in the 1970s and 1980s and as the electronic media forced the print media into more in-depth reporting, newspapers began turning to reporters who were specialists in certain areas: business, education, medicine, religion, environment, consumer news, the arts and other fields. Today more and more newspapers also are hiring specialists to cover fields that are particularly important in their locations, such as water, mining or the steel industry.

Unlike a beat reporter, who obtains stories by making daily stops at or phone calls to the courthouse, police station or county attorney's office, a specialty reporter's stories come from contacting a variety of experts and news sources or from following up ideas. Whereas the beat reporter usually is interested in news occurring now, the specialty reporter often is interested in long-range stories and the roots of problems.

It still is possible for a reporter to become a specialist by learning on the job, but today it is more and more likely that aspiring reporters specialize in one field before they look for jobs in the media. Reporters with doctorates are covering science for newspapers and television, people with master's degrees in business administration are writing financial news and physicians are practicing medical journalism. In many cases students who want to become specialty reporters have combined their journalism training with advanced training in another field. Sometimes reporters go back to school once they begin writing in a specialized area. And, yes, occasionally newspapers and the broadcast media hire experts in a particular field and hope they will learn reporting and writing skills on the job.

BUSINESS REPORTING

Many newspapers have specialists to cover business news. The phenomenal success of the Wall Street Journal (the most widely circulated daily newspaper in the United States), other financial publications and syndicated columns on personal finance all have shown that readers are keenly interested in news from the financial world. For years newspaper financial pages have carried listings of transactions on stock exchanges and/or handouts from businesses, industries and agencies, but in recent years they have broadened their coverage to meet a growing demand by readers. Today's business pages not only report the traditional financial news from bankers and brokers, they also explain to average readers what it all means.

There also is an increasing number of features on people in the business world. Newspapers still use handouts, annual reports and government reports for stories, but they also are sending reporters out into the field to uncover stories based on tips and ideas. This increased coverage requires reporters who are specialists in the complex field of business and who can develop contacts with many new sources.

The increased coverage in financial news has made business reporting more attractive to journalism students. To prepare themselves students are studying economics and business along with journalism. They are finding out that editors are impressed by reporters who understand how the government, stock market, money system and business world operate.

On the Job

Andrew A. Leckey, an economic and banking reporter and personal finance columnist for the Sun-Times in Chicago, is a specialty reporter who began his business training on the job and then went back to school for advanced training. He became a financial reporter when, having been on the job a month as a general assignment reporter at the Oregon Statesman in Salem, Ore., the business editor quit suddenly. The graduate of the University of Missouri School of Journalism found out quickly that the economy is a major story and financial reporters are in great demand.

"At first I had to bone up by reading every financial publication I could get my hands on," Leckey said. "I had to be willing to carefully ask questions, sometimes repeatedly, to get information right. There is a greater likelihood of screwing up information in financial and economic writing than any other area. You can't fake it, or you'll look like an idiot. In many cases you are dealing with a sophisticated audience. Your interview subjects test you, business people call to correct you and, in case of personal finance writing, your readers actually follow the advice within your columns with their hard-earned bucks."

The same basic reporting skills of accuracy, attribution and thorough research that are critical to surviving as a beat reporter also are paramount to a specialty reporter, and so Leckey approaches a financial story in the same hard-nosed manner that he would any type of assignment. He builds his sources by impressing them with the fact that he understands the nuances of what they are doing in big and small business. "The day when business reporting consisted of store openings and upbeat personality sketches alone is gone," Leckey said. "There are successes, of course, and people worth admiring, but the underlying philosophy must be, 'let the chips fall where they may.' Chronicling a failing company, worker layoffs, executive shakeups or an economy on the skids won't win you ticker-tape parades, but they are important."

After the financial reporting staff at the *Oregon Statesman* won a University of Missouri Business Award for a series on the lack of utility regulation in the Pacific Northwest, Leckey moved to the Phoenix Gazette, where he used his business and economics knowledge to cover the statehouse. Fast-buck artists were making millions of dollars in Arizona real estate, insurance and securities, and Leckey covered the governor and attorney general as they tried to reel in these "problem" industries.

While at the Gazette, Leckey received a Walter Bagehot Fellowship in financial writing at Columbia University in New York. He was one of 10 journalists to study at Columbia's Graduate School of Business for an academic year. "I spent time thinking about what the economy and business were all about, without having to file a story daily," he said. "It was not only an informative experience, it made me more employable as a financial reporter."

When he completed his fellowship, Leckey returned to his hometown, Chicago, to join the 14-member financial staff at the Sun-Times. First, he worked as a copy editor. Then he became economic and banking writer and later weekly personal finance columnist. On a regular basis he is in charge of making story assignments for financial reporters and selecting copy for editions. His experience also has led to his twice-weekly commentary on local public radio.

Tips on Business Reporting

Leckey gives the following advice to reporters who would like to specialize in financial writing:

- *Read as much financial material as possible*. Reading is important even if you do not become a financial reporter because business and economics affect many other areas requiring coverage, such as politics. Even reporters who do not cover business need knowledge of budgets, balance sheets and financial operating statements.

- *Learn how to say things simply and correctly.* Learn to cut the jargon that people you cover hide behind.

- *Try to take coursework in economics and business.* It is possible to fill in gaps through outside study, but some academic training is a big plus in helping you talk convincingly and in writing accurately. More and more financial reporters have had some type of formal training, and the number with MBAs is on the rise. That extra bit of training in business may mean the difference between getting or not getting a job in journalism.

- *If you are hired in journalism and are wasting away in an area you dislike, inquire about doing some financial reporting.* Financial staffs have grown rapidly in the last decade, but few are overstaffed. Most probably would appreciate some part-time help, and you would get an opportunity to learn.

- *Do not fear figures and other complicated financial data.* A good, solid reporter can become a competent financial reporter. A bad general reporter probably will not make it as a financial reporter. It takes homework to be able to ask the right questions; faking it will not work.

- *Remember that financial reporters can be tough.* Most newspaper managements realize now that financial reporting includes taking a hard look at businesses, even if they are major advertisers.

"Though many newspapers have increased their financial staffs in recent years, there still seems to be a continuing expansion, particularly at smaller dailies," Leckey said. "In addition, there are countless special interest financial publications, and television also is hiring financial reporters. The economy, the business world and what people do with their money will continue to be major stories."

CONSUMER REPORTING

Consumer reporting has come a long way in the last 15 years. It is one of the specialties that grew out of the advocacy journalism that became popular in the United States in the 1960s and early 1970s.

The Development of Consumer Reporting

Ralph Nader introduced consumer reporting to the nation in 1965 with his publication of "Unsafe at Any Speed," in which he took on General Motors. For a long time after that, consumer reporting consisted mainly of stories that compared various products or uncovered fraud in the marketplace. Journalists became advocates as consumerism, and mistrust of big business grew.

Today, however, consumer reporting consists of more than comparing grades of meat or prices of auto repairs. Issues such as Federal Trade Commission regulations, state and local consumer protection laws and consumer rights are being covered in-depth by consumer reporters at newspapers and broadcast outlets throughout the country. In many cases consumer reporters work in several specialty or general reporting areas while researching a single story. For instance a story on how to prepare for traffic court would require some police beat work, courthouse work and research into types of traffic violations, fines and sentencing. A story on the Federal Drug Administration's campaign against ineffective prescription drugs would require interviews with government officials, doctors, pharmacists and consumer advocates.

Another outgrowth of the consumer journalism of the late 1960s and 1970s has been "action line" columns, which have received tremendous support from readers. People write or phone in their problems, and reporters try to solve them.

Television is well-suited to hard-hitting consumer stories because actually showing steel-belted radial tires falling apart or toys exploding in children's faces has great impact. This type of reporting has become a specialty of such TV magazine shows as "20/20" and "60 Minutes," and many local television stations now employ consumer reporters.

Because their staffs are too small to cover consumer news extensively, many small-circulation newspapers must rely on consumer stories supplied by the wire services. The Associated Press and United Press International have consumer reporters, and they serve thousands of newspapers and broadcast outlets in the country.

There seems to be a never-ending supply of consumer stories. Antitrust violations, blatant price fixing, truth-in-lending violations and untrue advertising claims all are part of our vocabulary now and are fertile ground for reporters. But remember, never tell the public where or what to buy. Lay out the facts and the traps for readers and viewers and help them to understand the different products and regulations. Then let them make their own decisions.

Sources for Consumer News

Janet Key, a reporter at the Chicago Tribune who specializes in retail business reporting and consumer news, said her sources include local, state and national governmental agencies; various public action and consumer groups; corporate officials and public relations departments; economists; university professors, and stock analysts.

"I try to keep a file card on public action groups and other sources and list the people I talk to for a story," Key said. "Even if the person I write down is not the right source for my next story, it's easier to go back to one person and let him refer me to someone else."

Her card file includes:

- *Consumer spending sources.* These include university professors and corporate officials.
- *Consumer organizations.* These include Congress Watch, Consumer Federation of America, Consumers Union, Consumer Product Safety Commission, National Consumers League, National Council of Senior Citizens and Public Voice for Food and Health Policy.

"Some public relations people in big business also are good sources," Key said. "They can be good contacts at that business and notify you about things and other sources in their industry."

Before coming to the Tribune, Key was a reporter for United Press International, then a free-lancer and then a reporter for Business Week. She said that one important thing she has learned as a consumer reporter is to ask a source, "Is there anything else you feel I should have covered in my questions or is there anyone else you think I should be talking to? That will help get you new sources and responses and aid in establishing rapport."

S U G G E S T E D   E X E R C I S E S

1. Interview a local business leader. Before the interview, research the person and the business thoroughly so that you understand the language of the business. Write a personality profile on the person.

2. Here is a portion of a press release from Campbell Soup Co. Use the material to write a four-paragraph business news story:

Camden, N.J.—Campbell Soup Co. today reported increased sales and earnings for its second quarter and first half ended Jan. 30.

R. Gordon McGovern, President, said sales for the second quarter rose 9 percent to $886,741,000 from $816,140,000. Net earnings for the second quarter rose 1 percent to $47,042,000 from $46,656,000 in the second quarter last year.

Earnings per share were up 1 percent to $1.46 from $1.45 per share in last year's quarter.

For the first six months of Campbell's fiscal year, sales advanced 9 percent to $1,689,918,000 from $1,555,909,000. Earnings rose 4 percent to $89,866,000 from $86,109,000 reported in the first half of last fiscal year. Earnings per share climbed 4 percent to $2.79 from $2.67.

The second quarter was impacted by the company's decision not to accrue income resulting from an agreement of its Swift-Armour subsidiary with the Argentine Central Bank.

The Argentine government exchange insurance program is designed to moderate the effect of devaluation of debt of domestic companies denominated in other than the Argentine peso, in effect, converting dollar denominated loans into peso loans.

On a conservative basis the effect of the agreement would have been to add approximately $3,000,000 or about $.08 to the company's six months' results. Campbell, however, has decided to report the gains on a cash basis as received. The exchange insurance payments to the Swift-Armour subsidiary are expected to result in gains of more than $25,000,000 in total. Payments are scheduled throughout the period from 1984 to 1988.

The combination of the Argentine subsidiary results, the effect of the strong dollar and flat unit volume overseas resulted in a decrease in international sales of 4 percent for the six months period and 2 percent for the second quarter. Earnings are also down for both periods.

"Domestically, the company is performing well, with sales up 11 percent," Mr. McGovern said. "We are continuing our program of increased emphasis on marketing and holding price increases to a minimum."

3. Here is a statement, issued through a press release, by Robert A. Roland, president of Chemical Manufacturers Association. He is advocating decontrol of natural-gas prices. Use his statement to write a consumer news story:

The situation in which America and American gas consumers find themselves today is shameful—and the result of narrow and short-sighted energy policies.

Despite controls on natural-gas prices, consumers are paying more than 50 percent more for natural gas than they did merely four years ago.

What's worse, the nation's gas policy, as set out by the Natural Gas Policy Act, is doing precious little to ensure that we won't face severe shortages of natural gas in a few years.

Actually, the Natural Gas Policy Act is guaranteeing that consumers will not pay only higher prices, but the prospect of shortages.

The chemical industry, which is the largest industrial consumer of natural gas, applauds efforts presented by the Department of Energy and the Reagan administration to put competition back in the natural-gas industry.

This lack of competition that has been allowed to exist in the natural-gas industry has brought consumers to where we are today.

And the same people who a few years ago predicted that oil prices would climb to astronomical heights with the decontrol of oil prices are the same people who are spreading the doom and gloom predictions about natural gas prices.

They were wrong about oil decontrol—prices have come down. And they're wrong about natural gas.

By fostering competition in the natural gas industry, prices will come down. And competition will stimulate gas explorations, which will reverse the trend of our using up our natural gas reserves faster than we're replacing them.

We, as consumers, encourage the administration to push forward with plans to bring back competition in the natural gas industry.

Being a specialty reporter means dedication, a willingness to work as many hours as the job requires and an honest interest and knowledge in a particular subject. It also requires developing a network of trustworthy sources. This chapter examines specialty reporting through the eyes of actual reporters. They explain how they cover their specific fields, how they gain the respect of sources and how they write in language that their readers can understand.

You will be introduced to:

• Mary A.M. Perry, who covers the specialized field of water full time for the Arizona Republic in Phoenix. Perry has become as much an expert on water as many of the people she interviews.

• Bruce Buursma, religion writer for the Chicago Tribune. He believes religion writing can be the most-read news in any paper.

• Eric Mink, TV and radio critic of the St. Louis Post-Dispatch, who gives advice on how to be a successful specialty reporter and writer.

• Journalists in other specialty reporting areas: education, the environment, medical journalism and agriculture.

Bruce Buursma, religion writer for the Chicago Tribune, interviews Cardinal Joseph Bernardin of Chicago.

Chicago Tribune photo by Jose More

11 OTHER SPECIALTIES

Most people take water for granted. When they turn on the faucet, they expect pure water instantly for drinking or washing. For Mary A.M. Perry, however, water is more than a necessity delivered by others cheaply and quickly. It is a job.

Perry, one of a growing number of specialty reporters, covers water full time for the Arizona Republic in Phoenix. Water is a major political and emotional issue in Arizona and in the West generally, so what Perry writes is important to the newspaper's readers. To do her job effectively Perry has had to become an expert on many aspects of water.

WATER WRITING MAKES A SPLASH

Although Perry is not the first reporter at the Arizona Republic to write about water, she is the first to cover it exclusively. Because of increasing prices, a booming population and dwindling supplies, water has become a prime story in Phoenix. Perry has traveled throughout the state and the West and to Washington, D.C., to interview sources for her stories. The ideas seem endless: the Central Arizona Project to bring Colorado River water to Phoenix and Tucson, flood control, water quality, scientific advances in recycling water. As Perry sees it, "There is no shortage of ideas, only of water."

Perry didn't start her career as a water specialist. She completed her journalism degree in 1979 and later that year became a reporter at the Mohave Valley News, a 15,000-circulation, twice-weekly newspaper in northern Arizona. She covered everything: fire, police, schools, city and county government. She also carried a camera. "I averaged an 80-hour week," she said, "but I loved the opportunity to learn much of what it takes to produce a community newspaper."

Perry's next stop was the 44,000-circulation Mesa (Ariz.) Tribune. She worked in a seven-day-a-week zone publication of the Tribune, where she again reported on everything—and carried a camera. Twenty-one months after graduation she joined the staff of the 280,000-circulation Republic as a specialty reporter, a job she said required "total commitment."

During the first 10 days on the job, Perry met dozens of people in the water community, either by phone or in person. "Introduction of myself and my job was vital to obtaining future information," the reporter said. "People do not talk to strangers."

Her sources were logical: county and city health officials; the city water department; local, regional and national reclamation officials; the U.S. Interior Department; Indian communities, which have water rights on reservation lands that white men now want to "share"; water engineers, and Army Corps of Engineers officials. There were politicians to meet, too, because they must authorize and allocate funds for water projects.

Many of Perry's ideas for stories come from her own curiosity about water and the government process surrounding its allocation. Her stories deal with a variety of water issues, such as regulations from Washington, flood-control plans in Arizona and proposed dams on state rivers. All require reporter expertise.

Sources who trust her are the cornerstone to her success, Perry said. "I try to remember that my sources do not owe me a thing," she said. "I am asking them for their knowledge, which I then pass on to the public. Organization and doing your homework are critical to keeping doors open with sources. Also, I make it a point to let them know I am trustworthy, conscientious and dedicated to getting the story correct. No source likes a sloppy reporter. Sloppiness will be seen by the experts as irresponsible, and in specialty reporting, the community with which you work will pass the word. Doors open with good, accurate, honest work."

For Perry, being a specialty reporter means being dedicated, willing to work many hours and honestly interested in the subject she covers. "Anyone who thinks reporting is regular and leaves you time for planning a private life is nuts and in the wrong business," she said. "News does not happen during banking hours. If late-night phone calls to work bother you, don't get into reporting. Unless you love it, it could be a horrible chore, and that is not fair to the reader. Love it; that is the only way to survive it."

COVERAGE OF EDUCATION

Professor Ernest C. Hynds of the University of Georgia noted in an article published in Newspaper Research Journal, "Few, if any, topics covered by United States newspapers today affect more persons directly than education."

Indeed, the education beat is an important one at most newspapers. Hynds found that, in addition to regular coverage of education issues, approximately one-third of the nation's daily newspapers periodically publish a special page or section devoted to education. Yet fewer than half have one person assigned full time to education reporting, about 23 percent have one person who covers education part time and 16 percent have two persons who cover education part time.

Newspapers can help readers understand why schools succeed—and why they fail. (See Chapter 13 for a discussion of a major systematic study of the Philadelphia school system by the Philadelphia Inquirer.) Two decades ago, many newspapers thought they were covering the schools effectively if they printed lunch menus, honor roll lists and spelling bee winners. Newspapers—particularly in small towns—still publish those types of items, but coverage of education encompasses far more.

School systems today are complex institutions. No longer can newspapers adequately cover education merely by assigning a young reporter to "stop by the schools to see what is going on" after all other work is completed. A study of 330 school districts in Nebraska found that superintendents gave highest marks for accurate and insightful reporting to those newspapers that had a reporter with a strong layman's understanding of school issues covering the beat regularly.

Major School Topics

Recognizing the need to familiarize newspapers with today's complex educational issues, the Education Writers Association has published a booklet titled "Covering the Education Beat." It outlines 10 major issues that education reporters should cover in the 1980s: the "back-to-basics" movement, federal funding of education, violence and vandalism, student competency testing, declining enrollments, teacher negotiations and bargaining, desegregation, school financing, education for the handicapped and parent activism. The booklet provides sections on the history, current status and future outlook of each of these issues. Also included are tips on reporting them.

For example, in the section outlining coverage of teacher negotiations and bargaining, the booklet notes, "Formal negotiations and collective bargaining with teachers were almost unheard of prior to 1960. . . . Between 1962 and 1977, however, more than 35 states adopted collective bargaining laws that included teachers. School authorities generally agree that teachers were much better prepared for collective bargaining than were school boards and school administrators."

The booklet also recommends the following to reporters:

- Before covering negotiations obtain copies of teacher contracts dating back to the first one negotiated to isolate trends.

- Interview officials of the teachers' union dating back 10 to 15 years to better understand changes in teacher power.

- Interview school district administrators and board members, as well as representatives of parents' groups, to get their opinions about the growth of teacher powers.

- Interview teachers who are involved in politics because teacher unions "have begun wielding more political power in state and national elections."

The booklet also lists names, titles and telephone numbers of persons who might have "a national perspective on teacher power."

The booklet discusses key federal laws affecting education, how to report (and understand) school budgets and where to get more information about the following education issues: bilingual education, curriculum, reading, desegregation, educational governance, educational research and statistics, finance, education for the gifted, education for the handicapped, general trends, unionism, legislation, parent activism, private education, student rights, negotiations and strikes, testing, textbooks and urban education.

In addition to a discussion of these major topics, the booklet gives overviews of significant U.S. Supreme Court decisions on issues such as desegregation through racial balance, quotas and busing; due process for disciplined students; First Amendment rights for students; public support for non-public schools; prayer recitation and Bible-reading in the public schools, and corporal punishment.

William Grant, president of the Education Writers Association, said that the group decided to publish the booklet "because the public schools are probably the most demanding and challenging beat for reporters, especially new ones."

Award-Winning Stories

Winning entries in the Charles Stewart Mott Awards Competition sponsored each year by the Education Writers Association clearly show that coverage of education goes beyond the traditionally published safe education stories that deal with biographical information on new teachers and activities of the science club. Sociological, political, legal and economic issues often are explored in school stories today.

Rena Wish Cohen, a reporter for the Daily Herald and Sunday Herald (circulation 60,000) in Arlington Heights, Ill., for example, won a national award for a four-part series she wrote on sex education. Her series examined sex education in the northwest Chicago suburbs, trends in sex education, mothers who thought the schools had gone too far and whether sex education was effective.

Cohen's writing was crisp and vivid. In her story dealing with the reactions of two mothers to sex education in the schools, she led with:

> For Sharon Chavoen, it all started when she heard about a male teacher who was rumored to have told his junior-high-school students he was "glad he wasn't a woman because he didn't think he could cope with the menstrual cycle."
>
> For Sue Evenwell, it began when she read a book called "Raping Our Children," which links leaders of the country's sex-education movement to the Communist Party and tells a host of horror stories—like the one about a 12-year-old, fresh from sex-education class, who "practices" on his 4-year-old sister.
>
> The two mothers heard these things, and the red flags drew up faster than you can say the word *sex*.

In addition to probing issues such as sex education, good education writers also are doing more investigative reporting. Craig Brandon, writer for the Observer-Dispatch and Daily Press (circulation 38,000) in Utica, N.Y., put together a strong, award-winning series on who was moving into houses built by vocational education students. His stories were accompanied by a chart giving the names and occupations of the people who moved into the houses that were constructed by the Utica City School District students between 1955 and 1980. Brandon examined school and real estate records and conducted interviews with school officials, homeowners and those passed over on waiting lists to have the houses built. His lead:

> In the past 25 years vocational education students in the Utica City School District have built 23 houses. Of those, 15 were built for school employees and their relatives.
>
> Although the district says that anyone can get on a waiting list to have a house built by the students, an examination of the list shows numerous cases that resulted in preferential treatment for school and city employees.
>
> Under the program people can have houses built by paying only for the materials. The labor is supplied free by the students. Professional builders and owners of the homes estimate that this saves 20 to 50 percent of the cost of having a house built by a contractor.

Brandon's series was an excellent combination of skillful investigative reporting and good, clear writing. It is representative of the hard-hitting, well-researched stories being written by education reporters today.

ENVIRONMENTAL REPORTING

The story from United Press International said:

> CORPUS CHRISTI, Texas (UPI)—The nation's first seaborne incineration of 707,000 gallons of cancer-causing PCBs was completed aboard a ship Saturday by waste destruction experts.

Like consumer reporting, environmental reporting has changed in the last 15 years. In the 1960s and 1970s environmental reporters looked at problems that were visible, such as air pollution and filthy rivers and streams. In the 1980s they are concerned primarily with invisible problems, such as the cancer-causing PCBs (polychlorinated biphenyls) mentioned in the previous story, other industrial wastes, nuclear power and soil depletion.

Because energy and the environment are so vital to human survival, environmental reporting is likely to remain one of the most important jobs in the media. It has been and will continue to be Page One news. Environmental reporters never can divorce themselves from breaking news because events such as environmental crusades, OPEC price increases and nuclear protests always are popping up. Only when there is a lull are they able to search for the roots of environmental problems.

Most newspapers rely on the wire services to provide them with environmental news. When an environmental story does break in their areas, they assign general assignment or beat reporters to cover it as spot news. Metropolitan newspapers, however, treat environmental writing as a specialty, and a reporter who is an expert on energy and the environment covers both spot news and in-depth stories. Some newspapers even break up energy and the environment into separate specialties.

As always, the key to success as an environmental writer rests with the reporter's ability to question and test conventional wisdom that growth is good and more is better. However, today's environmental reporters face a bigger problem than did their counterparts of a decade ago because they now are dealing with the invisible problems, which are difficult to cover and for which public support often is difficult to enlist. Tackling such invisible problems requires that today's environmental reporters be better trained than ever before. First, of course, they must be good reporters and writers. Then they must be able to take complex technical jargon and explain it in simple, understandable language. Environmental writers therefore must spend as much time reading appropriate technical journals and learning the scientific language as the experts with whom they deal. As in any specialty reporting area, environmental writers must educate themselves in their field continually.

COVERING RELIGION

Religion writing—and newspapers' attitudes toward it—began to broaden and mature during the 1970s. This change resulted from a marked cultural shift in the United States toward privatism and introspection and from Southern Baptist Jimmy Carter's candidacy and presidency. At about the same time journalism schools began showing more interest in religion writing and students began considering the merits of covering religion. Still, most newspapers rely on wire services for religion news, except for spot news or weekly items from churches.

Religion writing is not new. The Religious News Service was established in 1933 and has served as both a weekly and daily service to hundreds of news outlets. Newspapers also rely on mailings from various church denominations. The growing emphasis on this specialized form of reporting is illustrated by an increase in annual awards for journalists who cover religion, such as the Louis Cassels Award of $200, which is given by the Religion Newswriters Association for religion writing in newspapers of 50,000 or less circulation. The contest was created to honor the late religion writer for United Press International.

Today, religion writing is gaining popularity as newspapers hire ministers-turned-reporters or other specialists who know the vocabulary and can explain complex religious issues to readers. Stories range from the opening of a new synagogue to the finances of a controversial priest to an in-depth look at an evangelist. "I'm convinced religion writing, done with sensitivity and verve, can be among the best-read coverage in any newspaper," said Bruce Buursma, religion writer for the Chicago Tribune. Before coming to Chicago, Buursma, whose father is a minister, covered religion at the Grand Rapids (Mich.) Press, the Courier-Journal in Louisville and the Dallas Times Herald. "There are many more people who attend a house of worship each week than purchase movie tickets," he said. "And in a one-week period, there are twice as many people in church as there are at a major league baseball stadium in an entire season. There are millions of people in America who order their lives according to a religiously informed conscience. Unless you understand the religious underpinnings of a culture, you cannot possibly fully understand the culture or how and why it behaves the way it does."

Besides writing hard news on a breaking story, religion reporters write features, profiles and analytical pieces. Because they are dealing with complex ideas based on a system of faith outside the realm of natural laws, religion reporters' work is demanding and at times tedious. A single story may require weeks of research, travel and interviews. For instance, when Buursma took on the task of researching an in-depth story on evangelist Oral Roberts, he had to go to Tulsa, Okla., home of Oral Roberts Evangelistic Association, Oral Roberts University and Roberts' City of Faith medical complex. Besides interviewing Roberts, he talked to friends and critics of the preacher and thoroughly researched the man who brought in more than $90 million in 1980 for his cause. Buursma then wrote an article for the Tribune's Sunday magazine. It began:

> In the beginning of his ministry, more than a biblical generation—40 years—ago, he was known as Brother Roberts, and he was a gangly preacher of the Pentecostal Holiness stripe. He toiled in the dustbowl towns of his native Southwest, pitching his tent on the parched prairie and invoking the high-voltage power of the Holy Ghost to descend on his caravan of miracles.
>
> Those were the days, he has recalled, of ecstasy and wonderment on the Hallelujah Trail. And today, in the latter years of his career, Granville Oral Roberts still is hankering for those supernatural signs, but now the stakes are much higher, and the competition has grown keener.

As in other specialties, advanced training is essential for reporters writing about religion. That does not mean only ministers—or their sons—can cover religion. It does mean that students interested in religion reporting should take as many courses as possible in religious studies. Most colleges and universities offer such courses, and they could be a ticket for landing a job.

THE ARTS

At small newspapers, where people do many jobs, beat reporters often spend their free time reviewing books, records, plays, concerts, movies, television and radio. It gives them the opportunity to be involved with things they are interested in, to take home records or books or to earn extra income. Metropolitan newspapers are different: They hire specialists to cover the arts. The larger the paper, the more the specialists. At big metros one reporter covers film, one is assigned to TV and radio, one reports on music, one reviews theater and so on.

Reporters who cover the arts deal in both fact and interpretation. They wear the hats of writer, analyst and critic. Often they must cover spot news, which means that they must know reporting skills. Other times they write reviews, which are filled with their own opinions.

Covering the arts is like covering any specialty field: Reporters must know the vocabulary in their fields and have many of the same skills as the people they write about. To cover the arts, they must be trained in architecture, music, theater, painting, film, photography, dance or sculpture so that they will be credible to their audience. Advanced training offered through university or college courses in the arts helps reporters develop the knowledge vital to the successful coverage of their specialities.

To review a play, for example, a writer must view it for enjoyment but also must look at the technical aspects. Was it fun to watch as a viewer? What about the scripts, the lighting, the sets? Is the play too long? Did the actors have trouble delivering lines? Could the audience hear them? There are scores of questions the writer must answer, and all require expertise.

Eric Mink, TV and radio critic of the St. Louis Post-Dispatch, is a good example of a specialized reporter who covers the arts. Much of what he does, and how he does it, exemplifies the work of arts writers throughout the country. He is obligated to write three columns a week—for the Monday, Wednesday and Friday editions—but he often writes four. He free-lances for other sections of the paper, and he covers breaking news if need be.

Mink has lived in St. Louis all his life, except for the four years spent at George Washington University, where he majored in English literature. He started working at the Post-Dispatch in May 1977. The paper had started a weekly consumer section, and Mink had been writing consumer stories at a magazine in St. Louis. He wanted a job at the newspaper, had written some free-lance articles for the Post-Dispatch and had friends on the staff, all of which helped him land the job.

In early 1979 the paper's new managing editor wanted to make a change in the TV–radio column. He wanted a different style and approach, something with more edge to it, something people would talk about. Enter Mink.

"There was sort of a bake-off for the job," he said. "I got into the competition late. The features director knew movies and TV were loves of mine, and he thought my writing abilities weren't being used as well as they could be in the consumer section. I really had to think about it because in addition to the TV column, I had a chance to switch to hard news. I finally decided that hard news always would be there, but there might not be another chance at getting a column with my name on it. The column would be a great challenge to my writing abilities. I got into the competition and eventually was selected."

Mink has been covering six television stations and about 35 radio stations and cable in St. Louis since March 1979. He described his job as "the oddest in the whole newspaper. Here, at least, one person does the job. That person must be a reporter, an analyst and a critic."

To be a successful TV—radio reporter, critic and writer, Mink said, "You need a willingness to take positions, to express opinions and to have enough confidence in yourself to put yourself on the line." The writer must look at the production as a viewer: Was it good? Is it believable? Does it have internal integrity? At the same time the writer must study the technical qualities of the production: Where is the camera? Are the people really where they are supposed to be? "Before I write, I look at a show both ways," Mink added. "I try to keep the technical analysis on a second level, especially if the show is working on the other level. Often a critic must put aside special knowledge and react to a show strictly as a viewer."

Mink's expertise, along with common sense, enables him to comment intelligently and communicate with his readers. He continually reads about the media, and he knows the vocabulary and business of broadcasting. He knows about ratings, how advertising is bought and sold, how people apply for licenses and how to read license applications. He is an expert, but when he looks in the mirror, he sees a writer. "I am a writer who must use my writing skills to criticize, to dig up facts, to be reflective and sometimes to be funny. It doesn't matter to me if I am writing about a local anchor known only in St. Louis or if I am writing an interview with the president of CBS sports. I don't think you can function effectively unless you are a good writer who reads a lot, constantly talks to the right people and continually develops sources."

Mink mingles with television and radio celebrities daily, but he said that does not make his job glamorous. "This job is 99 percent unglamorous," he said. "I am better known than most reporters in St. Louis, but that has not had any effect other than my family thinks I'm pretty neat. My job is non-stop. I am covering a 24-hour-a-day, 365-day-a-year industry. I never listen to the radio for pleasure. I may start with that intention, but as soon as I start listening, I start analyzing: What time of day is this? What song am I hearing. Are there a lot of public service announcements or have ads been sold? How many songs has the DJ played in a row? Is the DJ talking over the music? I am listed in the phone book, and I often get calls at home. They mostly are from sources, but occasionally a reader calls. I spend a lot of time on the phone in the evening."

MEDICAL JOURNALISM

As in other specialized reporting areas, the medical writer must be able to communicate with experts and write in language lay readers will understand. Medical writers deal daily with a highly specialized vocabulary, but they are writing for readers who demand understandable copy.

The job is easy for Lawrence K. Altman of the New York Times and Susan Okie of the Washington Post. They are medical writers, and they also are physicians. She works four days a week as a reporter on the Post's metro staff and spends one day a week working in a hospital emergency room or a local free clinic. He takes a sabbatical from the paper each year to practice medicine.

That Altman and Okie are physicians does not mean that a reporter must be a doctor to write about medicine. It does mean competition is fierce in this specialized field. Newspapers want specialists who can cover stories on health care, health policy, diseases and medical research intelligently and then write in easy-to-understand language. The better qualified the medical writer is, the better able the newspaper is to cover medicine as it would cover consumer news or environmental news.

Altman has searched for the cause of Legionnaire's Disease, written about the mental and physical health of the American hostages after they were freed from the U.S. Embassy in Iran in 1981 and explained the medical problems of the world's leaders. During the 1980 presidential campaign, he spent a week traveling with candidate Ronald Reagan. While interviewing the candidate, Altman discovered that Reagan's father suffered from senility. His article in the Times discussed senility and said that Reagan showed no symptoms of the disease. Shortly after the story ran, Reagan announced that he would step down from the presidency at the first sign of senility.

Medical writing consists of more than national stories. On a local level, hospitals are installing new, sophisticated equipment; millions of dollars in public money are being spent on health care; doctors are searching for new cures. All these issues require coverage by journalists who not only can write but who can communicate with and interview scientists, who usually are terrified of being misquoted. The secret is to talk their language and then report their statements accurately.

WRITING ABOUT AGRICULTURE

Agriculture is another specialized field whose coverage requires training and an uncanny ability to translate technical language into understandable terms. Agricultural news means more than covering the introduction of new tractors or reporting how many acres of corn were planted this year.

Contemporary agriculture has become a big, expensive business run by huge companies, which means that the number of small, independent farmers is decreasing rapidly. Thus fewer readers may be interested in agricultural news today than when America was rural, but those who are tend to be educated and sophisticated.

Because agricultural writers are dealing with big and little business, they must be knowledgeable about economics, politics and a host of other areas besides farming. Their sources include businessmen and politicians as well as farmers, and they must be investigators as well as interviewers.

THE FUTURE

Journalism will become even more specialized as readers become more knowledgeable and sophisticated. Indeed there are many more specialized reporting areas than those we have discussed, including women's news, transportation, science, food and human behavior. All are playing a bigger-than-ever role in contemporary America, and all require coverage by reporters who are, or can become, specialists able to communicate intelligently with experts and readers.

Specialty reporting is a never-ending educational process. The reporter must cover a story today while striving to be better at it tomorrow. That often means taking time off from daily reporting to go back to school or attend seminars. It means trading ideas with other journalists and professionals.

Because of daily deadline pressures, most media still are interested primarily in where and how somebody did something. They want to know what is happening now. However, more editors today appreciate the importance of the "why" of a story, which means that there will be an increasing need in the future of specialty reporters who can search for the roots of issues and explain their long-range effects.

S U G G E S T E D   E X E R C I S E S

1. What specialty reporting areas are particular to your part of the country? Are the local newspapers and broadcasters covering them adequately? How would you improve the coverage?

2. Make a list of courses taught at your school outside of journalism that would be helpful for specialty reporters. Are any of them required in your major?

3.   Obtain a copy of an agenda for an upcoming school board meeting. Carefully review the agenda. Get background on issues you do not understand. Attend the meeting and write a story.

4.   Review a movie, play or television show. Compare your story with those of your classmates and with a review in a local newspaper.

Today newspapers and broadcasters try to give their audiences a news mix: terse accounts of events that occurred in the last 24 hours and in-depth and investigative stories that go well beyond such accounts. This chapter examines the increased emphasis on in-depth and investigative stories.

You will be introduced to:

• The types of lead blocks that can be used in in-depth articles. Portions of an in-depth article are used to illustrate how the lead block is written to draw readers into the story.

• Weaving a thread through an in-depth piece to hold it together.

• The effective use of first-person in-depth articles. The chapter points out that a first-person article works well when the story deals with a highly intense and personal subject.

• The differences and similarities between investigative and beat reporters. William Recktenwald, an investigative reporter at the Chicago Tribune, offers tips to reporters involved in investigations. The chapter also describes an investigation by Tribune reporter Andy Knott of shoddy ambulance services in Chicago.

Mike Wallace, of CBS' "60 Minutes," prepares to interview investigators for the Better Government Association and a Chicago Sun-Times reporter for a segment on Mirage, a Chicago Near North Side tavern owned and operated for four months by the Sun-Times and the BGA to investigate public and private corruption in the tavern business. The interview took place in the basement of the Mirage.

Marc Harris

217

12 IN-DEPTH AND INVESTIGATIVE REPORTING

Most American newspapers find space in their news holes each day for in-depth articles, which include news features, investigative reports and even first-person articles. These stories now are commonplace on pages that only a few years ago carried nothing but terse, inverted pyramid accounts of news events that had occurred within the preceding 24 hours. Both newspapers and broadcasters now provide their audiences with a mix: They report the news, and they also provide in-depth information that allows people to lead more enjoyable, profitable or better informed lives.

Some newspapers devote a single section to in-depth pieces, often daily; others use such stories throughout. This increased emphasis on longer, more comprehensive stories that require extensive research and interviews is giving reporters an opportunity to be more than technicians following a rigid set of guidelines. It is giving them the chance to be creative, to become a part of their readers' emotional lives.

In-depth articles are choice assignments because they allow reporters to thoroughly explore a topic, learn things that most people do not have a chance to learn and tell a story without the fear of its being cut to 6 inches for a small hole on Page 4. An in-depth allows a reporter to interview many people and thoroughly research a single topic. The final story may be written as hard news or soft news. It may be one long piece that starts on Page 1 and jumps to one or more inside pages, or it may be a series that runs several days.

Assignments for in-depths usually are grueling because they require the reporter to spend days, or even weeks, researching a topic in the library and in the field, asking questions and writing. Often reporters work on in-depths while they continue their regular beats.

HOW IN-DEPTHS ARE WRITTEN

Assignment: Take an in-depth look at the emergency room in the county hospital. Spend as many days as it takes to learn what it is like to be a doctor or a nurse in a demanding, emotional setting where every second counts. Find out all you can about these doctors and nurses who keep some people alive or watch others die.

For this article on emergency room treatment, the reporter had to spend nights and weekends in a hospital because those were the busiest times. There was little time for such personal things as a family or social life because, in fact, the reporter had to live like a doctor or a nurse, learning and seeing things in a few weeks that most people would not experience in a lifetime.

Besides the field work, this story took hours of research and many more hours of writing. To produce such an article in language people can understand requires long and stressful hours, but the reward is a piece of writing with the reporter's brand—a byline—on it.

What Type of Lead?

Summaries are the most common leads on hard news stories, but on in-depth articles, reporters may use anecdotal, contrast, direct address or other types of leads that do not summarize the story in the first paragraph. Of course, a summary lead can be used on an in-depth, but because the story is longer than a news account, the reporter often wants to paint a picture and draw readers deep into the story before giving them the climax. To do that the reporter writes a *lead block,* and readers must stick with the story for several inches before they realize where the reporter is taking them. The climax of the story even may be saved until the end.

For instance, here is the lead block on the emergency room story, which ran in the Minneapolis Star:

Saturday, 9:30 p.m.
"413, Code 3 to Third Avenue and Franklin. A shooting."
The Minneapolis Police Department has called the Hennepin County Medical Center's ambulance service. Owen Strandburg, a 38-year-old dispatcher, is managing the switchboard, which resembles the cockpit of an airplane. It's his job to get a two-member team of paramedics in an advanced life support ambulance to a person in need anywhere in the county as quickly as possible.

He has been told there was a shooting in front of an apartment building at Third Avenue and Franklin. He calls ambulance No. 413.

Now, it's lights, siren and action. Unit 413 is en route at 9:39. Every second counts.

Soon, another patient will be wheeled into the medical center's emergency room and then to its stabilization room, where the critically ill are brought.

Doctors and nurses call it the stab (pronounced with a long a) room. The sign outside labels it the "Red Room." The 24 × 30-foot room is filled with gadgets only doctors understand—things with names too hard to spell or remember.

It smells clean.

In the middle of the room are two tables on wheels. Red lines are painted around them so the doctors will know the optimum area in which to work. Each of the tables—they're called hospital carts—has a blue paper cloth over it.

The only people who walk into this room are doctors, nurses and other hospital employees. Patients are wheeled in and minutes later, out, some to other parts of the hospital for treatment, others to the morgue.

The medical people who work in the stab room can, indeed, save lives. People do die in their hands. Inside, it's loud and it's bloody. Outside, families scream.

By now, the writer has painted, with anecdotes, a vivid picture for the readers. They know the story is going to be about life—and death—in the emergency room, and like the patient, they were brought to the emergency room by ambulance. Soon both the patients and the readers will be in the thick of the action. The patients have no choice. The readers do, but the anecdotes should keep them interested enough to continue.

The simplest formula to follow when writing anecdotes is to have one of the characters in the story doing something. The object is to evoke some type of emotion from the readers, to make them feel that they are part of the action. A reminder, though: Stay away from cliché-filled "atmospheric" phrases, such as "It was a dark and stormy night" or "As the sun crept slowly over the mountain."

The Story Thread

The key to a successful in-depth article is a strong "thread" throughout to keep readers interested. The thread may be a real-life situation, strange twists or suspense leading to a surprise ending, but it is used to evoke some type of emotion from readers so that they will want to continue with the story. For example, an in-depth on child abuse would examine many areas of the problem, but it may begin by describing a man who is accused of abusing his daughter. Numerous sources would be named and quoted, and readers would be given the necessary statistics on child abuse, but incidents from the case involving the man would be sprinkled throughout the story. In fact, his case becomes the thread that weaves throughout the story and holds it together. The readers should develop an emotional attachment to the man. By combining the facts and figures of child abuse with a story about a father who beats his child, the writer produces a readable "people story."

In the case of the emergency room story, Saturday night was the thread that wove throughout the story. It started with a Saturday night shooting, moved to statistics about emergency room care, came back to another Saturday night, went into more quotes and information on the emergency room and then ended on a Saturday night. By the end of the story, readers had been introduced to a variety of patients and doctors and nurses working on busy Saturday nights, but the readers also were educated on what emergency room care is all about and what doctors and nurses have to go through.

As the drama of the first Saturday night unfolded for the readers, different doctors and nurses were introduced. Readers also were told that about 200 patients are seen here each day. "Six doctors work full time and three work part time," the story said. "Together, these people take care of everything from cardiac arrest to drug overdoses to cut fingers in an area that's open 24 hours a day, seven days a week, 365 days a year." Readers also were told how much the doctors earn, how much schooling they go through and even some of the funny things that can occur in such a sad environment. The head of the emergency room was interviewed. Doctors were interviewed at work and off work. Nurses and interns were quizzed night after night.

About midway through the story, the readers were brought to another Saturday night:

It's winter. Another Saturday night.

Ramona Hodgeman, a 17-year-old high school senior, is walking to her home at 2813 S. Columbus Ave. from a nearby supermarket. Like always, she is taking a shortcut down the alley. While she is rounding a curve, two men come up to her. One of them has a knife. He stabs her in the chest, ripping through her breast, between her ribs, through the front of her heart and out the back. One of her lungs is torn open.

Ramona runs home, opens the front door and collapses. Her 21-year-old brother, Raymond, calls an ambulance.

As Ramona fell, the story shifted back to the hospital and an ambulance's being dispatched much as one was at the beginning of the story. Now readers were introduced to another case, more doctors and nurses, different types of medical procedures. In the case of the shooting described at the beginning of the story, the victim died on the operating table despite frantic efforts by doctors and nurses in the stab room to save him. In the second case, Ramona lived. She was saved on the operating table:

Once again, the doctors are ready in the stab room, but the cast has changed. The pit boss (the doctor in charge) is Ellen Vancura, a 29-year-old doctor in her third and final year of residency.

Vancura knows what she has to do. It's called a thoracotomy, cutting open the chest. The object is to get to the heart as quickly as possible and release blood from the pericardial sack that encloses it. When the heart is punctured, it fills the sack with blood, which then restricts the beating motion of the heart. If the heart can't beat, it can't pump blood, and the patient will die.

Once the heart has quit pumping, the only thing that can save the patient is opening the chest, releasing the blood and "plugging the dike," that is, putting a finger over the hole in the heart until it can be sewn by surgeons.

The procedure has a high mortality rate, and takes 30 to 60 seconds to perform. Time is critical. Within four to six minutes after the heart stops, the patient suffers brain damage.

Within seconds after Ramona is lifted onto the cart, Vancura slices open the teen-ager's chest and pericardial sack. Blood gushes out.

The biggest problem is a hole in her left ventricle. Vancura has to plug it as quickly as possible because Ramona is near death. The doctor puts her finger over the hole. The heart starts beating. Ramona wakes up, and has to be given medication for pain.

This time it works.

Ramona was in the stab room for 15 minutes. When she left to be wheeled upstairs to surgery, Vancura accompanied her, holding a finger over the hole in her heart.

Night after night, the reporter and a photographer went to the emergency room. During the day the reporter poured through medical documents to learn about the procedures doctors mentioned. Ramona would be interviewed to find out how she felt about the doctor who saved her life. Police would be interviewed to find out if suspects had been arrested in the stabbing.

Throughout the story anecdotes were used. Real names were used and real cases explained so that readers could be emotionally attached to the story. Facts, figures and other often-dull statistics were given in between the anecdotes. Then the story ended much the same way it started:

> There's a soap opera a minute in the emergency room, where a small sign near one of the patient areas says, "Cubicle, Sweet Cubicle."
>
> While her mother is inside receiving treatment for a scalded arm, an 8-year-old girl from Arizona sits outside, watching the ambulances pull in. "Daddy, you should have seen this old man. His face looked so bad. It was like porridge was coming out of his nose and mouth."
>
> There's a woman lying on a cart in the middle of the hall because all of the cubicles are full. "You are dehydrated," a doctor tells her. "You have to quit drinking. No, you can't stay here today. You'll have to go home. We are too crowded."
>
> The people who work in this room see it all. Drugs. Stabbings. Shootings. Murders. Suicides. Car wrecks. Burns. Scratches. Bruises.
>
> They try to comfort the patient and the families. They want to save everyone, even when they know it's hopeless.
>
> In a cubicle, a doctor in a green scrub suit is talking to a woman lying on a cart with the side rails pulled up. "Why don't you want to talk to us? Are you depressed? Are you suicidal?"
>
> A man is brought in who has overdosed on "angel dust." He's cussing. He does not want treatment. A guard is called to stand over him.
>
> An ambulance brings in a woman, another stab room case. Her daughter stands outside, screaming, "I want to see my momma. I want to see my momma."
>
> It's another Saturday night.

FIRST-PERSON ARTICLES

News stories seldom are written in the first person, for reporters are taught to stay out of their writing, to be completely unattached to the subject. In the name of objectivity reporters are trained to be middlemen— to witness an event and then recall it in words so that readers who were not there can read the news story and feel that they were. The reporters are the eyes and ears of the public.

Unlike a hard news story written in an inverted pyramid, an in-depth piece meant to involve its readers can be effective in the first person. In a first-person story, the writer invites the readers into a personal experience, and by the end of the story, the readers should feel that they are a part of the writer's life. First-person articles can make a highly intense and personal subject much more real. Examples of first-person articles are "I was an inmate in the county jail," "I worked as a guard at the state prison" or "I was an orderly in an emergency room."

Another good example of a first-person in-depth is this story written by a female journalism student whose husband was dying of cancer. The story worked better in the first person because it allowed a talented writer to tell her story directly to readers. The article, which was purchased by Arizona, the Sunday magazine of the Arizona Republic in Phoenix, began:

> I was standing at the kitchen sink washing fresh vegetables for dinner. Dennis walked in from work and said he had just heard a song on the radio that described how he felt.
>
> "Better be good to yourself cause you're no good for anyone else," he said while he kissed me and reached around for a glass. (Dennis is in a low mood, and I had better just drift with him for awhile, I thought.)
>
> My husband Dennis is 24 years old. We've been married 2 1/2 years, but are never sure how much longer we have together. Dennis has cancer of the soft tissue. His doctors have told us his cancer is a rare form and they can do no more than experiment with various drugs in their search for a cure. The doctors have said that the longer he goes without another growth the greater his chances of survival.
>
> We think the will to live is the most important factor. Somehow, this will carry us through even the lowest moods.

In this story the reporter wrote a lead block that described a real situation—a moment before dinner—with which readers could identify easily. Then she left the kitchen for awhile to develop her story. She went back to their wedding day and mentioned the trouble Dennis had kneeling. Then she explained what they went through when they found out he had cancer. In her research she also interviewed doctors and studied records to report to readers the statistics on cancer of the soft tissue. Periodically, she returned to the kitchen, the thread that kept the readers personally involved in the story.

> While Dennis mixed a drink, he asked me, "Do you realize how short a time we've been married and how much of that time I've had cancer. I don't want you to always go through this."
>
> We've had conversations like this before and I know what they lead to. I dropped my eyes from his and moved around him to the refrigerator.

The thing that makes first-person stories so powerful for the readers also makes them emotional for the writer, who has to relive a personal and sometimes painful experience, revealing it to thousands of eyes. In the cancer story the reporter had to talk about her insecurities, her finances and the rest of her family. None of that was easy to do. She ended the story as she and her husband were eating dinner:

> The drugs and cobalt have left Dennis sterile. The doctors can't say whether it is only a temporary condition. We no longer discuss the children we would like to have. We just wait.
>
> While Dennis ate and talked about the possibilities of investing in a home, I realized, gratefully, that he'll never give up.

First-person stories also can deal with many people. Three months after three guards were killed and three others injured during a riot in the state prison in Pontiac, Ill., Chicago Tribune reporter William Recktenwald applied for and got a job as a guard at the prison. His in-depth investigation became a series in the Tribune. Much of the series was in first person. The headline over the first day's main story was "I was a guard in Pontiac prison." Here is how it started:

> The cellblock was filled with trash, excrement and spoiled food, all of it soaked with water that collected in puddles. The air reeked of tear gas, MACE and smoke. A pile of bedding was on fire, and all the windows were closed. Men in the cells began screaming and clanging the bars.
>
> This may sound like a description of the Pontiac state prison at the height of the riot there last July, when three guards were killed and three others seriously injured. And so it might have been in July.
>
> But this was Pontiac on Oct. 11, almost three months after the riot; it was the scene as I entered the segregation cellblock to begin my first day as a prison guard.

INVESTIGATIVE ARTICLES

Journalists always have been civic watchdogs, and so they always have been involved in investigations. The idea that investigative journalism is something new—a result of the Watergate era—is a misperception, as is the notion that an investigative reporter is anything different from any professional news gatherer.

In a way all in-depth stories are investigative stories because they require a great deal of research, digging and writing. Also, all reporters are investigators who are trained to ask questions, uncover information and write the most complete story possible.

Some reporters, however, concentrate solely on investigations of wrongdoing by a person or agency. They deal with reporter-source adversary relationships that usually are not found in regular in-depth or beat coverage. These reporters are trying to ferret out well-guarded information from often hostile sources.

William Recktenwald, the Chicago Tribune reporter who worked as a prison guard, is one of two permanent members of the Tribune's task force, which is formed periodically with different reporters to carry out scores of investigations. Recktenwald calls himself a general assignment reporter. He started his professional career as an investigator for the Cook County state's attorney's office in Chicago in 1962, when he was 21 years old. He was hired to do undercover work for the state's attorney's 110-member police force.

In 1967 Recktenwald went to work as an investigator for the Better Government Association in Chicago, which provides investigators to work with newspaper and broadcast reporters to uncover corruption and mis-management in government. As a BGA investigator he trained reporters in investigative journalism.

Recktenwald worked on dozens of stories with reporters while he was at the BGA. In 1977 as chief investigator for the BGA, he played a major role in the Chicago Sun-Times' investigation of the shakedowns and payoffs that plagued small businesses throughout the city. The Sun-Times purchased a tavern, renamed it the Mirage and with the BGA ran it for four months. Recktenwald worked as a bartender there.

In early 1978 the Sun-Times ran its Mirage series. The stories de-tailed payoffs to city inspectors to ignore health and safety hazards, shakedowns by state liquor inspectors who demanded cash for silence about liquor violations, illegal kickbacks from jukebox and pinball machine operators and misconduct by public employees who loafed on the job.

Recktenwald left the BGA for the Tribune in 1978. He now helps coordinate investigations for the newspaper and helps develop young reporters interested in doing investigative work.

Tips on Carrying Out an Investigation

Recktenwald gives the following advice to reporters who are involved in investigations:

- *Be briefed completely in an area before starting to investigate it.* If you are going undercover, remember that your first duty is to do the job right and not jeopardize anyone's life. For instance, if you are going to work in a nursing home, your duties in your job come first. If a firm is paying you to do a job, do it, and then be a reporter. (The ethics of undercover journalism are discussed in Chapter 18.)

- *If something is not there, do not make it up.* Do not embellish. Never encourage people to break the law so that you can get a story.

- *If you are going undercover, and you have to use a phony background, make it as close to the truth as possible.* If you must use a false name, at least use your real first name. That way you will not hesitate if someone calls out your name. Use your real birthday, where you were reared, where you went to school and where you have worked (except as a reporter). It always is easy to say you worked someplace for two years when you might have been there only six months. Most of the time your background is not checked. Remember, you cannot lie on forms where you have to give an oath, such as on a driver's license. You *never* should break the law. The news *gathering* process is not protected by the First Amendment. Ninth Circuit Court Judge Shirley Hufstedler made clear in a 1971 court decision *(Dietemann v. Time, Inc.)* that the "First Amendment has never been construed to accord newsmen immunity from torts or crimes committed during the course of news gathering."

- *Avoid leak journalism.* In this way of handling investigations, you must rely on unnamed sources. Instead, rely on *enterprise journalism:* Just stay enthusiastic and work at it. Dig through those boring records. The key to success is perseverance and digging—and digging.

Recktenwald also said the best commandments a reporter involved in an investigation can follow are found every day on the editorial page of the St. Louis Post-Dispatch. It is the Post-Dispatch platform, written by Joseph Pulitzer on April 10, 1907. In describing his newspaper, Pulitzer said:

> I know that my retirement will make no difference in its cardinal principles. That it will always fight for progress and reform, never tolerate injustices or corruption, always fight demagogues of all parties, never belong to any party, always oppose privileged classes and public plunderers, never lack sympathy with the poor, always remain devoted to the public welfare, never be satisfied with merely printing news, always be drastically independent, never be afraid to attack wrong, whether by predatory plutocracy or predatory poverty.

Recktenwald said that it is impossible to overdo stories on topics such as child abuse, government corruption, medical fraud or prison reform because problems always are popping up. "I don't think the cost of the investigation should be a factor in if it should be done, either," he added. "The object is to look at the results of the investigation and put the story together. You can't tag that to costs. How can you compare money to human suffering?"

An Example of an Investigation

One of the young reporters at the Tribune who has worked with Recktenwald is Andy Knott, who came to Chicago as an intern after his senior year at the University of Tennessee. The Tribune hired him permanently at the end of the summer, and Knott was assigned the 5 p.m. to 1 a.m. shift as a general assignment reporter.

"I wanted to be an investigative reporter, but working at nights you only do fires, speeches, murder, rape and squalor," the 26-year-old reporter from Georgia said. "I had some ideas for investigations, but they kept getting kicked back. Some of my ideas were accepted, but they were assigned to older, more experienced reporters."

Then Knott did a wise thing. He went to the newspaper's morgue and read many of the stories resulting from the investigations the Tribune's task force had done over the years. He was impressed with the investigation of private ambulance companies done a decade earlier by William H. Jones (who was now managing editor of the Tribune), and he thought that it would be a good idea to see what had happened in the 10 years since the Pulitzer Prize-winning series ran. He took the idea to Recktenwald, who went to Jones, who approved both the idea and the choice of Knott as the reporter. That started in motion an investigative process that would last nearly a year and change Knott's life forever.

In June Knott started the three-month course for certification as an emergency medical technician (EMT) required of all attendants or drivers for private or public ambulances. It met for two nights a week, so Knott was several hours late for work those two nights. When people asked where he was, he would say, "I was out on a story." At this point only Knott and four other people at the Tribune knew what he was doing.

On his application for the class, Knott used his real name: Thomas A. Knott. "It would have been too complicated to use a fake name because at the end of the class you have to get a license from the city, and you have to use your driver's license," he said.

Knott told his classmates he was a college student from Georgia who was in Chicago for the summer and was interested in taking the course. No one suspected anything else. Forty-five people started the demanding class. Knott and 21 others finished it.

Three weeks after the class ended, Knott found out that he had passed his final exam and was certified by the national registry of EMTs. At that point, his editors told him to get a city license and go out and find a job.

Meantime the Tribune had a separate phone line installed in Knott's apartment with the number he would use on all of his work applications. That way, if that phone rang, Knott would know to answer it as Tom Knott, EMT. He shared the apartment with two other Tribune reporters, and so they were told about the story.

Within three days of getting the approval from his editors to find a job, Knott was working. In the next three months, he would work for 500 hours for five of Chicago's private ambulance services. "They hired me on the spot," he said. "There is a quick turnover. Most companies will hire anyone with a city license. I just went to them and told them I was out of school and wanted a job."

He worked 10-hour shifts, six days a week. His base pay was $3.50 an hour, but he received time and a half for any work over 40 hours. And he suddenly disappeared from the schedule at the Tribune. "I called the night city editor, who had been alerted to the project, and told him I was going undercover," Knott said. "He just took me off the schedule. The word also spread to the assistant city editors that I was on a project, which meant a task force assignment. They were to tell no one. If anyone called, they were to take a message and then call me. After I had been gone about a week, people started talking in the newsroom. Reporters are inherently curious, so they started picking Recktenwald's brain. He wouldn't tell them a thing."

On the job nothing suggested that Knott was anything else but a hillbilly from Georgia. "I really laid on the accent, so to them I was just a hick," he said. "I was driving an old car. I just kept my mouth shut and did my job." After working his 10 hours, Knott would come home and write memos for one or two hours. He took notes during the day on little pieces of paper and stuffed them in his pocket. Ambulance attendants are always writing, and so it was relatively easy for him to take notes. He dated each memo and typed two or three pages of notes a night. When his job ended in November, Knott had 250 pages of notes.

During his undercover work Knott was not allowed to discuss his story with anyone except those authorized to know about the project. He was told to go straight home at night and not to stop at a bar for a drink. "This is a very competitive town, so the biggest fear was that the Sun-Times or a television station would find out about the story," he said. "I had no social life. There was no one to talk to about the story. I had no way to vent off steam. At times I was so depressed. I could not leave for the weekend. I would call Recktenwald at home and talk to him, but I did not want to bother him. It was very strenuous work. I would come home exhausted. After lifting a couple of 300-pound people in a day, I was so tired."

After the actual work experience had ended, the next step in the investigation was to set up a scam to check the condition of the ambulances. That involved two more reporters, photographers and two automotive experts who could inspect the ambulances for wear and tear—without the private companies' knowing about it. It worked this way.

A top-floor apartment in a Chicago high-rise was remodeled to look like the apartment of an invalid, who would be portrayed by one of the older Tribune reporters. A female reporter would play his daughter. She would select a private ambulance firm from the Yellow Pages, call it and ask it to transport her "father" from one residence to another as a non-emergency patient. On the street, in a borrowed van, Knott, the photographers and the two experts would wait for the ambulance to arrive. Knott would wear his EMT uniform, just in case someone, especially police officers, wondered why the people were going through the ambulance.

In January, after several dry runs, the reporters, photographers and experts were ready to go. Ten ambulances were called in three days. As each ambulance arrived, Recktenwald, who portrayed the sick man's son, stood out in the street and signaled the ambulance to park in an alley. Once the crew entered the building, Recktenwald radioed the van in the garage that the attendants were on their way.

With the ambulance parked in the alley, hidden from view from the street, the team came out to do the inspections. The reporter playing the sick man also locked himself in a bathroom in the apartment, which gave the inspectors extra time, but they still had only about 15 minutes to examine the ambulance from top to bottom. Because the team was so well-trained, most inspections only took about eight minutes, and none of the crews ever realized their ambulances had been checked.

While the experts worked the photographers made pictures from all angles. What the experts found was shocking: damaged doors that would not close completely, bare tires, steering columns not secured to dashboards, fire hazards because of faulty wiring, emergency lights not working, speedometer cables broken, brake lights out and more. By the time the inspections were completed and the experts had filed their reports, Knott was armed with information that would produce an explosive series.

Writing the Story

Knott wrote all of February in a separate office he was given in the Tribune building. The photographers were given a separate darkroom. A copy editor, a photo editor and graphics people—all sworn to secrecy—were brought in on the series. Knott wrote—and was told to rewrite—a six-day series. He wrote 50 inches for each day—a 35-inch main story and a 15-inch sidebar—on his experiences as an attendant and on what the experts had found in their investigations. He also called owners of the ambulance firms, told them what he had done and asked for their reaction.

On March 15, nine months and one day after Knott started his class, the series began. A promotion box in the Tribune on the Thursday before the series started told readers, and the competition, what was coming. By the time the promotion ran, 40 people at the Tribune were authorized to know about the project.

"It was my first shot at investigative reporting," Knott said. "It was very intense. I checked everything many times. I knew that if I ever wanted to do it again I had to do it right this time."

In the beginning Knott assumed he would write the series in third person, as a narrative, but because it would carry a single byline and because his experience was so emotional, Knott was given the approval to write in first person. All of the main stories, except the last one, were written that way.

The first story began:

> I'm exhausted after a long, tense day of high-speed ambulance riding through the streets of Chicago.
> This day began at 7 a.m. When we finally limp back to the garage 13 hours and two ambulances later, we have no beacon lights, no siren, no power steering, no shock absorbers. The brakes are in terrible shape.

My partner, Bob, who's driving, isn't doing much better. He stopped twice to drink beer today and he says he's popping Valium "to keep going."

At one point, I thought I'd be killed. With a beer can in one hand and the other on the wheel, he almost lost control of the ambulance as we wove at high speed down a South Side street.

We were "running hot" at the time—lights flashing and siren blaring—even though it was a non-emergency call. I don't know how fast we were going; the speedometer didn't work.

On this day, I also saw fraud and theft. And I can't forget how we terrified the lunchtime crowds as we zipped down busy Michigan Avenue on the wrong side of the street.

I'm expecting more of the same tomorrow and I'm not sure how much longer I can take it.

Today was by no means my worst day. What I've described happened again and again in the 500 hours I worked undercover as a certified emergency technician (EMT) for five of the city's private ambulance services.

Many of their ambulances are dangerous. In my three months on the job, our service to the sick and injured was rarely efficient or safe.

The Results

For six days Knott told readers what he discovered. The results of his series were immediate. Chicago and the State of Illinois announced while the series was running that they would beef up their policing of ambulances. Knott said there were other results:

- Three ambulance firms were shut down temporarily. One went out of business.

- The federal General Services Administration decided to review its guidelines on ambulance specifications for city and state agencies that wanted federal money to help buy ambulances.

- The public was more aware of ambulance abuses. Knott said people started asking more questions about companies they called.

- Chicago police began cracking down on ambulances that were running hot, which forced drivers to be more careful.

- Hospitals that used private ambulance firms to transfer non-emergency patients were much more careful about which firms they called.

The question, of course, in any type of investigative work is, How long will its positive results last? That question is impossible to answer, but it does mean that there always will be fertile ground for investigative journalism. Such abuses are not only city problems, either, so reporters in any size market should be encouraged to investigate problem areas.

1.   How does the daily newspaper in your area treat in-depth articles? Do some in-depths start on Page 1 and jump inside, or is there a separate section?

2.   Select a single subject, such as the rising costs of medical care, and write several lead blocks on it. Use the following leads: summary, anecdotal, contrast, staccato, direct address, question, quote and delayed.

3.   Find examples in your area newspaper of each type of lead on in-depth articles. Rewrite each one into another type.

4.   Select an inverted pyramid news story on Page 1 of a newspaper. How would you change it to make it an in-depth article? What thread could you use to hold together the story?

5.   What are several investigations that need to be done in your community? How about your school?

During the past decade newspapers have accelerated their use of survey research to gather information for stories. Newspapers are relying more and more on electronic computers to assemble and analyze huge, complicated amounts of information. This chapter discusses how reporters can make use of survey research.

You will be introduced to:

• The basics of survey research—how to form survey questions, gather information, analyze information and, most importantly, report information in understandable, human terms.

• Sophisticated projects, aided by computer analysis, that are conducted by metropolitan newspapers. The chapter traces how reporters at the Philadelphia Inquirer blend well-grounded reporting skills with computer analysis.

• Reporting projects that can be performed with low-budget computer help at small- and medium-circulation newspapers. The chapter examines a computer-aided project of the Telegraph Herald in Dubuque, Iowa.

• Ways that college journalism students can stay within limited budgets and still use fresh, relevant computer-generated data for stories.

Reporters in the 1980s are basing more stories on systematically gathered statistical information.

© George Bellerose/Stock, Boston

233

13 USING SOCIAL SCIENCE METHODS

The tasks were demanding.

Reporters at the Philadelphia Inquirer were asked to conduct a systematic study of the city's school system—a district with 26,000 employees, 224,000 children enrolled and an annual budget of more than $700 million.

Reporters at the Telegraph Herald in Dubuque, Iowa were asked to determine what 169 doctors thought about the practice of medicine in the nine-county Dubuque Health Service Area.

Reporting students at the University of North Carolina were asked to write stories about reactions of state residents to a proposed library on the Duke University campus to house former President Richard Nixon's papers.

In each instance the reporters could have checked their morgues for background information and interviewed dozens of persons before blending the information into a series of articles that undoubtedly would have been labeled an *in-depth*. They went beyond these traditional news-gathering techniques, however, and turned to computers to get a more precise basis for their stories.

In a book published in 1973, Philip Meyer alerted working reporters and editors to the feasibility and practicality of using social science methods to gather information. The methods he advocated were quantitative—the use of numbers to measure and evaluate.

The title of Meyer's book, "Precision Journalism," is appropriate. The theme that runs throughout is that social science research methods—methodologically sound sampling procedures and computer analysis—can be used to gather facts, leading to more accurate news stories.

Meyer, who credited the title of his book to Professor Everette E. Dennis of the University of Oregon, wrote that reporters and social scientists in the first half of the twentieth century were "much more alike than they are today." During the 1950s and 1960s, however, social scientists took advantage of electronic computers to gather and analyze vast amounts of information.

Journalists, in the meantime, continued to limit their information-gathering techniques primarily to conducting interviews and scouring documents. Then, more often than not, they would draw "armchair conclusions."

As a reporter for the Beacon Journal in Akron, Ohio, in 1962, Meyer grew frustrated when hand-tabulating 500 voter-preference forms in an attempt to analyze the state's gubernatorial race. He concluded that technology indeed had passed beyond traditional reportorial techniques for gathering news, and he decided to do something about it. He took a year as a Nieman Fellow at Harvard, where he discovered that social scientists were doing "what we journalists like to think of ourselves as best at: finding facts, inferring causes, pointing to ways to correct social problems and evaluating the efforts of such correction."

Meyer put his newly found knowledge to use when he became a correspondent in Knight-Ridder's Washington bureau. He used surveys and other social science methods as a working reporter, and he quickly gained a national reputation for his expertise.

Meyer advised his fellow journalists thus:

> We can save ourselves some trouble, some inaccuracy, and some lost opportunities by merely paying attention to what the social scientists are doing and finding out. More importantly and of more direct value, we can follow their example by abandoning the philosopher's armchair, giving up the notion that a few facts and common sense will make any problem yield, and make the new, high-powered research techniques our own. The task is difficult, yet not so formidable as it might seems at first glance.

In 1978 Professor John N. Rippey of The Pennsylvania State University sent questionnaires to 817 of the nation's 1,750 daily newspapers and received 437 responses. He then published a study in Journalism Quarterly, in which he stated that 37 percent of the newspapers responding to his survey had conducted opinion polls to gather information on which to base news stories. He also found that more than half of the newspapers that had conducted surveys did so for the first time after 1970.

Rippey said his study indicated "an acceleration during the 1970s of the survey research aspect of precision journalism." He also concluded that larger-circulation newspapers were more likely to use survey techniques but that small circulation need not discourage polling.

According to Rippey's study the vast majority of the respondents who conducted polls said that their newspaper staffs did much of the survey work themselves. A "substantial majority of all respondents" said that their news staffs had prime responsibility for determining questions, conducting interviews and analyzing results. Still, many of the newspapers— particularly those with larger circulations—used outside consultants and university researchers to aid more sophisticated polling efforts.

Editors of newspapers that did not conduct surveys during the 1970s singled out lack of staff time as the primary reason. Several editors also pointed to lack of qualified staff to conduct and analyze the surveys as well as limited budgets. About 10 percent of the respondents whose newspapers did not conduct surveys said that they did not believe polling was a valid news-gathering technique.

Despite doubts by some, journalists likely will continue to make greater use of social science techniques to gather information. Several of the country's journalism schools now require courses in research methods and computer science in an effort to better prepare tomorrow's journalists for the increasingly technological field they will be entering.

BASIC SURVEY CONSIDERATIONS

Reporters are not expected to be experts on research design or polling procedures, but a working knowledge of these techniques is helpful. This section is not intended to serve as an "everything you ever will need to know about survey research" overview. Rather, its purpose is to provide a look at some basic survey considerations that are of value to reporters.

A fictional scenario will be constructed to illustrate most effectively these basic considerations. In this example Mike Walters covers the board of education for the Riverdale Daily News, an afternoon newspaper of 12,000-circulation published in a community of 20,000. As is often the case in communities of this size, residents strongly support the public schools.

A current issue, however, has divided the townspeople. Two school board members recently were elected on the platform that modular scheduling should be eliminated in the public schools. Under modular scheduling, students attend 20 class modules of 20 minutes each day. The newly elected board members favor a return to the traditional 7-period day with each period lasting 57 minutes. During their election campaigns, the board aspirants said that modular scheduling was fine for independent, highly motivated students, but average and below-average students—the majority of those enrolled—would be served best by a traditional system.

Walters is apprehensive at the first school board meeting after the election. No one really knows what the newly elected board members might do. When it comes time for new business, one of the newcomers moves that the board mandate a return to the 7-period day. The other newcomer seconds the motion. The motion does not carry—several members object on procedural grounds—but the board does agree to hire outside consultants to measure the effectiveness of modular scheduling in Riverdale.

Walters returns to his office. He tells his editor that he would like to interview several district patrons to determine what community opinion is. Walters says that he intends to station himself at various school buildings around town and interview mothers and fathers as they pick up their children after classes. He will supplement these interviews with comments from teachers, principals, the school superintendent and board members. His editor, Susan Kelly, suggests that a survey would provide a better barometer of community sentiment.

Kelly says that she is familiar with survey basics, but she wants Walters to talk to a professor at Riverdale College for additional guidance. After conversations with the professor, Walters realizes that he must get to work on the project immediately. He must form questions, gather data, analyze the data and then write a story based upon the data.

Forming the Questions

The main goal is to develop a focal question. Here the primary issue is whether most residents favor modular or traditional scheduling. First, Walters writes a brief introductory statement that capsulizes the difference between modular and traditional scheduling. He then formulates several questions, with each fitting under the broad umbrella of the focal issue. Questions are framed so that people will understand them. Generally, it is easiest to structure closed-ended questions, which build answers into the question. Walters decided on the following question: "The Riverdale School Board is considering changing from modular scheduling to traditional 7-period scheduling. Do you prefer modular scheduling or the traditional 7-period scheduling?"

This type of question generally is preferred to open-ended questions, such as "Which type of scheduling do you prefer in the Riverdale schools?" Answers to closed-ended questions are easier to code and tabulate. Walters also structures a handful of other questions. He starts with general questions, such as the number of years the repondent has lived in Riverdale, and then proceeds to issue-oriented specific questions. He reasons that this will help put the respondent at ease.

Walters asks his editor and the college professor to look over his questions for improvements. After getting their reactions, he pretests the questions on some non-editorial department employees at his newspaper who have children in the public schools. Several of them have difficulty understanding the wording of one of the questions, and so Walters makes the language clearer.

Walters is satisfied that his questions are understandable and will indeed help to determine what Riverdale really thinks about modular scheduling. He is ready to pose his questions.

Gathering the Data

Walters now must select the best way to gather the information. Kelly promises him that he can use four general assignment reporters to help conduct the survey. Basically, Walters can use one of three methods to gather the information: mail questionnaire, face-to-face interviews or telephone. All these methods are acceptable; choice of method depends on the situation.

Walters realizes that the *mail questionnaire* is relatively inexpensive, but he is concerned about the possible low rate of return. Also, he wants to get the survey completed as soon as possible and does not want to have to conduct a follow-up if the response rate on the first mailing is low.

Face-to-face interviews would be good, Walters thinks. This way, the reporters conducting the interviews could probe extensively during the questioning process. But this method would take the most time, and also Kelly likely would question the overtime pay.

Walters finally decides that the best way to conduct the survey would be by *telephone*. The telephone affords the luxury of follow-ups and the clarification of answers, which mail surveys are too cumbersome to handle, and it is faster than face-to-face interviewing. He realizes, of course, that his questions must be very clearly drafted and that he must pare them down so that they can be asked in a few minutes. He does not want to irritate the persons being interviewed by asking long irrelevant questions.

Kelly and Walters decide that they are most interested in the opinions of parents who have children in the Riverdale schools. These are the people they want to interview. Random telephone dialing would provide a cross section of the community, but it would not isolate households with school district children. Kelly suggests that Walters talk to the school superintendent. The district should have a list of parents, their addresses and their telephone numbers.

Walters tells the superintendent that the newspaper would like to conduct a survey to determine the opinions of parents. He suggests that the superintendent allow the newspaper to make random selections from the list of parents. For the selection to be random, each household must have an equal chance of being included in the survey.

The superintendent agrees that the survey has merit, but he contends that the names and addresses cannot be released. Finally, a compromise is struck: The superintendent agrees to provide a list of telephone numbers of the parents. He will, however, protect the confidentiality of the parents by not providing their names and addresses.

Thirty-two hundred students are enrolled in the Riverdale schools. Because several parents have more than one child in school, however, Walters finds that 1,500 households have children enrolled. Walters does not have the time to call all the households. The professor suggests that if Walters samples 350 of the 1,500 households, the reporter will be within an acceptable sampling level of confidence (see the section on "Writing the Story," pages 239–241).

The professor tells Walters not to expect all numbers dialed to result in usable responses (some persons will not answer their telephone; others will refuse to participate in the survey). The professor tells Walters to expect about a 70 percent response. Thus, by randomly selecting 500 numbers to be dialed, Walters has a good chance of getting 350 usable responses.

The professor then tells Walters to divide the population—the number of households (1,500)—by the number of calls he will make (500). In this case, Walters will call every third household. Instead of necessarily starting with the first number on the list, however, Walters put the numbers 1, 2 and 3 in a hat. He draws 2. Thus he circles the second telephone number on the list and every third (the *skip interval*) thereafter. He now has a systematic sampling; based upon the "luck of the draw," every household on the list had an equal chance of being included in the survey.

Kelly and Walters then go over the questions with the four reporters who have been assigned to help conduct the survey. They decide to make their calls after 6 p.m., when working parents more likely will be home. The estimate was accurate—500 calls result in 350 usable responses.

Walters could hand-tabulate the results, but the professor offers to show Walters how to computerize the data. It takes Walters about three hours to punch the data into the computer terminal. The professor quickly programs the material. In less than a minute, the computer spits out the results. Walters primarily is interested in percentages.

Analyzing the Data

Walters goes through the information, isolating percentages that he thinks will be of most interest to his readers. He turns to the printout of the survey's key question: "The Riverdale School Board is considering changing from modular scheduling to traditional 7-period scheduling. Do you prefer modular scheduling or the traditional 7-period scheduling?"

Overall 350 persons were asked the question. The responses: modular, 210 (60 percent); traditional, 118 (34 percent); don't know, 22 (6 percent).

Next, Walters looks at the breakdown according to age. Of the 350 who responded, 70 were under age 30; 120 were between ages 30 and 39, 100 were between ages 40 and 49, and 60 were age 50 or older.

The responses:

	Modular	Traditional	Don't know
Under age 30	42 (60 percent)	23 (33 percent)	5 (7 percent)
Ages 30–39	73 (61 percent)	39 (33 percent)	8 (7 percent)
Ages 40–49	65 (65 percent)	29 (29 percent)	6 (6 percent)
Age 50 and older	25 (42 percent)	32 (53 percent)	3 (5 percent)

Walters examines the results of other questions, but he decides to build his lead around this information. He is ready to write his story.

Writing the Story

The percentages show that more than half of all parents polled preferred modular scheduling. In fact, 60 percent of the 350 persons surveyed said that they favored modular scheduling. But how reliable are these figures? After all, not all the parents in the school district were interviewed.

The professor consults a chart and tells Walters that, for a random sample of 350, the *sampling error* is 5.2 percent, which according to most social scientists meets the minimum requirements. In other words, the percentage of the entire population may be 5.2 percent above or below the estimate obtained from the sample of 350. Thus, by finding that 60 percent favor modular scheduling, Walters knows that the true answer lies somewhere between 54.8 percent and 65.2 percent—clearly more than half the population.

Walters learns that a sampling error for any survey based on random selection should be reported. A *confidence interval* is calculated to state the likely error because of chance variations in the sample. The most common interval is the 95 percent level of confidence. This means that the chances are only 1 in 20 that the true answer is not within the range found. The sampling error at the 95 percent level of confidence becomes smaller as the sample size is increased and larger as the size is decreased.

For example, the professor tells Walters that if he were to have randomly selected 600 parents for the modular survey, the sampling error would have been 4 percent. Thus, if he had talked to all the households, there would have been only 1 chance in 20 that the findings would vary from the results of the poll by more than 4 percentage points.

With this in mind Walters writes his lead:

More than half of the parents of Riverdale schoolchildren prefer modular scheduling, a Daily News poll shows.

Walters continues his story with specific results of the survey:

Sixty percent of those surveyed said they preferred modular scheduling; 34 percent said they preferred traditional scheduling; 6 percent said they did not know.

The major opposition to modular scheduling, according to the poll, comes from parents 50 years or older. Of those surveyed in this age bracket, 53 percent said they favored traditional scheduling; 42 percent said they preferred modular scheduling; 5 percent said they did not know.

Walters' story goes on to detail other findings of the survey. He also inserts the following:

The Daily News randomly interviewed 350 parents in the Riverdale School District. Telephone interviews were conducted last Wednesday and Thursday evenings by Daily News reporters.

As with all sample surveys, the results of the Daily News poll can vary from the opinions of all school district parents because of chance variations in the sample.

For a poll based on 350 interviews, the results are subject to an error margin of 5.2 percentage points each way because of such chance variations. That is, if one could have talked Wednesday and Thursday to all Riverdale School District parents with telephones, there is only 1 chance in 20 that the findings would vary from the results of surveys such as this one by more than 5.2 percentage points.

Walters, who conducted his survey in a relatively short time and at little expense, inserted the explanatory paragraphs to keep within the guidelines suggested by the National Council on Public Polls. The Associated Press Stylebook suggests that editors and reporters consider the guidelines before using a story about a canvass of public opinions.

The guidelines are as follows:

- Who paid for the poll?
- When was the poll taken?
- How were the interviews obtained?
- How were the questions worded?
- How were the people chosen?
- How many people responded?
- How big was any smaller group on which conclusions are based?

"The New York Times Manual of Style and Usage" states that occasionally all polling details cannot be included in a story. The manual concludes: "If there ever is a doubt, the reporter should include as much of the information as possible. The responsible editors can then decide how much should be used."

The Times manual also cautions that terms such as *opinion poll, poll, survey, opinion sample* and *cross section* "should be limited to truly scientific soundings of opinion. They should not be applied to stringer roundups and man-in-the-street stories by reporters."

THE PHILADELPHIA INQUIRER PROJECT

Mary Bishop was hired as the education writer for the Philadelphia Inquirer in January 1979. Executive Editor Gene Roberts told her that sometime in the future she would be asked to conduct a major, systematic study of the Philadelphia School District. Bishop worked the education beat for about a year and a half; she reported on board of education issues, school finances, labor matters, teacher contract disputes and deployment of personnel. The job helped train her for the challenging project she was destined to undertake.

In June 1980 Bishop was given the assignment she had been waiting for: She was to write a series of articles that focused on the school district. She and reporter Tom Ferrick were told to work full time on the enormous undertaking.

How would they even begin to dissect an urban school district? The size of the Philadelphia system was staggering.

"Tom and I sat down and discussed all the things we thought were wrong with the district," Bishop said. "Since I had been covering the education beat for 18 months, I filled him in on the hierarchy of the system. We discussed possible topics. Already, the task seemed enormous, but it became bigger as work on the project progressed. We thought patronage, contracts, educational quality, racial bias, budget management and school board politics were possible topics."

Bishop and Ferrick checked whether any other newspaper had attempted an analysis of an urban school district to the extent the reporters envisioned. They found no precedents. "After six months we discovered why no other newspaper had attempted it—it was so damn tough," Ferrick said.

Bishop and Ferrick discussed the most efficient, reliable ways to gather information for the series. Traditionally, reporters would talk to teachers, principals, students and community leaders. Budgets and other statistics supplied—and interpreted—by the district would be examined; bottom-line operational expenses would be reported. A profile of the district as told by people who have a stake in it would emerge.

The Inquirer reporters, however, wanted more than basic school district stories to constitute the series. "We wanted to do something empirical in the sense that we would take the district apart piece by piece, gather our own data, set it out on the table, get our own perspective on how the district operated and then go out to talk to people about what we found," Ferrick said.

To arm themselves with an extensive arsenal of information, the reporters looked at minutes of school board meetings, budgets and other public documents. They examined the 7,200 contracts let by the Philadelphia School District from 1975 through June 1980. The data they gathered were so diffuse that it became obvious that they would need the help of a computer to lay the groundwork for the project.

"The school board has to approve all contracts," Ferrick said. "These appear chronologically in board meetings. So we went through all the minutes and grouped into categories all the contracts that were let. For example, we created categories for money spent on books, on audio visual supplies, on paint and on other such items. The school district's budget did not break these types of expenditures into component parts, so we used the Inquirer's IBM computer to help us."

Bishop and Ferrick were given a brief lesson on how to operate IBM computer terminals, quite different from the terminals they used in the newsroom. The reporters holed up in a 9- by 15-foot room on the 13th floor of the Inquirer's building at 400 N. Broad St. The reporters moved in two cafeteria tables, two chairs, two telephones and two computer terminals. The walls were lined with pictures of schoolchildren to serve as a reminder of what the undertaking was all about.

The project required patience. It took three months to feed the contract data into the computer terminals. A fourth month was required to proof it. "This was not a job for reporters who require daily bylines in order to feel productive," Ferrick said.

When they had logged all that data into the computer, a printer spat out a foot-tall stack of printouts on district spending. Then they turned to the gathering of other information on each of the district's 273 schools: age of the main buildings and annexes, pupil capacities, enrollment breakdowns over a 5-year period, racial breakdowns over 5 years, student and teacher attendance, the percentage of inexperienced teachers assigned to each school, results of California Achievement Tests over a 5-year period and other data. And, from their printouts on school contracts, they had expenditures for outside maintenance done at each school.

All the information was gathered from public records. "We found most of it in the city library," Ferrick said. "We punched it on the computer cards, but after we were through compiling the information, we needed help to interpret it."

Using Statistical Analysis

Ferrick went to Miami to meet with Knight-Ridder Newspaper researcher N. Reilly Kirby. Using the Statistical Package for the Social Sciences (SPSS), Kirby ran statistical tests on the information Ferrick sought. SPSS is a preprogrammed computer package that produces most commonly used statistics from raw data.

"I had no knowledge of the capabilities of SPSS," Ferrick said. "I knew what information I wanted, though, and Kirby got it for me. He made it look easy."

Ferrick returned to Philadelphia loaded with statistics, but the battle was only beginning. He and Bishop realized that they would be hard pressed to put together general interest stories from the data. It was time to conduct the field work. In November they were joined by a third reporter, Donald Kimelman. During the winter and spring months, the three reporters visited dozens of schools and conducted hundreds of interviews. They checked out tips on patronage. They accompanied maintenance crews to check on the condition of various district schools.

"We worked hard to make sure our stories were not merely a compilation of statistics," Ferrick said. "Reporters must be careful not to get bogged down in the data when putting together stories of this type."

Indeed, statistics can be fascinating, but developing stories based in part on social science research methods involves three steps: (1) gathering the information, (2) synthesizing it and (3) presenting it to the public in understandable form.

"In journalism you must get the reader's attention," Ferrick said. "You cannot clutter a story with data. It is easy to become so fascinated with the information that you want to spit it all out, to tell it to everyone in excruciating detail. But people won't read that. Reporters must learn to humanize the statistics. You must show the human face."

How did Bishop, Ferrick and Kimelman humanize the cold, hard figures the computer gave them?

Headlines that appeared over stories published in the week-long series help tell the story:

- "How Philadelphia's children are neglected by the system"
- "Philadelphia's failure: Educating its children"
- "District gets poor marks in survey of residents"
- "The city and the suburbs: How the money is spent"
- "The patronage game: It's not what you know, but who"
- "How inept teachers thrive in the district"
- "Absent teachers: A costly presence in the school district"
- "Despite obstacles, some keep a shine on the apple"
- "Buildings, through neglect, are falling apart at the seams"
- "Also neglected: The tools students use to learn"
- "The new segregation: It's largely a matter of brains"
- "Principal's diary: He tells it like it is"
- "Junior highs: An idea whose time has passed"
- "Those big test gains are but a small step in learning"
- "The final test: No leadership for the schools or the students"
- "A tale of two students and a teacher who cared"

An Extensive Series

Bishop, Ferrick and Kimelman quickly grabbed readers' attention in the overview article for the series:

> In the struggle over who gets what in the Philadelphia School District, it is the children who lose out.
>
> Plaster crumbles from their classroom walls because too little money is budgeted for maintenance. Books, paper, crayons, pencils, musical instruments and athletic equipment are in short supply. Homework is often not assigned because there are not enough textbooks to let students take them home.
>
> The teachers do better for themselves.
>
> They get more money and fringe benefits than teachers in any other large urban district in America. They also rank first in absenteeism. They work shorter hours than teachers elsewhere, and their union shelters the lazy and incompetent from removal and imposes work rules that are costly and restrictive. Through a combination of frequent strikes and skillful lobbying, the teachers' union has come to dominate the system.

The reporters supported their sweeping assertions with statistics—hard, cold facts.

One of the most basic statistically generated stories in the series was built around a survey of district residents. The newspaper wanted to find out what Philadelphians thought about their school district. The Inquirer commissioned a research firm (at a cost of $1,500) to conduct a survey that consisted of telephone interviews of a random sample of 752 adults who lived in Philadelphia. One of the most significant findings of the survey was that 81 percent had no children in the public schools; they had no school-age children or if they did they were keeping them out of the public school system. The reporters concluded that "the vast majority of Philadelphians have no direct stake in the school system and that their opinion of its performance has not been formed through direct experience."

The Inquirer put into perspective its statistical analysis of the money spent for building maintenance, textbooks and supplies by comparing it with the money spent by the other school districts in the country that ranked in the top 10 by size: New York, Houston, Baltimore, Chicago, Detroit, Miami, Dallas, San Diego and Los Angeles. The statistics showed that only New York spent less per pupil on these items than did Philadelphia.

Another story in which precision journalism methods were used was in a districtwide analysis of the results of the California Achievement Test (CAT). So often, newspaper stories on school test scores merely compare the most recent scores to those of previous years. That is simple enough. But the Inquirer reporters wanted a more meaningful analysis. They examined five years of test scores from each school in the district. The scores were obtained from official school district documents. The information was fed into a computer and the results were analyzed using the SPSS. A wide variance among schools was found.

But the reporters did not stop at reporting the variance in scores. They examined the information available on the schools and their students in an attempt to determine what *caused* the variance. Without the use of the computer to isolate the factors that could affect scores, the journalists merely could have drawn armchair conclusions by interviewing school district employees. At best their story would have been built around educated speculation. By using the computer, however, the reporters were able to develop an empirical answer. Their conclusion: "Race of students or teachers, age and condition of school building, teacher attendance and class size had only minor effects on the CAT scores." The two factors "with the greatest influence were poverty and student attendance. In other words, schools with the fewest poor students and the lowest absentee rates tended to do the best on the CAT."

An impressive thing about the Inquirer's series was the way reporters Bishop, Ferrick and Kimelman were able to construct several stories around computer-generated facts without hammering readers with a barrage of statistics. To emphasize how poorly equipped the Philadelphia district was (as clearly indicated by the comparison of dollars spent for necessary supplies in other urban systems), the reporters led a story with this vivid word picture:

It is an interesting world that unfolds in a seventh-grade geography textbook used at Beeber Junior High School in West Philadelphia.

It is a world where Main Street is lined with trees and with Hudsons and DeSotos; where Dwight D. Eisenhower is President, the United States leads the world in oil production, women work happily in their kitchens and Negroes pick cotton in the South.

It is a world of promise. Someday, great superhighways will link our cities. Someday, the African nations will be free from colonialism. And someday, in the distant future, man might even land on the moon.

Most Philadelphia textbooks aren't nearly this out-of-date, but some are. The reason that any stay in use is simple, but sad: This is one of America's poorest equipped urban school systems.

Clearly, the Inquirer reporting team's 15-month project was an awesome combination of excellent planning, excellent reporting, excellent writing and excellent use of human *and* computer resources. The series shows that newspaper reporters can make effective use of social science methods to strengthen people-oriented stories.

Certainly, the people of Philadelphia were provided with a penetrating analysis of their city school district. And though it was coincidental, two days after the series concluded, Philadelphia's teachers struck. Fifty days later they returned to their classrooms.

THE DUBUQUE TELEGRAPH HERALD PROJECT

Large-circulation dailies, with huge labor power and economic resources, naturally produce more stories based on social science research techniques than do dailies with circulations under 50,000. The Philadelphia Inquirer can afford to free two reporters for a 15-month project. The Telegraph Herald (circulation 41,500) in Dubuque, Iowa, is not in a position to do that, but the Telegraph Herald, which has a long record of state and national awards for excellence, has engaged in some excellent precision journalism projects without tying up reporters and extra dollars for extended periods.

James A. Geladas, former managing editor of the Telegraph Herald and now its manager of project research, pointed to one of the many impressive projects undertaken by his staff: A series that examined physicians' attitudes about the practice of medicine in the Dubuque area.

The series cost $280 out of pocket and required 185 staff hours. The staff hours did not include planning sessions.

"By virtue of our early exposure to precision journalism techniques, we got the jump on most papers our size," Geladas said. "We quickly learned that precision journalism requires a strong commitment from management, but it is well worth it, in my opinion."

Reporters Jack Brimeyer and John McCormick put together the series. Just as the Philadelphia Inquirer reporters did, Brimeyer and McCormick carefully blended statistics with human angles. Using a direct address lead in their overview story, the reporters wrote:

If you're typical, you'll see a doctor almost five times this year. If your doctor is typical, he won't have time to give you the care he'd like.

There are 252,000 of you swamping 177 of them in the nine-county Dubuque Health Service Area.

And swamped they are, they said in response to a Telegraph Herald survey of physicians.

Through their offices will pass 1.2 million patients this year. Our doctors will visit another half-million patients at hospitals and, contrary to stereotypes, they'll make 11,000 housecalls.

The overview article outlined main survey findings: Two of 10 of the doctors had been sued for malpractice; medical care was good, but could be better; almost all the physicians said that their jobs were satisfying, but six of 10 said that their lives were getting worse, and half of the small-town doctors had "noticed an increase in the number of patients with imaginary illnesses since America's economy began to sour."

The series also examined the average age of the physicians, their religions, their average tenure in the Dubuque area, their average incomes, their total billings for services during the year and the average number of hours they work each week. The reporters supplemented these statistics with interviews with area physicians and hospital officials.

Statistical information was generated from a mail questionnaire sent to the 169 physicians who had full staff privileges at one or more of the 17 hospitals in the Dubuque area; 131 of the doctors completed the four-page questionnaire.

According to Brimeyer and McCormick the newspaper used the University of Iowa's IBM 360 computer to tabulate the findings. It produced 812 pages of statistical findings. The Telegraph Herald used a specialist in physician studies from Ohio University to help plan and analyze the survey.

The Dubuque project certainly was not as immense as the Philadelphia Inquirer's school series, but it was a superlative effort by a medium-circulation daily to blend computer-generated statistics with quotations and information gleaned from personal interviews and other medical sources. The physician series clearly illustrates that by combining staff resources, university resources and management support, newspapers do not have to be metropolitan in size to produce precision journalism articles.

PRECISION JOURNALISM IN COLLEGE CLASSES

The use of social science research methods to gather information for news stories need not be limited to daily newspapers. According to an article by Patty Courtwright in the UNC Journalist, students in the mass communication research class and the advanced reporting class at the University of North Carolina at Chapel Hill combine their efforts each year to produce and report a survey called The Carolina Poll.

Students in Professor Robert L. Stevenson's research methods class make use of the theoretical concepts outlined in their textbook by designing the questions, conducting the poll and analyzing the results. Students in the advanced reporting class taught by Professor Philip Meyer reduce the statistics to layman's terms and write stories that are distributed by the university's news service to papers throughout the state.

Many profit: Students in the research class have an opportunity to apply the theory they study; students in the reporting class have a chance to base their stories on fresh, relevant, computer-generated data; newspapers in the state that could not afford to commission or conduct a statewide poll receive stories from the UNC news service to publish, and readers of North Carolina are enlightened about contemporary issues.

Journalism students involved in the 1981 poll received some assistance from the professional media. The Knight Publishing Co., which publishes the Charlotte (N.C.) News and the Charlotte Observer, provided a computer-generated random list of telephone numbers for the poll. This list served as the basis of the sample. Each student enrolled in the two courses spent at least eight hours making telephone calls to 592 people randomly selected from the state's 100 counties. The students also received help from the UNC Center for Public Television, which provided telephones and paid for the long-distance billings. Clearly, it was a team effort; contributions from the academic and professional communities blended well.

The stories, written by advanced reporting students, were given good play in the state's newspapers. Of particular interest to the state's residents were the stories written in 1981. That year a controversial issue developed in North Carolina when Duke University President Terry Sanford announced that the institution had been negotiating with former President Richard Nixon to build a library to house Nixon's presidential papers.

Student Harry Greyard's story began:

> Public opinion in North Carolina is divided on the proposed Nixon library at Duke University, although a large number of the state's residents say they do not know if the library should be built.
>
> Thirty-eight percent of the population favors construction of the library on the Duke campus, 38 percent opposes the project and 24 percent does not know.
>
> The figures are from the Carolina Poll, a public opinion survey conducted by the School of Journalism at the University of North Carolina at Chapel Hill and cosponsored by the UNC Center for Public Television.

Greyard went on to discuss other results of the poll: More men than women supported the plan (44 percent compared with 30 percent); more whites than blacks supported the plan (41 percent compared with 26 percent), and more persons whose family incomes exceeded $20,000 supported the plan than did those whose income was less than $20,000 (42 percent compared with 36 percent).

Greyard also included quotations from Duke faculty members who commented on the poll and the effect it would have on the controversy.

Mike Spear's story on North Carolinians' approval of the Reagan presidency also received good play in the state's newspapers. Spear compared the Carolina poll results with a national survey:

> North Carolinians think Ronald Reagan is doing his job all right, according to a statewide public opinion survey conducted last month.
> Sixty-two percent of those polled gave the president a favorable job performance rating, a higher mark than the 57 percent he received in a nationwide Louis Harris poll conducted in August.
> The Carolina Poll also suggested that the president had picked up some support in the state, where he won an electoral victory last year with only 49 percent of the vote.
> But Reagan's political power base appeared to be largely among whites. The poll found 26 percent of the whites questioned said Reagan was doing an excellent job, compared to 5 percent of the blacks.

Spear went on to give the precise question that persons surveyed were asked: "How would you rate the job Ronald Reagan has been doing as president—excellent, pretty good, only fair or poor?"

The story was laced with direct quotations from some of the people who responded. The story concluded with an explanation of the sample surveyed and the sampling error and revealed when the poll was conducted.

The North Carolina students never could have written authoritative stories on the issues merely by interviewing a handful of people. Statistically reliable social science survey methods, combined with accurate interpretation of data and straightforward reporting in layman's terms, helped to provide North Carolina newspaper subscribers with readable stories that summarized public opinion on important state issues.

Students who are exposed to social science reporting methods and who have the ability to analyze computer-generated data could find themselves valued staff members when they take their first reporting jobs. Student journalists should not complain about the irrelevancy of required computer science or research methods courses. Rather, they should make every effort to develop an understanding of these important concepts. Journalists of the future likely will make increasing use of these methods.

DANGERS OF POLL PROLIFERATION

Social science reporting methods most commonly are used at newspapers during election campaigns to measure opinions about candidates and major issues. Of course, as has been discussed, social science methods also can be used to augment newspaper stories on topics ranging from an analysis of lower achievement scores in some grade schools to an analysis of doctors' opinions about health care in Dubuque, Iowa. Newspapers of various circulations can enter the precision journalism arena relatively easily. Only those newspapers that have the labor power, the expertise and the available money to do the job right, however, should base stories on precision journalism methods.

Richard Wirthlin, pollster for the Republican National Committee in 1980, told the American Society of Newspaper Editors that newspapers should use polls to measure attitude, which would produce more analytical reporting. Polls should not merely be used to predict who will win or lose an election.

Peter Hart, another expert who has done polling for the Democratic National Committee, suggested that newspapers run their normal poll stories on prominent news pages but then list all poll questions and results in agate type in another part of the newspaper where space can be sacrificed.

According to Editor & Publisher, Hart urged editors not to leap into polling only during an election. He suggested that editors get an expert to conduct their polls if no one on the staff has expertise in both politics and polling research.

James Gannon, executive editor of the Register and Tribune in Des Moines, Iowa, told the American Society of Newspaper Editors that it is "not hard to find plenty to criticize about polls and the way they were handled by newspapers, especially in election year 1980." Here are Gannon's main criticisms:

- There was "overkill" in polling. "Polls proliferated like mushrooms in the sweaty, competitive atmosphere of an election-year climate. More and more newspapers and television stations cranked up their own polls. According to one count I've seen, there were more than 140 published polls operating in 1980." Quite simply, "Polls became a bore."

- Prominent display of polls in newspapers suggested an "over-fascination with survey data."

- Too many polls that newspapers published did not give readers all the information they needed to understand totally the significance—or lack thereof—of the surveys.

1.   Ask a professor at your school who specializes in research methods to provide your class with some raw computer data. Write news stories that translate the data into understandable language for the layman.

2.   Clip news stories based on surveys from area newspapers. Do all of the stories include the information suggested by the National Council on Public Polls?

3.   Invite a polling expert to your class to discuss political surveys. Does he or she think journalists adequately report survey findings?

4.   Clip articles from area newspapers. Discuss which of the articles could have been improved by the use of social science research methods. Outline how you would have conducted the precision project.

Some of the worst writing in contemporary newspapers is published on the sports pages. Significantly, however, some of the best writing also is published on sports pages. This chapter examines contemporary sportswriting and sports coverage.

You will be introduced to:

• The differences between writing game stories for morning newspapers and writing stories based on the same games for afternoon newspapers.

• Different philosophies of covering high school and college sports.

• The intense preparation necessary for solid sports coverage. The discussion focuses on planning behind Omaha (Neb.) World-Herald coverage of that perennial national football power, the University of Nebraska.

• Different writing approaches reporters from various newspapers use when covering the same football game.

• Basic considerations for writing sports features.

• The types of news events that are covered not only by sports reporters but also by general assignment reporters.

For sports reporters, intense coverage of an athletic conference begins long before the players take the field and continues long after the final play is over.

© Anthony Neste/Focus on Sports

14 IN THE PRESS BOX

Critics long have contended that too many newspaper sports page stories read something like this:

> The powerful, invincible Clay Center Wildcats, behind sizzling sophomore sensation Billy "Wild Horse" Gratopp, rambled roughshod over an outmanned, underweight but scrappy Harvard contingent 36-0 in high school football Friday.
>
> The Wildcats, riding the broad shoulders and strong legs of Gratopp, roared to a 21-0 halftime advantage and were never headed.
>
> "Billy came to play," said his coach, Bobby "Big Red" Johnson. "He's a coachable kid who always gives 110 percent. If I had two more just like him, nobody could touch us. He's been like a son to me."
>
> Harvard coach Scott Blatchford agreed. "The kid plays with intensity," he said. "But what it boils down to—the bottom line—is Clay Center wanted this game more than we did. Football is a game of inches—and they got the breaks today. They out-quicked us off the ball; we didn't play aggressively. Our kids just plain flat out didn't take it to them."
>
> Instead, it was the sturdy, tough Gratopp who did all the taking.
>
> Gratopp, a 6-1, 195-pounder with a 19-inch neck, played like the combination gazelle-battering ram he closely resembles. Harvard defenders bounced off him like rebounded basketballs as he ran for 239 yards in total offense. His five touchdowns—on runs of 32, 41, 18, 44 and 16 yards—set a school record.
>
> It was his 51-yard scamper that ended short of paydirt, however, that had the crowd abuzz. The lightning bolt dash set up Clay Center's first six-pointer of the evening.

Lewis Gannett, book reviewer for the old New York Herald Tribune, once wrote, "Most sports writers suffer from hyperthyroid congestion of adjectives and are dope fiends for forced similes."

Cliché-riddled stories are not gone from today's sports pages, but they are found less frequently. Sportswriting has matured; the trend is away from cheerleading and toward a more critical approach. The verbs remain strong—as well they should—but unquestioning, lavish, profuse praise is used more sparingly. No longer should all sports reporters be thought of as second-raters who failed to mature into serious journalists.

Wick Temple, Associated Press general sports editor, said that the transition from gushy adoration to "legitimate journalism" began in the late 1960s. Critics continue to contend, however, that sportswriting still is too "gee-whiz" and "rah-rah," but some prominent coaches claim that this is not so. Editor & Publisher quoted Penn State football coach Joe Paterno as saying, "Journalists usually refer to us as 'the other side.'"

More than writing style has changed on the sports page. Wally Provost, sports columnist for the Omaha (Neb.) World-Herald and former sports editor, said the biggest changes in sports page content over the past 30 years are "due to television's glamorizing of certain sports, and by the advent of recreational sports stemming from affluence and added leisure time."

Provost cites professional football, basketball and golf as prime examples of television's influence. "They receive far more coverage now," Provost said. Amateur baseball and golf are among sports page items receiving generally less coverage today. Sports sections carry more on leisure activities—from water sports to hang-gliding. Provost said that some of this may "reflect a prod from similar coverage from Sports Illustrated," where excellent writing abounds.

David Shaw, media critic for the Los Angeles Times, in a 129-column-inch article about the evolution of sports coverage, said sportswriting in earlier eras consisted primarily of adjectives, scores and statistics—sometimes called "meat and potatoes" reporting. Shaw wrote, however, that "the times—and the nation's sports pages—they are a changin', and it is now no longer sufficient to write sports stories by the numbers . . . or by the clichés." Shaw said the sports department has gradually shifted "from its traditional image as the toy department of the newspaper."

DIFFERENCES BETWEEN AM AND PM SPORTS COVERAGE

For the most part, morning and afternoon newspapers cover the same athletic events played the night before, but the writing angles should be different. Traditionally, morning newspapers offer a more straightforward account of the preceding night's game; readers who open their morning newspapers might not even know the score of the game they are interested in. The reporter who covers the game generally is rushed to make his deadline; the story must be complete, but quite often there is not sufficient time to conduct extensive interviews or develop a feature lead.

By contrast, sports reporters working for afternoon newspapers have time to write comprehensive stories that encompass not only the essential ingredients (victor, score, team records and so on) but also a unique angle or feature lead. They therefore lose the standard alibi given for a poorly written story—they cannot contend that they were under extreme deadline pressure. These sports reporters should analyze the game they cover, for most of their readers know the score before they open their newspapers. They should combine a synopsis of the game, a statistical summary and an angle not covered in morning newspapers or by the electronic media. The afternoon account should not be a play-by-play rehash.

When Arizona State University's nationally ranked basketball team was upset by the University of Kansas in the second round of the NCAA basketball playoffs on a Sunday, the Monday morning Arizona Republic and the afternoon Phoenix Gazette used different leads.

Using a relatively straightforward approach, with the score mentioned high in the story, Dan Daly wrote for the Republic the following:

WICHITA, Kan.—Arizona State went quietly Sunday in the second round of the National Collegiate Athletic Association basketball tournament. Not only that, the Sun Devils were beaten at their own game.

Kansas guards Tony Guy and Darnell Valentine literally ran ASU into the ground at Wichita State's Henry Levitt Arena. They combined for 52 points, many of them off fast breaks, to lead the Jayhawks (24-7) to an 88-71 upset victory and a spot in the Midwest Regional semifinals in New Orleans.

Guy, 6-foot-6, had an extraordinary game, scoring a career-high 36 points on 13-for-15 shooting from the field.

By the time readers opened their Monday afternoon newspapers, most of them knew the score of Sunday's game. Structuring a lead around the fact that several of the nation's top-rated teams had been beaten in the early rounds of the tournament, Jerry Guibor wrote this in the afternoon Phoenix Gazette:

WICHITA, Kan.—It was not as if Arizona State was unaware that something dreadful was happening to the nation's top basketball teams.

"We were talking about it at breakfast," said sophomore guard Byron Scott. "We knew we had to go out and play well."

The truth of the matter is that the Devils didn't.

Instead, the Devils stood around, shot poorly—except for Scott—and, as they grew more impatient with a clogging zone, watched their growing aspirations to win the NCAA title go down the drain.

The Kansas Jayhawks were the spoilers, blowing ASU out of the 48-team tournament in the second round, 88-71, before 10,666 fans at Henry Levitt Arena Sunday.

Kansas (24-7) advanced to the Midwest Regional at New Orleans where the Jayhawks will face bitter rival Wichita State (25-6) Thursday for the first time since 1955.

Ten more paragraphs of player and coach quotations followed, each trying to explain what had happened to the Sun Devils. It was not until the bottom one-third of the story that Guibor focused on the performances of Guy and Valentine.

It is imperative that sports reporters for afternoon dailies devise game story angles that are markedly different from those used in morning editions, but details of the game itself still must be provided. Normally, statistical details are in the bottom halves of the stories.

HIGH SCHOOL SPORTS COVERAGE

Coverage of high school sports often is the first assignment a sports reporter directly out of college receives. The prep sports beat can be viewed as the best and worst of assignments. Colorado Springs Gazette-Telegraph Prep Sports Editor Terry Henion described it:

It is a genuine pain in the neck sometimes to have to keep statistics and never get to see the game. It's a pain to listen to a wild-eyed mother question your roots because you misspelled her daughter's name in a summary. It's a pain—and somewhat frightening—to have a father scream wildly at you because you are not giving his son enough "ink." It's a pain to cover six or seven games a week and rarely see your family.

But it's a pleasure to watch an awkward and timid sophomore develop into a poised and polished senior. It's a pleasure to see kids play games for the fun of it without the pressure and hard sell of college and pro sports. It's a pleasure to see the smiles on their faces and in a way a pleasure to see their tears when they lose because the emotions are honest.

Henion said, in the long run, "the pleasures of covering high school sports greatly outweigh the pains, and that's why I enjoy it so much. High school sports are what sports were always meant to be: kids playing kids' games."

At most high schools, there is no sports information director cranking out play-by-play charts, keeping statistics and providing player quotations after the game. The work must be done by the sports reporters, who usually find themselves walking the sideline at a football game or crammed into tight quarters at a basketball game. *Covering* a prep game almost is a misnomer, according to Henion. He thinks that *documenting* might be a better description. Henion, who also covers college athletics, said that the prep writer cannot always concentrate on doing what a good writer should do—answer the human interest questions fans would ask if they had access to the locker room. Instead reporters must keep the statistics (or rely on a 14-year-old student manager who tends to inflate his team's numbers), interview the coaches and players and then formulate a readable game account. Often the work is done under deadline pressure.

Some high school coaches also prefer that reporters not talk to players after games. The wise reporter will respect those wishes. A quote taken out of context can harm the player, the coach or the entire program. An important thing to remember when interviewing a high school athlete, though, is that these are youngsters—they are not poised athletes in college or professional programs.

As Henion said, "You're dealing with kids who usually never have felt the sting of a razor, let alone the cutting edge of a perhaps cynical and bored writer. Temperance is the word when quoting high school athletes." Henion labeled the use of quotations as being possibly "the touchiest area of covering high school sports."

COLLEGE SPORTS COVERAGE

Coverage of major college football is a choice assignment; it also is a difficult one. The conscientious reporter does not merely arrive at the stadium five minutes before kickoff, pick up the sports information office's statistics after the game and peck out a routine 750-word story.

Planning for a Saturday afternoon game begins the Sunday before the contest in the sports department at the Omaha World-Herald. Stories are published daily starting Monday about the upcoming University of Nebraska-Lincoln opponent (occasionally the newspaper hires a stringer to staff the foe's open practice sessions). The articles focus on injuries, lineups and general preparation for Saturday's game. Of course, daily stories also are published that center on Nebraska preparations.

On football Saturdays in Nebraska, Cornhusker football is a news event from 6 a.m. until 6 p.m. Saturday morning World-Herald editions lead with an advance on the game, lineups and season records for both teams. If the game is televised, the paper publishes a complete roster, in large type, for the convenience of the reader–viewer.

Though Saturdays might be festive for fans, it is a grueling workday for the 19 World-Herald reporters, editors, desk people and photographers who shape their schedules around the game. Sports Editor Steve Kline arrives at his Omaha office at 6 a.m., reads the morning newspapers and leaves for Lincoln—50 miles away—at about 7 a.m. He coordinates coverage from the press box. Three writers are assigned: one to do the primary game account; one to do sidebar material and the Nebraska postgame locker room, and a third to walk the sideline for fan sidebars, to cover the opposing team's locker room and to interview the opposing team's coach. The reporters exchange quotes and information. In addition, a team of photographers shoots sequential photos—one set in black and white, one in color—of every play. Photographers are stationed around the field, two shooting color, the rest shooting black and white.

Normally there is ample space in the Sunday edition for this extensive coverage. Copy desk editors constantly plan their pages as the game is played. Between 65 and 70 news columns are reserved for the Sunday sports section during football season—nearly double the space on other Sundays. The World-Herald makes the most of it; during an important Nebraska–Oklahoma game played in Lincoln, nearly half the section was devoted to the contest.

The Cornhuskers, rated third in the nation going into the game, lost 21-17. Many newspapers around the country carried a concise, straightforward wire service account of the game similar to this:

Oklahoma scored a game-winning touchdown with 56 seconds remaining to lift the Sooners to a 21-17 Big Eight Conference football victory over Nebraska in Lincoln Saturday.

It was the ninth time in the last ten games the Sooners have prevailed.

If Oklahoma beats Oklahoma State Saturday, the Sooners will represent the Big Eight in the Orange Bowl. Nebraska will be relegated to the Sun Bowl.

Newspapers in regions directly affected by the game, however, approached the story from different perspectives. Each focused on details most relevant to their readers. For example, Tom Ash wrote for the World-Herald:

> Blinded by flashbacks and the luster of a youngster called Buster, Nebraska gulped hard and swallowed yet another stunning setback by Oklahoma Saturday.
>
> The Sooners, working into a south wind that had decidedly favored the downwind offense to that point, cooked up an 80-yard touchdown drive that carried into the final minute and topped off a stirring 21-17 victory.
>
> With a one-yard touchdown by freshman halfback George "Buster" Rhymes in the final 56 seconds another great depression settled over Huskerland.
>
> The majority of a boisterous Memorial Stadium turnout of 76,332 had gathered to cheer on a Cornhusker team that both sides agreed was more talented. A first outright Big Eight championship since 1971 and a trip to the Orange Bowl awaited. The sidelines and end zones were littered with oranges, the result of a blizzard that accompanied Nebraska's early 10-point advantage.

In the first 150 words of his story, Ash gave the essentials: the score and the victor. He also told how the game was won, who was responsible for the Sooner victory, the weather conditions, the mood of the Husker crowd, the attendance and the results of 10 previous games. He also made it clear that Oklahoma, not Nebraska, would be going to the Orange Bowl—the scattered citrus of several Nebraska fans to the contrary.

Orange Bowl officials, prior to the game, had made it no secret that they wanted Nebraska to win. With this in mind John Meyer wrote in the News-Sentinel of Fort Lauderdale, Fla.:

> The Orange Bowl's grand scheme to become the stage upon which college football's national championship is settled suffered a grievous wound Saturday, thanks to an Oklahoma freshman who longed to see his native Miami Jan. 1.
>
> George "Buster" Rhymes, an alumnus of Miami's Northwestern High who paid absolutely no attention to home-state recruiters last year, didn't want to "spend the rest of my life in Miami."
>
> Almost certainly he denied Nebraska a trip to his hometown for the holidays. It was a pair of Rhymes' runs in the game's waning moments which gave Oklahoma a spectacularly improbable 21-17 victory.

Also localizing the story was Michael Janofsky of the Miami Herald:

> It is becoming increasingly difficult to call this a rivalry anymore. Whereas, in the past Nebraska versus Oklahoma might have conjured up demonic thoughts and disrespect and hatred, the last few years have shown us something altogether different.

If there is a rivalry, it exists only within the Nebraska team itself. . . .

The Big Eight championship it coveted, the national championship it had hoped to play for New Year's Night against Florida State in the Orange Bowl—gone. Poof!

Nobody knows the sequence (nine Oklahoma wins in 10 games) better than the Orange Bowl committee, which had two representatives here Saturday.

"Amazing how this turned out," said one of them, Stan Marks. He was walking from the winner's locker room to the loser's, and it wasn't exactly a smile he was wearing.

He and his traveling companion had wanted Oklahoma about as much as they wanted the flu.

Al Carter of the Daily Oklahoman also focused on the hometown angle for Rhymes and the Nebraska depression:

In a sea of misplaced citrus, a homesick freshman helped the Oklahoma Sooners peel off a stunning 80-yard drive Saturday that killed Nebraska's high hopes of an outright Big Eight Conference championship in the final minute.

Buster Rhymes, the celebrated freshman from Miami, Fla., set up two Sooner touchdowns with long runs, the second a 43-yard dash with 2:32 left. With just 56 seconds remaining, Rhymes devastated a Memorial Stadium crowd of 76,332 with a one-yard leap into the end zone.

Just 34 seconds before Rhymes' key romp to the Nebraska 14-yard line, quarterback Jeff Quinn scored on a yard sneak that gave the Huskers a 17-14 lead and sparked a torrent of oranges from strong-armed fans, delirious over what looked like an Orange Bowl-clinching victory.

World-Herald coverage did not stop with the main story, which ran nearly 1,000 words. Coverage after the Oklahoma game included the following: a sidebar feature on Rhymes, an interview with Oklahoma coach Barry Switzer, a wire service story from Salt Lake City that told of the barrage of complaints received at an ABC affiliate station there that had switched away from the Nebraska-Oklahoma game to do a pregame presentation on Utah and Brigham Young University, a feature on reactions of Nebraska players about going to the Sun Bowl, a short story on Nebraska players who had been injured, a sidebar on Husker All-America halfback Jarvis Redwine's taunting of an Oklahoma player after Redwine had sprinted 89 yards for the game's first touchdown, a feature on how Nebraska's equipment manager had lost his Big Eight championship ring when hurling an orange from the field, a full picture page with text, a sidebar on the sideline presence of the University of Oklahoma president, an interview story that focused on depressed Cornhusker fans, a story written about Nebraska coach Tom Osborne's post-game television show, an article on ticket policy for the Sun Bowl and complete game statistics. Photos were scattered throughout the section.

THE SPORTS ILLUSTRATED STYLE

Newspaper sportswriters often are criticized for being content to put together game stories from publicity handouts and official game statistics. Writers at Sports Illustrated, however, are more thorough.

Naturally, few newspaper sportswriters have the luxury of working full time to prepare for a single game as writers at Sports Illustrated do. Still, the intense preparation for coverage of a single game by a Sports Illustrated writer is something all reporters—regardless of age or size of newspaper they work for—should be aware of and in turn appreciate. Young sports reporters should emulate—to the extent their circumstances allow—the organized and intense preparation of Douglas S. Looney, a senior writer for Sports Illustrated who specializes in college football.

Looney seldom watches an entire game from the press box with fellow writers. Instead, he sits in a coaching booth or walks the sidelines, feeling that this provides him with special insight into the contest. His game coverage strategy is the culmination of nearly a week of preparation.

His week:

Monday—His New York editor calls him. Looney is to cover the Oklahoma–Nebraska football game in Lincoln Saturday. Looney calls the sports information directors at both institutions to inform them that he will cover the game. He then makes travel arrangements.

Tuesday—Looney always goes first to the home of the visiting team, so he flies to Norman, Okla. He spends Tuesday and Wednesday there, talking with players and coaches. He watches game films with the team and on his own. "I talk to everyone I can think of who is connected with the program," Looney said. He looks for insights: What is Oklahoma doing to prepare for the game? Why does Oklahoma win with such regularity?

Thursday—The writer flies to Lincoln. He spends two days doing the same things he did in Norman Tuesday and Wednesday.

During his visits Looney might go out to dinner with coaches or persons associated with the football program. He tries to interview the coaches at their homes. "Coaches are in a more relaxed frame of mind if you can interview them away from the university," Looney said.

"I am very boring to be with during the week leading up to a game," Looney said. "I try not to do anything during the week that will not directly affect the story. I don't want to go to dinner with anyone unless it relates to information about the game. I am oblivious to everything else in the world except that week's game. I get home and my wife tries to make conversation about something the president said during the week. But I won't have a clue as to what he said. I dismiss myself from the world around me, focusing on the upcoming football game."

Game day—Looney spends part of the morning scrutinizing his notes. He roughs out stories that can be used if either team wins—not formal drafts but notes that are in order. He has a stock of several anecdotes to use depending on who wins—or by how much.

Before the game Looney tries to spend time around the players and in the locker room. Naturally not all writers enjoy this kind of access; this is an advantage to working for Sports Illustrated.

During the game Looney focuses on areas "other writers might overlook." He does not statistically chart the game like many writers; he depends on the sports information director's statistics. "I think it is foolish to chart the game—somebody else is doing that for me. I try to analyze the game. I've spent half of some games watching only a linebacker. You get a different view of the game when you do that."

After the game Looney talks with significant players and coaches. As soon as he has conducted his interviews, he picks up the statistics and heads to his motel. "This is when I earn my money," he said. Looney generally sits at the typewriter all night. "I won't get up from my desk until 6 a.m. or so." By then he has put together a 1,500-word story. He must call his story in by 10 a.m. New York time.

Looney boards a Sunday afternoon flight home. Monday morning his editor calls, gives him his next assignment and the week begins.

Looney's routine illustrates his philosophy: "To do good game coverage or pregame coverage, you should throw yourself into it—totally. Immerse yourself in it." He said that in this era of television and radio game coverage writers should not spend so much time trying to reconstruct games play by play. Rather, writers should think in terms of how to get behind the scenes. "I look for things that our readers could not pick up on while watching the game on television or listening to the radio."

Looney also places great importance on listening. "I hear some of the most atrocious interviewing going on," he said. "Part of the problem is lack of listening. Listening is a developed skill. Sometimes it is hard to listen; it requires total concentration."

WRITING GAME STORIES

Outstanding game coverage of any sport is predicated on one principle: preparation. Sports reporters should do a thorough job of pregame preparation. If reporters have an arsenal of significant background facts, they can work the facts into the game story, where appropriate, with a minimum of stop-and-go writing.

Wally Provost of the Omaha World-Herald, who for many years covered University of Nebraska football, said that there "always is a temptation to formulate a lead while the game is in progress (which the wire service writers must do), but I believe it is more satisfactory to take a few minutes at the conclusion of the game to 'sit back' and try to picture the broad view of what has happened rather than leap into the lead with a preconceived angle."

Provost said that if preparation has been adequate, the "various angles and little brighteners will fall into place when the writing does begin." Provost's preparation includes a review of the previous year's meeting, a review of the teams' current season, a brushup on player profiles in the press guides, a study of statistics to date, knowledge of the coaches' philosophies (which might help explain some tactic or twist in the game), an awareness of the fans' attitudes and expectations and an idea of what is happening in terms of betting.

Much of the preparation material Provost seeks is available in the newspaper's morgue. If not, when covering college athletics, sports information directors should be called. Don Bryant, longtime sports information director and assistant athletic director at the University of Nebraska, said that sports reporters could adequately cover a football game without watching it. "All they have to do is sit there; we'll pass all the information to them," he said.

Statistics crews staff press boxes at most universities; they provide pregame dope sheets, number changes, lineups, pregame statistics for both teams, halftime statistics, halftime play-by-play, "quickie" statistics immediately after the game, and then complete game individual and team statistics, substitutions, scoring summaries, time of possession summaries (football) and quotations from both locker rooms within 45 minutes after a game.

The first paragraphs of a Provost story written only minutes after a Nebraska–Oklahoma football game illustrate his preparation for the contest. Provost's story could be broken down like this:

Straightforward Summary Lead

Who—University of Nebraska football team
What—Suffered a defeat
When—Saturday
Where—Norman, Okla.
Why and How—Oklahoma Tailback Steve Owens had a brilliant game.

Historical Perspective

Norman, Okla., was the site of Nebraska's last humiliating defeat—more than a decade earlier.

Significance of the Nebraska Defeat

Possible bowl bid not likely to materialize.

Tieback to Owens Reference in Lead

Statistical documentation of record-shattering day.

Narrative Highlighted Account of Game

Scoring details, major plays and quotations from coaches and players provide the meat of the story.

Reference to Upcoming Games

Dates and opponents for next games of both teams are discussed.

The first paragraphs of Provost's story follow. Note how he was able to weave significant statistics into the game flow without ruining the rhythm of the writing:

OWEN FIELD, NORMAN, Okla.—The University of Nebraska football team suffered its most shattering defeat in a dozen years Saturday as Tailback Steve Owens' Big Eight-record scoring led Oklahoma on a 47-0 spree.

Not since the 1956 Huskers were smeared 54-6 in this same bull ring had the Lincolnites been whipped so decisively.

Among the broken bits left in the wake of Owens' brutalizing five-touchdown performance was an offer for Nebraska to play Mississippi in the Liberty Bowl at Memphis.

There had been no official mention of the bid by the N.U. staff, but it was understood that the offer was good—and that acceptance would be automatic—had the Cornhuskers upset the defending Big Eight Champions.

It is safe to assume that any and all bowl feelers were snatched back at the half, when Oklahoma already was riding a 28-0 lead on the rangy junior tailback's first four touchdowns.

A robot-rushing son of a Miami, Okla., truck driver, Owens retired in the fourth quarter after carrying 41 times for 172 yards. He also caught two passes for eight yards as Oklahoma overwhelmed N.U. in total yardage, 414-184, and outdowned the visitors by 27-7.

With the Oklahoma State game remaining, Owens has collected 1,416 yards to expunge the one-season conference record of 1,342 set by Nebraska's Bobby Reynolds in 1950.

Saturday's accomplishments included these additional records:

—Most points in a conference game, 30; old record 28 by Ralph Graham, Kansas State, 1932, against Kansas Wesleyan.

—Most points by an O.U. back in one season, 120; old record of 117 by George (Junior) Thomas, 1949.

—Most touchdowns by an O.U. back in one season, 20; old record 19 by Thomas in 1949.

Owens already had wiped out the school's one-season rushing record held by Billy Vessels, and the league's two-season rushing record held by Gale Sayers.

Unfortunately for the Cornhuskers' "image," the game was televised nationally.

That was a mistake. The presentation belonged on the Educational TV Network with a title announcing, "Oklahoma Exhibition of Big-Time Football."

Nebraska never was in the running.

Provost's story then flowed into a narrative account of the game.

Skillful use of available statistics, good preparation, strong verbs and the ability to analyze turning points obviously aid the reporter in writing a story for any sport.

Just as responsible newspaper editors should not send reporters to cover the courthouse without a lesson on reading court documents, sportswriters should not be dispatched to cover a game without a lesson on deciphering statistics. Reporters quickly learn to cull the significant from the stat sheets. Statistics provide the skeleton for a good game story; insight, analysis and quotations provide the soul.

WRITING SPORTS FEATURES

Tom Allan, roving reporter for the Omaha World-Herald, whose sideline coverage of University of Nebraska football games dates back more than three decades, tells young reporters it is commendable to strive for a front page headline and Pulitzer Prize. He emphasizes, however, that while doing so, "don't forget to stoop and pick a daisy along the way." Allan plucked one after the 1972 Orange Bowl game. Nebraska crushed Alabama 38-6 to clinch its second consecutive national championship. Allan labels the story "the night tears fell on the game ball."

Allan describes the circumstances:

> Johnny Rodgers, who the next year would win the Heisman Trophy, was in the spotlight in the middle of the locker room. Forgotten in a corner was Rex Lowe, a teammate who was dying of Hodgkins Disease, but who had come to the game and had sat on the sidelines in a wheelchair.
>
> The press was interested in Rodgers' finest moment, his game-breaking 72-yard touchdown run. But Rodgers' finest moment that night came after the game.
>
> I was helping cover the Husker locker room that night since the game had been so one-sided and it had resulted in a national crown. Thus I was able to catch that magic moment with my camera and pen when Johnny, clutching the game ball, slipped through the crowd as gracefully as he had the Crimson Tide to kneel by Lowe's side.
>
> "Buddy, this game ball belongs to you," Rodgers said. "You're the greatest."
>
> Then they clutched each other in an embrace and their tears fell on the game ball.

Allan described the story as "a daisy I picked up that I could have missed trying to get to the coach or other stars."

Post-game locker room coverage often can bring about a unique, readable story angle. It also has its pitfalls. Allan and fellow sportswriters were almost hit by a flying roast beef sandwich after Nebraska edged Kansas 21-17 when Pepper Rodgers was the Jayhawk coach. A late-game pass interference call had put the Cornhuskers in scoring position, and they went on to win.

In the KU lockerroom Allan knelt beside the dejected Rodgers and said, "Tough way to lose a ballgame, coach." Rodgers snarled an obscenity and added, "Let's see you print that."

Later, during the post-game questioning, Rodgers was handed a sack lunch. The coach, angered that the loss was his second last-minute defeat in two weeks, said that he had "no comment" on the officiating. Irritated at another question, Rodgers rolled his sack lunch into a ball and hurled it against the wall behind the interviewers. Thud.

"How about that," Rodgers shouted. "There's your story. Rodgers throws sandwich against the wall with vengeance—and by the way, it was a beef!"

STORIES THAT REACH BEYOND THE PLAYING FIELD

Game stories, pregame articles and player features account for most of the material printed in sports sections. Some stories, though, extend beyond the playing field. Articles about NCAA investigations, player trades, contract disputes, litigation and strikes by professional athletes are found with increasing frequency.

An example of a story that extended beyond the playing field was the announcement by Fiesta Bowl officials that this post-season football game, played at Arizona State University's Sun Devil Stadium in Tempe, would be moved to New Year's Day. The story was important to non-sports fans, too. The news event was handled a number of ways. The Tempe Daily News carried the announcement as a straight news story in the sports section. The story began:

> The 11th Annual Fiesta Bowl will be played on New Year's Day, subject to certification by the NCAA Extra Events Committee, Bowl officials announced Saturday.
>
> Don Meyers, a member of the Fiesta Bowl Board of Directors, said he has been negotiating with NBC to televise the game at 11:30 a.m., Arizona time.

The story went on to explain that the change from a late December game should bring about increases in attendance and television ratings. Also, participating teams would get a larger payoff. One paragraph near the end of the story mentioned the effects of the change on the area economy.

The story carried by the Arizona Republic's sports section focused on reactions to the change by other bowls. Though Phoenix-area residents generally were pleased with the change, the enthusiasm was not widespread. The Republic's story started this way:

Rival bowls and television network officials withheld applause Saturday upon learning that the Fiesta Bowl plans to hold its game on New Year's Day.

"I'm a little surprised," said Field Scovill, chairman of the Cotton Bowl selection committee. "The football fan will not be treated right when he won't have the opportunity to see the Fiesta, Sugar and Cotton. With all the bowls at the same time, the loser is the fan."

Under the new schedule, the Cotton Bowl will start 30 minutes later than the Fiesta Bowl.

It is understood that the Fiesta move was prompted because of Sugar Bowl plans to go to an evening starting time.

On the day that the Republic and the Daily News carried the stories on their sports pages, the Republic also published a Page One story that emphasized the economic impact of the game change:

The Fiesta Bowl will be moved to New Year's Day, improving the game's ability to draw top teams and possibly bringing the Valley up to $16 million more in revenue, bowl and tourist officials announced Saturday.

The bowl thus will begin its second decade on Jan. 1, 1982, placing it in an elite group with the Big Four—the Cotton, Orange, Rose and Sugar bowls—that traditionally have been played on New Year's Day.

Bruce Skinner, executive director of the bowl, said the new date is on a one-year "trial" basis, "but it's our intent to play on that date every year."

Television ratings and other considerations will determine if the format is continued, Skinner said.

With the new date, officials estimate that 10,000 more visitors will attend the bowl game than last year and will stay longer, tripling the game's economic impact on the Valley.

The bowl is estimated by the Phoenix and Valley of the Sun Convention and Visitors Bureau to have generated $4.5 million in 1980. Ted Sprague, the bureau's executive director, said the date change will mean a minimum of $10 million to as much as $20 million in revenues generated by the bowl in the future.

Sports-related stories obviously are not limited to the sports pages. Depending on the writing angle, stories that were once thought to be the exclusive property of the sports pages are finding their way to general news sections. And angles that sports staffs once avoided (economic impact stories and court battle pieces, for example) are now being tackled with enthusiasm by qualified sports reporters.

S U G G E S T E D   E X E R C I S E S

1.   Clip from morning and afternoon newspapers the account of a game played the night before. Compare to see how the writing approaches differ.

2.   Read sports stories from two newspapers for one week. Look for examples of cheerleading in the writing. Does one of the papers have more examples than the other? Is one particular writer responsible for most of them?

3.   Read the featured college football game account in Sports Illustrated for a given weekend. Notice the detail. Find a newspaper article written about the same game. What are the similarities? What are the differences?

4.   Invite the sports information director at your school to your class. Ask for all statistics made available to the press after a football game and basketball game. Practice writing short stories based only on the statistics the sports information director provides.

5.   Cover a "minor" sport event at your college or university. Write an AM and a PM account of the event.

6.   Get press credentials to cover a major sport event at your school. Write a complete account by using statistics, interviews with coaches, interviews with players and comments from representatives of the opposing team.

Reporters deal with wire services—primarily The Associated Press and United Press International—on a daily basis. More than 2,000 journalists in the United States work for the wire services, but many more daily newspaper reporters work indirectly with the services, either by providing information to them or by gleaning information from them. This chapter discusses the wire services and their reporting practices.

You will be introduced to:

• Wire service terminology and operational procedures. A day at the Phoenix, Ariz., AP Bureau is discussed.

• Wire service hiring practices. AP Chief of Bureau for Iowa and Nebraska, Edward C. Nicholls, discusses the qualities he looks for in reporters.

• Ways in which wire service reporters and daily newspaper reporters pool their resources.

• Methods the wire services use to update developing stories. The chapter discusses how the services strive to provide different lead material for stories to be published in both AMs and PMs.

• Procedures in overseas wire service bureaus. The discussion focuses on UPI reporter Leon Daniel.

Reporter Walter Berry, foreground, waits for a story transmission as News Editor Neil Bibler, center, and Chief of Bureau Gavin Scott examine copy at the Associated Press office in Phoenix, Ariz.

Russell Gates

15 THE WIRE SERVICES

Joe Morris capsulized the philosophy of the wire services when he wrote in the preface to his history of United Press, "Deadline Every Minute":

> It is the nature of a press association that men and women scattered from St. Louis to Bombay spend their days and nights hunting not only headlines but the small scraps of news that will interest readers in Centerville, Iowa, or Albany, New York, or Santa Barbara, California. There is endless routine and endless drudgery and there are times when a correspondent feels that the press association does possess certain physical assets after all—it possesses *him*. At other times, when his story skims over the wires for thousands on thousands of miles, carrying his excitement and perhaps his name into hundreds of newspapers around the world, he may feel that he is the press association. But day after day, the wires are always open, always waiting for him to produce. Day and night, on holidays and on days of disaster, the wire is always waiting.

And so it is at the hundreds of wire service bureaus around America and the world: The wire is always waiting.

HOW THE SERVICES OPERATE

From wire service facilities flows news of presidential assassination attempts, devastating hurricanes, billion-dollar budgets and international strife. Like many Associated Press offices around the country, the Phoenix, Ariz., bureau occupies space in a newspaper building. This building, owned by Phoenix Newspapers, Inc., also houses the morning Arizona Republic and afternoon Phoenix Gazette.

The Phoenix AP bureau—like most wire service offices around the country—is not pretentious. Metal desks and video display terminals occupy most of the 750-square-foot glassed-in newsroom. Electronic gadgetry fills about one-fifth of the floor space. Doors lead to smaller glassed-in offices for the bureau chief and chief of communication.

The area is not a picture of orderliness: Stacked newspapers cover desks; coffee cups are scattered everywhere; bulletin boards are littered with memos; a blackboard contains some scribbled reminders; waste baskets are filled to overflowing; maps and log sheets are strewn about.

A Busy Day

On a typical day four persons, including bureau chief Gavin Scott and news editor Neil Bibler, are handling the endless flow of news. The third staffer has been with the AP for less than a year; the fourth is a temporary replacement just out of college.

The first staffer to arrive reports at 5 a.m. to process the early needs of the state's newspapers and broadcast stations: the weather fixtures, broadcast news and sports. Interruptions keep him from getting the news stream under control by the time Bibler arrives at 7 o'clock.

Three telephones ring almost simultaneously; three member newspapers request that overnight stories be transmitted again. Their computer terminals malfunctioned, and they missed part of the cycle's stories.

Bibler retransmits the stories. Repeating dozens of stories on an old AP slow-speed (66 words per minute) wire would have been a heavy burden. But many newspapers today, including these Arizona publications, use high-speed wires (1,200 words per minute computer-to-computer transmissions). Thus the task is performed efficiently.

By 7:30 early weather, sports and broadcast deadlines have been met and the retransmission requests have been handled. Bibler focuses on today's needs. He scans national stories on the A and B wires to see if any should be localized.

The main national news wire of both the AP and UPI is called the *A wire,* often written as *AAA* or *Aye*. National and international news of secondary importance is carried on the *B* (or *BBB*) *wire*. In addition, both services offer financial wires, sports wires, state wires, stock market wires and various regional wires. There also are wires labeled "SNO" for "state news only" and "single circuit" wires that carry a complete basic report for smaller circulation newspapers. Both the AP and UPI also offer broadcast wires for radio and television stations.

If Bibler finds stories on the A or B wires that can be rewritten with an Arizona angle, he will assign it to a staffer. Bibler also is in touch with AP reporters in Tucson and at the State Capitol in Phoenix, where the Legislature is in session.

At about 9 o'clock Bibler examines stories written by reporters at member newspapers throughout the state. Before the news business was revolutionized by computer technology, member newspapers had to assign reporters or editors to telephone the AP with local stories of statewide interest. An AP staffer in turn had to type the story as it was dictated. Several of Arizona's papers now transmit news copy originating locally directly from their computers to the regional AP computer in Phoenix. These simultaneous transmissions are called *electronic carbons*.

After scanning the electronic carbons, Bibler processes the stories, sending rewritten and edited material on the general news circuits for all members. A primary advantage of the computer system is that it permits all afternoon newspapers to print today's stories today. Under the more cumbersome non-electronic method, by the time the story was dictated, rewritten and transmitted, early afternoon newspaper deadlines often had passed.

As he selects and transmits the electronic carbon stories, Bibler again talks with the AP's Tucson-based reporter and with the two State

Capitol reporters. They soon will file news stories and enterprise pieces for statewide distribution.

Bibler also is in telephone contact with Walter Berry, a new AP staffer just two years out of college who is covering the trial in Phoenix of former Arizona State University football coach Frank Kush. Kush is defending himself against a $2.2 million lawsuit brought by a former punter who accused Kush of punching him in the face during a Pacific 10 Conference game and then using physical and verbal tactics to force him to quit the team.

The story, a major one, is being carried by most newspapers around the country. The first phase of the trial started nearly three months ago, but a jury verdict in the trial's second phase is expected today. Berry's updates will be carried on the national wire.

Berry is putting in 16-hour days to keep pace with developments of the trial. He is filing stories for the AM and PM cycles. The *AM cycle* runs from about noon Eastern time until midnight; the *PM cycle* runs from midnight until noon. Copy slugged AM indicates that morning newspapers have first use. Copy slugged PM means that evening newspapers have first use. Copy given a *BC* (*both cycles*) designation is for use by either AM or PM papers immediately.

The lead paragraph of Berry's PM cycle story, written shortly after midnight, reads:

> PHOENIX (AP)—A jury of six women and two men began deliberations today on a verdict which attorneys claim could legally define the disciplinary methods of college football coaches for the first time.

At 11:50 a.m. Berry calls Bibler with a new lead to his story. It is transmitted under an urgent priority code and runs 300 words. It begins:

> PHOENIX (AP)—Jurors deliberated for more than three hours Monday without reaching a verdict in the $2.2 million damage suit filed by former Arizona State punter Kevin Rutledge against his ex-college coach Frank Kush.
>
> Rutledge, now a student at the University of Nevada-Las Vegas, is suing Kush, the university and former Arizona State assistant coach Bill Maskill, claiming verbal and physical harassment which forced him to quit the team in 1979 and forfeit his scholarship.

Berry's new lead moves in time for afternoon newspapers in the West. Because of the three-hour difference in the East, it moves as an AM story there.

Most daily newspaper reporters are covering the Kush trial in a less hurried atmosphere. Morning newspaper reporters can gather their thoughts, organize their notes and type a wrap-up story at the end of the day. Afternoon reporters won't have to worry about processing a late-afternoon verdict quickly. It will not make their editions until the following day. This, however, is a luxury Berry cannot enjoy.

The wire is always waiting.

The work is like nothing Berry had done in his first job as a reporter at a medium-circulation daily newspaper. Covering the Kush trial is without a doubt a good AP baptism under fire for the young reporter.

Back at the AP bureau, staffers are nearing the end of a busy morning. As noon approaches, the AP-written stories from Tucson have been filed, the AP-written stories from the state Legislature have been transmitted, bureau chief Scott has tracked down information on a Chicago photo that a small-circulation Arizona daily had requested and, of course, Berry's story has cleared.

Meanwhile, the wire still is waiting for more—it wants a jury verdict in the Kush trial.

PM papers won't get it, though. It is now past 2:30—and the verdict still is not in. Shortly after 4 o'clock, however, the jury returns. Berry scrambles for a telephone. Bibler, who is getting ready to turn things over to the nightside crew, takes the call and transmits a new, 200-word lead to the story. At 4:30 p.m. the priority item begins:

> PHOENIX (AP)—A jury of six women and two men found in favor of the defendants on all claims Monday in the second phase of a $2.2 million damage suit against former Arizona State University football coach Frank Kush and others.
> In the suit brought by former Sun Devil punter Kevin Rutledge, the jury voted 5-3 in favor of Kush and ex-assistant coach Bill Maskill on the allegation that they drove Rutledge off the team through physical and verbal harassment.

Berry's job is not over. He examines his notes of previous interviews with persons involved in the case. He had saved them for quick transmission once a verdict was reached. Now Berry moves quickly to get juror reactions. He telephones his story to the bureau. At 5:05, again under an urgent priority code, another new lead—this one 450 words—is transmitted. It begins:

> PHOENIX (AP)—Citing "a lack of sufficient evidence" a Maricopa County Superior Court jury found in favor of former Arizona State University football coach Frank Kush and three other defendants Monday in the second phase of a $2.2 million damage suit.
> Former Sun Devil punter-defensive back Kevin Rutledge filed suit against Kush claiming his ex-college coach had physically and verbally harassed him into quitting the team in 1979 and forfeiting his scholarship.

The story goes on to quote Kush, his attorney, his wife, Rutledge's lawyer and three jurors.

Berry returns to the office, examines his 5:05 story, tightens it and transmits his last revision at 6 o'clock.

This day at the Phoenix AP bureau was hectic. But some days move even faster. For, as Morris said, the wire is always waiting.

The Need for the Services

During the Kush trial, scores of daily newspapers around the country budgeted space for its coverage. The story focused on litigation involving one of America's best-known football coaches.

Certainly, in every city in which college football was extensively covered—in places such as Austin, Texas; Lincoln, Neb.; Ann Arbor, Mich.; Columbus, Ohio; Oklahoma City, Okla.; Tuscaloosa, Ala.; Fayette-ville, Ark., and Athens, Ga.—this story was relevant. The trial was not so important, however, that newspapers in these cities would dispatch a reporter to cover it. Only a handful of the nation's 1,750 daily newspapers can afford to staff bureaus around the country and world. Obviously, most newspapers do not have the economic resources to hire reporters to cover developments in their state Legislature, Congress, the executive branch, the administrative agencies and hundreds of foreign countries. They certainly cannot afford to send reporters to Phoenix to cover a trial.

How, then, do newspapers published in the cities named above—to say nothing of newspapers in Emporia, Kan.; Casa Grande, Ariz.; Carbon-dale, Ill.; Tupelo, Miss., or Ocala, Fla.—provide their readers with region-al, state, national and international news?

The wire services.

America's oldest cooperative news-gathering service, The Associated Press, was conceived in May 1948 in New York City. Representatives of six newspapers met to see if there was not a more efficient means of gathering information for stories. They decided it would be cheaper for all of them if they shared the news. Telegraph cables would be the vehicle to transmit the information.

Costs and labor power were important considerations in that era—just as they are today. It was pure economics: Substantial savings could be realized by publishers if they sent a single messenger to collect and distri-bute dispatches to all the newspapers involved.

The AP, as the news service was called, continued to grow during the 19th century. Due to differences with its controllers, however, two of the country's most powerful publishers formed their own wire services to compete with the AP in the 20th century's first decade.

E.W. Scripps established the United Press Associations in 1907; William R. Hearst founded the International News Service in 1909. Over the ensuing years others also attempted to found wire services. One of the most interesting attempts was Transradio Press, established by the broad-casting industry in the mid-1930s in response to an effort by newspaper publishers to squeeze radio out of the national news-reporting field. By 1958 only the AP, UP and INS remained, and in that year INS and UP merged to form United Press International. On June 2, 1982, UPI was sold by the E.W. Scripps Co. to Media News Corp. Today, then, there are two "basic" news services in the United States—the AP and UPI.

In addition to the AP and UPI, newspapers can subscribe to supplemental news services. For a fee, these supplemental services provide newspapers with materials ranging from cartoons to in-depth political analysis pieces. Scores of supplemental services are available. Small-circulation newspapers generally subscribe to only one. Some newspapers—particularly those with larger circulations—subscribe to several.

Most supplemental services mail their material to subscribing newspapers. Their stories, which usually are not timely, are sent *camera ready*—that is, they do not have to be reset in type at the newspapers. Some services, which transmit timely copy that would diminish in relevance if tied up in the mail for two or three days, contract to provide an electronic transmission vehicle to deliver material.

Supplemental services include the Field Newspaper Syndicate, the King Feature Syndicate, the Los Angeles Times Syndicate, the New York Times News Service, the Newspaper Enterprise Association, the North American Newspaper Alliance, the Register and Tribune Syndicate, Inc., the United Feature Syndicate and the Universal Press Syndicate.

The New York Times News Service is among those supplemental services that provide Washington coverage, but most newspapers rely almost exclusively on the AP and UPI for Washington and foreign news. Widespread coverage of national and international affairs would be an economic impossibility to most newspapers were it not for the wire services. Each day, the wire services take people to all parts of the world for on-the-spot coverage.

WANTED: GOOD REPORTERS

Naturally, the wire services constantly are looking for good reporters. Working for the services has a certain prestige; scores of experienced journalists spend careers with them. It is not uncommon, however, for extremely promising journalists with relatively little professional experience to land reporting or editing jobs with the services.

The AP, in fact, has few firm rules for hiring; the bureau chief is given discretion. A journalist can take AP employment tests and make application at any Associated Press bureau. Testing includes the AP News Test, which involves writing four stories from notes included in the test, editing some sample sentences or paragraphs and completing a 50-word spelling test. There also is a 100-word vocabulary test and a Wonderlic test of basic intelligence. The applicant must pass all of them to be considered for employment.

Applicants indicate on their forms whether they would work in any AP bureau in the country or whether they have specific geographic restrictions.

Edward C. Nicholls, AP chief of bureau for Iowa and Nebraska, likes to hire applicants with about two years' experience. "This is not a hard rule," he said. "Some persons are hired with no experience, others are hired with many years."

Applicants with some—but not extensive—experience are hired at a lower pay level. The amount of full-time news experience with a broadcast station or daily newspaper determines the salary level at which an applicant should begin, according to Nicholls.

Applicants who pass all the tests and have good interviews with the bureau chief may be considered for employment. If the bureau chief who administered the exam has an opening, he can seek approval from the New York headquarters to hire the applicant. If the bureau does not have an opening or is looking for someone on a different pay scale, the applicant's tests and application can be forwarded to New York to be sent on a circular to all bureau chiefs.

The circular summarizes the applicant's test results, strengths and other qualities. Any interested bureau chief can then contact the applicant directly. If the bureau chief wants to hire the applicant, approval still must be sought from New York.

"It is my experience, generally, that applicants without at least some full-time news experience are likely to find themselves overwhelmed by the pace and volume of copy to be handled in an AP bureau," Nicholls said. "I would, therefore, recommend that aspiring employees get one to two years good experience before applying to the wire services."

Once hired, new employees are on probation for six months. They can be terminated at any time during that period. After passing probation, they become regular members of the staff and termination is possible only for cause, as spelled out in the contract between the Wire Service Guild and the AP.

WORKING WITH THE WIRE SERVICES

The AP and UPI have the same purpose: the transmission of accurate, comprehensive news. But the AP and UPI differ in structure. Newspapers and broadcast stations that receive news from the AP are called *members*. The AP is a not-for-profit cooperative. Newspapers and broadcast stations that receive news from UPI are called *clients* or *subscribers*. UPI is a privately held corporation.

Under the AP bylaws, members are considered news-gathering agents for the cooperative. They are obligated to share their news with the AP for possible widespread distribution. UPI operates differently. Because it is not a cooperative, its clients are not obligated to share news with the service. UPI pays "stringers," who often are local newspaper or broadcast station reporters, to telephone news in their areas to the nearest bureau.

With the coming of age of electronic carbons, cooperative efforts between newspapers and AP bureaus are increasing. Stories written by reporters at member newspapers are evaluated at regional AP bureaus for possible transmission to all members. Reporters should be pleased when the AP "picks up" their stories; this often is recognition of a solid, interesting story.

The Salt Lake City bureau chief, for example, decided that a story written by Salt Lake Tribune staff writer JoAnn Jacobsen-Wells would be of interest to other member papers. The feature focused on an attorney who had taken more than a year off to set up a homestead on five acres of rural ground. His family stayed behind while he lived in a tent, built a cabin, did a lot of reading, hiked, rode horses, ran the river and did some consulting work. The Thoreau-type story, which was of interest to all readers tired of the 9 to 5 workday drudgery, is the kind of feature story that the AP is interested in circulating—one that reaches beyond the immediate circulation area of the newspaper in which it first appears.

Here is how Jacobsen-Wells began her story:

> Former Salt Lake County Attorney Paul VanDam, who took 15 months off to "unwind and do what ever I wanted," has come home.
>
> Following a lengthy retreat to the hills of Pine Valley, 18 miles northwest of St. George, a more relaxed VanDam is again in his native Salt Lake City practicing law—an occupation on which he doesn't depend, but now suits him.
>
> Sitting in his unpretentious law office, the bearded, casually dressed attorney said, "One of my great realizations (while away) was I didn't need to be a lawyer. I could get by doing a tremendously lot of things for a living."

The AP rewrote the story for widespread dissemination. Though the facts were not changed, the literary flow was.

Here is how the AP started its story:

> SALT LAKE CITY (AP)—After 15 months in the hills of southwestern Utah, former Salt Lake County Attorney Paul VanDam has returned and is again practicing law.
>
> "One of my great realizations was I didn't need to be a lawyer. I could get by doing a tremendously lot of things for a living, such as carpenter, boatman or consultant," he said.
>
> "For my own status, my own ego, it became clear to me that it wasn't essential to be a lawyer just to say I was a lawyer," he said.
>
> But VanDam also found that, examined alongside other jobs, being a lawyer was pretty good, "mainly because you can make a reasonable living and control your own schedule."

Individual newspapers also can rewrite or localize a wire story. When the space shuttle Columbia was circling the globe in spring 1981, Americans watched, hoping to be able to see the spacecraft.

UPI moved a story datelined Cape Canaveral, Fla., that began:

Hurtling through the heavens at 17,500 miles per hour, the space shuttle Columbia looks like a moving star—a speck of light visible one minute and gone the next.

Callers from around the world have deluged the Kennedy Space Center since launch time Sunday wondering when to look skyward to catch a glimpse of the shuttle.

NASA spokesman Rock Raab said the best time for viewing is shortly before the sunrise when the sun's reflection illuminates the orbiter in the darkened sky.

The story went on to list several cities around the world, giving information about the best time to see the shuttle. Included was Chicago: "visible at 4:23 a.m. moving southwest to east for four minutes at 20 degrees 450 miles distant."

When the Chicago Tribune received the transmission, the national desk editor asked a rewrite person to localize the story. Illinois residents, after all, likely were not interested in a rundown of sight times in such places as Denver, Phoenix, Perth and Tokyo. And they would likely want more details about the Chicago sighting. The rewrite person's instructions were to call Chicago's Adler Planetarium to ask where a person could stand in the city for the best sighting. The result was this story:

Chicagoans will have two chances to see the space shuttle Columbia as it hurtles through the heavens at 17,500 miles an hour on its maiden voyage.

The best sighting, according to officials from the National Aeronautics and Space Administration (NASA), will be at 4:23 a.m. Tuesday. The shuttle will be 450 miles southwest of Chicago, but will be visible for about four minutes as a shining, moving object in the darkened sky, NASA said.

To see the Columbia, turn southwest. Make a fist, point your straightened arm southwest and line up the bottom of your fist on the horizon. Make a fist with your other hand and place it on top of the first. The Columbia should pass from right to left at the height of the top fist.

The Columbia will also be visible almost directly overhead, passing over Champaign, Ill., at 9:55 a.m. Tuesday, an Adler Planetarium spokesman said. It will be hard to see because the sky will be bright, but the sun glinting off of it will be visible for about 15 minutes.

Turn west, look for the glint overhead, and follow it east, the planetarium spokesman said.

Reporters, particularly when writing roundups, often make extensive use of wire copy. If the newspaper subscribes to a particular service, it can use the copy as it sees fit. Ethically, though, attribution should be made when logical to do so. For example, a reporter in Wichita, Kan., is assigned to do a story on hail damage to the area wheat crop. The reporter should check wire service copy that could be used for background or additional information. When the reporter puts the story together, combining her local angle with wire service information, the story would look like this:

Southern Kansas and northern Oklahoma farmers watched helplessly as golf ball size hail pelted area wheat fields Friday.

John Jones, Wichita farmer, estimated his crop loss at 75 percent.

State agriculture officials are expected to release damage figures tomorrow. Early estimates place total losses to county farmers in excess of $25 million, said county extension agent Michael Walters.

Northern Kansas also was hit by the late spring storm. The Associated Press reported hail and damaging winds near Oakley had caused "severe" damage to the maturing wheat crop.

The storm weakened as it moved into south central Nebraska. No crop damage was reported there, according to United Press International.

Wichita area farmers are deciding whether to plow the damaged wheat under or to harvest what they can, a spokesman at the Emerald Elevator said.

The Wichita reporter was able to capsulize the local situation from her interviews and by incorporating wire service copy, write a complete story of interest to area farmers. Status of the wheat crop in other parts of the midwest would have an impact on summer grain prices.

WRITING FOR THE WIRE SERVICES

The wire services strive to be impartial gatherers of news. Staffers carry a mandate to be as objective as possible. They are instructed to be accurate and to write concisely. Wire service staffers do not interpret the news (unless the copy is clearly marked *analysis*)—they report it. Though this is always sound journalistic practice, the logic behind it in the services' early years was purely pragmatic. With hundreds of clients, it was imperative that the services steered clear of any political or ideological biases. If they had not the number of subscribing papers undoubtedly would have been reduced.

The inverted pyramid writing style has been a staple of the newspaper wires. The most important material runs early in the story, the least important information at the end. This of course makes it easier for newspaper editors to slice story length.

Naturally, with the wire services always striving to meet deadlines, some copy is transmitted that is not as concise as it should be. Newspaper editors then must edit the material carefully.

In addition to constantly updating developing stories, the wire services also must transmit separate stories for morning and afternoon newspapers. New leads, angles or writing approaches are imperative. If a story first appears in a morning newspaper, afternoon papers that subscribe to the wire obviously do not want to print the same story—even if no particularly significant new developments have occurred.

Bob Kuesterman, an Associated Press reporter in Salt Lake City, wrote a 300-word story for afternoon newspapers that moved at 7:38 a.m.

The story focused on a document that was said to shed new light on Mormon Church succession. The article was of particular interest in Utah, where the Mormon Church is headquartered. Kuesterman began his story for PM papers thus:

> SALT LAKE CITY (AP)—A document in which Mormon Church founder Joseph Smith Jr. says his son is to succeed him as church leader could present a "real problem" to those who believe Brigham Young was Smith's legitimate successor, a Protestant minister says.
>
> A Mormon Church spokesman confirmed Wednesday that the document had been obtained by the church historical department.
>
> The Protestant minister, the Rev. Wesley Walters of Illinois, disclosed contents of the document Wednesday. Walters says he is a student of Mormon documents.
>
> Mormon Church spokeman Jerry Cahill said Smith gave church leaders instructions on succession shortly before his death and the Mormon Church, or Church of Jesus Christ of Latter-day Saints, follows these instructions.

The story went on to quote Cahill, who did not dispute the authenticity of the document. He said that it would be given to the Reorganized Church, which was founded by Smith's son and which is headquartered in Independence, Mo.

During the day Salt Lake City AP staffers tracked new information to incorporate into a lead for AM newspapers. The 650-word morning story, written by Larry Werner, had considerably more information and was a total rework of the PM version that moved before it. It began:

> SALT LAKE CITY (AP)—Discovery of a 137-year-old document in which Joseph Smith Jr. promised his son the presidency of the Mormon Church—a post instead claimed by Brigham Young—will make no difference in how church leadership is now transferred, Mormon officials said Thursday.
>
> The document, discovered by a collector of Mormon records, apparently is the text of a blessing given by church founder Smith in 1844. It promised his then 12-year-old son, Joseph Smith III, that he would one day become the leader of the church. Six months later, Smith was shot to death by a mob in Carthage, Ill.
>
> After Smith's death, Young led the main body of the church to Salt Lake City.

The story went on to quote Earl E. Olson, assistant Mormon Church historian, who said that the document would have little effect on his church's doctrine of "apostolic succession" because the blessing was "conditional" and "never presented to the body of the church for its acceptance."

The PM and AM versions of this story illustrate that wire service staffers constantly are seeking and revising update information.

Occasionally, particularly on the sports wire, the services will provide optional leads for same-cycle papers. In the National Collegiate Athletic Association's basketball West Regional, Kansas State University was the surprise team. Doug Tucker, AP sports writer, began his 200-word story for AM papers:

> Tim Jankovich, Ed Nealy and Rolando Blackman hit crucial free throws in the final minutes Thursday night as Kansas State held on to slip past 18th ranked Illinois 57-52 in the semifinals of the NCAA West Regional.
> In the regional championship game beginning at 11:24 MST Saturday morning, Kansas State will meet fourth-ranked North Carolina, which beat Utah in the other semifinal Thursday, 61-56.

Tucker continued the story, which moved at 11:35 p.m., with specifics on Kansas State's win over Illinois. Less than a half-hour later, at two minutes past midnight, Tucker transmitted an optional lead for AM papers with a more featurized lead:

> After three straight NCAA tournament upsets, Kansas State, which plays with the precision of a Marine marching band, is becoming known as Jack's giant-killers.
> Controlling the tempo—and the lead the entire game—the unranked Wildcats defeated No. 18 Illinois 57-52 Thursday night in the semifinals of the West Regional.
> "I'm extremely proud of my basketball team," said Coach Jack Hartman. "Their concentration, their poise and their shot selection. We knew we had to control the game."

These excerpts show the tight, factual writing apparent in most wire service reporting. Though the writing is straightforward, wire service staffers still work diligently to constantly update and to focus on revised writing approaches for same topic stories transmitted for morning and afternoon newspapers.

OVERSEAS ASSIGNMENTS

When reporters are hired by the wire services, domestic bureaus likely will be their first assignments. Those staffers who remain with the services for several years, however, can receive overseas assignments. Leon Daniel, national reporter for United Press International, has spent about half of his nearly 30-year UPI career abroad.

As editor for Europe, the Middle East and Africa, he was based in London. He reported to a vice president and general manager for the same region, also based in London, and to the foreign editor, based in New York. Daniel's job was both editorial and administrative.

"I made staffing decisions and also approved expense accounts," he said. "I did not spend much time actually editing copy but I did frequently go to the scene of a major story to direct operations and to help cover it."

During his three years in London in the late 1970s and 1980, Daniel spent a lot of time in Iran and helped cover papal visits to Poland and Ireland and U.S. presidential visits to various European and Middle Eastern countries. He was just as busy during his three years as editor for Asia, based in Hong Kong. He covered the fall of South Vietnam and remained in Saigon for six weeks after the takeover.

It is traditional for UPI editors to participate directly in news coverage by editing copy on the desk. However, because he always had strong desk people, Daniel usually tried to make his contribution "by reporting and making staff decisions from the scene of major news stories."

Daniel also was based in New Delhi as chief correspondent for South Asia and in Manila as chief correspondent for East Asia. Both were roving jobs. "I functioned as sort of a fireman, traveling frequently," Daniel said. He also had stints in Tokyo (three years) and Saigon (13 months) as a correspondent. He returned to Vietnam often over a nine-year period to help out. He also spent three years in Thailand as manager until he was expelled by the government "for writing stories it considered unfriendly."

In addition to unfriendly governments, the fluctuating U.S. dollar also has caused problems for wire service staffers stationed abroad. When Daniel first arrived in London, he could buy a pound sterling for about $1.85. When he left, the price was $2.40. "Living allowances," however, help to alleviate the economic situation for staffers living abroad.

Despite inherent difficulties, overseas work is exciting and challenging. It requires a special type of person. When selecting reporters who aspire to work abroad, Daniel looks for candidates "with a highly developed sense of competition, someone who enjoys pressure and stiff opposition. We say a good overnight staffer is one who actually *enjoys* getting people out of bed to answer questions."

Though he has known correspondents with widely different backgrounds, Daniel said "the best ones seem to be the ones who enjoy competing." Also, a "demonstrated talent for languages" is an advantage. "I have always liked the self-starters, the kind of people who could hit the ground at the scene of a disaster and begin filing a story," Daniel said. "The name of the game still is accuracy and speed, with the former still more important than the latter."

S U G G E S T E D E X E R C I S E S

1. Invite to your class the chief of the United Press International or Associated Press bureau that serves your area. If possible arrange to visit the bureau to observe the daily routine.

2.   Read the front page of a newspaper that carries UPI stories. Read the front page of a newspaper that carries AP stories. Compare stories on the same issue or event. What are the differences and similarities? Find a story about this same issue or event published in a newspaper that subscribes to both AP and UPI. Did the newspaper combine portions of both services' stories?

3.   Look at morning and afternoon editions of an area newspaper. Compare AM and PM versions of a wire story dealing with the same issue or event.

4.   Clip examples of stories in which local reporting and wire service material are combined. Note how the newspaper handled the attribution of wire service material.

5.   Clip three major articles from your campus newspaper. Rewrite them for wire service dissemination.

Qualified journalists can function effectively at newspapers or broadcast stations, but there are some basic differences between print and electronic reporting. This chapter discusses the basics of electronic news reporting and compares the reporting and writing styles used by print journalists with those used by broadcast journalists.

You will be introduced to:

• Writing in a conversational style for broadcast. Associated Press stories written for newspapers are compared with AP stories on the same subjects for radio and television.

• Differences in the news coverage philosophies of print and electronic journalism. Tucson, Ariz., television reporter Dan Fellner discusses his conversion from print to broadcast journalism.

• Typical working days of reporters in broadcast markets of different sizes. The chapter traces a day on the job with Paul Louderman, one-man news staff at KHAS Radio in Hastings, Neb. It also traces a day on the job with Tucson television reporter Fellner.

• The legal status of cameras in courtrooms. Relevant U.S. Supreme Court decisions are discussed.

A television reporter checks her story for accuracy before the evening news.

© *Tim Carlson/Stock, Boston*

287

16 BROADCAST NEWS

When Walter Cronkite anchored his last CBS "Evening News" program in March 1981, about 18.5 million people watched. Both rival networks reported Cronkite's departure. Accolades flowed. The Associated Press said that "the final broadcast was the highlight of a day that brought Cronkite an outpouring of tribute and affection normally reserved for a national hero." Eric Sevareid, a longtime CBS News colleague, noted that Cronkite's departure received "more publicity and attention . . . than (Jimmy) Carter got leaving the presidency."

Clifford Terry wrote in the Chicago Tribune Magazine: "Walter Cronkite *is* a star. He is the Mr. Goodwrench of electronic journalism—solid, dependable, reassuring. Middle-of-the-road and Middle America."

Broadcast journalist Cronkite is proud of his print heritage. When he stepped down from the anchor slot, he was quoted by the wire service as saying that he worried "about the truncated nature of much of broadcast journalism." As a result, he reasoned, "a whole class of people, many of whom are capable only of doing the first paragraph of a story," have emerged. But, Cronkite commented, "If you don't know what belongs in the 34th paragraph of a story, how can you know what belongs in the lead?"

Still, a Gallup Poll conducted in 1981 showed that a majority (71 percent) of people believed that network television did a better job of providing accurate, unbiased news than anyone else. Local television rated next at 69 percent.

It is ironic, then, that several top broadcast journalists were trained in the print field. Cronkite dropped out of the University of Texas to go to work for the Houston Post. After two years there, he joined United Press and eventually became Moscow bureau chief. Later he joined CBS.

Cronkite told the wire services that at CBS he tried "to supply the principles that had long been laid down in print journalism. When I came into the business, there was a tendency toward superficiality." Even today electronic media newscasts often do not provide much more than headlines. Critics are quick to point out that on most 30-minute newscasts the total number of words spoken would not fill the front page of a daily newspaper. It must be remembered, however, that television is first and foremost a visual medium. Pictures can convey a tremendous amount of information—sometimes with more impact and with more accuracy than can hundreds of words.

Without doubt electronic media journalism is easy for listeners to absorb; a person has to work much harder when reading than when listening. It is important, however, for electronic media reporters to write clearly and simply. The terse who, what, why, where, when and how lead can be a tongue twister and extremely difficult to articulate. Writing style for radio, as it developed through the years, became increasingly conversational. The evolution from crisp newspaper style to conversational radio style was natural.

Television news writing style also evolved gradually. The style developed to suit a medium that differed somewhat from radio news writing.

For instance, the pauses necessary to coordinate words with film are taken into consideration. Writing often is in phrases, not complete sentences, because it is geared to available pictures. A story on coal mining in eastern Kentucky accompanied by aerial video of mining operations, the eastern Kentucky landscape and an underground shot of a mechanical miner clawing the earth could begin like this: "Kentucky. Largest coal producer in the country . . . Eastern Kentucky . . . where most of that coal is mined . . ."

BASICS OF BROADCAST STYLE

Though broadcast journalists are not as tied to stylistic detail as their print counterparts, hundreds of style rules or specific writing practices are widely observed.

The wire services have established broadcast style rules, and many broadcast news departments have adopted additional rules of uniformity unique to their operations. Broadcast journalists should be familiar with these guidelines.

Guidelines for Writing Broadcast Copy

Professor Donald E. Brown, who has taught at the University of Illinois and Arizona State University, has synthesized suggestions on stylistic practices that are followed in the broadcast industry. Practices can vary among broadcasting outlets, but Brown, in his "Radio and Television News Style Sheet," provides his students with the following guidelines on preparation of copy, use of numerals, time references, use of quotations, use of abbreviations and punctuation.

Preparation of Copy
- *Use a typewriter with pica type.* A few reporters, especially in television, prefer a special machine with even larger type.
- *Write on standard size sheets of paper (8 1/2 × 11 inches).* Avoid small fragments of paper that tend to get dropped or misplaced. Do not use a stiff bond paper that is noisy when handled near a sound-sensitive microphone.
- *Double-space or triple-space all copy, and write on one side of paper only.*
- *Type a slug line consisting of one or two words that clearly identify the story in the upper left-hand corner of each page.* Examples: President's speech, truckers' strike, highway closed. In a newsroom where several people are employed, the writer's name should be typed below the identifying slug.

- *For radio, type lines that are approximately 70 spaces in length, with 1-inch margins on each side.* Keep the margins uniform so that lines can be counted and scripts timed with reasonable accuracy.

- *For television, divide the page vertically, with the left-hand side to be used for video cues.* The column at the right is for narration copy.

- *Omit date lines.* Make sure necessary place references are incorporated in the story.

- *Use an end mark that clearly designates the end of a story.* If a long story or roundup is not completed on one page, pencil a long horizontal arrow in the lower right corner or write "MORE" at the bottom of the page.

- *Keep paragraphs reasonably short.* Experience shows that the average announcer reads with more expression and emphasis when he does not get bogged down in long paragraphs.

- *Keep copy as clean as possible.* Dirty copy often hampers good reading on the air, and it may lead to errors in pronunciation or in fact.

- *Avoid most of the copyreading symbols that are used so liberally in newspaper copy.* If time does not permit retyping, black out completely any material that is to be stricken. Print any insertions neatly and boldly so they can be read easily at a single glance.

- *In most instances, keep individual stories on separate pages.* Scripts can thus be quickly organized and late-breaking stories inserted at appropriate places.

Use of Numerals

Of all the categories customarily covered in style sheets, the section concerning numerals is perhaps of greatest importance to the beginning writer of broadcast news. Three premises should be established: Certain types of news stories involve so much statistical information or numerical detail that they are not suited to oral presentation and should be left to newspapers where they properly belong; some stories, such as the national budget, may have a great many large figures, but they are of such significance that they deserve intelligent coverage (with such stories, reporters must decide which figures are of paramount importance and must weed out those that are not essential), and, if a journalist decides to write a story that presents numerical information, it should be written in such a way that the announcer can read it easily and that the listener can readily comprehend and remember it. To facilitate the process, the following suggestions are given:

- *Whenever reasonable, simplify complicated numbers.* It will be convenient and honest to use terms such as "approximately," "more than," "about " and "almost."

- *Vary wording to help both the announcer and the listener.* To avoid repetition and to make trends or changes more clear, use phrases such as "dropped sharply," "tumbled 40 percent," "more than doubled," "cut in half" and "slightly more than 15 percent."

- *Spell out numbers under 10.* Use numerals for numbers from 10 to 999.

- *Use a hyphenated combination of numerals and words to express large numbers.* For example: 21-million families and 35-thousand farmers.

- *Translate many figures, especially large ones, into round numbers whenever feasible:* $2,001,897.46 in most cases should be written as "slightly more than 2-million dollars."

- *Spell out symbols for dollars and cents:* 29-dollars and 60-cents.

- *Write fractions as words and hyphenate them:* two-thirds.

- *Remember that in most stories, ages are not essential.* In obituaries or special situations where the age is needed, do not use this common newspaper style: "Marvin Smith, 6, was honored." For broadcasting, write "Six-year-old Marvin Smith was honored."

- *For certain types of numerical information, such as automobile licenses and telephone numbers, use a hyphen to break the sequence into its component parts in the manner that they ordinarily would be read aloud:* "Kansas license number J-U-M-8-3-2."

Time References

Because the element of immediacy is one of the biggest assets of the broadcast media in their reporting of news, every effort should be made to give up-to-the-minute reports and to write copy in a way that makes it sound fresh and timely. With this in mind, a number of authorities have encouraged heavy usage of the present tense. Frequently, the present tense can be used honestly and effectively, but this does not justify its use when it sounds forced and inappropriate. Striving too hard for an effect of immediacy can be damaging. It sounds awkward to say, "Senator Jones says the state income tax will have to be raised. Jones made his comments at a legislative session last night." This awkward shift from present to past tense within the story should be avoided. Some suggestions on time references are:

- *Avoid emphasizing old time elements as much as possible.* Be wary of emphasizing "yesterday" or "last night" in lead sentences. Look for a new development and fresh approach when possible.

- *Strive to avoid undue repetition of "today."* In some instances, break the day into its component parts: late this morning, this afternoon and so forth.

- *In capitalizing on immediacy, be alert to occasional uses of interest-catching time references.* These include: "at broadcast time this noon," "within the past half-hour" and so forth. There is, however, no defense for stations falsely referring to a "late bulletin" that was transmitted an hour earlier.

- *Note that the present-perfect tense can be functional.* For example, "Striking truckers have not decided when they will return to the highways." The precise time element can be pinpointed as the story processes.

Use of Quotations

The newspaper-oriented reporter shifting to broadcast writing faces an important change when quoting sources. Newspaper reporters commonly make extensive use of direct quotations. Broadcast stories should contain fewer quotes because there is no time for extended quotations, since stories are shorter; it usually is possible to summarize content more briefly and more understandably than to give complete verbatim quotes; the listener cannot see quotation marks and can be confused as to who said what, and stations know that if a speech is of paramount importance they can broadcast it, live or recorded. If quotations are called for in broadcast copy, attribution can be handled a number of ways. The reporter could introduce direct quotations with phrases such as "in what he called," "which she described as" or "in these words."

Use of Names and Titles

Most broadcasters agree that writers never should start a lead sentence for radio or television with a person's name. It is too easy for the listener to miss the name entirely or to misunderstand it, unless there is a "warm-up" for the ear. The newspaper style "John Jones, 42, 2020 W. Norwood St., Hill City, was named chairman" would become in broadcast style "A Hill City man—John Jones—today was named chairman." Other suggestions:

- *Begin news stories with titles preceding names:* Nebraska Senator J. J. Exon.

- *If an official is well known within a given listening area (as the governor of the state in which the station is located), it is possible to omit the first name:* Governor Babbitt.

Use of Abbreviations

One sentence can provide functional advice on use of abbreviations in broadcast writing: Eliminate the use of almost all abbreviations. Even on common abbreviations of states such as Pa. and Me., there is the possibility of the announcer's making an error. More probable than error is the possibility of hesitating while trying to make mentally sure that each abbreviation is accurately identified.

Common sense should be exercised in handling names of governmental agencies or other phrases that are sometimes conveniently identified by a series of letters. The four letters "YMCA" have as much recognition value to the average listener as the more cumbersome "Young Men's Christian Association."

Punctuation

Correct punctuation for other forms of writing is also correct for broadcast news. Punctuation marks are highly valuable to the silent reader; they are even more valuable to the person at the microphone who is striving for instantaneous interpretation, for inflections, for phrasing, for emphasis and for other qualities that will make the reading more intelligible and more interesting to the listeners.

There are two somewhat unconventional punctuation practices that are popular among broadcasters. Many announcers feel the dash is useful in setting off certain types of explanatory or identifying material. For example, "The new chairman of the budget committee—Senator Sam Smith—will make his recommendations to the entire legislature." The other device is a row of periods as a guide for a long pause or dramatic timing. For instance, "He gingerly touched the flywheel of the new machine, adjusted his safety mask, reached for the switch and . . . . . . a deafening explosion rocked the laboratory."

Writing Tips

In addition to stylistic considerations, broadcast journalists always should write to express—not impress. Professor Brown cites several taboos in broadcast writing: rhyming, alliteration, dialects, slang, profanity, technical terms, uncommon scientific terms and professional jargon.

Brown lists three points for sentence structure in broadcast copy:

- *Avoid long separations of subjects and predicates.* Do not write, "John Jones, *a resident of the Fourth Ward who was elected mayor of Riverdale by the largest margin in the city's history,* will present his acceptance speech today." Instead, write, "Riverdale's new mayor, John Jones, will present his acceptance speech today. A resident of the Fourth Ward, he was elected by the largest margin in the city's history."

- *Break up lengthy sequences of modifiers.* Do not write, "John Jones caught *a well-thrown, expertly timed, 45-yard pass* from

Henry Smith in Friday night's football game." Instead write, "John Jones caught a 45-yard pass from Henry Smith in Friday night's football game. The pass was well-thrown and expertly timed."

- *Avoid the common newspaper structure in which the attribution is tacked on after a quotation.* Do not write, " 'I am going to win the election,' *John Jones said.*" Instead, write, "John Jones said he will win the election."

Examples of Differences Between Broadcast and Print Styles

Differences between print and broadcast styles can be illustrated by examining stories transmitted on the Associated Press newspaper wire and stories transmitted on the AP radio wire. When Edward M. Richardson entered a plea to a charge of threatening to kill President Reagan, the AP moved this story on the newspaper AAA wire:

> NEW HAVEN, Conn. (AP)—Edward M. Richardson, arrested in New York carrying a loaded gun last spring, pleaded guilty Monday to two counts of threatening to kill or harm President Reagan.
>
> Richardson, 22, of Drexel Hill, Pa., had pleaded innocent in a hearing on June 2 in U.S. District Court, but he told Judge Ellen Burns on Monday that he understood the charges against him and would accept his punishment.
>
> Each of the two counts carries a maximum penalty of 10 years in prison and a $2,000 fine.
>
> Richardson was arrested April 7 after he arrived by bus in New York City carrying a loaded, .32 caliber revolver. He had left two letters in a New Haven hotel, one addressed to actress Jodie Foster, a Yale University freshman, in which he said "R. R. must die."
>
> His arrest came just a week after Reagan was shot and wounded while leaving a hotel in Washington, D.C. John W. Hinckley Jr. has been charged in that attack. [Hinckley later was judged to be innocent by reason of insanity.]

Brad Kalbfeld, AP's deputy broadcast editor, said that the newspaper version can go into the story straight ("Edward M. Richardson, arrested in New York carrying a loaded gun last spring, pleaded guilty Monday to two counts of threatening to kill or harm President Reagan.") A broadcaster reading such a lead would run out of breath and "turn blue in the face if he tried to take such an approach in the lead sentence of his story," he said.

As a result, when the AAA newspaper story was rewritten for the broadcast wire, a narrative approach was used to briefly explain what the Richardson case was all about. This story moved on the broadcast wire:

BACK IN APRIL, EDWARD RICHARDSON WAS ARRESTED IN NEW YORK CITY FOR ALLEGEDLY THREATENING THE LIFE OF PRESIDENT REAGAN. TODAY, THE 22-YEAR-OLD MAN FROM DREXEL HILL, PENNSYLVANIA PLEADED GUILTY TO TWO COUNTS OF THREATENING TO KILL OR HARM THE PRESIDENT.

RICHARDSON HAD PLEADED INNOCENT IN A HEARING IN U-S DISTRICT COURT IN NEW HAVEN, CONNECTICUT LAST MONTH. BUT TODAY HE TOLD JUDGE ELLEN BURNS THAT HE UNDERSTOOD THE CHARGES AGAINST HIM AND WOULD ACCEPT THE PUNISHMENT.

RICHARDSON WAS ARRESTED ON APRIL SEVENTH AFTER ARRIVING BY BUS IN NEW YORK CARRYING A LOADED .32 CALI-BER REVOLVER. HE'D LEFT TWO LETTERS BEHIND IN A NEW HAVEN HOTEL, ONE ADDRESSED TO ACTRESS JODIE FOSTER—A FRESHMAN AT YALE—IN WHICH HE SAID "R. R. MUST DIE."

THE ARREST CAME JUST ONE WEEK AFTER REAGAN WAS SHOT WHILE LEAVING A HOTEL IN WASHINGTON. JOHN W. HINCKLEY JUNIOR HAS BEEN CHARGED IN THAT ATTACK.

Though the story's post-lead structure parallels the newspaper wire version, the writing style definitely is more conversational. Also, style changes are apparent. Newspapers would, for example, abbreviate Pennsylvania and Connecticut (states that follow cities); put periods after U.S. instead of using a hyphen to separate the letters; write "April 7," not "April seventh," and abbreviate the "junior" reference to Hinckley.

Broadcast journalists also were faced with a difficult story concerning an infestation of Mediterranean fruit flies in California. The newspaper version—which ran nearly 1,000 words—read in part:

SAN JOSE, Calif. (AP)—Without issuing a formal ruling, a judge said today he will not allow aerial pesticide spraying over populated areas to combat the Mediterranean fruit fly infestation until a hearing on the issue is completed.

The hearing could take two days, and Malathion spraying was to start at 2 a.m. PDT Tuesday.

"There is not going to be any aerial spraying until I am satisfied that it's legally valid," said Santa Clara County Superior Court Judge Bruce Allen. "As far as I'm concerned, there is no rush."

But Allen took no official action on a request by Santa Clara County and three of its cities to stop the government from spraying Malathion. That means there is nothing to prevent the spraying from going on as scheduled.

The request for an injunction is similar to one denied Friday in federal court by U.S. District Judge William A. Ingram.

The newspaper story went on to give the possible health dangers of Malathion, background on the order for the aerial spraying by Gov. Edmund G. Brown Jr., comments from Agriculture Secretary John R.

Block on the possibility of quarantining crops from the entire state and comments from residents planning to leave because of the spraying.

Kalbfeld pointed to the difficulty in converting this complicated story to the broadcast wire. The AAA story lead paragraph made it sound as if the spraying would not go on—but in the fourth paragraph the reader learns how much uncertainty exists. This is accurate, but on the broadcast wire, such a lead would sound misleading. Thus the broadcast desk editors decided to more directly state the confusion that existed:

> JUST AFTER MIDNIGHT TONIGHT, HELICOPTERS LADEN WITH INSECTICIDE ARE SUPPOSED TO BEGIN SPRAYING FOR MEDITERRANEAN FRUIT FLIES IN PARTS OF CALIFORNIA. BUT IT'S STILL NOT CLEAR WHETHER THAT SPRAYING WILL ACTUALLY TAKE PLACE. A CALIFORNIA JUDGE SAID TODAY HE WILL NOT ALLOW ANY SPRAYING OVER POPULATED AREAS UNTIL A HEARING ON JURISDICTIONAL AND SAFETY ASPECTS OF THE SPRAYING IS COMPLETED. AND THAT COULD TAKE TWO DAYS. THE CATCH IS THAT THE JUDGE HAS ISSUED NO OFFICIAL RULING. THAT MEANS THAT RIGHT NOW—LEGALLY—THERE'S NOTHING TO PREVENT THE SPRAYING FROM TAKING PLACE. AND A SPOKESMAN FOR THE ERADICATION PROJECT SAYS PLANS ARE TO GO AHEAD WITH THE SPRAYING.

The informal language, the difference in structure, and the more conversational flow are apparent.

These examples illustrate *back-in leads,* but not all broadcast leads begin this way. This fact is apparent when comparing newspaper and broadcast stories that dealt with the 1981 air traffic controllers' strike.

A 960-word newspaper version began:

> WASHINGTON (AP)—President Reagan, confronting his stiffest labor challenge, faced a showdown today with the nation's air traffic controllers, who had to decide whether to return to work or be fired.
>
> But the striking controllers, who forced cancellations of almost 30 percent of all regularly scheduled commercial flights, appeared to be holding their ranks despite the dismissal ultimatum and multi-million dollar fines that increase each day of the strike. Robert E. Poli, president of the Professional Air Traffic Controllers Organization, says their resolve has not diminished.
>
> "If they show up on their shifts they will have their jobs," Transportation Secretary Drew Lewis told reporters Tuesday. Those who don't will be dismissed and barred from federal employment, Lewis said.
>
> But the government's ultimatum appeared to be having little effect as the 7 a.m. shift reported for work at Eastern Airlines.

The broadcast wire version—written with sentences that are easy on the ear—began with:

THERE MAY BE A FEW STRIKING AIR TRAFFIC CONTROL-
LERS WHO AREN'T WATCHING THE CLOCK THIS MORNING—
BUT PROBABLY NOT MANY. ABOUT AN HOUR FROM NOW, CON-
TROLLERS ON THE DAY SHIFT WILL LOSE THEIR JOBS IF THEY
DO NOT REPORT TO WORK. THE DEADLINE WAS SET BY PRESI-
DENT REAGAN HIMSELF, WHO MAINTAINS THE CONTROLLERS
ARE VIOLATING THEIR OATH NOT TO STRIKE.

AND DESPITE THE THREAT OF BEING FIRED, CONTROLLERS
ARE CONTINUING TO STAY OFF THE JOB ON THIS, THE THIRD
DAY OF THEIR WALKOUT. OF 214 CONTROLLERS DUE TO WORK
AT FIVE AIRPORTS IN AND AROUND NEW YORK CITY THIS
MORNING, ONLY THREE PEOPLE REPORTED. AND MUCH OF THE
SAME IS TRUE AT WASHINGTON'S NATIONAL AIRPORT, LOGAN
AIRPORT IN BOSTON, AND BALTIMORE-WASHINGTON INTERNA-
TIONAL AIRPORT IN MARYLAND.

Naturally, one does not write a newspaper story or broadcast story by
strict formula, but these versions of same-subject stories show that different writing approaches are necessary.

BROADCAST COVERAGE VS. PRINT COVERAGE

Dan Fellner, an honors broadcast-journalism graduate of Arizona State
University, served internships at the Phoenix Gazette (an afternoon newspaper with a circulation of about 100,000) and at KPNX-TV (an NBC
affiliate in Phoenix) before he finished degree requirements. Very early in
his career Fellner cultivated an appreciation for the differences between
covering a story for print and for broadcast purposes.

As a Gazette intern Fellner was assigned to work with a regular staff
reporter who covered the county courts. On a slow Friday afternoon the
reporter suggested that Fellner check with the county's marriage license
bureau to compare statistics from previous periods. Fellner learned that
the bureau had just completed its busiest month in history. He talked with
two of the bureau's workers for direct quotations. Later, he called some
bridal stores; employees told him business was booming.

His 450-word feature story earned Page One play. It began:

Whoever said marriage is a dying institution?
Certainly not the clerks at the Maricopa County Marriage License
Bureau who in May issued more marriage licenses than in any other
one-month period in the bureau's history.
And if the first 12 days of June are any indication of what is to come,
this month could easily shatter May's record, despite a sluggish economy
and a divorce-rate high enough to scare off any couple from tying the
matrimonial knot.

"No matter what people have said, marriage hasn't gone out of style," said Rita Hill, a clerk at the bureau for six years. "It's always been here."

In May the bureau issued 1,700 licenses, toppling the June 1978 record of 1,657.

Fellner went on to quote the bureau's supervisor and spokespersons from area businesses that provided food, clothing, music and flowers for weddings. He closed with an anecdote about a young man who, before he finished filling out his license form, said he had to go to the restroom. He never came back.

About five months after Fellner had written the newspaper story, he was back at the same court building covering a story for television station KPNX. On a hunch he stopped by the marriage license bureau to see if business had fallen off. It had not. Indications pointed to a record-breaking year. Fellner wrote his assignment editor a note, suggesting a story on the local marriage boom. The editor liked the idea and instructed him to put the story together. The assignment editor suggested that Fellner look in the station's film-tape library to see if there was some stock video of a wedding ceremony that could be used to illustrate the story. Fellner and a photographer then went out to shoot video tape of the rest of the story. The cameraman taped some couples waiting in line for licenses and then shot video tape of the swearing-in process that they had to go through to get the document. Interviews were conducted with some couples and three of the bureau's workers.

"I feel it is important to interview as many people as possible," Fellner said. "That way you hopefully have a greater selection of interesting 'sound bites' to choose from when putting together the story. In this case, none of the married couples I interviewed was that interesting, so I ultimately did not include them in the finished product."

Fellner and the photographer then went to a bridal shop for video of practically everything in stock—from flowers to wedding gowns.

He and the photographer looked over the video tape to make sure that it was technically of acceptable quality; it was. Fellner then reviewed the interviews and selected portions. He avoided detailed statements that exceeded 20 seconds, selecting instead brief statements from two license bureau employees and one from the bridal shop owner.

Writing was easy.

"I just had to make sure we had the pictures to go with my words," Fellner said. "After having a producer approve the script, I went into an audio booth and cut the audio-track for the story."

The next day the photographer edited the piece on video tape. Fellner, like many reporters, likes to be present when his work is edited. The editing process took about an hour; the story was ready to be aired.

Total time, including the anchor lead-in, was about one minute forty-five seconds.

It went like this:

Video	*Audio*
Anchorperson on set.	Anchor lead-in: If you think marriage is a dying institution, you're wrong . . . at least not here in the Valley. In fact, as Dan Fellner reports, more Valley couples have tied the knot this year than ever before.
Couples getting their marriage licenses at the license bureau.	Reporter: Officials at the county's marriage license bureau say they've been busy this year. By the time 1980 ends, more than 15,000 couples will have come into their office to get a marriage license. That's substantially more than any other year in history. This has occurred despite a sluggish economy and a divorce rate high enough to scare any couple from taking the plunge.
Sound on video tape. Bureau worker with her name superimposed on the screen.	There are all ages of people coming in and I really don't know why they would be doing it now more than ever. Every age has been in here so it must be throughout society . . . people are getting married.
Another interview with a bureau worker	I think people are tired of short-lived romances. I think they want something more permanent.
Shots of a bridal shop. Name and address supered on the screen.	Valley businesses which sell anything you'd ever want for a wedding ceremony are benefiting greatly from all this. Some say 1980 has been their most profitable year ever. And the outlook for 1981, they say, is even better.
Sound on video tape. Store owner.	We were really surprised to find that the month of January—which is what we're figuring for right now—is 50 percent over January of last year. And we're anticipating we'll have the biggest year we've ever had in business.
Wedding ceremony.	(Wedding music from ceremony up full for seven seconds—then under narration:) But wedding-type businesses aren't the only ones to benefit from the marriage boom. If current statistics hold true, in a couple of years there's going to be an awful lot of busy divorce lawyers. Dan Fellner, TV-12, Action News.

Though Fellner dealt with the same topic in his newspaper account and television account, his approach and preparation were emphatically different.

TIPS FROM A PRO ON MAKING THE CONVERSION

What is it like to make the conversion from print to broadcast journalism? Fellner, who now is a reporter for KOLD-TV, the CBS affiliate in Tucson, Ariz., described it as "sort of like asking a brain surgeon to perform a heart operation. While many of the same principles apply in both areas, each requires quite different techniques and modes of operation."

Fellner, who took both broadcasting and print journalism courses in college, provides his perceptions of the differences between working for newspapers and working for television:

> To the uninitiated, broadcast reporting might appear to seem much easier. And in some ways it is. Reporting does not have to be as detailed. Minor facts that would be included in the bottom paragraphs of a newspaper article can be cast aside by the broadcast reporter. He or she simply does not have enough time to include them.
>
> While working in the City Hall pressroom, covering the same stories as newspaper reporters, it would not be uncommon for me to bang out a television story in the same amount of words as their first two paragraphs. There isn't a whole lot you can say when your story is allocated 30 seconds by the 6 o'clock producer.
>
> Another aspect of broadcast reporting that I found to be easier is interviewing. As a newspaper reporter I would write at a furious pace, trying to get enough words on paper so I could quote accurately and frequently when putting together the story. In television, the camera does all that for you. True, it is still necessary to take notes for background information. But in terms of quoting sources, all the television reporter generally has to do is look back over the video tape and select the appropriate "sound bites." It eliminates the possibility of misquoting and enables the reporter to concentrate on more important things during the interview.
>
> But while broadcast reporting is easier in some ways, in others it is much more difficult. True, stories are usually shorter and less detailed. This, however, can make life miserable for a broadcast reporter. Deciding how to condense a complicated story into four sentences is never easy. No doubt, important points have to be omitted for the sake of time. And this can be frustrating.
>
> While print reporters put words down on paper for people to read to themselves, broadcasters write for them or someone else to read out loud over the airwaves. So stories have to be put together with this in mind. Writing has to be less formal and more conversational. And sentences should be short and concise. Television anchors do not like having to read

stories that leave them gasping for breath. This was perhaps the most difficult adjustment for me to make when switching from print to broadcasting. My old newspaper habits had a tendency to show up in my television stories. It was not uncommon for producers to return my scripts, telling me to cut some of the sentences in half.

Another difficult transition to make when switching from print to television reporting is the sudden importance pictures have in telling the story. The television reporter constantly has to be thinking about the visual aspects of a story. And it is imperative that his or her writing fits with what the film or video tape is showing. Sometimes semi-important parts of a story will have to be left out because there is not any suitable video with which to visualize the information. Occasionally, entire stories will be discarded for this reason. It was not uncommon for my television assignment editor to reject a story because its visual possibilities were severely limited. "That's a good story for the newspapers," he would tell me. "Let them write it."

I have found print and broadcast reporting different in many ways. Yet when it comes right down to it, basic ingredients of both are the same: the gathering and dissemination of information in an accurate, fair and interesting manner.

ON THE JOB

Vernon A. Stone, in "Careers in Broadcast News," said that "radio and television are the most powerful and exciting news media. The camera and microphone transmit actuality—the sights and sounds of events as they happen, of history being made." Stone noted that the thousands of newcomers entering the job pool each year "usually find jobs in broadcast journalism if they are willing to start with realistic entry-level positions." According to Stone, about 30,000 persons work in radio and television news. Because of turnover, jobs are there—but it is a competitive field.

With approximately 4,500 AM radio stations, 3,000 FM radio stations and 900 television stations, it would indeed seem that qualified graduates could find jobs in broadcast journalism. Jobs and titles vary, depending on the market size, but most stations have at least one person on the news staff. Television stations in medium-size markets generally have from 10 to 40 persons on news staffs. Large stations in New York, Chicago or Los Angeles often have 100 or more. The networks also employ hundreds.

So the jobs are available, but they will differ from broadcast market to broadcast market, depending on size. To see why, let's look first at the one-person news staff of KHAS Radio in Hastings, Neb. (population 23,500) and then at a medium-size television market in Tucson, Ariz., with 27 persons on the news staff.

Working in Hastings

John Powell, general manager of KHAS Radio, looks for college graduates who have mass communication degrees and who have some professional experience to fill his news director's position. The job is demanding; the news director at KHAS, who is responsible for nearly all the local news that airs in Hastings, works an average of 12 hours a day, six days a week.

Paul Louderman, a graduate of Northern Illinois University, is Powell's news director. Powell demands no less than six local stories each day. Louderman must gather, write and edit them himself.

When hiring news directors, Powell places the greatest emphasis on the candidate's sensitivity to community interests. He looks for persons who understand local government, are confident of their abilities and possess "a degree of aggressiveness that is not offensive."

Powell realizes, however, that as soon as a news director at KHAS has "learned the ropes," he likely will move on to more money, a bigger market and fewer hours. Louderman's two immediate predecessors both landed jobs at larger stations: One became news director of a four-person staff in Illinois, and the other became news director of a four-person staff in California.

Louderman's days are long—and busy. Normally he reports to work at about 9 a.m. He checks for telephone messages and then starts on his beat. His first stop is the police station. He examines a sheet that lists crimes of the past 24 hours. If something seems significant, he asks for the full report. He then stops by the dispatcher's office to look at accident reports.

After 20 minutes at the police station, he goes to city hall. He talks with the civil defense director, city clerk and other local government office holders. He then drives to the county courthouse. He stops in to check on activities at most offices there, including the clerk's office, sheriff's office, recorder of deeds and county attorney's office.

By 10:30 he is back at the station preparing for his noon newscast. If time permits, he makes phone calls to begin developing leads for the next day's stories. On this particular day, however, he spends most of the time gathering information on an early morning blaze at the Hastings Coal Fire Plant. The early morning news carried little detail about the fire:

HASTINGS FIREFIGHTERS CONVERGED ON THE HASTINGS COAL FIRE PLANT EARLY THIS MORNING TO FIGHT A BLAZE THAT BEGAN IN A DUST COLLECTOR UNIT. HASTINGS ASSISTANT FIRE CHIEF JIM MITERA DESCRIBED DAMAGE AS "CONSIDERABLE." HE SAID TODAY NO MONETARY ESTIMATE OF DAMAGES HAS BEEN MADE. THE FIRE WAS REPORTED AT APPROXIMATELY 2-40 THIS MORNING.

Louderman expanded his noon newscast story to include two *actualities* (excerpts from an audio tape of newsmakers):

DAMAGE IS TERMED EXTENSIVE TO A METAL DUST SUP-
PRESSION MACHINE AT THE HASTINGS COAL FIRE PLANT FOL-
LOWING AN EARLY MORNING BLAZE TODAY. ABOUT FORTY
FIREFIGHTERS WERE CALLED IN BY THE HASTINGS UTILITIES
STAFF AT ABOUT 2-40 THIS MORNING. THE DUST COLLECTOR IS
LOCATED ON THE SOUTH ROOF OF THE MAIN BUILDING. IT IS
USED TO SEPARATE THE COAL DUST AND AIR MIXTURE.
PLANT AND FIRE OFFICIALS MET THIS MORNING TO DETER-
MINE THE CAUSE. PLANT SUPERINTENDENT GLENN HORNER
TELLS REPORTERS HOW IT HAPPENED:
"... TO DISCHARGE TO COAL." :21

(This is the *end cue*—the last words of the actuality excerpt and the
time elapsed.)

DAMAGE IS ESTIMATED UNDER 100-THOUSAND DOLLARS,
BUT HORNER WOULD NOT ALLOW REPORTERS TO SEE THE
DAMAGE UNTIL THE INSURANCE COMPANY LOOKS AT IT.
ASSISTANT FIRE CHIEF JIM MITERA CALLED THE FIRE "TOTAL-
LY INVOLVED."
"... ADEQUATE NATURE." :18
THE FIRE WAS UNDER CONTROL ONCE FIREFIGHTERS
WERE ON THE TOP OF THE BUILDING. NO INJURIES WERE RE-
PORTED. A FULL INVESTIGATION IS EXPECTED.

After his noon newscast, Louderman must write and tape headlines
for the afternoon. (KHAS airs five-minute newscasts on the hour.) He
spends the afternoon interviewing people for a second-day follow on the
coal story. Louderman talks with the assistant fire chief, the civil defense
director, two volunteer firemen and the mayor. At 7:30 p.m. he covers a
meeting of city and union officials that focuses on an upcoming contract.
After the meeting he visits with some union officials; it is off-the-record.

By the time Louderman puts together news stories about the meeting
and pieces together an update on the coal fire based upon his interviews, it
is 2:30 in the morning.

Louderman's day—a typical one—illustrates why Powell thinks
"stamina is a major requisite in the makeup of a small-station radio news
director." This is especially true during annual nightly budget hearings by
the city council or county supervisors.

Working in Tucson

Arizona State University graduate Dan Fellner keeps a busy pace as a
reporter for KOLD-TV, Tucson, but he puts in a conventional 40-hour
week. He is part of a 27-person news team that includes the news director,
an executive producer, three producers, a production assistant, an assign-

ment editor, seven anchors (weekday and weekend), seven reporters and six camerapersons.

KOLD-TV's local coverage often focuses on events at the University of Arizona, on city and county government and on the weather. High school sports are given much more attention than in larger markets. Stations in this size market (Tucson is a city of about 335,000) normally do not hire reporters straight out of college, but Fellner is an exception.

One day recently he developed a major, lengthy story and a shorter piece for the evening news. At 8:30 a.m. Fellner is assigned to do a follow-up story on the preceding day's major tanker truck spill of a dangerous chemical. It forced the evacuation of 2,000 people in Blythe, Calif., a community about 265 miles northwest of Tucson. The assignment editor asks Fellner to check with state officials to determine how they attempt to keep such accidents to a minimum.

By 9:30 a.m. Fellner has made several telephone calls and has arranged to ride with a hazardous-cargo investigator who is with the state's Corporation Commission. Fellner also checks the station's news files for background material.

Between 9:30 and 11:30 Fellner and a photographer ride with the hazardous-cargo investigator during routine inspections on the highway north of Tucson. They shoot an interview with the investigator and one of the truckers he stops. They also shoot a reporter stand-up at the scene of the inspection.

After lunch Fellner and the photographer return to the station to look over the 20 minutes of tape they shot. The best portions are selected from the interviews, and they get an idea of what video to use. Between 1 o'clock and 1:45, Fellner writes the script. He is given a minute and 45 seconds by the producer. At 2 o'clock the producer approves the script.

Minutes later a story comes over the wire indicating that the University of Arizona president has appointed a committee to investigate alleged improprieties in the athletic department. Fellner is told to go to the university to get a quick interview with the president. Fellner calls to set it up, but the president refuses to discuss the matter on camera. "Once you turn on the camera, it has a tendency to do strange things to people," Fellner said. The president does, however, provide some information on the telephone; Fellner then writes a 35-second story for the anchors to read on the 5 o'clock news.

At 3 o'clock Fellner checks the wires and writes a 30-second read-over on the latest about the tanker mishap. It will run immediately before his story on tanker truck inspections.

Between 3:30 and 4:30, the photographer edits Fellner's story on video tape. Fellner is there to make suggestions about what shots to use. The story turns out to be a little shorter than expected, so Fellner selects another seven-second sound bite to insert midway through the story.

Between 4:30 and 5 o'clock, Fellner meets with his assignment editor to discuss story ideas for the following day. On the 5 o'clock news, his main story airs. The anchor begins with a lead also written by Fellner:

Video	*Audio*
Tanker truck accident.	Anchor lead-in: About 300 residents of a Blythe trailer park remain forced out of their home for the second straight day. The trailer park is directly in the path of a cloud of acid vapor which spilled from a tanker truck yesterday on Interstate-10. The accident forced the evacuation of about 2-thousand people. Most of them have now been given the go-ahead to return home. The Arizona Corporation Commission is faced with the difficult task of keeping such accidents to a minimum. But as Dan Fellner reports, it's a tough job easier said than done.
Commission car parked in the bushes by the highway. Suddenly, he pulls out in pursuit of a truck.	Reporter: Ed Neasakowski parks his car every day near the freeway and keeps a watchful eye on traffic. But he's not looking for speeders. He's searching for truckers loaded with hazardous materials . . . who may be violating state law.
Interview with Neasakowski with name supered on screen.	He discusses the importance of his job . . . (12 seconds).
Neasakowski pulling over trucker for inspection.	Every day some 12-hundred trucks pass through Tucson . . . hauling dangerous cargo like explosives, chemicals and fuel. And some of them . . . like this trucker, are pulled over for routine inspections.
Neasakowski talking to trucker.	He tells the trucker why he was stopped . . . (8 seconds).
Shots of the inspection and the truck's discharge valve.	As it turned out, the trucker was not in compliance with the law . . . one of more than a hundred such vehicles found every month. He's hauling a dangerous explosive . . . ammonium nitrate. This discharge valve was missing a cover and there could have been a leak.
Shots of chemical inside the discharge valve.	Neasakowski explains what could have happened had the chemical started leaking . . . (5 seconds).
Shots of truck's wheels. Neasakowski writes a citation and puts an out-of-service sign on the truck.	Also, two of the truck's wheels were cracked . . . and eventually . . . could have fallen off. For the safety violations, the trucker faces a stiff fine and is put out of service until he makes the needed repairs.

Fellner standing in
front of a tanker truck
with a "Warning . . .
Flammable" sign on the
truck next to him.
(reporter stand-up)

Truckers hauling hazardous loads are required by law to post warning signs like this one. But officials say many will skip the sign to avoid inspections.

Trucks on highway.

It's truckers like that officials are most worried about . . . people who try to skirt the rules and at the same time, risk the public's safety. For the News, Dan Fellner reporting.

TIPS FOR BROADCAST JOURNALISTS

Professor Ben Silver of Arizona State University, a former CBS newsman, offers the following suggestions to students who aspire to broadcast journalism positions:

- *Learn not only how to report and write but how to perform as well.* After all, stories that are written are aired on news *shows.* Because of the emphasis on live coverage in broadcast reporting, reporters should learn to speak extemporaneously.

- *Learn the production techniques and the capabilities and limitations of the equipment used in both broadcast news gathering and news presentation.* In radio, reporters are expected to record and edit audio tape. Reporters in small-market television news are expected to know how to use a minicam and video editing equipment.

- *Recognize that television is a unique medium—a visual medium that can show action.* Therefore, the kind and quality of visual material available for a given story frequently determine the length and position the news producer will allot to it. It is not unusual for a producer to ask a reporter, "What kind of film or video tape do we have on the story?" One of the challenges of the TV news reporter is to get motion pictures of the story.

- *Learn to think visually.* To a certain extent this is the cameraperson's job. But it is also the reporter's responsibility. News event coverage is a team effort, with the reporter in charge. If there is a communication breakdown and the reporter does not let the cameraperson know what will be said in the script, the reporter often winds up with a well-written story but without the necessary footage to visually tell it.

- *When putting together stories for television, make sure that the words match the motion pictures.* If they do not, the words compete with the pictures. Nothing gets through to the listeners. The picture is saying one thing, and the words are saying something else. Although the words should match the picture, they should not tell viewers what they can see for themselves. Let the picture tell part of the story, and use the words as a supplement—to explain or reinforce the picture or to tell the audience what the picture does not show. Words compete with the picture when there is too much narration.

- *Remember that the last sentence of a broadcast news item is the second most important part of the story.* Only the lead is more important. The final sentence is the wind-up line, the "punch line." Winding up with the least important fact in a broadcast story would sound like a balloon with the air running slowly out of it. The reporter should use a summary line or a future angle to end the story.

EXTENDED ELECTRONIC COVERAGE IN COURTROOMS

Television news teams constantly strive to coordinate pictures with words. In 1981 the U.S. Supreme Court handed down a decision that pleased broadcast journalists who long had advocated the televising of state court proceedings. The question that faced the court was whether, consistent with constitutional guarantees, a state could provide for radio, television and still photographic coverage of a criminal trial for public broadcast— even when the accused objected. It was not an overnight issue. In 1937 the American Bar Association had passed Canon 35—a "suggestive code"— that banned cameras in state courtrooms. In 1952 an amendment was approved that included television cameras in the ban. All but a handful of states adopted the rationale of Canon 35. In 1972 the Code of Judicial Conduct replaced the Canons of Judicial Ethics and Canon 35 was replaced by Section 3A(7). Rule 53 of the Federal Rules of Criminal Procedure— enacted in 1946—effectively banned cameras in federal courtrooms.

By the mid-1970s, however, some states had launched movements to allow camera coverage of state court proceedings. In 1978 a Washington Post survey showed that 56 percent of the lawyers, state supreme court justices and law professors favored electronic coverage of trials. About 31 percent disapproved; 13 percent were uncertain.

The only previous time the U.S. Supreme Court had considered the camera issue was in 1965 (*Estes v. Texas*). In that case the Supreme Court held that Billy Sol Estes, a financier charged with theft, swindling and embezzlement involving the federal government, had been deprived of a fair trial because of cumbersome camera coverage of portions of it. The decision, of course, was based upon the state of the technology at that time. Justice Tom Clark, who wrote the majority opinion, said that the cameras had an impact on the jurors, the quality of the testimony and the defendant. He said also that the cameras placed additional responsibilities on the judge to control the courtroom.

Chief Justice Earl Warren wrote a concurring opinion. He said that television was "one of the great inventions of all times and can perform a large and useful role in society. But, the television camera is not entitled to pervade the lives of everyone in disregard of constitutionally protected rights."

Justice John Marshall Harlan's concurring opinion, however, kept *Estes* from becoming a blanket constitutional prohibition against televising state criminal proceedings. He said that the door should be left open for future camera coverage as the technology became sufficiently sophisticated.

When the Supreme Court considered the question of the constitutionality of cameras in state courtrooms in January 1981, more than 20 states were experimenting or already had experimented with them. The issue was ripe for adjudication.

In July 1977 Noel Chandler and Robert Granger were charged in Florida with conspiracy to commit burglary, grand larceny and possession of burglary tools. The counts covered breaking and entering a restaurant on Miami Beach. Chandler and Granger were Miami Beach policemen. Interestingly, the state's main witness was an amateur radio operator who had overheard and recorded conversations between Chandler and Granger on their police walkie-talkie radios as they planned the burglary. These factors made the case particularly newsworthy. The case was widely publicized.

Chandler and Granger's counsel sought to ban electronic coverage of the trial. The judge refused. A television camera filmed proceedings during an afternoon in which the state presented the testimony of the chief witness. No camera was in place for presentation of defense arguments. Some two minutes and 55 seconds of the trial were broadcast. The jury returned a guilty verdict on all counts. Chandler and Granger appealed, claiming that because of the television coverage, they had been denied a fair and impartial trial. Lower courts said they had not.

The U.S. Supreme Court voted 8-0 to affirm the lower courts. Chief Justice Warren Burger said that *Estes* did not announce a constitutional rule that *all* photo, radio and television coverage of criminal trials was inherently a denial of due process. Burger said, "It does not stand as an absolute ban on state experimentation with an evolving technology, which in terms of modes of mass communication, was in its relative infancy in 1964, and is, even now, in a state of continuing change."

Burger said that any criminal case "that generates a great deal of publicity presents some risks that the publicity may compromise the right of the defendant to a fair trial." Trial courts would have to be "especially vigilant to guard against any impairment of the defendant's right." Still, an "absolute ban" on camera coverage could not be justified "simply be-

cause there is a danger that, in some cases, prejudicial broadcast accounts
. . . may impair the ability of jurors to decide the issue of guilt or innocence
uninfluenced by extraneous matter."

Burger also talked about the Florida program. The experiment began
in July 1977 and continued through June 1978. When the pilot program
ended, the Florida Supreme Court reviewed briefs, reports, letters of
comment and studies. The court also studied the experience of six other
states that had experimented with electronic coverage of state trials.

The chief justice seemed pleased with the safeguards built into the
Florida program, which were similar to those of other states. The Florida
guidelines provided the following: Only one television camera and technician were allowed in the courtroom; coverage had to be pooled; there could
be no artificial lighting; equipment had to be placed in fixed positions;
video taping equipment had to be remote from the courtroom; film could
not be changed when the court was in session; the jury could not be filmed;
the judge had sole discretion to exclude coverage of certain witnesses, and
the judge had discretionary power to forbid coverage whenever satisfied
that it could have a "deleterious effect on the paramount right of the
defendant to a fair trial."

Media Law Reporter quoted J. Laurent Scharff, of Pierson, Ball &
Dowd, Washington, who represents the Radio Television News Directors
Association. He said that the court "is no longer willing to assume the
worst about broadcasting." Richard J. Ovelmen, of Paul & Thompson,
Miami, who represented public television stations in Florida in a friend-of-
the-court brief, however, said that *Chandler* "turns almost entirely on
federalism and on the failure of the defendants to show actual prejudice,
and doesn't deal with the positive aspects of television."

Despite some misgivings electronic media journalists generally regarded the *Chandler* decision as a much-deserved victory. The American
Bar Association's House of Delegates in August 1982 reacted in a positive
way to the *Chandler* decision. The delegates repealed Section 3A (7),
passed in 1972. Undoubtedly more and more states will permit cameras,
microphones and recorders on an experimental or permanent basis. When
the delegates repealed the section, some 38 states already were experimenting or already had adopted electronic coverage of trials on a
permanent basis.

S U G G E S T E D   E X E R C I S E S

1. Invite a local broadcaster who has print experience to your class. What were the
main adjustments the reporter had to make when the switch from print to electronic journalism was made?

2. The following two stories were transmitted on the AP's newspaper wire. Rewrite them in broadcast form:

ELOY, Ariz. (AP)—An anonymous call led Pinal County sheriff's deputies to the body of a man 315 feet down an abandoned irrigation well near here, Sheriff Mike Reyes said Monday.

Reyes said the call came Saturday night but that deputies were unable to see a body in the 30-inch-diameter well until Sunday night after special search equipment using television cameras was brought from Phoenix.

He said the partially decomposed body appeared to be that of an Anglo male but that identity, cause of death and how long the body was in the well couldn't be determined until an autopsy was completed.

PHOENIX, Ariz. (AP)—Gov. Bruce Babbitt's nominations of Bill Jamieson and Tim Barrow as department directors won the unanimous recommendation of the State Government Committee Monday.

Sent to the full Senate were the recommendations for Jamieson, 39, as head of the Department of Administration and Barrow, 49, as director of the new Racing Department.

Jamieson, who headed the Department of Economic Security for 4 1/2 years, was reshuffled at his own request to the Administration Department in December. His work as DES director was praised by Republican Sen. Jacque Steiner of Phoenix and House Democratic Leader Art Hamilton of Phoenix.

3. Cover a news event. Write one story in newspaper style, the second story in broadcast style.

4. Invite the communication law professor at your school to visit your class to discuss the First Amendment protection extended to the print media and the First Amendment protection extended to the electronic media.

5. Find out whether cameras are allowed in courtrooms in your state. If they are allowed, what are the conditions?

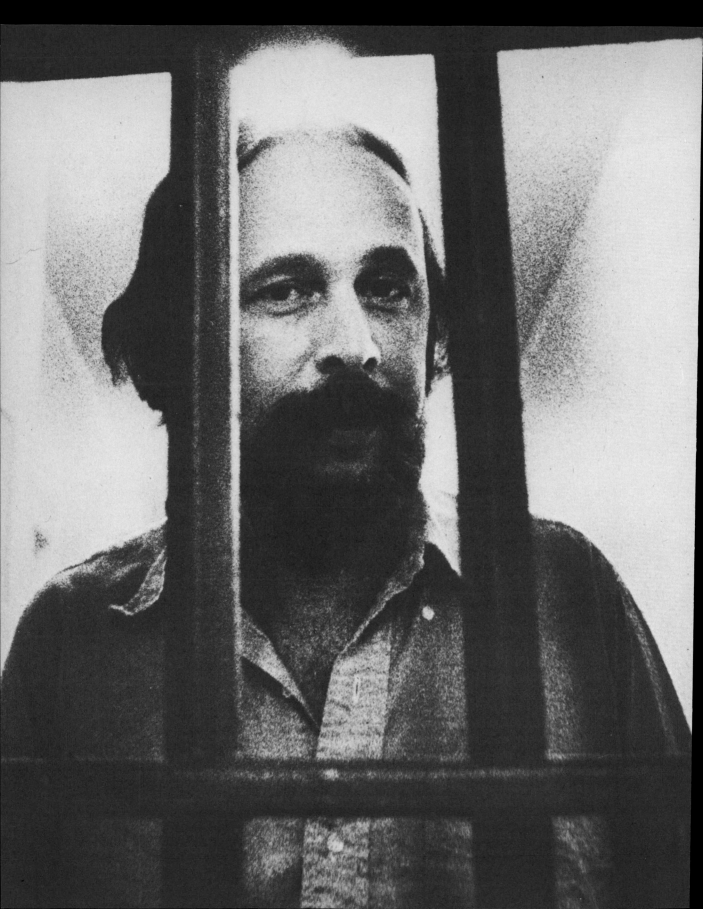

In a national survey, more than two-thirds of the editors polled said that their newspapers had been involved in litigation during the past five years. This chapter discusses legal areas of practical concern to journalists.

You will be introduced to:

• Court cases and federal statutes concerning newsroom searches by law enforcement officers. The chapter discusses procedures reporters should follow if ever confronted with a newsroom search.

• Court cases and laws relevant to journalists asked to reveal confidential information or names of sources.

• Libel, the area of greatest legal danger to reporters. The chapter discusses significant court cases, available defenses and "Red Flag" words that reporters and editors should handle carefully.

• Invasion of privacy considerations. The chapter discusses the four branches of privacy. Stories that brought about privacy suits are examined.

• The conflict between the rights of the press to report court proceedings and the rights of the accused to receive a fair trial. The chapter describes significant court cases and provides advice to reporters covering closed trials.

New York Times reporter Myron Farber peers from behind bars. Farber was jailed for refusing to turn over his notes relating to a murder trial.

Wide World Photos

313

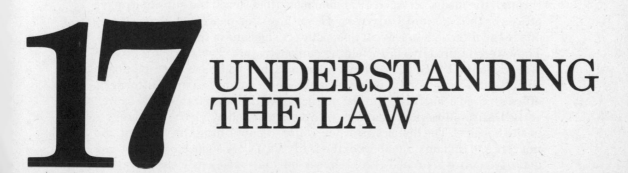

17 UNDERSTANDING THE LAW

The reporter's lot when dealing with controversial stories would be secure if the First Amendment meant precisely what it says: Congress shall make *no* law abridging freedom of speech or press. That, of course, is not the case. Only seven years after ratification of the First Amendment, Congress passed the Alien and Sedition Laws of 1798, the latter designed to stifle criticism of the government. Those laws expired when the Thomas Jefferson administration took office in 1801, but more than a century later, in 1918, Congress approved another Sedition Act for basically the same reason.

The U.S. Supreme Court, in *New York Times Co. v. Sullivan* (1964), essentially put to death the concept of seditious libel in this country, but the courts repeatedly have held that the First Amendment is not an absolute. Very simply, there are exceptions to its seemingly ironclad language.

The courts constantly are called upon to decide whether actions taken by the press are legally permissible. As the courts consider issues on a case-by-case basis, journalists are obligated to stay abreast of significant decisions.

A national survey reported in Journalism Quarterly showed that editors are increasingly cognizant of the need to keep pace with communication law developments in the 1980s. Student journalists—as well as professionals—certainly need to be aware of the effects of court decisions on reporters and editors. Applicable court decisions should not be looked at as esoteric ramblings by scholarly justices; working journalists should view the decisions as fragments of wisdom that help them to function effectively—day by day.

Areas of particular concern to reporters are newsroom searches, protection of sources, libel actions, invasion of privacy suits and the fair trial/free press controversy.

NEWSROOM SEARCHES

A case decided in 1978 (*Zurcher v. Stanford Daily*) sent shockwaves through the media. In April 1971 demonstrators seized the administrative offices of the Stanford University Hospital. After peaceful efforts to persuade the intruders to leave failed, police rushed one of the hospital wings. They were injured by club-wielding demonstrators. Two days later a special edition of the Stanford Daily was published complete with photos of the altercation. The next day the Santa Clara County district attorney's office secured a warrant from the municipal court for an immediate search of the Daily's offices for negatives, film or pictures showing the occurrences at the hospital. The district attorney's office, in obtaining the warrant, did not contend that any members of the Daily staff were suspected of criminal activity. Police searched the premises but did not open locked drawers and rooms. The lower courts held that the First Amendment precludes searches of innocent third-party newspapers except "in rare circumstances" in which authorities feel certain that the materials in question would be destroyed or removed from the premises.

On May 31, 1978, however, the U.S. Supreme Court reversed the lower court ruling holding that neither the First nor 14th Amendments were violated by issuance of a search warrant to obtain criminal evidence reasonably believed to be at the newspaper office. Justice Byron White said that precedent cases clearly showed that the state's interest in enforcing the law "is the same, whether the third party is innocent or not." White rejected Stanford Daily arguments that searches of this nature would be physically disruptive, impeding publication schedules; cause confidential news sources to dry up; disclose internal editorial deliberations, and lead to self-censorship by the press.

The possibility of police ransacking newsrooms suddenly became real. According to the "Survival Kit for Reporters, Editors and Broadcasters" (1980), issued by the New York State Newspapers Foundation, if police obtain a warrant to search a newspaper's premises, the warrant must contain:

- The name of the issuing court and signature of the issuing judge.
- The identity of the police officer or department to whom it is addressed.
- A description of the premises or person to be searched.
- A description of the property to be seized.
- An instruction as to the time the search may be executed.
- A direction that the seized property must be returned without delay to the court that issued the warrant.

If newspaper personnel refuse to allow the authorities to enter, the police may use physical force to execute the warrant.

Court Precedent Is Offset

When authorities show up at a newspaper's front door with a search warrant, there is no warning. Recognizing this problem, President Jimmy Carter signed a bill in October 1980 that to a certain extent offset *Stanford Daily*. The bill prohibited federal, state and local law enforcement agencies from conducting surprise newsroom searches except under *exceptional circumstances*.

The bill required government officials to obtain a subpoena—rather than a search warrant—when seeking information from a person who has collected it "with a purpose to disseminate to the public a newspaper, book, broadcast or other similar form of public communication." Journalists generally are pleased with the law. Subpoenas must be issued in most cases—thus giving newspapers a chance to delay on technical grounds. Fighting subpoenas has, in fact, become a major ordeal for many American newspapers. This was made clear at the First Amendment Survival Seminar, an all-day session sponsored by 16 media organizations that was held in Washington, D. C., in March 1979. The National Press Foundation and the Philadelphia Inquirer funded and published a transcript of the seminar.

Christopher Little, vice president and general counsel for the Washington Post, told the seminar that "an increasingly large percentage of our monthly legal bill relates not to defending libel suits, but to fighting subpoenas. One reason is there are a lot of lazy lawyers. One of the easiest ways to get a witness who knows something about a case is find out who has been writing about it for the local paper and subpoena them."

Contingency Plans for Newsroom Searches

Though subpoenas generally must be issued, it is important that reporters, editors and publishers formulate contingency plans to be implemented should they find themselves in a situation similar to that of the Stanford Daily staff. At the First Amendment Survival Seminar, Sam Klein, counsel to the Philadelphia Inquirer, recommended that journalists follow these procedures if a police officer walks into the newsroom with a search warrant:

- Do not make any physical attempt to stop the police.
- Attempt to delay the police until your attorney can arrive.
- Read the warrant and review it; take your time, giving your attorney time to get there.
- Question the police officer about the search.
- Advise the police that they are going to be searching in areas that contain confidential information.
- Notify the photography department; get a photographer to follow the police around, taking pictures.
- Log in items that police look at or examine.
- Get signed receipts itemizing all property seized.
- Do not help the police. You cannot interfere, but you do not have to aid them.

REPORTERS AND THEIR SOURCES

Reporters historically have guarded the identities of anonymous sources. It is theorized that once a reporter betrays a confidential source, the reporter's other anonymous contacts soon will vanish. Why, after all, would sources who wished to remain unnamed give information to reporters if the sources thought they might be betrayed?

The problem has become more acute during the past decade. Attorneys and police have turned with increasing frequency to reporters for information. As investigative reporting increases, it is only logical that reporters will, in some instances, obtain information that could be helpful to authorities. To date, the U.S. Supreme Court has considered only one case that focuses on journalists' privilege. In 1972 the Court held that the First Amendment does not provide a testimonial privilege to reporters who have witnessed a crime if they are called upon to testify during a criminal investigation (*Branzburg v. Hayes*).

The Branzburg Case

Paul Branzburg, a Louisville Courier-Journal reporter, had witnessed illegal drug use and had written articles about it. He was subpoenaed and asked to testify before a grand jury. He refused, claiming a First Amendment privilege. Justice Byron White, who wrote the majority decision for the High Court, said that to contend that it is better to write about a crime than to do something about it is absurd. White's opinion, though not well received by the press, did provide some hope. He emphasized that official harassment of the press in an effort to disrupt the reporter's relationship with his sources would not be tolerated. White also said that states were free to implement statutory laws—shield laws—to protect reporters.

Justice Lewis F. Powell Jr., in a concurring opinion, attempted to put *Branzburg* in perspective. He said that the ruling was "limited"; courts would still be available to newsmen who think that their First Amendment rights have been violated. Furthermore, the press could not be annexed as an "investigative right arm" of the government or judiciary, and if the requested testimony was "remote," news reporters could move to quash the subpoena. The information sought had to be relevant and go to the heart of the issue; it could not be a fishing expedition by the authorities.

Professor George Killenberg of Southern Illinois University-Edwardsville has emphasized the flexibility of *Branzburg*; though the decision went against the Louisville reporter, portions of the opinion did provide the rationale for lower courts to halt any blatant abuses of a reporter's First Amendment rights. Killenberg wrote in Journalism

Quarterly, "Judicial developments have shown that *Branzburg* was not a death knell for press freedom."

In fact, it allowed lower courts to interpret as broad the boundaries established by the High Court. A number of state and lower federal courts have in turn upheld the right of news reporters to protect their sources under certain conditions. In other circumstances, however, several lower courts have not upheld the reporter's rights.

Shield Laws

Though the Supreme Court made it plain that the First Amendment would not provide absolute protection for journalists called to testify, it did leave the door open for states to pass laws that would shield reporters from testifying. More than half the states have done so. Some states have relatively stringent *shield laws* that provide a great deal of protection, whereas others have qualified shield laws. It is important to remember, however, that even the most stringent laws likely have some loopholes.

Nebraska has one of the country's more stringent laws. The Nebraska law is designed to ensure the free flow of news and other information to the public and to protect the reporter against direct or indirect governmental restraint or sanction. The statute states that "compelling such persons to disclose a source of information or to disclose unpublished information is contrary to the public interest and inhibits the free flow of information to the public." The law protects reporters from testifying before any federal or state judicial, legislative, executive or administrative body.

No matter how ironclad shield laws appear, however, they are subject to interpretation by the judiciary. The constitutionality of most shield laws has never been contested, and even if their constitutionality were upheld, hostile judicial interpretation could strip protection from the reporter. In essence, it is better to work in a state with a shield law than in a state without one, but reporters should not make the assumption that the law will always keep them out of jail.

The New Jersey shield law, for example, did not provide sufficient protection to New York Times reporter Myron A. Farber. Farber had written two 3,000-word articles about mysterious deaths in a suburban New Jersey hospital. The deaths occurred in 1965 and 1966; Farber's articles appeared 10 years later. His articles prompted the state to reopen an investigation of the deaths, and a doctor was indicted for allegedly murdering five patients.

At the doctor's trial Farber was subpoenaed and asked to turn over his notes. Farber refused. The subpoena sought the production of *all* statements, pictures, memoranda, recordings and notes of all interviews with the defense and prosecution witnesses. More than 100 persons were on the list. The defense counsel merely signed an affidavit that "on information and belief" all documents were "critical" to the defense. In essence, the defense counsel was asking to conduct a search of countless documents with no proof that any were necessary or relevant. The trial judge asked to inspect the items privately to see whether the state shield law applied. Farber also refused this request. The result: Farber and the Times were hit with both criminal and civil contempt citations, and Farber was sentenced to jail.

The Supreme Court never reviewed the *Farber* case, for the doctor was found innocent, and the reporter was released from jail—after 40 days of confinement. Still, the case should serve as a warning to journalists. Though *Branzburg* seemingly limited subpoenas to situations in which authorities could show the relevancy of the information sought—information not available from other sources—Farber was not given this benefit. Furthermore, the Times had to pay more than $275,000 in fines and legal fees. The newspaper has declared its intention to help its reporters protect their informants despite high costs, but most newspapers do not have the economic resources to make this guarantee. Thus, though states might have shield laws, reporters should not mistake them for infallible saviors if called upon to testify in official proceedings.

The common law does not provide protection to journalists who are called upon to reveal their sources (unlike the common law privilege extended to doctors, lawyers and clergy). Nor does the First Amendment provide an absolute protection, though, on occasion, courts have said that the Constitution does provide some qualified protection when government requests are not specific, relevant and essential. Finally, state shield laws, though better than nothing, do not provide ironclad protection when reporters are asked to reveal their sources.

In addition to worrying about revealing names of confidential sources during investigations of criminal wrongdoing, reporters also must face the possibility that plaintiffs while bringing suit for libel will seek the identities of persons who supplied the information on which the story was based. In fact, shield laws in some states specifically say that protection is not extended to journalists under these circumstances. Though shield laws might not help journalists involved in libel actions, the journalists are not without protection.

In December of 1970, for example, Jack Anderson's syndicated "Washington Merry-Go-Round" newspaper column reported that United Mine Workers' president Tony Boyle and general counsel Ed Carey had been seen removing boxfuls of documents from Boyle's office. Later, Carey made an official complaint to Washington police that burglars had stolen a boxful of "miscellaneous items." Because the United Mine Workers union was under investigation by the Justice Department, Carey contended that the column had, essentially, falsely accused him of obstruction of justice.

Carey brought a libel suit against Anderson and reporter Brit Hume. Crucial to Carey's proving that Anderson and Hume had acted in "reckless disregard for the truth"—a necessary condition to collect damages—was his showing that Anderson and Hume had obtained their information from an unreliable source. The Court of Appeals for the District of Columbia reasoned that this was a heavy burden to meet and that the identity of the source therefore was critical to Carey's claim. Hume was prepared to go to jail for contempt, fully intending not to reveal his source. However, the source, a former UMW employee, voluntarily stepped forward to testify at the jury trial. This likely saved Hume from going to jail.

Circumstances were similar in another libel suit brought against Jack Anderson and his "Merry-Go-Round" column (*Shelton v. Anderson*). Turner B. Shelton, former ambassador to Nicaragua, sought damages for a column critical of his performance as a public official. Shelton claimed that several of the allegations made against him were false. As had Carey, Shelton attempted to compel Anderson to reveal confidential sources who had supplied information. Anderson supplied the names of several non-confidential sources, but he refused to supply the names of those persons who had been promised anonymity. The District Court for the District of Columbia reasoned that because Shelton had made no effort to question any non-confidential sources, one could hardly conclude that the identities of unnamed sources were *essential* to his case. Thus Anderson was not forced to reveal the names.

It becomes apparent, then, that the flexibility of *Branzburg* can be used to protect journalists who are asked to reveal their confidential sources, particularly when the information sought is not directly relevant to the issue or if other equally valuable sources have not been tapped. Killenberg, though, cautions against taking an overly optimistic view of post-*Branzburg* developments. He wrote that though reporters have successfully fought revealing their sources on some occasions, this trend "cannot be viewed too optimistically because, despite some victories for newsmen, many judges still believe newsmen's privilege is an unjustified impediment to the judicial system's search for the truth."

LIBEL LAW BOUNDARIES

Possibly the area of greatest legal danger to a reporter is libel. Libel—holding someone up to public hatred, ridicule or scorn—is the communication of information that damages an individual in his personal reputation and good name, in his right to enjoy social contacts and in his profession, business or calling. Three requirements that must be met before a libel action can be successfully brought are: (1) publication (communication to a third party); (2) identification (though not limited to calling an individual by name), and (3) harmful effect.

William Prosser of the Hastings College of the Law wrote: "There is a great deal of the law of defamation which makes no sense. It contains anomalies and absurdities for which no legal writer ever has a kind word." Indeed, libel law is complex. Large-circulation newspapers have the luxury of retaining attorneys with special expertise in this area; most smaller-circulation papers retain lawyers, but they probably do not specialize in communication law. Knowing that virtually every story is potentially libelous is enough to make any reporter timid. It is imperative, therefore, that reporters have at least a basic understanding of libel law. Reporters can then free themselves from the albatross of calling an attorney—particularly one who does not specialize in communication law—every time a controversial story is written.

In fact, veteran Supreme Court reporter Lyle Denniston thinks that reporters are too dependent on attorneys. Though possibly an overstatement, Denniston wrote in Quill magazine that lawyers in the newsroom are "as much of a threat to the press as judges sitting on the bench deciding what we can print. I think you have to go hell for election with your stories and then take the consequences—and I do mean prepare to go to the slammer." Translation: Newspaper attorneys are retained to keep their newspapers out of court; the easiest way to do so is to avoid printing controversial stories.

Most libel suits, however, do not grow from hard-hitting, aggressive reporting of monumental importance. Instead, the majority of suits evolve from—to use the newsroom vernacular—stupid, idiotic mistakes. Bruce Sanford, a reporter-turned-attorney who represents United Press International and Scripps-Howard, said at the First Amendment Survival Seminar that the "chief cause of libel suits is plain old unromantic carelessness." Sanford estimated that 80 percent of all libel suits flows from "the simple, routine story that nobody would have missed if it hadn't appeared in the newspaper or been broadcast." Sanford cautions that reporters must be very careful with rewrites, condensations and summaries.

In an attempt to head off careless oversights, Sanford listed the following "Red Flag" words in "Synopsis of the Law of Libel and the Right of Privacy." Reporters and editors should handle these words carefully:

adulteration of products	buys votes	drunkard
adultery	cheats	ex-convict
altered records	collusion	false weights used
ambulance chaser	communist (or red)	fascist
atheist	confidence man	fawning sycophant
attempted suicide	correspondent	fool
bad moral character	corruption	fraud
bankrupt	coward	gambling house
bigamist	crook	gangster
blackguard	deadbeat	gouged money
blacklisted	deadhead	grafter
blackmail	defaulter	groveling office seeker
blockhead	disorderly house	humbug
booze-hound	divorced	hypocrite
bribery	double-crosser	illegitimate
brothel	drug addict	illicit relations

incompetent	plagiarist	sold his influence
infidelity	price cutter	sold out to a rival
informer	profiteering	spy
intemperate	pockets public funds	stool pigeon
intimate	rascal	stuffed the ballot box
intolerance	rogue	suicide
Jekyll-Hyde personality	scandalmonger	swindle
kept woman	scoundrel	unethical
Ku Klux Klan	seducer	unmarried mother
liar	sharp dealing	unprofessional
mental disease	short in accounts	unsound mind
moral delinquency	shyster	unworthy of credit
Nazi	skunk	vice den
paramour	slacker	villain
peeping Tom	smooth and tricky	
perjurer	sneak	

Attorney Richard Schmidt, general counsel for the American Society of Newspaper Editors and the Association of American Publishers, Inc., told the First Amendment Survival Seminar that reporters and editors cannot limit their scrutiny of fine detail to major, probing stories. Schmidt said that care must extend to "all the articles that come across a desk."

Reporters must be particularly careful when working with late-breaking, deadline stories. Stan Mortenson, a Washington, D.C., attorney, told the seminar he often is called by reporters who ask for information about a case and say, "I've got a story to write, and I've got a deadline a half hour away." Mortenson said the reporter then asks for a five-minute condensation of three years of litigation. "And they're going to go ahead and write a story, having no background whatsoever."

No matter how careful a good reporter is, though, libel suits can materialize.

Libel Defenses

If a libel suit is filed, a defendant can use a number of defenses. Some defenses are *conditional* (they are viable if certain conditions or qualifications are met); others are *absolute* (if proven, there are no conditions or qualifications).

Conditional Defenses
In their book, "Libel: Rights, Risks, Responsibilities," Robert H. Phelps and E. Douglas Hamilton, noted authorities on libel law, discuss complete, but conditional, defenses that have evolved through the *common law* (judge-made law based on prior court decisions) and statutory law. These defenses include:

- *Truth*. Truth is an absolute defense in some states, but in most it is conditional. The conditions are that the article must have been published for justifiable ends and with good motives.

- *Privilege of reporting*. This defense flows from fair and accurate reporting of official proceedings—city council meetings, state legislative sessions, congressional hearings and so forth—and the fair and accurate reporting of information contained in official documents and court records. Obviously, it is a defense that is often cited by reporters. As emphasized, however, the defense is limited to fair and accurate reporting. Extraneous libelous matter cannot be intertwined. If, for example, during a city council meeting the mayor accuses the council president of embezzling city funds, the reporter is free to report that the charges were made—so long as the story accurately conveys what the mayor said. Any elaboration or interpretation of the mayor's remarks by the reporter would not necessarily be protected.

- *Fair comment and criticism*. This defense applies only when writing *opinions* about matters of public concern. The defense does not protect erroneous factual reporting. It must be clear that the allegedly libelous statement—whether it appears in an editorial, book review or personal viewpoint column—is a statement of *opinion,* not an expression of *fact.* This defense is not available to the reporter who covers an event and then writes a factual news account. However, if a reporter were to comment upon the news event and offer an analysis of it in a personal column, this defense could then be utilized.

- *Neutral reportage*. In 1977 the 2nd U.S. Circuit Court of Appeals accepted neutral reportage as a conditional defense; that is, it is defensible to report charges made by one responsible person or organization about another when both parties are involved in a public controversy. This defense has not been widely accepted, and one circuit court has flatly rejected it. Where it applies, however, it makes available additional protection to the libel suit defendant. The defense was cited in *Edwards v. National Audubon Society* where a New York Times reporter wrote a story concerning accusations by officials of an Audubon Society periodical, American Birds, that scientists who contended that the insecticide DDT did not have a negative impact on bird life were being paid to lie. The Times' story included a short denial by some of the named scientists, who had sent to the reporter extensive research material to refute the charges. The 2nd U.S. Circuit Court of Appeals said that even when a newspaper seriously doubts the truth of the charges, the publication is protected under the defense of neutral reportage—objective and dispassionate reporting of both the charges and the denials.

Absolute Defenses

The following are absolute defenses:

- *Statute of limitations.* This is the most ironclad of the defenses. If a suit is brought after a specified period—in most states the statute of limitations on libel is one, two or three years—the plaintiff has no standing to sue.

- *Privilege of participant.* This defense applies to participants in official proceedings: a city councilman's remarks during a meeting, testimony of a witness during a trial, a U.S. senator speaking on the protected floor of the Senate. This, then, is not a defense reporters generally would be able to use. Reporters normally report the news—not make it.

- *Consent or authorization.* If a reporter writes a libelous passage, calls the individual in question and gets his permission to publish it, this defense can be used. Obviously, this situation is not likely to happen.

- *Self-defense or right of reply.* If publicly criticized, the recipient of the criticism has a privilege to respond. He must, however, be careful to keep his response within the framework of the original accusation. Journalists would not often have occasion to use this defense. An example of its use would be if a newspaper's drama critic treats the opening of a play harshly. The star of the play could respond, but the privilege covers his response to the original criticism. The star, in other words, could not launch a salvo critical of the reviewer's home life.

Partial Defenses

If conditional or absolute defense cannot be used successfully (including the conditional New York Times actual malice defense, which will be discussed in the next section), the defendant likely will be assessed damages. He or she can, however, cite *partial defenses* to mitigate the damages. Partial defenses represent good faith on the part of the defendant, and a judge can take them into consideration when levying damages. Partial defenses include publication of a retraction (a clear admission of erroneous reporting), or of facts showing that, though the newspaper erred, there was no gross negligence or ill will or that the reporter relied on a usually reliable source.

The New York Times Rule

Clearly, then, the reporter is not without common law and statutory defenses. However, these defenses are severely limited compared with the *federal rule* (commonly called the *actual malice defense*), a constitutional defense first articulated by the U.S. Supreme Court in 1964. In the landmark *New York Times Co. v. Sullivan* case, the Court nationalized the law of libel to provide a constitutional defense when public officials are plaintiffs. Suit was brought against the Times for publication of an advertisement in 1960 that, in essence, said that the civil rights movement in the South was being met with a wave of aggression by certain Southern officials. L.B. Sullivan, a Montgomery, Ala., commissioner, filed the suit. Portions of the advertisement were false and under existing statutory and common law, a defendant had to prove the literal truth of the statements. The Alabama courts awarded Sullivan $500,000 in damages.

The U.S. Supreme Court, however, reversed this ruling. It held that, to collect damages, a public official—which Sullivan clearly was—would have to prove that the defendant acted with "actual malice"—with reckless disregard of whether its allegations were true or false. Justice William Brennan wrote that the advertisement, "as an expression of grievance and protest on one of the major public issues of our time, would seem clearly to qualify for the constitutional protection." The media would be protected against suits brought by public officials, even when the statements were false—so long as the statements were not made with actual malice.

The conditional actual malice defense provides reporters with a primary defense to add to their arsenal of common law and statutory defenses. The condition upon which the Times rule was based, of course, is that the publication must concern a public official. From 1964 on, the status of the plaintiff—whether public or private—has been the first consideration a defendant makes when formulating possible defenses against a libel action. In 1967 the U.S. Supreme Court said that public *figures*—in addition to public officials—also have to show actual malice to recover libel damages.

The message is clear: As a reporter, you don't want to get tied up in a libel action; but if you do, there is more protection if the plaintiff is a public person.

Libel protection again was extended in 1971. The court said in *Rosenbloom v. Metromedia* that private persons involved in events of general or public interest also have to show actual malice to recover libel damages. The press was elevated to its most protected position ever regarding libel defenses. In 1974, however, the press was dealt a setback. In *Gertz v. Robert Welch,* the court said that it had gone too far in *Rosenbloom* and that unless a libel suit plaintiff were to be awarded punitive damages, private persons involved in events of general or public interest need only prove a lower fault standard—presumably negligence—to receive damages. Negligence certainly would be easier to prove than actual malice, the standard still required of public officials and public figures. In addition to stripping the press of some of the protection it had grown to enjoy as a result of *Rosenbloom, Gertz* also restructured the definition of a public figure. The court said that to be categorized as a public figure, an individual must "voluntarily thrust" himself or herself into the vortex of the particular controversy that gave rise to the litigation with the intention of influencing its outcome, or he or she must assume a role "of especial prominence" to the extent that, for all purposes, he or she is to be considered a public figure (for example, Henry Kissinger).

The court also said that each state would define the appropriate level of liability—*negligence*—when suits were brought by non-public persons involved in events of general or public interest. More than half the states have since defined *negligence,* but few definitions are uniform. Some states define it as "gross negligence," others as the "failure to act as a reasonable person." Two states—Colorado and Indiana—have clung to the actual malice standard: reckless disregard for the truth. In any event, it is important that reporters check to see the definition that applies in the states in which they work. Many state supreme courts agreed to review cases for the sole purpose of defining the standard liability for libel of private persons involved in public events. In reviewing such a case, for example, the Arizona State Supreme Court said that negligence is "conduct which creates an unreasonable risk of harm. It is the failure to use that amount of care which a *reasonably prudent* person would use under like circumstances." (Italics added.)

As emphasized earlier, with the status of the plaintiff an all-important consideration when defending against libel actions, *Gertz* took away some of the certainty editors and reporters had when deciding who might be categorized as a public figure. In *Gertz,* for example, the plaintiff was a well-known Chicago attorney who had been reasonably active in civic affairs. But the court reasoned that his reputation as a lawyer was not pervasive enough to stamp him as a public figure for all purposes and in this particular case, he had not thrust himself to the forefront of the controversy.

In another far-reaching case in 1976 (*Time, Inc. v. Firestone*), it became even more apparent that reporters and editors would have difficulty distinguishing between public figures and private individuals. The High Court said that the wife of a prominent, wealthy industrialist who held press conferences during the course of her divorce proceedings, who subscribed to a press clipping service to keep pace with articles written about her and who was well-known in Palm Beach, Fla., society was, for the purposes of libel law, to be considered a private person.

The U.S. Supreme Court continued its conservative flow of libel decisions in 1979 when it said that to show that a defendant acted in reckless disregard for the truth, a libel plaintiff could probe the state of mind of the defendant and inquire into the "predecisional communications" between editors and reporters (*Herbert v. Lando*).

Justice White, who wrote the opinion for a six-member majority, said that courts have "traditionally admitted any direct or indirect evidence relevant to the state of mind of the defendant . . . necessary to defeat a conditional privilege or enhance damages." White said that he was aware of the First Amendment rights of the press but that the courts were obligated also to consider the individual's interest in his reputation.

Also in 1979 the court ruled that a man—a research director at a state mental hospital and an adjunct professor at a university—who had received hundreds of thousands of dollars in federal grant money was not, for libel purposes, a public figure (*Hutchinson v. Proxmire*). That same term, the court held that persons engaged in criminal conduct do not automatically become public figures for purposes of libel law application (*Wolston v. Reader's Digest*).

Obviously, the substantial protection the press had grown to enjoy, particularly between 1971 and 1974, has been eroded. The status of the plaintiff is the key consideration. The press has most protection when plaintiffs are either public officials or public figures; if the plaintiffs are so categorized, they must prove the defendant acted in reckless disregard for the truth to recover damages. When plaintiffs are private persons involved in events of general or public interest, they must prove the defendant acted with negligence—a less stringent standard to meet. Reporters naturally do not want to become embroiled in libel suits. If they are, however, the chance of a successful defense would be much greater if the plaintiff is a public official or public figure.

Guidelines for Libel Defendants

Concern over libel actions is real enough that the New York State Newspapers Foundation, in its "Survival Kit for Reporters, Editors and Broadcasters," provides this advice for the potential defendant:

- *Be courteous and polite.* Nothing is gained by antagonizing the individual who claims to have been libeled.

- *Do not admit an error when a person initially complains that he or she has been libeled.* Take advantage of the complexity of the law. Even though you conceivably have libeled the individual, the wrong may not be sufficient to sustain a libel suit.

- *Agree to look into the matter.* If nothing else, this will get the caller to leave you alone at least temporarily.

- *If an attorney calls you about the potential libel, refer the call to your attorneys.* Libel law is full of traps for the unwary; do not assume that you can discuss a case on an attorney's turf. The attorney probably knows the territory; you do not.

- *Notify your editor or attorney at the first mention of libel.* Reporters should not attempt to resolve the problem without proper advice or counsel.

PRIVACY CONSIDERATIONS

Reporters are finding themselves increasingly involved in invasion of privacy suits. Perhaps this is only logical; there is a growing concern over the lack of privacy in today's technological world. Though libel has been a fear of journalists for centuries, privacy is a relatively recent problem. Samuel Warren and Louis Brandeis, in a Harvard Law Review article in 1890, first contended that Americans had a right to privacy—"a right to be let alone." New York was the first state to recognize a statutory right to privacy (1903), and Georgia, in 1905, was the first state to recognize a common law right. More than 80 percent of the states now recognize either a common law or statutory right to privacy. A handful of states have neither recognized nor denied the right.

The late Dean Prosser divided the broad area of privacy into four branches: (1) intrusion into an individual's solitude (this could be a physical intrusion or could extend to such things as electronic surveillance or eavesdropping), (2) appropriation of a name or likeness for commercial gain, (3) public disclosure of embarrassing private facts and (4) false light (painting a false, though not necessarily defamatory, picture of a person or event).

As with libel suits, reporters have defenses available to them. There are no solid defenses for physical intrusion (which is akin to trespass), though the courts have recognized "newsworthiness" as a defense to the post-intrusion publication. Consent, in writing, is a viable defense for appropriation. Newsworthiness is a defense in suits brought because of the public disclosure of embarrassing private facts. Truth and actual malice are defenses when defending against false light suits.

The Intrusion Branch

The four branches of privacy are best understood by examining suits brought under each branch. The intrusion branch, for example, is illustrated by a suit brought by former U.S. Sen. Thomas Dodd of Connecticut (*Dodd. v. Pearson*). The U.S. Court of Appeals for the District of Columbia decided the case in 1969. Four of Dodd's office workers or former employees became disenchanted with the differences between the senator's public posture and his real dealings. The employees were convinced that Dodd was converting public campaign funds to private use. They considered taking their allegations to the Senate Ethics Committee or the Federal Bureau of Investigation but decided that both institutions were capable of glossing over the alleged wrongdoing. Thus, they decided to convey their concerns to columnists Jack Anderson and the late Drew Pearson.

Anderson met with the employees; a list of 50 "questionable practices" was drawn up. Anderson said that he would need verification of the allegations. The employees then took materials from Dodd's personal files, made copies of them and replaced the original documents. The copies were turned over to Anderson. During an 18-month period in 1966 and 1967, Anderson devoted more than 120 "Washington Merry-Go-Round" columns to the Dodd story. Dodd sued. He sought $5.1 million in damages for libel and invasion of privacy. It did not take the trial court long to dispose of the libel case; as a public official, Dodd would have to show actual malice to receive damages. Because the information came from the senator's own files, it was highly unlikely that he could show that Anderson and Pearson had acted in reckless disregard for the truth.

Regarding the privacy suit, brought under the intrusion branch, the court clearly distinguished between the actual physical intrusion and the subsequent publication. The Court of Appeals for the District of Columbia struck down the privacy claim against the columnists. The court said that there were two distinct elements in most intrusion cases: the trespass and the publication. The court said that because Pearson and Anderson had not participated personally in the theft of the documents, they could not be held liable. Publishing the information was newsworthy and thus protected. The court made it clear that journalists would be held responsible for breaking the law—personally participating in a theft—but that they would not be held legally responsible for publishing newsworthy information turned over to them by a third party.

A similar suit brought by A.Λ. Dietemann against Time, Inc., illustrates a potential problem for reporters. Two Life magazine reporters had posed as husband and wife while visiting the private home of Dietemann, who styled himself as a "healer" by using clay, minerals and herbs. While Dietemann was examining a lump on the breast of the woman, the other reporter was taking photos with a concealed camera. Also, the conversation was being broadcast through a hidden microphone to authorities waiting in a car outside. When Dietemann later was arrested for practicing medicine without a license, Life carried the story and published the pictures. The trial court awarded Dietemann damages for invasion of privacy as a result of the use of the concealed microphone and camera. The 9th U.S. Circuit Court affirmed in 1971. Judge Shirley Hufstedler ruled that the "First Amendment has never been construed to accord newsmen immunity from torts or crimes committed during the course of news gathering."

Dodd and *Dietemann* show that reporters must be aware of potential legal problems when using hidden cameras or procuring documents by illegal methods. Such awareness is increasingly important in an era of increased investigative reporting.

The Appropriation Branch

Appropriation is a branch of privacy that should not pose much danger to reporters. Reporters generally are dealing with newsworthy items in the public domain. Stories are written to inform the public—not for the primary purpose of reaping a financial windfall at the expense of the subject. The electronic media reporter has more to fear than the print media reporter in this privacy area. In 1977 the U.S. Supreme Court held that the First Amendment did not afford a television station the privilege of filming an *entire* 15-second act by entertainer Hugo Zacchini in which he was shot from a cannon into a net some 200 feet away (*Zacchini v. Scripps-Howard*). Justice White emphasized that filming a performer's entire act posed a substantial threat to the economic value of the performance. Presumably, if the television station had aired only a portion of the act, it would have been justified legally.

The Embarrassing Private Facts Branch

Reporters could be drawn into suits brought under the publication of embarrassing private facts branch. This is, at best, a hazy area. Newsworthiness, as mentioned earlier, is a defense, and the courts have been relatively liberal in applying it. Essentially, the courts use as a test whether the material complained of violates the standards of "common decency" perceived by persons of "ordinary sensibilities."

In 1942, for example, the Missouri State Supreme Court affirmed an invasion of privacy suit against Time magazine, which had published a photograph of a hospitalized woman who suffered from an unusual disease (*Barber v. Time, Inc.*). Though the woman consumed huge amounts of food, she continued to lose weight. A photographer rushed uninvited into her hospital room and took pictures without her permission. Time published the picture and labeled her "the starving glutton." Though the *common decency test* is somewhat vague, reporters clearly do not have unbridled discretion to trample the innermost feelings of their subjects.

In another case brought under this branch by William James Sidis, the 2nd U.S. Circuit Court of Appeals saw things differently. Sidis, a famous child prodigy during the early part of the 20th century, was featured in a New Yorker article in 1937. Sidis, who was graduated from Harvard College at age 16 and who was recognized as a mathematical genius, brought suit based upon the publication. The article told of Sidis' marvelous talents but said that instead of using them, he had reverted to a private life and the occupation of clerk. The court said that, admittedly, the article deprived Sidis of the privacy for which he obviously yearned, but that nevertheless he was the object of considerable interest and discussion. The court said that his right to privacy did not render off limits press scrutiny of truthful, unexaggerated aspects of his life. Though the common decency criteria is not ironclad, one can, at least on an emotional level, discern differences between the *Barber* and the *Sidis v. F-R Publishing Corp.* cases.

The False Light Branch

The false light branch has been described as a "second cousin" to libel. Suits brought under this branch are occurring with increasing frequency. Attorney Richard Schmidt told the First Amendment Survival Seminar that, "Today, in many instances, we see the movement toward actions for invasion of privacy being intermingled with defamation actions. And when you get sued, you're probably going to get sued for both."

The first privacy case that involved the mass media to be heard by the U.S. Supreme Court was brought under this branch (*Time, Inc. v. Hill*). Life magazine reviewed a play based on the captivity by three escaped convicts of the James Hill family in their suburban Philadelphia home in 1952. Life's account included pictures of the actors in the house where the incident took place but from which the Hill family had moved. The play, which elevated the Hill family to the role of heroes, was adapted from a novel written about the incident. The novel added some fictionalized violence to a story that actually had been somewhat docile, considering the circumstances. Hill brought suit for invasion of privacy. The U.S. Supreme Court held in 1967 that for a plaintiff to recover damages under the false light privacy branch, he or she would have to prove actual malice. The Life article and photographs were newsworthy; they focused on the premiere of the play. Despite the lapse of time and fictionalization of the violence, Hill chose not to pursue the suit further; actual malice would have been difficult to show.

One plaintiff, however, was able to prove actual malice. In *Cantrell v. Forest City Publishing* (1974), a woman brought suit based on an article in the Cleveland Plain Dealer that exaggerated the poverty of her family. Her husband had been killed in a bridge collapse a year earlier, and the reporter was doing a follow-up story. In an apparent effort to strengthen his story, however, he implied that he had seen and talked to the widow. She was not, however, even present when he visited her house. The court concluded that the reporter had written "calculated falsehoods," and had, indeed, acted in reckless disregard for the truth.

Though the actual malice protection is considerable, reporters should guard against fictionalization techniques or attempts to exaggerate the significance of a story. Indeed, reporters constantly must consider the privacy ramifications of stories on which they are working.

THE FAIR TRIAL/FREE PRESS CONTROVERSY

Cases involving the inherent conflict between the First Amendment rights of the press to report and the Sixth Amendment rights of the accused to a speedy and public trial by an impartial jury have surfaced with regularity during the past two decades. The dilemma, however, has been ever-present. As early as 1807, Chief Justice John Marshall was confronted with the responsibility of seeing that Aaron Burr was not deprived of his constitutional rights during a treason trial that gained widespread public attention.

Journalists long have contended that the press is entitled to cover litigation. Reporters recognize the Sixth Amendment rights of defendants but argue that these rights can be maintained without trampling on freedom to report. Procedural safeguards such as *change of venue* (changing the location of the trial), *change of venire* (bringing in jurors from another jurisdiction), *sequestering jurors* (keeping them away from news reports) and effective *voir dire examination* (questioning potential jurors to determine their level of prejudice) are available to judges who wish to ensure that the defendants are not deprived of the judicial serenity and fairness to which they are constitutionally entitled.

Though procedural safeguards are available, they sometimes are not used. In fairness to the judiciary, however, publicity for some particularly notorious trials has been so prejudicial and pervasive that the safeguards might not have provided sufficient protection. This was evident in some cases during the early 1960s. In *Irvin v. Dowd* (1961), the U.S. Supreme Court, for the first time in history, reversed and remanded a state criminal conviction solely on the grounds of prejudicial publicity. The publicity barrage leveled at Leslie Irvin in Evansville, Ind., was so intense—it even included roving man-on-the-street interviews by a radio station to determine what kind of punishment a yet-to-be-found-guilty Irvin should receive—that of 430 potential jurors examined under *voir dire,* 370 said that they believed Irvin was guilty.

Two years later, the court considered a case in which a Lake Charles, La., station had televised, complete with sound, a sheriff securing a confession from a man accused of murder (*Rideau v. Louisiana*). The height of press irresponsibility, however, likely came in the trial of Dr. Sam Sheppard, who had been accused of murdering his wife (*Sheppard v. Maxwell,* 1966). His trial later was described by the U.S. Supreme Court as a "carnival" that rendered virtually impossible any private communication between the defendant and his attorney. Reporters jammed the 26- by 48-foot Ohio courtroom. Only 14 seats were reserved for family members.

Seven of the 12 jurors had one or more Cleveland newspapers delivered to their home; local papers cried for "justice" in Page One editorials. Not surprisingly, the High Court reversed and remanded the case, contending that "bedlam reigned at the courthouse."

Cases such as these that focused on media irresponsibility at its crudest brought the dilemma to the forefront. Shortly after *Sheppard* the American Bar Association's Advisory Committee on Fair Trial and Free Press released its findings. The committee sought to provide guidelines that would balance the conflicting constitutional rights. Though the report was aimed primarily at lawyers, law enforcement officers and judges, it had an indirect effect on the press. Also, the committee recommended that judges use the contempt power against reporters who communicate information that could be damaging to the accused.

The committee also recommended that lawyers and law enforcement officers refrain from talking about the prior criminal records of the accused, the existence of confessions, the results of tests or medical examinations and prospective witnesses and also refrain from making public statements about their opinions regarding the guilt or innocence of the accused. Dissemination of routine information such as facts of arrests, text of the charge or future scheduling of trials would be permitted. Though the press was not stopped from digging out information on its own, the guidelines in effect shut off a valuable information pipeline.

Another major case involving a fair trial/free press question reached the U.S. Supreme Court in 1975. Jack Murphy—who often was referred to as "Murph the Surf"—was convicted in Dade County, Fla., of breaking and entering. He had a criminal background. The Florida press gave substantial coverage to his arrest and subsequent trial. Murphy sought a reversal based on prejudicial publicity. The High Court refused, emphasizing that prejudicial publicity is not necessarily synonymous with pervasive publicity. The majority distinguished *Murphy* from *Irvin, Rideau* and *Sheppard.* In *Murphy,* though the media coverage had been extensive, it had been responsible. *Voir dire* examination did not reveal pervasive hostility.

A grave threat to press coverage of criminal trials came in the autumn of 1975 when a Nebraska judge issued a *gag order*—a protective order—prohibiting the press from publishing some information from a public murder trial (*Nebraska Press v. Stuart*). The Reporters Committee for Freedom of the Press estimated that there had been 174 cases involving gag orders between 1967 and 1975, with 62 of the instances occurring in 1975.

Obviously, the controversy was ripe for adjudication. Among other things, a Nebraska district county judge, Hugh Stuart, prohibited the press from reporting contents of a confession that had been mentioned in open court, statements made by the accused to others, medical testimony that had been introduced at the preliminary hearing and the identity of sexual assault victims (six members of the Henry Kellie family of Sutherland, Neb., had been killed; some were assaulted sexually). In addition Stuart gagged the press from reporting the contents of the gag.

The U.S. Supreme Court in 1976, however, reversed the ruling, holding that though the First Amendment is not absolute, barriers to a constitutional prior restraint on the press are high. A "heavy burden" would have to be met to justify the issuance of a prior restraint on the press, and in this instance, that heavy burden had not been met. Justice Burger, in his majority opinion, criticized the trial judge for not exploring available procedural safeguards before resorting to a gag order. The majority conceded, however, that under the most extreme circumstances, some gag orders conceivably could be upheld as constitutional. In a concurring opinion Justice William Brennan said that there never could be a prior restraint placed on the press in covering litigation.

Because *Nebraska Press* did not slam the door on the possibility of the press's sometimes being excluded from coverage of litigation, it was only logical that future cases would develop. In 1979 the U.S. Supreme Court held that the Sixth Amendment is for the benefit of the *defendant*—not the media (*Gannett v. DePasquale*). The majority said that the Constitution does not give the press an "affirmative right" of access to criminal trials. In a concurring opinion Justice Burger noted that the ruling applied only to pretrial hearings. Justice William Rehnquist, however, disagreed. In his concurring opinion, he said that it applied to all stages of a public trial. Rehnquist said that the First Amendment was "not some kind of sunshine law." Confusion prevailed. After the decision several justices took contrasting stances during public speeches about what the decision meant. Critics of the decision contended that lower court judges would take advantage of the uncertainty of the ruling and close trials, as well as preliminary hearings, without substantial reason to believe that the press would deprive the defendant of the right to receive a fair trial.

Fortunately for the press a case that could clarify the *DePasquale* ruling already was making its way up through the judicial system. Reporters had been denied access to a Virginia murder trial upon the request of the defense attorney. As had been the case in *DePasquale,* the reporters present did not object to the closure. A few hours later, however, attorneys for the newspaper asked that the order be vacated. The court refused. Though the case was technically moot, the U.S. Supreme Court agreed to hear it (*Richmond Newspapers, Inc. v. Virginia*). Exactly one year to the day after *DePasquale,* the court held that the Virginia closure was not proper. The majority said that the First Amendment guarantees the right to attend public trials, absent "overriding considerations." The 7-1 decision helped clarify the murky waters left by *DePasquale.* Though it had long been assumed, *Richmond Newspapers* was the first formal articulation by the court that the press had a right of access under the First Amendment to gather news at public trials. Justice Burger, author of the majority opinion, distinguished the case from *DePasquale.* He emphasized that *DePasquale* applied only to pretrial hearings. Burger also criticized the trial judge for failing to explore available procedural safeguards.

The media welcomed the clarification. The Reporters Committee for Freedom of the Press noted that there had been 260 attempts by judges to close or uphold closings of criminal proceedings during the year after *DePasquale*. Extensive interest in the *Richmond Newspapers* case was evidenced by the fact that 56 newspapers, including the New York Times, the Los Angeles Times, the Wall Street Journal and the Washington Post, along with the three television networks, filed friend-of-the-court briefs.

Though the court made clear in *Nebraska Press* and *Richmond Newspapers* that reporters could be banned from covering public litigation only in the most extreme circumstances and that a heavy burden would be placed on the individual requesting a closure to show that the defendant would otherwise be deprived of a fair trial, reporters undoubtedly will continue to be confronted with similar situations. The rulings should make judges hesitant to close public trials to the press, but the courts can continue to place *indirect gags* on the media through sealing records, instructing attorneys, witnesses and other court participants not to give information to the press and through the closing of preliminary hearings to both the public and press.

Also, reporters should obey court mandates, even when they know them to be unconstitutional. *United States v. Dickinson* made clear in 1972 that no matter how constitutionally infirm a court mandate might be, the reporter is bound to obey it until a higher court overturns it. A court of appeals emphasized that chaos would ensue if reporters could ignore court directions—even directions that were obviously unconstitutional.

In the event a trial is ordered closed, several media organizations and newspapers have prepared cards for their reporters to carry. Printed on each card is a brief statement of objection that the reporter is urged to read for the court record. The Gannett group card reads:

> Your honor, I am _____, a reporter for _____, and I would like to object on behalf of my employer and the public to this proposed closing. Our attorney is prepared to make a number of arguments against closings such as this one, and we respectfully ask the Court for a hearing on these issues. I believe our attorney can be here relatively quickly for the Court's convenience and he will be able to demonstrate that closure in this case will violate the First Amendment, and possibly state statutory and constitutional provisions as well. I cannot make the arguments myself, but our attorney can point out several issues for your consideration. If it pleases the Court, we request the opportunity to be heard through Counsel.

Time clearly is important to any reporter involved in closed proceedings. Editors and attorneys should be notified promptly. It also is important that reporters attempt to state on-the-record that they object to the closure. Of course, reporters do not have a right of access to *all* judicial proceedings. Grand jury proceedings and juvenile hearings are examples of judicial situations from which the press normally is barred. But basically the public's right to know what goes on in the courtroom through unrestricted press coverage generally should be protected.

S U G G E S T E D   E X E R C I S E S

1. Locate and read in your school's library or law library a significant U.S. Supreme Court decision that has a profound effect on you as a working journalist. For example, read *New York Times Co. v. Sullivan,* 376 U. S. 254 (1964) or *Gertz v. Robert Welch, Inc.,* 418 U.S. 323 (1974). After you have read one of these important libel decisions, write a news story that capsulizes the important segments of the decision.

2. As you read the discussion of *Gertz v. Robert Welch, Inc.,* in this chapter, you should have noticed that the decision left it up to the individual states to define appropriate levels of fault—negligence—when libel suits are brought by private persons involved in events of general or public interest. More than half the states have since defined *negligence.* Ask the communication law professor at your school to visit your class. Ask if your state has defined it. If so, how is it defined for purposes of defending against libel suits?

3. Invite to class an attorney who has some expertise in communication law or the professor at your school who specializes in media law. Discuss recent decisions that have an impact on the working media.

The First Amendment gives journalists the freedom to report and edit, but it does not mandate responsibility in return. The Constitution makes no mention of a trade-off: press freedom in exchange for press responsibility. Society, however, is calling for more journalistic accountability. This chapter examines the relationship between the press, the government and society.

You will be introduced to:

• Primary press theories—the authoritarian, the libertarian, the Soviet Communist and the social responsibility theories.

• Situations in which journalists must make difficult decisions on whether or not to publish sensitive information.

• Problems that can flow from the use of *new journalism* techniques—mixing fiction and reporting to create composite characters. The Janet Cooke episode is examined.

• Efforts on the part of national journalism organizations and individual media outlets to establish acceptable codes of behavior.

• Ethical dilemmas that can confront reporters in everyday situations.

When they covered Watergate, reporters Bob Woodward, left, and Carl Bernstein of the Washington Post had to make many difficult decisions about whether or not to write sensitive information.

UPI

339

18 RESPONSIBILITY TO SOCIETY

Media critics constantly are evaluating the role of the press as an American social institution. Privately owned newspapers understandably have resisted any type of governmental control, but during recent decades critics of the press increasingly have called for codes of ethics and greater professionalism on the part of reporters.

Reporters must recognize that today's society expects them to behave responsibly. This expectation fits in with the "social responsibility" theory outlined by Theodore Peterson in "Four Theories of the Press," a book he wrote nearly three decades ago with Wilbur Schramm and Fred S. Siebert. Peterson wrote that "freedom carries concomitant obligations; and the press, which enjoys a privileged position under our government, is obliged to be responsible to society for carrying out certain essential functions of mass communications."

THEORIES OF PRESS SYSTEMS

Siebert, Peterson and Schramm grouped the press systems of the world under four headings: authoritarian, Soviet Communist (which we will not discuss here), libertarian and social responsibility. In an *authoritarian system* criticism of the government is not tolerated. Content is controlled by the state through licensing. If newspapers want to stay in business, they print what the state wants them to print. Courageous colonial American journalists sought to escape suppression by the authoritarian system.

As authoritarian controls on the press were resisted, the *libertarian system* developed. Under this philosophy, newspapers provided information on a variety of topics—particularly government—so that citizens could be in a position to make enlightened decisions. This romantic concept flourished during the early 1800s.

As might have been expected, the libertarian philosophy opened the door for unscrupulous reporters to be blatantly irresponsible. Some nineteenth-century American newspapers were particularly vicious and irresponsible. They were, however, regarded as the primary instrument for checking on the government and its officials.

In reaction to perceived press shortcomings under the libertarian system, the Commission on Freedom of the Press was formed shortly after World War II. Made up of scholars and philosophers, it was concerned about the decreasing number of newspaper voices (the number of daily newspapers had been declining since shortly after the turn of the century) and the accompanying loss of marketplace philosophies. The commission said that the press should exercise more responsibility; it should make a concerted effort to discuss divergent views, even if the views were not compatible with those of newspaper management. The commission said

RESPONSIBILITY
TO SOCIETY

that it was the responsibility of the press not only to present diverse viewpoints but also to interpret them responsibly.

What has been labeled the *social responsibility theory* of the press emerged from the commission's report. According to this philosophy everyone who has something to say should be given access to the press, which is bound by professional ethics. Community opinion helps to keep the press in check. And if the press fails to live up to its obligations of social responsibility, government can step in to ensure public service.

In exploring the evolution of the social responsibility theory, Peterson wrote:

> A rather considerable fraction of articulate Americans began to demand certain standards of performance from the press. . . . Chiefly of their own volition, publishers began to link responsibility with freedom. They formulated codes of ethical behavior, and they operated their media with some concern for the public good—the public good as they regarded it, at least.

Today's reporters, then, find themselves working in a libertarian system that is making increasingly strong demands for journalistic responsibility. The challenge is formidable.

The courts have not been willing to impose a responsibility standard on the press. In 1974 Chief Justice of the United States Warren Burger wrote in a court opinion: "A responsible press is an undoubtedly desirable goal, but press responsibility is not mandated by the Constitution and like so many virtues it cannot be legislated. . . . A newspaper is more than a passive receptacle or conduit for news, comment and advertising. The choice of material to go into a newspaper . . . constitutes the exercise of editorial control and judgment."

Americans, however, have grown increasingly outspoken in their criticism of perceived media irresponsibility. A national opinion poll conducted by the Public Agenda Foundation in 1980 showed that the majority of Americans surveyed support laws requiring fairness in newspaper coverage of controversial stories or political races.

The message to the media is clear: Society is demanding responsibility. As a public service for The First Amendment Congress held in 1980 in Philadelphia, George Gallup's organization conducted a survey to determine public perceptions of the press. In an article published in Editor & Publisher, Gallup wrote: "The press in America is operating in an environment of public opinion that is increasingly indifferent—and to some extent hostile—to the cause of a free press in America."

The Gallup Poll revealed that Americans thought that present curbs on the press were "not strict enough," rather than "too strict," by a 2-1 margin. Many respondents said that more stringent restrictions should be placed on the press. The poll also showed that Americans think that "newspapers sometimes publish information that is not in the best interests of the nation and should be kept confidential."

THE H-BOMB STORY

Some of the respondents undoubtedly remembered an incident that had occurred one year earlier: The U.S. government had sought to enjoin the Progressive, a magazine of 40,000-circulation published in Madison, Wis., from printing an article on the hydrogen bomb. The article, "The H-Bomb Secret: How We Got It, Why We're Telling It," was the culmination of more than six months of research and writing. Howard Morland, a free-lance writer, wanted to show that information thought to be top secret was available to almost anyone who wanted to search for it.

The federal government based its request for suppression of the article on the Atomic Energy Act of 1954. The act prohibits anyone from communicating or disclosing any restricted data "with reason to believe that the data will be utilized to injure the United States or to secure an advantage to any foreign nation." The Progressive decided to fight the government request. Several major newspapers supported the magazine editorially. Others, including the Washington Post, advised the Progressive to reconsider publishing the article because it could lose if the Supreme Court heard the case. Editor & Publisher editorialized that the case would "prove to be detrimental to the cause of a free press no matter which way the court or courts decide."

Erwin Knoll, Progressive editor, felt the heat. Nearly two years later, in the opening lecture for Iowa State University's Institute on National Affairs, Knoll said that he had learned a painful lesson during the litigation. Editor & Publisher reported that Knoll said many American newspapers and electronic media "didn't give a damn about our First Amendment rights when they came under attack." He said that the magazine was "advised by some of America's greatest newspapers, by distinguished columnists, by prominent commentators, that we should not contest the government's unprecedented attempt at censorship, that we should censor ourselves, lest we jeopardize the First Amendment by incurring an adverse court decision."

Knoll said that Americans had grown cynical about the press because of its "wolf-crying" about the First Amendment. To worsen matters the "First Amendment has been invoked for the shabbiest and sleaziest of reasons. It has been invoked to promote legislation fostering newspaper monopolies and media conglomerates that threaten to swallow up the few remaining and independent voices left in the country."

The government had pressed hard its claims of national security in the case it brought against the Progressive. In issuing a preliminary injunction, federal District Court Judge Robert Warren emphasized how difficult it was to write such a decision; he noted his respect for the First Amendment. Warren conceded that the article did not provide a "do-it-yourself" guide for the hydrogen bomb, but he did think it provided "sufficient information to allow a medium-size nation to move faster in developing a hydrogen weapon. It could provide a ticket to by-pass blind alleys." Warren pointed out that only five nations had a hydrogen bomb, thus casting some doubts on the Progressive's assertions that the information contained in the article was relatively easy to obtain. Warren concluded that the government had "met its burden" under the Atomic Energy Act; it had shown that grave, direct, immediate and irreparable harm could come to the United States if the information were published.

Before the case could advance further, though, it was rendered moot by another publication's releasing the information. Still, nearly a year passed before the Justice Department stopped trying to keep the Madison-based magazine from publishing its story. Judge Warren finally dismissed the government's suit.

Professor Ben H. Bagdikian, former Washington Post ombudsman, wrote in the Quill that "despite many courageous and expensive court fights by some news organizations, much of the press, including some of its most powerful representatives, acquiesce in the worst restrictions on their own freedom." Bagdikian labeled the Progressive issue "the greatest leap yet into the destruction of freedom of expression and, consequently, of an open society."

Though reporters and editors are not often called on to make decisions as great as those required before publishing the H-bomb article, hardly a day passes that journalists are not confronted with stories that, some contend, might be best let alone. In fact, many Americans feel that journalists should exercise greater restraint in choosing the stories to publish or to air. The 1980 Gallup Poll showed that Americans think the media "exaggerate the news in the interest of making headlines and selling newspapers," and that the media "rush to print without first making sure all facts are correct." Not long after the survey, a dramatic event at one of America's most powerful newspapers seemed to confirm these fears. The event brought concerns about journalistic excesses to the forefront.

THE JANET COOKE EPISODE

When readers opened the Washington Post on Sunday morning, Sept. 28, 1980, they saw several solid, hard news stories displayed on Page 1. Most eyes, though, probably focused on a story accompanied by artwork that showed a needle piercing the thin arm of a small youngster. The all-capitals hammer headline read: "JIMMY'S WORLD." The main headline read: "8-Year-Old Heroin Addict Lives for a Fix."

The story carried the byline of Janet Cooke, a Post staff writer who was in her mid-20s. The lead was compelling:

Jimmy is 8 years old and a third-generation heroin addict, a precocious little boy with sandy hair, velvety brown eyes and needle marks freckling the baby-smooth skin of his thin brown arms.

Powerful stuff.

Miss Cooke went on to describe the "comfortably furnished home in Southeast Washington" that Jimmy lived in with his mother, Andrea, and her lover, Ron. The story said that every day someone "fires up Jimmy, plunging a needle into his bony arm, sending the fourth grader into a hypnotic nod."

The story contained direct quotations from Ron and Andrea. The quotations were vivid. "I let him snort a little and, damn, the little dude really did get off," Ron said.

Interspersed with several direct quotations by Jimmy, Andrea and Ron were authoritative facts about the growing heroin problem in the District of Columbia; information from medical experts on the increase in the number of deaths from heroin overdoses in the district, and opinions of a social worker about the family structure of homes like Jimmy's. Names and titles of authorities were used.

The story drew to a powerful conclusion. It described Ron sliding a needle "into the boy's soft skin like a straw pushed into the center of a freshly baked cake." It ended with a direct quotation from Ron: "Pretty soon, man, you got to learn how to do this for yourself."

Before the story was published, Cooke told her editors that Jimmy existed, as did his mother and boyfriend, but she could not use their real names. In fact, she said that the boyfriend had threatened her life if she told anyone—and that included her editors—their real identities. Assistant City Editor Milton Coleman agreed to the procedure of anonymity. So did Bob Woodward, metro assistant managing editor.

After publication Washington, D.C., police tried to find Jimmy. Two weeks later they gave up. Police Chief Burtell Jefferson was convinced that "Jimmy" did not exist. Skepticism about the story spread beyond city officials; several reporters—including Cooke's roommate—and editors at the Post also had doubts.

Despite the doubts by some about the authenticity of the article, it won a Pulitzer Prize.

Before Cooke could bask in Pulitzer glory, however, her world started to shatter. The biography she had supplied the Post said she was a magna cum laude graduate of Vassar and that she had a master's degree from the University of Toledo. Vassar officials told the Post that she was not a graduate; Associated Press staffers in Toledo, making a routine check, found that Cooke did not have a master's degree—she had a bachelor's—from the university there.

When alerted to these inaccuracies, Post editors started to fidget about the veracity of "Jimmy." After intense interrogation by Post editors—which drew to a close in the early morning hours of Wednesday, April 15, 1981—Cooke admitted that Jimmy did not exist, that he was a composite of several drug users.

Reactions from the Press

The following day, the Post carried a Page One story that said the Pulitzer Prize Committee had withdrawn its feature-writing prize after Cooke "had admitted that her award-winning story was a fabrication." The article quoted Post Executive Editor Benjamin Bradlee:

> It is a tragedy that someone as talented and promising as Janet Cooke, with everything going for her, felt that she had to falsify the facts. The credibility of a newspaper is its most precious asset, and it depends almost entirely on the integrity of its reporters. When that integrity is questioned and found wanting, the wounds are grievous, and there is nothing to do but come clean with our readers, apologize to the Advisory Board of the Pulitzer Prizes, and begin immediately on the uphill task of regaining our credibility. This we are doing.

Bradlee assigned Post Ombudsman Bill Green to write an account of how "Jimmy's World" came about. Green responded with a series of articles that filled nearly four full pages in the Sunday, April 19, edition. Green interviewed 47 persons (Cooke was not one of them) as he told of "the failure of a system that, in another industry, might be called 'quality control.' On newspapers, it is called editing." Green found that "Jimmy's World" made its way "through the cycle of news reporting and editing like an alien creature, unimpeded by ordinary security devices."

The ombudsman mentioned a newsroom "mythology" that leads young reporters to think that Watergate blockbusters are routine occurrences and that heavy pressures are placed on reporters to produce Page One copy. Green quoted Lewis Simons of the Post's metro staff, who said: "Pressures are so great to produce, to go beyond excellence to the 'holy s——' story. Everyone knows that's what the editors want. The pressure is to get the incredible story, the extraordinary story."

The Gallup Organization conducted a poll for Newsweek magazine shortly after the Cooke incident. When asked whether the Janet Cooke hoax was an isolated incident, 33 percent replied that reporters "often make things up."

The nation's newspaper editors and reporters also reacted. Editor & Publisher printed some of the reactions.

Chuck Thomas, executive editor of the Ventura County, Calif., Star-Free Press, wrote that it was the " 'I've Got a Secret' school of journalism inspired by Watergate that led to the ultimate anonymous quote—an entire story fabricated . . . and published."

Jane Perlez, media critic of the New York Daily News, was quoted in Time magazine as saying: "Other fabrications, on a less spectacular scale, go by every day in news stories. Every day, reporters 'embellish' quotes from an individual to make them 'sound better' or to fit the point of the story."

Possibly the Washington Star, the Post's competitor until it folded in 1982, provided the most thoughtful media reaction to the controversy. The Star editorialized that "certain tendencies in journalism need critical review." The Star pointed to the spread of new journalism techniques—when fiction and reporting are mixed—to newspapers, to the increasing use of soft news pegs to "illuminate larger political and social problems" and to the everyday emergence of the anonymous source. The Star said, "In the rush to engage the reader, nothing invites abuse like the anonymous source."

Nagging Questions Raised

What can be learned from the Janet Cooke episode? Are there lessons for working professionals as well as college journalism majors?

Certainly, there is a need to closely examine several pertinent questions: When are new journalism techniques proper in newspaper writing? Is there too much pressure to write blockbuster stories? Do the media need to examine their procedures on quoting anonymous sources? Do the media need to build more credential verification procedures into their hiring practices? Are there circumstances when press freedom should give way to a greater social need? For example, if "Jimmy" had been real, should the Post have felt a social obligation to divulge his identity to authorities?

It is, of course, ironic that the Cooke journalistic embarrassment involved the Post, a newspaper that Ombudsman Green labeled the "proud house of Watergate investigations." The Post, less than a decade earlier, had openly and defiantly challenged President Richard Nixon and his administration. Solid investigative reporting by the Post—spearheaded to an extent by Woodward—led to the crumbling of the Nixon adminstration.

ETHICS AND RESPONSIBILITIES OF REPORTERS

American presidents often have been at odds with the press—but none like Richard Nixon. From the beginning of his political career, Nixon was leery of the media. He came under intense media pressure during Watergate. The press received generally good marks for investigative reporting during this troubled era, but a portion of the public was not particularly impressed; some people felt that Nixon had been badgered from office by a vindictive, out-of-control press. A Lou Harris poll conducted in August 1973 found that 66 percent credited the press with exposing Watergate. Still, 50 percent said that the media had given more attention to the scandal than it deserved.

One month before Nixon's resignation, a Harris poll showed that 47 percent thought the president had been the victim of unfair media attacks. Just after Nixon's resignation, a Roper poll showed that 24 percent did not think that the press performed well during Watergate. Woodward and Carl Bernstein conceded in their book, "All the President's Men," that they had been guilty of journalistic ethical excesses.

Woodward told the First Amendment Survival Seminar, held in 1979 in Washington, D.C., that "power is not simply the raw mechanics of having the upper hand—and this is not to say that the press has the upper hand—but that in the last 10 years because of Vietnam and Watergate and a lot of other things, there is this feeling that we do not have limits, either imposed by the outside or by ourselves. Certainly, power or the sort of power and responsibility we have has a lot to do with moral authority. I at least hope . . . that we the press don't lose our ability to react to unjustness."

In a Frank E. Gannett Memorial Lecture in 1978, John B. Oakes, former senior editor of the New York Times, said that the American press "would be living in a fool's paradise if we believed that we could continue to enjoy support for our constitutional protection under the First Amendment if we forgot our implied responsibilities under it." Oakes told the National Conference of Editorial Writers in 1976 that a newspaper has "an obligation" to its readers "to explain and interpret the events that it is reporting every day, to provide some kind of philosophic standard through the maze of conflicting premises and special interests."

Indeed, Woodward told the First Amendment Survival Seminar that the "big question" in journalism today "is not what we can publish . . . but what should be covered and how thoroughly." Woodward recalled the great prominence the Post gave to a story about Congressman Wayne Hays' having a girlfriend on his payroll "at the mammoth expense of $16,000 a year." However, each day, stories about $100 million being wasted by government inefficiency often are given two inches of space, according to the reporter.

Woodward said that the "immediate battle" the press should be concerned with is not "so much a battle of the government or the courts, but, to a certain extent, the battle with ourselves." Newspapers should "turn the dial a little bit on the agenda and focus more on what, I think, fairly would be called the public interest." He said journalists need to develop a "self-consciousness" about their failings that they are "not always inclined to have."

THE INDUSTRY RESPONDS

Many newspapers have looked inward to determine, address and find solutions to the shortcomings for which they have been criticized. Some have appointed ombudsmen to see that readers' complaints are acted upon. A few metropolitan newspapers, such as the Los Angeles Times, have hired *press critics*—reporters who write stories about the strengths, weaknesses and trends of newspaper coverage.

The Press Critic

David Shaw has been press critic for the Times since 1974. Times editor William H. Thomas asked Shaw, who then was a general assignment reporter, to write in "exhaustive fashion" about the American press and the Times. Shaw was somewhat unsure of his turf.

But Thomas quickly cleared the air. In his book, "Journalism Today," Shaw wrote that Thomas told him that "the one thing the press covers more poorly today than anything else is the press." Shaw paraphrased Thomas: "We don't tell our readers what we do or how we do it. We don't admit our mistakes unless we're virtually forced to under threat of court action or public embarrassment. We make no attempt to explain our problems, our decisions, our fallibilities, our procedures." Thomas wanted the press critic to confront these issues directly.

Shaw wrote that his job was unique—he was to function neither as beat reporter nor ombudsman. Thomas wanted him "to provide long, thoughtful overviews on broad issues confronting the press today, to analyze, criticize and make value judgments, to treat my own newspaper as I would any other."

Shaw's stories often appear on Page 1. They have included such topics as the ethical ramifications of reporters secretly tape-recording telephone conversations with sources, the influence of editorial endorsements, the shortcomings and changes in contemporary sports pages, the relationship between the press and the police and the influence of film critics.

Shaw's pieces are not always greeted with enthusiasm by fellow journalists who come under scrutiny, but the Times has been a pacesetter in media introspection.

The Ombudsman

The Washington Post has been a pacesetter in the use of ombudsmen. An *ombudsman* is a "middle person"—a theoretically objective employee of the newspaper—who listens to complaints from readers and when they are justified, passes them along to the appropriate editors or reporters. Most newspapers that have ombudsmen instruct reporters and editors to respond to, not ignore, complaints or suggestions forwarded by the ombudsman. These responses take several forms—argument, agreement, disagreement, rebuttal, frustration or even anger—but the reporters and editors must respect the independent position of the ombudsman. Staffers might be required to respect the position, but to establish rapport with and gain respect from these reporters and editors, each ombudsman must be scrupulously fair and unbiased. It is not an easy job.

The Post created the position in 1970—one year after the Louisville Courier-Journal did—and since then a long line of distinguished persons has filled the job.

Robert J. McCloskey, who in 1981 became the sixth person to serve as ombudsman at the Post, said that his job is to "let the readers know there is somebody at the newspaper who at least will listen to their comments and complaints and, in turn, can bring some influence to bear on the editors."

The Post's ombudsman receives about 75 letters each week and about a dozen telephone calls each day with complaints about the newspaper. McCloskey, a retired ambassador who for 10 years was the State Department's press spokesman, sifts through the complaints and passes on to editors and reporters what he considers to be the legitimate concerns. He is in a position to "call it as I see it because I have no further aspirations with the paper."

According to McCloskey an ombudsman can funnel complaints primarily in three ways. He can (1) go directly to the editor or reporter involved, say that an issue has been raised that should be considered and pose a possible solution, (2) write memos, which are distributed to senior editors and the publisher, outlining complaints and possible solutions or (3) write a column outlining shortcomings and posing solutions. The column is published.

"I don't want to make any great claims that I have affected policy changes," McCloskey said. "Newspapers never want to acknowledge that they are changing anything, except possibly the price of the paper."

Still, McCloskey said the Post editors and staffers take seriously his suggestions. "I am sure, however, that there are people on the staff who resent my position as 'second guesser,' and you do bruise some egos, but that goes with the job."

Bill Green, who was the Post's ombudsman during the Janet Cooke episode and who was McCloskey's predecessor, is a firm believer in the positive effect an ombudsman can have on a newspaper.

"The position, after all, does establish a link between readers and newspapers—or it can if it is filled well," said Green. "It has some influence on the paper's credibility."

Green acknowledged that many newspapers cannot afford to hire an ombudsman (about two dozen dailies have full-time ombudsmen), but he said that it was important for newspapers to make it known to readers that their comments and observations are welcome and will be considered.

Some newspaper editors, for example, set aside time each week to meet personally with readers who have complaints. Some newspapers run advertisements that invite readers to write editors with their complaints.

Green, who returned to his job as director of university relations at Duke University after his one-year stint at the Post, said that complaints received by the ombudsman range from significant to trivial. He constantly was bombarded with letters from a reader whose primary interest was to analyze the lead paragraphs of Post stories to see if the remainder of the stories justified them. Another irate reader would call to complain about missing commas in stories.

Green said that one of the difficult jobs for editors at the Post is deciding how to cover the frequent demonstrations in the nation's capital. "It becomes a very difficult judgment for the city desk and the ombudsman to determine if coverage of a particular group is justified," Green said. "While I was at the Post, we were charged with being pro-Israel (by one group) and anti-Israel (by another group). We were charged with being pro-women by some and anti-women by others. Once, we were charged with being anti-Methodist. I never did figure that one out."

Codes of Ethics

The 1970s witnessed a growing concern about media ethics and responsibility. The Associated Press Managing Editors Association, the American Society of Newspaper Editors, the Society of Professional Journalists (Sigma Delta Chi), the National Conference of Editorial Writers and the Associated Press Sports Editors were among groups that revised existing codes during the 1970s. The American Society of Newspaper Editors Statement of Principles, for example, was adopted in 1975. It replaced the 1923 Code of Ethics. A 1978 survey showed that 52 percent of the 150 newspapers questioned had written policies on ethics; 45 percent reported oral policies.

Journalists recently have taken a harder look at their ethical conduct—particularly when it comes to accepting free travel from news sources. This is apparent from examining results of surveys conducted by the American Society of Newspaper Editors' Ethics Committee in 1972, 1974, 1977 and 1979.

In 1972, for example, 78 percent of the editors who responded said that they would accept free travel from tax-supported agencies for reporters and photographers. This dropped to 32 percent in 1974, 25 percent in 1977 and 11 percent in 1979.

In a 1974 survey 38 percent of the editors said that their sportswriters accepted free transportation to travel with teams. That percentage dropped to 25 percent in 1977 and 8 percent in 1979.

These surveys show that the press is indeed making an extensive effort to get away from "freebies." But they also show that some newspapers continue to accept free transportation from news sources.

Sigma Delta Chi's Code of Ethics

The codes developed by national groups that sincerely wished to strengthen the profession were broad statements of principle. The Society of Professional Journalists, Sigma Delta Chi, adopted the following code in 1973:

The Society of Professional Journalists, Sigma Delta Chi, believes the duty of journalists is to serve the truth.

We believe the agencies of mass communication are carriers of public discussion and information, acting on their Constitutional mandate and freedom to learn and report the facts.

We believe in public enlightenment as the forerunner of justice, and in our Constitutional role to seek the truth as part of the public's right to know the truth.

We believe those responsibilities carry obligations that require journalists to perform with intelligence, objectivity, accuracy, and fairness.

To these ends, we declare acceptance of the standards of practice here set forth.

Responsibility
The public's right to know of events of public importance and interest is the overriding mission of the mass media. The purpose of distributing news and enlightened opinion is to serve the general welfare. Journalists who use their professional status as representatives of the public for selfish or other unworthy motives violate a high trust.

Freedom of the Press
Freedom of the press is to be guarded as an inalienable right of people in a free society. It carries with it the freedom and the responsibility to discuss, question, and challenge actions and utterances of our government and of our public and private institutions. Journalists uphold the right to speak unpopular opinions and the privilege to agree with the majority.

Ethics
Journalists must be free of obligation to any interest other than the public's right to know the truth.
1. Gifts, favors, free travel, special treatment, or privileges can compromise the integrity of journalists and their employers. Nothing of value should be accepted.
2. Secondary employment, political involvement, holding public office, and service in community organizations should be avoided if it compromises the integrity of journalists and their employers. Journalists and their employers should conduct their personal lives in a manner which protects them from conflict of interest, real or apparent. Their responsibilities to the public are paramount. That is the nature of their profession.
3. So-called news communications from private sources should not be published or broadcast without substantiation of their claims to news value.
4. Journalists will seek news that serves the public interest, despite the obstacles. They will make constant efforts to assure that the public's

business is conducted in public and that public records are open to public inspection.

5. Journalists acknowledge the newsman's ethic of protecting confidential sources of information.

Accuracy and Objectivity

Good faith with the public is the foundation of all worthy journalism.

1. Truth is our ultimate goal.
2. Objectivity in reporting the news is another goal, which serves as the mark of an experienced professional. It is a standard of performance toward which we strive. We honor those who achieve it.
3. There is no excuse for inaccuracies or lack of thoroughness.
4. Newspaper headlines should be fully warranted by the contents of the articles they accompany. Photographs and telecasts should give an accurate picture of an event and not highlight a minor incident out of context.
5. Sound practice makes clear distinction between news reports and expressions of opinion. News reports should be free of opinion or bias and represent all sides of an issue.
6. Partisanship in editorial comment which knowingly departs from the truth violates the spirit of American journalism.
7. Journalists recognize their responsibility for offering informed analysis, comment, and editorial opinion on public events and issues. They accept the obligation to present such material by individuals whose competence, experience, and judgment qualify them for it.
8. Special articles or presentations devoted to advocacy or the writer's own conclusions and interpretations should be labeled as such.

Fair Play

Journalists at all times will show respect for the dignity, privacy, rights, and well-being of people encountered in the course of gathering and presenting the news.

1. The news media should not communicate unofficial charges without giving the accused a chance to reply.
2. The news media must guard against invading a person's right to privacy.
3. The media should not pander to morbid curiosity about details of vice and crime.
4. It is the duty of news media to make prompt and complete correction of their errors.
5. Journalists should be accountable to the public for their reports and the public should be encouraged to voice its grievances against the media. Open dialogue with our readers, viewers, and listeners should be fostered.

Pledge

Journalists should actively censure and try to prevent violations of these standards, and they should encourage their observance by all newspeople. Adherence to this code of ethics is intended to preserve the bond of mutual trust and respect between American journalists and the American people.

Newspapers Formulate Policies

Guidelines established by national organizations, though helpful, are inherently vague. Recognizing this, individual newspapers have formulated more concrete policies. These policies often are prefaced with remarks similar to those made by William H. Hornby, editor of the Denver Post: "These guidelines are issued because this is an era in which the news media are increasingly subject to public criticism and scrutiny, and in many cases public misunderstanding."

The Burlington (Vt.) Free Press has a written policy that lists specific things that "without exception" should be rejected: expense-paid trips; free admission to sports events; entertainment, political or other events with an admission charge (except for the strict purpose of covering a news event occurring within); complimentary or discounted books, records, food, liquor, cosmetics, consumer items and news products; free lunches, and drinks. The Free Press policy stresses the importance of impartial editing and reporting. The newspaper even cautions reporters and editors against formal "chance remarks" that could show "a prejudicial viewpoint on a current topic."

The Louisville Courier-Journal has formulated a very specific set of guidelines. Among other things the policy emphasizes the importance of avoiding any conflicts of interest: "These efforts to protect our newspaper's integrity are extremely important. They are probably more important now than ever before, since newspapers' 'credibility' is so much in question. If our readers do not believe we are acting in good faith, we are no longer rendering a public service; we are simply another business enterprise."

Courier-Journal policy does not allow regular staffers to "write for pay for any company or organization, profit or non-profit," and does not allow them to appear for pay on radio or television stations in its circulation area. The policy does allow free-lance work for publications headquartered outside the Courier-Journal's circulation area. It allows staffers to make public speaking engagements and to teach at educational institutions—but the policy states that staffers must clear such activities through the editor and publisher or executive editor. The policy does not prohibit staffers from performing voluntary services for religious, cultural or social organizations but warns that staff members should not prepare publicity for any organization, "except for a professional organization of journalists in hope of Courier-Journal coverage."

The formulation of codes shows an awareness by individual newspapers that ethics are a growing concern. A former managing editor of the Washington Star, however, contended that most codes "share a weakness—they are toothless." Charles B. Seib wrote in Presstime:

My belief that codes of ethics are of limited value is based on examination of a number of codes and on my own experience. I have come to the conclusion that while codes have some use as broad statements of standards and as prior restraints on disgraceful conduct and bases for action in response to such conduct, their natural resting place is the back of the desk drawer.

No matter how transparent some codes are, they do represent legitimate attempts by the industry to police its own ranks. The codes often are helpful—particularly to the working reporter—but journalists regularly are confronted with ethical and moral dilemmas that must be reacted to on a case-by-case basis.

ETHICAL DILEMMAS

Do reporters adhere to the same stringent ethical standards for which they hold public officials accountable? Journalists are trained to report the first hint of governmental impropriety. Government officials, after all, have a responsibility to their constituents. Reporters should remember, however, that they, too, have a responsibility to their readers. Should reporters:

- Jump at the chance for free movie tickets? What could it hurt?
- Stock personal libraries with review books sent out by publishers?
- Look forward to gulping down free liquor from friendly sources?
- Expect—and accept—small favors in return for complimentary stories?

Though the acceptance of "freebies" often is the first thing that comes to mind when discussing reporter ethics, dilemmas faced by journalists sometimes are considerably more complicated.

Reporter Misrepresentation

Should reporters misrepresent themselves when working on stories? Yes? No? Sometimes?

Chicago Sun-Times reporters grew frustrated when gathering information for a story focusing on corruption in small business. They reasoned that because small businessmen were hesitant to talk about extortion and payoffs to ensure protection, the best way to write the story would be to start a small business. The newspaper bought a tavern. Sun-Times reporters worked as tavern employees. A revealing story of city inspector payoffs was written. The story was significant—one that should have been told.

Critics, though, questioned the reporting method. Had the newspaper gone too far?

Many editors do not allow this type of investigative journalism at their newspapers—ever. They view undercover journalism as a form of entrapment.

David Shaw, after conducting a non-random survey of reporters across the country, wrote in the Los Angeles Times: "Most journalists argue that it is unethical for a reporter to pretend he is not a reporter—or to fail to identify himself as a reporter—when interviewing someone."

Still, particularly at some metropolitan newspapers, this type of undercover journalism occasionally is practiced. Generally, however, it is only after editors and reporters have concluded that the story is extremely significant and that there would be no other means of obtaining it. Many journalists widely criticize undercover journalism, whereas others view it as a necessary means of gathering information, particularly when criminal activity is being investigated. In those situations some newspaper editors and reporters contend that the ends justify the means.

Certainly, most editors and reporters realize that this type of reporting is susceptible to abuse and should be considered only as a last resort. Many editors, however, would go a step farther; they would follow an inflexible rule that never—under any circumstances—should reporters misrepresent themselves.

Working with Quotations

How much leeway do reporters have when working with quotations? How precise should reporters be when quoting directly?

An associate editor of Portland's Oregonian was suspended in 1980 when then Gov. Dixy Lee Ray protested that two of the editor's stories contained trumped-up quotations. Ray had been interviewed several times by the editor, but according to her press secretary, she was "quite distressed with the stories" because of the "profuse use of quotes . . . she didn't say." In reponse to such incidents, Editor & Publisher has surveyed several metropolitan dailies to determine policies on the use of direct quotations. The magazine reported that the general response was, "We tend not to set down hard-and-fast rules. Good sense is still the best guide."

The problem with such a policy is obvious: Defining *good sense* is like defining *obscenity*. The definition varies.

Quote marks mean that the reporter is relaying the precise words of the speaker. However, many newspapers allow editors to "fix" grammar and insert occasional words to make a complete sentence. Of course, the words should not alter the thrust of the quoted passage.

To guard against accusations of misquoting, the no-longer-published Minneapolis Star had a policy that required reporters to identify themselves as employees of the newspaper when they approached a source. The policy reminded reporters that most sources are unfamiliar with ground rules on interviewing: They should make it absolutely clear at the beginning of an interview that the interviewee is likely to be quoted.

Dealing with Threats

Most reporters have been threatened with, "Do you want to be responsible for the consequences if you print this story?" The threats occur with frequency, but even veteran reporters never grow completely calloused to them. It is not uncommon for court reporters—particularly those who work for small dailies or weeklies—to be confronted by persons charged with criminal offenses. One would be surprised at how many of them have relatives with heart trouble or other medical problems—conditions that would quickly worsen if a story were published. Most reporters have received telephone calls from ministers or other community leaders urging that a drunken driving story not be printed because of the disastrous effects such a story could have on the family of the accused. Generally, the story is published and the matter forgotten.

This was not the case, however, when the Dallas Times Herald carried a Page One story about a 69-year-old retired engineer who had been a Soviet spy and an FBI double agent. The man threatened the Times Herald that he would commit suicide if the story were published. He made good on his threat.

Newsweek magazine said the man had threatened suicide on four occasions, but reporters never believed that he was serious. After the incident Newsweek surveyed several editors; most supported the Times Herald's decision to print the story—an exposé based on three months of interviewing and fact gathering. However, Washington Post editors told Newsweek that on at least two occasions, they had withheld stories when a check of those who had threatened suicide revealed a history of psychiatric problems.

Local Situations Most Delicate

Does the public *always* have a right to know?

Rod Deckert, managing editor of the Missoulian, in Missoula, Mont., knows what it is like to be faced with such a problem. His dilemma was explored in a Quill article by Jack Hart and Janis Johnson.

When Missoula native Cindy Herbig, 21 years old, was stabbed to death on the streets of Washington, D.C., the Missoulian carried the story on Page 1. At the time the circumstances of the death were not known. Most of the community remembered Cindy as a model student, member of the All-State Orchestra, recipient of a scholarship to Radcliffe (though she dropped out in her freshman year) and member of a respected local family.

Shortly after the death the Washington Post carried a front page story that described Cindy as a "$50-a-trick prostitute" who had worked the city's streets. Editors and reporters undoubtedly handled the story carefully, but they probably lost little sleep in deciding whether to publish it. Missoulian editors were alerted to the Post's story; because the article was to be distributed by the Post's news service, it was apparent that its contents soon would filter to Missoula.

Should the Missoulian carry the story? Cindy's mother and father, director of the Missoula Youth Symphony, pleaded that the story not be run. Cindy, an honors graduate of a local high school, was, after all, more than a name in a news story. She was a real person who had hundreds of friends and acquaintances in Missoula. What purpose would the story serve? Cindy was dead. Her family was hurt.

But did the newspaper have a responsibility to its readers—to parents of local teen-age girls? When Deckert discovered that Miss Herbig had been recruited out of a Missoula bar by an East Coast pimp, he decided to publish the story. Missoulian editors deleted the "$50-a-trick prostitute" description and carried the article on Page 12 under a banner headline: "Cindy Herbig 'shouldn't be dead,' friend says." Despite efforts to humanize the story as much as possible, editors and reporters at the Missoulian were struck by a torrent of adverse public opinion. Why did the paper print such "garbage"? What good did it do now? Had the newspaper no ethical standards?

What do you think?

S U G G E S T E D   E X E R C I S E S

1. Invite a panel of area reporters and editors to class to discuss ethical dilemmas with which they have been confronted. Make sure weeklies, small dailies and larger dailies have representatives on the panel. Formulate some hypothetical situations for them to discuss. Would the circulation of their newspaper make a difference in the way they would handle certain situations?

2. Discuss with the area reporters and editors how their newspapers deal with unnamed sources. Do their newspapers have written policies to deal with this issue? Do their newspapers have written codes of ethics?

3. Discuss with the area editors their procedures for verifying the academic and professional credentials of job applicants.

4. Discuss with the area editors and reporters whether they think there is too much emphasis on winning awards and gaining front page bylines.

5. Bring to class examples of stories published in area newspapers that raise ethical questions about the way they were handled. Discuss how you would have handled the stories.

6. Discuss in class the ethical dilemma that confronted editors and reporters at the Missoulian when deciding how to handle the Cindy Herbig story. Would you have done differently?

More than 15,000 students receive college degrees in mass communication fields each year. Competition for jobs is fierce. If they actively seek it, however, the best qualified graduates usually find media work. This chapter discusses the job market.

You will be introduced to:

• The experiences of recent college graduates who landed media jobs in various size markets. The chapter presents their satisfying experiences—and their frustrations.

• Steps college students can take to better prepare themselves for careers in mass communication.

• The status of the newspaper industry—its circulation, advertising revenues and employment practices.

• Jobs in non-newspaper media work such as television, radio, public relations, advertising, wire services and magazines.

Senior journalism students at Arizona State University check bulletin board for employment opportunities.

Ken Krehbiel

361

19 THE JOB MARKET

Good journalism jobs—even in a tight market—await adequately prepared graduates. These jobs, however, will not instantly materialize upon graduation. Aspiring reporters need to build a firm academic and professional foundation to make themselves more marketable.

Casey Bukro, environmental writer for the Chicago Tribune, used the Chicago Headline Club newsletter as a forum to give this advice to graduating print journalism students: "First, know what you want to do. Determine what your skills are and what you do best. Declare your preference early. If you have a special interest in a certain field, tell someone. If you have to, develop stories in your interest on your own time whether it be in labor, education, courts, the environment."

Paul Davis, news director at WGN-TV in Chicago, advised students interested in television careers to first seek jobs in smaller markets. Davis said that it was too easy to "get caught in a rewrite experience and not get a chance to do any real reporting" when starting in large markets.

Each year, thousands of newly minted journalism graduates seek jobs. Some land media positions, are happy with their work and spend a lifetime. Some find media work, grow frustrated and leave the field. Some who lack adequate academic and professional training—or desire—are not able to find media jobs. They turn elsewhere.

SOME EXPERIENCES

The following accounts describe real situations. The names, however, are fictional.

A Successful Career

Ken Dassner had considerable newspaper experience before he was graduated from college. In addition to working for the campus newspaper, where he gained both reporting and editing experience, he worked summers and weekends at the Tribune, the local 20,000-circulation daily.

He enjoyed his work. Primarily, he was a sports reporter covering area high school events. He also reported on events at his college and wrote a lot of news and sports features. Occasionally he would write a signed sports column. He built up a fat clip file.

As a 20-year-old sophomore he felt in control of his life. He was paid to do what he enjoyed most: watch and write. The hours were bad, but he was young and unmarried, and the job was enjoyable. The work extended into the early morning hours on weekends, but in a sadistic sort of way, it was fun calling area coaches at 3 a.m. to ask them why they had not telephoned the results of their games.

While working part time at the newspaper, Dassner got to know the regular staffers. The editor told him there would be a spot for him after he finished college.

Dassner did not even send out job applications during his senior year. He was looking forward to starting his newspaper career at the Tribune. Some of his friends were seeking jobs on bigger newspapers, but that did not interest Dassner. He was content at the Tribune and comfortable in the community. He looked forward to spending several years there.

After five years at the newspaper—during which he served first as sports editor, then general assignment reporter and eventually city editor—Dassner had to make a decision. Should he remain at the Tribune—and almost certainly be named managing editor—or should he look for a reporting or editing job on a bigger daily?

Dassner chose to stay. The Tribune—an award-winning newspaper with a young and enthusiastic staff—is where he plans to spend the rest of his career. There are jobs at other papers that pay more, but Dassner feels that none can give him more satisfaction than he gets now from putting together solid, hard-hitting news stories that have a significant impact on the community he loves. His byline is more than a name to the town's residents; it represents a person most of the town knows and respects.

Dassner's first—and only—newspaper job evolved naturally. Each step in his career, from the time he was hired as a 19-year-old part-time sports reporter, was logical and anticipated. Dassner never learned the feelings of frustration and discouragement that so often go hand-in-hand with that first news job.

An Unhappy Ordeal

Julie Harrison did feel frustrated and discouraged.

She wanted to work on a newspaper larger than the Tribune. She feared that she would be burdened with writing obituaries, doing features on soapbox derby winners and filing clips in the newspaper morgue. She wanted none of that. She did not want to write the "fluff" stories that weeklies and small dailies often publish.

Harrison's grades were excellent; she was graduated summa cum laude. She had earned a summer internship at the state's largest daily, had edited the campus newspaper and had done some stringing for the local Tribune.

Harrison yearned to use her talents at a metropolitan newspaper. Seldom does a journalism school graduate, two weeks out of college, get hired by an 80,000-circulation daily in a metro area, but Harrison did. She had to leave her home state for the job, but she was eager.

Six months later, she was back on campus. She told her journalism professors that the experience had been a disaster:

Why didn't you tell me what it was like out there? My editors didn't care about putting out a good newspaper. They were just interested in filling the news hole and meeting deadlines. They kept telling me I had more talent than other first-year reporters they had hired.

But how did they reward me? They gave me all the crap jobs. I could understand having to write an obituary here or there. But do you know what else I had to do? They made me answer the switchboard on Saturdays when the operator took her lunch break. Can you believe that?

Fridays were something else. I worked the night shift. At first, I didn't think I would mind. I figured it would give me time to put the finishing touches on some enterprise reporting. What else was there to do on a Friday night? I had some good stories to pursue. You know, such things as nursing home care, graft in the police department, lack of qualified staff at the local hospital and irregularities at the county jail. But did my editors want me to look into these stories? Hell no.

What did they have me doing on Friday nights? I couldn't believe it. Football scores. I took football scores over the telephone. They were high school scores. At least they could have been college scores. I didn't know why I had to help the sports department with high school football scores. Nobody in sports ever helped me at the courthouse when several cases were pending.

I had no real complaints about my pay. It wasn't good, but it wasn't bad. I had no illusions about getting rich. That wasn't it. It was a combination of editors who didn't care, of having to answer the switchboard and of having to take those damn football scores.

Obviously, newspaper work entails more than working on blockbuster stories and winning awards. Young journalists need to realize that. Job satisfaction is an internal feeling. Ken Dassner enjoys—or at least tolerates—taking time from a major story he is working on to answer a call from a local mortuary. When everyone else in the office is tied up with something, he does not mind helping with the small chores. It is part of the job. He understands that.

Julie Harrison never did. She got out of the business.

Climbing the Ladder

Andy Tackett, a third journalism graduate, wants to make it all the way to a major metropolitan newspaper, and he is willing to work any jobs at any paper until he does. After college, where he worked on the campus daily and had internships for two summers, he started at an 18,000-circulation evening daily. "At least the hours weren't bad; I worked Monday through Friday 8 to 5," he said. "But I wanted more, and still do. I'd like more money, a better reputation. I want to make it to New York, Los Angeles, Chicago or Washington, D.C. I'll answer phones and work insane hours if that's what it takes."

Two years after graduation, Tackett is at another evening paper. This one has a circulation of 180,000, but it is dropping quickly. Staffers talk often about the paper's folding. It is being clobbered in advertising and news reporting by a much stronger morning paper.

"I won't be here long," Tackett said. "Just like in my senior year of college, I am sending out resumes again and making phone calls. I'll land on my feet. I really do love journalism, and I won't stop until I get to one of the best papers in the country.

"There is something about seeing your byline on a story, about interviewing famous people, about revealing secrets. I feel so good, so fulfilled in this profession that I'd never consider doing anything else."

A Lack of Preparation

Terry Alleman never even got into the business. He was a below-average college student, never had an internship, was not interested in working on the campus paper because he thought its staffers were egotistical and "cliqueish" and regarded stringing for the local daily as "no big deal."

He knew he was not strong in writing fundamentals—"Who really cares whether you should use a colon or semicolon?"—but he always felt he would get a job on a good newspaper or with a public relations firm. After all, he liked to write, and he enjoyed being with people. He considered himself a "creative writer":

> I took the reporting course in college because it was required. I sure didn't take it to learn anything. Anybody can cover a school board meeting, write a speech story, cover a press conference and write 35-word leads. I didn't have to sit in a classroom an entire semester to learn those things.
>
> The worst thing about my reporting class was that instructor. He didn't appreciate creative writing. He kept bugging me about attribution, punctuation and style. I'd be rich if I had a nickel for every time that guy asked me, "What does the stylebook say?"
>
> I'm intelligent, certainly more intelligent than my grades show. You know, I never was challenged as a student. Few teachers got my creative juices flowing.

During his last semester in college, Alleman went to a local printer and ordered 100 copies of an elaborate resume. Granted, he did not have many accomplishments to put on it. He thought the part about "I'm willing to take any job that is challenging and will enable me to be creative" was a nice touch. Clichés, however, do not get many journalism graduates jobs these days.

FINDING A JOB

Good students generally can find work in the media. Sometimes average students with strong desire can, too. But the market is tight enough that students with low grade averages, no experience and little desire will find job hunting frustrating and unsuccessful.

In the November 1970 careers issue of the Quill, an ad urged newspeople to "consider journalism opportunities offered by the Journal Company of Milwaukee, Wisconsin." The ad said the company "now employs a staff of 3,200 full and part time in the newspaper and broadcasting operations. The evening and Sunday Milwaukee Journal is by far the largest and best known newspaper in Wisconsin. The morning Milwaukee Sentinel, which the company bought from the Hearst Corporation in July 1962, is Wisconsin's oldest and largest morning newspaper. . . ." Other companies also advertised in the magazine. They needed good people, and the nation's journalism schools couldn't supply them fast enough.

Also in 1970, newspaper editors, wire service bureau chiefs and broadcasting executives visited journalism departments and schools each semester, hoping to recruit graduates. Most people with journalism degrees were able to find jobs; often they were able to choose from several offers.

All that has changed. Today only the top graduates land good jobs. Everyone has to go out searching, applying and hoping. In most cases jobs are easier to find at smaller newspapers and broadcasting outlets, mainly because most graduates still shoot for the big newspapers or television stations where the pay and exposure are best.

From the standpoint of those who hire for the print and broadcast media, the glut of capable journalism graduates is welcome. They usually have more than one graduate applying for entry-level jobs, and so they are able to pick the best. Thus the journalism graduate most likely to get a media job upon graduation is the one who has worked for the campus newspaper or radio station, has had an internship and has earned good grades.

Today's job market is tight, but it is not impossible to crack. Most graduates simply have to realize that they are not going to be hired right out of school by one of the giant metros, one of the networks or by a major public relations firm. Graduates may not be able to work in exactly the town or area they want. Still, jobs often are available at small dailies and weeklies and in small broadcast markets, but competition tends to be fierce at every level.

In its "Journalism Career and Scholarship Guide," the Newspaper Fund said, "Editors closely scrutinize the educational and job backgrounds of applicants to find sure signs of applicants' training for and interest in a media job. A journalism education gives editors one of these 'signs,' and a graduate with a journalism degree usually gets the job over grads without academic and practical preparation. It is getting harder every year for an aspiring journalist to find media work without a journalism education background."

Newspaper Fund statistics bear out these contentions. Sixty percent of the entry-level positions in 1970 in news went to journalism majors. The percentages rose to 72 percent in 1973, 77 percent in 1974 and 83 percent in 1980.

The Newspaper Fund report continued: "Some professional newspeople may advise you to avoid journalism subjects in college because they did. But chances are they are not aware of what is happening in modern journalism education. Most young people who find media jobs studied journalism in college, had professional media internships during college, or both."

Preparing to Enter the Job Market

Journalism students can do several things to prepare for careers in mass communcation. Recent graduates mentioned some of the following tips in the "Journalism Career and Scholarship Guide":

- *Keep grade point averages as high as possible.* Employers often will look first at experience (campus newspapers, internships, summer media work, part-time assignments) but logic dictates that a student with a 3.2 grade average will be hired instead of a student with a 2.2 grade average if other credentials are comparable.

- *Sample liberal arts offerings.* Courses in political science, history, management, economics, English and sociology are among those that can provide valuable background for aspiring reporters.

- *Get to know working media professionals.* These people can offer insights into journalism that can be valuable in deciding whether to choose journalism for a profession. Contacts within the media also can sometimes lead to jobs.

- *Work for the campus newspaper, campus radio station or student magazine.* Campus experience can be invaluable, for here a student first gets a feel of the real world of journalism. Students learn the inner workings of the business—the thrill of reporting, the missed meals, the emotions, the pride of a job well done—while gaining on-the-job experience. At many campus papers and radio stations, students have to compete for jobs, which helps them learn what they will be facing when they graduate.

- *Compile a clip file.* Save all stories. Employers want to see samples of an applicant's work. Clip and paste stories on a regular basis. No employer will be particularly impressed if an applicant submits a tattered, yellowed set of clippings.

- *Master writing fundamentals.* Surveys generally show that the best way for students to prepare for the job market is to master language skills—spelling, punctuation and syntax.

- *Develop all-round journalism skills.* This is particularly important for students who seek jobs on smaller dailies and weeklies. Reporters on some newspapers are expected to be able to cover a school board meeting, explain developments at the city utilities, write in simple fashion about the letting of revenue bonds, write an editorial about city hall, sell an advertisement to a department store manager or take a picture at a track meet.

- *Try to get internships.* They enable college students to taste the professional world and to get feedback from experienced professionals. They also can lead to a first full-time job.

- *Seek summer work.* Journalism majors might be able to earn more money working in construction or in fast-food restaurants during the summer, but prospective employers will be more impressed if those summers were spent working in the media.

- *Monitor trade journals for job openings.* Keep regular tabs on media openings around the country. The ads should provide examples of the type of employee in demand, the most plentiful jobs, the sections of the country with the most openings and salary ranges. They also show how mobile journalists can be once they have several years' experience.

- *Become familiar with video display terminals.* It is unlikely that technological advances in the profession will replace working reporters. Instead, these technological advances will enable reporters to do their jobs quicker and better. Many of the ads in trade journals today say that knowledge of VDTs is necessary.

- *Prepare updated resumes.* Employers appreciate organized, neat, complete resumes. Keep cover letters concise. Proofread application materials several times. Editors do not take kindly to typos or grammatical errors.

- *Prepare mentally and physically for job interviews.* Editors are most likely to react positively to applicants who are articulate and well-dressed.

- *Do not give up.* If you feel you are qualified for a job, go after it aggressively. Write a letter and resume. Wait a couple of weeks and then send another letter if you have not received a response. Follow up the second letter with a phone call. Most employers like people who are aggressive and ambitious, and so if there are no openings today, keep checking in. Without making a pest of yourself, keep reminding the employer that you want the job.

The Newspaper Industry

Despite reports of newspapers folding in cities where they are buried by strong competition, American newspapers attained all-time records in advertising revenues, employment and number of Sunday editions as the industry entered the 1980s.

According to statistics compiled by the American Newspaper Publishers Association from trade and government sources:

- Newspaper employment rose from 420,700 to 432,100 and ranked first in the Department of Labor's listing of the nation's largest manufacturing employers.

- Daily circulation of 1,750 newspapers exceeded 62 million.

- Sunday newspapers reached an all-time high of 735. Circulation increased to a record of more than 54 million.

- Weekly newspapers numbered 7,602, with circulation of 40.9 million.

- Advertising revenues for U.S. daily newspapers reached a record of $15.6 billion—more than television and radio combined.

With most American newspapers doing well financially, many news departments either are holding stable or are expanding in size. A check of the classified ad pages of each week's Editor & Publisher, trade magazine of the industry, reveals scores of job openings. Recent journalism school graduates realistically can compete for many of the openings.

A survey of 124 randomly selected newspapers conducted in 1980 by Professor Warren W. Schwed of Fordham showed that of those persons they had hired recently, 48.5 percent were hired from other papers, 12.5 percent were hired from other media jobs, 28.5 percent from journalism schools, 6.1 percent from other college majors and 4.1 percent from miscellaneous sources. E & P published the results.

The Newspaper Fund reported in its "Journalism Career and Scholarship Guide": "Superior graduates will continue to find the best media jobs. Grads with lesser records will have more difficulty finding media jobs because newspaper editors who hire college graduates ask journalism professors to send them only the best student writers and editors."

What Else Is There?

Remember, a degree in journalism does not limit a graduate to working only for a newspaper or broadcast news operations. According to Newspaper Fund statistics published by Quill, of the journalism graduates of 1980, 14.5 percent went to work for daily newspapers. And the others?

- Weekly newspapers took 4.7 percent.
- Wire services, 0.4 percent.
- TV stations, 3.3 percent.
- Radio stations, 3.5 percent.
- Public relations, 10.4 percent.
- Advertising, 4.7 percent.
- Magazines, 3.2 percent.
- Other media, 12.4 percent.
- Graduate or law school, or another undergraduate school, 7.8 percent.
- Sales/management/clerical, 12.3 percent.
- Other fields, 12.4 percent.
- Unemployed; not looking for media work, 2.2 percent.
- Unemployed; looking for media work, 8.2 percent.

The figures have not changed much over the years. According to statistics published in Quill in 1970, daily newspapers took 16.5 percent of the journalism school graduates of 1969. Weekly newspapers got 2.5 percent, wire services 1 percent and public relations 9.7 percent. Television news employed 2.6 percent of the 1969 graduates, compared with 3.3 percent in 1980, indicating the outlook has improved for students interested in that area of journalism.

Journalism degrees prepare people for more than working in a news operation. Trade magazines, for instance, often are willing to take a chance on a recent graduate. Some graduates plan careers as photojournalists or as teachers. The point is that journalism graduates should be able to put their experience in writing, reporting and editing to work in a variety of areas.

And the Pay?

Before Barbara Walters signed her contract with ABC, she got a hairdresser, a limousine and her own press agent. She also got $5 million. Her negotiating was done by the William Morris Agency, which represents some of the world's best-known entertainment stars.

CBS newsman Bill Kurtis is represented by Don Ephraim of Chicago, who represents about 30 broadcasting and newspaper figures in Chicago. When Kurtis was an anchor at WBBM-TV in Chicago, his $500,000 Ephraim-negotiated salary made him the highest paid local anchor in the country.

Yes, there are some big salaries in journalism today. And many working newspeople are represented by media agents, who negotiate salaries; assist in tax, investment and retirement planning, and advise on career moves. In television a reporter without an agent is regarded as naive. In the nation's largest markets, newspaper columnists also turn over their contract and career negotiating to agents. Some newspeople are represented by unions. Indeed, journalism has become a big business.

There are excellent salaries in journalism for those who become stars in the profession, and the salaries are getting better all the time. And although most journalists are not represented by agents, the high salaries at the top have brought a much better standard of living for all newspeople. In the last few years, newspapers and broadcasting outlets have started to catch up with other industries in salaries and benefits, although in some areas of the country they still lag behind.

In most cases journalists with more than five years' experience can figure on a middle-class lifestyle. They probably will not be living on the lake or driving a Mercedes-Benz, but their children will go to good schools, they will be able to eat at some nice restaurants and there should be some money for an annual vacation.

IS IT WORTH IT?

Is journalism worth going into? It depends. For a young person who is willing to work, there possibly is no better profession. It is fun. It opens the door to the real "real world." It provides an opportunity to hobnob with the great, the powerful and with all those trying to be.

So is it worth it? It is for many.

SUGGESTED EXERCISES

1. Invite upper-echelon editors of small- and large-circulation dailies, editors of weekly newspapers, news directors who work in the electronic media and public relations executives to hold a panel discussion for your class. Ask them to discuss qualifications they look for in job applicants. Ask them also to discuss salaries and working conditions.

2. Invite recent graduates of your institution who have gone into media work to your class. Ask them to discuss their jobs. Did college adequately—or realistically—prepare them? Do they think they will be working in a media-related job in five years?

3. Start a clip file of your work.

4. Begin a subscription to a newspaper, public relations or broadcasting trade journal. Read it regularly.

5. Write your résumé. Check with professors in your department and with campus job placement officials for examples.

Index

About the Authors

Douglas A. Anderson is associate professor of journalism at Arizona State University. His teaching specialties are reporting, editing and communication law. Professor Anderson is author of "A 'Washington Merry-Go-Round' of Libel Actions" and co-author of "Electronic Age News Editing," and has written articles that have appeared in such academic and professional publications as Journalism Quarterly, Newspaper Research Journal, APME News and Grassroots Editor. Formerly managing editor of the Hastings (Neb.) Daily Tribune, he was a graduate fellow at Southern Illinois University, where he received his Ph.D.

Bruce D. Itule works in the City Room of the Chicago Tribune, where he has been a copy editor, makeup editor and graphics editor. He has been a reporter and copy editor at the Arizona Daily Star in Tucson, the Phoenix (Ariz.) Gazette, the Boulder (Colo.) Camera, the Denver Post, the Minneapolis Star and the Montrose (Calif.) Ledger. He also has taught reporting and editing at New Mexico State University and Arizona State University. Mr. Itule has written numerous articles on journalism for professional journals, including The Quill, Journalism Educator, Grassroots Editor and the Associated Press Managing Editor News.